Zaner-Bloser

SPELLING CONNECTIONS

J. Richard Gentry, Ph.D.

7

Series Author
J. Richard Gentry, Ph.D.

Editorial Development: Cottage Communications

Art and Production: PC&F

Photography: George C. Anderson: cover, pages 1, 4, 6, 7, 254, 255, 256, 257; Corbis Bettmann: p. 12, © Dean Conger; p. 18, © Bob Krist; p. 24; p. 30, © Phil Schermeister; p. 48, © Mark Gibson; p. 54, © Lowell Georgia; p. 90, © Philip James Corwin; p. 108, © Joe McDonald; p. 126, © Joseph Sohm; p. 132, © Joseph Sohm; p. 168, © Richard Cummins; p. 216, © Bojan Breceli; p. 268, © Lake County Museum; p. 269, © Lester V. Bergman; p. 272, © Lois Ellen Frank; p. 274, © David Muench; p. 275, © John Heseltine; p. 276, © Joseph Sohm; ChromoSohm Inc.; p. 277 ; p. 279, © Richard Hamilton Smith; p. 281, © Henry Diltz; p. 282, © Massimo Listri; p. 283, © Bettman; p. 285, © Roman Soumar; p. 286, © Owen Franken; p. 288, © Adam Woolfitt; p. 289, © Charles E. Rotkin; p. 291, © David A. Northcott; p. 292, © Raymond Gehman; p. 293, © Roger Ressmeyer; p. 294 ; p. 295, © Peter Smithers; p. 297, © Paul A. Souders; p. 298, © Pal Almasy; p. 301, © Bob Rowan; Progressive Image; p. 302, © Paul Seheult; p. 303; p. 305, © Kevin R. Morris; p. 306, © Roger Ressmeyer; p. 307, © Philip Gould; p. 310, © Roger Ressmeyer; p. 313, © David Lees; p. 314, © Roger Ressmeyer; The Stock Market: p. 36, © Tom & Dee Ann McCarthy; p. 66, © Ariel Skelley; p. 144, © Jon Feingersh; p. 210, © 96 Jose Pelaez; p. 304, © 97 Don Mason; p. 311, © 98, A. & J. Verkaik; © Index Stock Imagery: p. 60, p. 120, p. 174, p. 192, p. 280; Tony Stone Images: p. 72, © Linda Burgess; p. 84, © Greg Pease; p. 96, © Kelvin Murray; p. 102, © Michael Orton; p. 138, © Ralph H. Wetmore II; p. 156, © Baron Wolman; p. 180, © David Hiser; p. 198, © Davies & Starr; p. 267, © Jim Corwin; p. 271, © World Perspectives; p. 278, © Bruce Ayres; p. 287, © World Perspectives; p. 309, © Renee Lynn; p. 312, © Andrew Hall; FPG International: p. 162, © Paul & Lindamarie Ambrose; p. 204, © VCG; Artville ©: p. 273; SUPERSTOCK ©: p. 290, p. 296, p. 299, p. 300, p. 308

Illustrations: Laurel Aiello: pages 123, 124, 146, 147, 148, 149, 226, 230, 231, 232, 235, 239, 242, 243, 245, 247, 250, 253; Dave Blanchette: pages 21, 22, 27, 51, 63, 129, 201, 213; Len Ebert: pages 57, 81, 105, 117, 118, 136; Kate Flanagan: pages 15, 16; Ruth Flanigan: pages 11, 17, 23, 29, 35, 47, 53, 59, 65, 71, 83, 89, 95, 101, 107, 110, 119, 125, 131, 137, 142, 143, 155, 161, 167, 173, 179, 191, 197, 203, 209, 215; Bill Ogden: pages 38, 40, 41, 74, 75, 76, 77, 93, 106, 165, 182, 184, 195, 218, 220, 221; George Ulrich: pages 9, 10, 33, 45, 69, 153, 172, 189, 207

ISBN: 0-7367-0112-5

Zaner-Bloser, Inc., P.O. Box 16764, Columbus, Ohio 43216-6764 (1-800-421-3018)

Printed in the United States of America   00 01 02 03 04 QP 5 4 3 2

Contents

Spelling Study Strategy

Look ➡ **Say** ➡ Cover ➡ **See** ➡ **Write** ➡ Check

1 **Look** at the word.

2 **Say** the letters in the word. Think about how each sound is spelled.

3 **Cover** the word with your hand or close your eyes.

4 **See** the word in your mind. Spell the word to yourself.

5 **Write** the word.

6 **Check** your spelling against the spelling in the book.

Spelling and Thinking

READ THE SPELLING WORDS

1.	newsroom	*newsroom*	The reporters waited in the **newsroom**.
2.	edition	*edition*	I read today's **edition** of the paper.
3.	sportscaster	*sportscaster*	The **sportscaster** gave the game's score.
4.	media	*media*	Will the **media** cover the story fairly?
5.	headline	*headline*	I read the **headline** above the article.
6.	copy	*copy*	He typed the **copy** for the story.
7.	editorial	*editorial*	Her **editorial** supported a dress code.
8.	newscast	*newscast*	I saw you on the six o'clock **newscast**!
9.	caption	*caption*	I read the **caption** under the photo.
10.	commentary	*commentary*	His **commentary** was informative.
11.	newsprint	*newsprint*	This thin paper is called **newsprint**.
12.	verify	*verify*	The eyewitness can **verify** what happened.
13.	deliver	*deliver*	He will **deliver** papers to earn money.
14.	footage	*footage*	We watched live **footage** of the storm.
15.	masthead	*masthead*	The editor's name is on the **masthead**.
16.	exclusive	*exclusive*	One reporter got an **exclusive** interview.
17.	update	*update*	The news gave an **update** on the story.
18.	coverage	*coverage*	All channels provided live **coverage**.
19.	newsreel	*newsreel*	Have you ever seen an old **newsreel**?
20.	dateline	*dateline*	A story's **dateline** tells when and where.

SORT THE SPELLING WORDS

1.–11. Write the words with two syllables. Draw a line between the syllables. Use the **Spelling Dictionary** if you need help.

12.–18. Write the words with three syllables. Draw a line between the syllables.

19.–20. Write the words with four or more syllables. Draw a line between the syllables.

REMEMBER THE SPELLING STRATEGY

Remember that the English language includes many words that relate to the media.

Word Meanings

Write a spelling word for each definition.

1. to prove or confirm
2. not shared by others
3. a set of explanations, interpretations, or remarks
4. a single press run or copy
5. an opinion piece
6. a short film about current events
7. to bring to a person or place
8. the extent to which something is observed and reported

Word Structure

Change the underlined part of each compound word to write a spelling word.

9. <u>bed</u>room
10. <u>fore</u>head
11. <u>under</u>line
12. up<u>stairs</u>

13. sports<u>wear</u>
14. <u>fore</u>cast
15. <u>foot</u>print
16. head<u>ache</u>

USING THE Dictionary

The **pronunciation key** in the front of a dictionary matches the symbols you see in a phonetic spelling to the sounds of words you already know.

Match the vowel sound in the first syllable of each phonetic spelling in Column A with the word in Column B that has the same sound. Then write the spelling word for each phonetic spelling. Use the **Spelling Dictionary** if you need help.

A	B
17. /kŏp′ ē/	a. h<u>a</u>t, ă
18. /mē′dē ə/	b. p<u>o</u>t, ŏ
19. /foot′ ĭj/	c. t<u>oo</u>k, oŏ
20. /kăp′ shən/	d. b<u>e</u>, ē

Spelling and Reading

newsroom	edition	sportscaster	media	headline
copy	editorial	newscast	caption	commentary
newsprint	verify	deliver	footage	masthead
exclusive	update	coverage	newsreel	dateline

Solve the Analogies Write a spelling word to complete each analogy.

1. **Teacher** is to **classroom** as **reporter** is to _____.
2. **Wool** is to **sweater** as **wood pulp** is to _____.
3. **Printing** is to **newspaper** as **filming** is to _____.
4. **Credits** are to **movie** as **staff list** is to _____.
5. **Title and author** are to **bibliography** as **time and place** are to _____.

Complete the Sentences Write the spelling word that could replace the underlined words in each sentence.

6. The person who reports athletic events will observe the teams from a special box overlooking the stadium.
7. You can listen to descriptions and explanations on the game.
8. During the game, we will give current information about the scores of games being played in other areas.
9. Computers will check the accuracy of all scores and statistics.
10. This channel will show live lengths of film of the game.
11. The extent of reporting will include postgame ceremonies.
12. During the game, we will present possessed-by-one-source-only interviews with the athletes.
13. Your local broadcast of news events will air after the game.

Complete the Paragraph Write spelling words from the box to complete the paragraph.

editorial
headline
deliver
media
edition
caption
copy

Mary Liston, a reporter for our school newspaper, was voted Reporter of the Year. She was chosen by students and teachers involved in school __14.__, including the newspaper and the school television station. Mary was recognized for her __15.__ in last week's __16.__ of the paper. The __17.__ of her article was "School needs better lunches." Under the accompanying photo was the following __18.__: "Students eating in the lunchroom." Mary not only writes and edits __19.__, she is also willing to __20.__ the papers to classrooms.

Spelling ^{and} Writing

Proofread an Editorial

Six words are not spelled correctly in this editorial. Write the words correctly.

SCHOOL NEWS

We need to update the equipment in our school's medea center. New computers will help everyone. The school television station could use computers to produce a newzcast. Reporters for the school newspaper could use computers to write copie for each eddition of the paper. Computers would help students to research and verafy facts. Teachers could use them to diliver e-mail to parents. Ask your parents to go to this month's school board meeting and support new computers for our school!

Proofreading Marks

≡ Make a capital.

/ Make a small letter.

∧ Add something.

℮ Take out something.

⊙ Add a period.

⌗ New paragraph

(SP) Spelling error

Write an Editorial

Persuasive Writing

Choose an issue or an idea that you have a strong opinion about or a problem that you think needs to be solved. Write an editorial to influence others.

- Begin with a sentence that states your opinion.
- Use supporting facts to persuade your readers to agree with your opinion.
- Suggest a solution that is clear and reasonable.
- Follow the form used in the proofreading sample.

Use as many spelling words as you can.

Writing Process

Prewriting
⇩
Drafting
⇩
Revising
⇩
Editing
⇩
Publishing

Proofread Your Writing During

Proofread your writing for spelling errors as part of the editing stage in the writing process. Be sure to check each word carefully. Use a dictionary to check spelling if you are not sure.

Vocabulary

Review Words: Media Words

Write a word from the box to complete each sentence.

assignment	bureau	business
	career	license

1. The columnist in the network's London _____ reported on the Queen.
2. The _____ section of the paper has job listings and financial news.
3. If you want a _____ as a reporter, you should study journalism.
4. The reporter was on _____ in the jungle.
5. A station needs a _____ to broadcast.

Preview Words: Media Words

Write the word from the box that matches each clue.

administer	advertisement	digital
	executive	gaffer

6. expressed numerically, like computer data
7. a person having authority in an organization
8. a notice or announcement to persuade a consumer to buy a particular product or service
9. to be in charge of or to manage
10. the person in charge of lighting on a movie or television set

Connections

Content Words

Write a word from the box to complete each sentence.

choreographer	designer	playwright
producer	stagehands	

1. A _____ writes the script for a play.
2. In a theater production, the _____ arranges funding for the project.
3. A _____ plans the sets and scenery.
4. The _____ creates dances to match music.
5. During the show, the _____ are busy backstage with the lights, curtains, and sound.

Social Studies: Sports

Write the words from the box that complete the paragraph.

bleachers	enthusiasm	referee
scoreboard	teammate	

I looked up and saw the crowded __6.__. It seemed as if the whole school had come to our game! Everyone cheered and clapped with lots of __7.__. When the __8.__ called my __9.__ out at first base, the crowd gasped. But at the end of the game, the __10.__ showed that we had won!

Apply the Spelling Strategy

Circle the content word you wrote that best relates to the media.

13

Spelling and Thinking

READ THE SPELLING WORDS

1.	transmit	*transmit*	A messenger can **transmit** your reply now.
2.	indicate	*indicate*	Signs will **indicate** the way to the party.
3.	enroll	*enroll*	Chan plans to **enroll** in that class.
4.	rustic	*rustic*	The Barrets live in a **rustic** country cabin.
5.	comfort	*comfort*	The child found **comfort** in his father's arms.
6.	enclose	*enclose*	Do not forget to **enclose** a recent snapshot.
7.	culprit	*culprit*	I will find the **culprit** who is responsible!
8.	ambition	*ambition*	My **ambition** is to play professional soccer.
9.	parachute	*parachute*	The **parachute** billowed open and floated down.
10.	elegant	*elegant*	The state dinner was very **elegant**.
11.	mistake	*mistake*	Juan rarely makes a **mistake** in grammar.
12.	campus	*campus*	The school **campus** was crowded with students.
13.	property	*property*	He planted a hedge on his **property**.
14.	support	*support*	Please **support** me for class president.
15.	witness	*witness*	A **witness** to the crash described what he saw.
16.	picnic	*picnic*	Roberta forgot the **picnic** basket.
17.	improve	*improve*	The weather should **improve** by the weekend.
18.	extreme	*extreme*	Cacti thrive in the **extreme** desert heat.
19.	dignity	*dignity*	The official greeted the guests with **dignity**.
20.	wisdom	*wisdom*	The owl is a symbol of **wisdom**.

SORT THE SPELLING WORDS

Write the words whose first syllable contains the following sound.

1.–4.	**short a** spelled **a**	16.	**short o** spelled **o**
5.–7.	**short e** spelled **e**	17.	**short u** spelled **o**
8.	**short i** spelled **e**	18.–19.	**short u** spelled **u**
9.–15.	**short i** spelled **i**	20.	**schwa**

Draw a vertical line between the syllables of each word. Use the **Spelling Dictionary** for help.

REMEMBER THE SPELLING STRATEGY

Remember that short vowel sounds may be spelled in a variety of ways.

Word Meanings

Write a spelling word that could replace the underlined words in each sentence.

1. Some people prefer <u>simple, country</u> surroundings.
2. Lynnette showed <u>good judgment</u> in her choice of friends.
3. Students are not allowed to leave the <u>school grounds</u> between classes.
4. In her first speech as class president, she displayed great <u>poise and stateliness</u>.
5. Hurricane winds destroyed their <u>home and possessions</u>.
6. She is talented and has <u>a strong desire to succeed</u>.
7. The furniture in their home was <u>tasteful and expensive</u>.
8. The police arrested the <u>person responsible for committing the theft</u>.

Word Analysis

Write the spelling word with the same prefix as the given word.

9. <u>transfer</u>
10.–11. <u>engage</u>
12. <u>imperil</u>
13. <u>inspire</u>
14. <u>expel</u>

USING THE Dictionary

In a dictionary, the part-of-speech label follows the phonetic spelling of an entry word. When a word has more than one part of speech, the different parts of speech may be listed in a separate entry.

cop•y[1] **/kŏp′** ē/ *n., pl.* **-ies. a.** An imitation or reproduction of something original. **b.** A manuscript to be set in type.

cop•y[2] **/kŏp′** ē/ *v.* **-ied, -y•ing, -ies. a.** To make a copy of. **b.** To imitate.

15.–20. Write the spelling words that can be used as both nouns and verbs. Use the **Spelling Dictionary**.

Spelling AND Reading

transmit	indicate	enroll	rustic	comfort
enclose	culprit	ambition	parachute	elegant
mistake	campus	property	support	witness
picnic	improve	extreme	dignity	wisdom

Solve the Analogies   Write a spelling word to complete each analogy.

I. **Mansion** is to **estate** as **school** is to _____.

2. **Deep-sea diver** is to **scuba gear** as **skydiver** is to _____.

3. **Amaze** is to **astound** as **surround** is to _____.

4. **Roof** is to **protect** as **foundation** is to _____.

5. **Free** is to **freedom** as **wise** is to _____.

6. **Commend** is to **hero** as **blame** is to _____.

Reword the Headlines   Write the spelling word that best replaces the underlined word or words in each newspaper headline.

7. Architect makes major <u>error</u> in developing plans for new city hall

8.–9. Lawyers argue as <u>observer</u> gives testimony with <u>poise</u>

10.–11. Weather stations <u>send</u> reports that <u>point out</u> a serious change in weather patterns

12.–13. Annual town <u>outside meal</u> to be held at <u>rural</u> site near old gristmill

Complete the News Article   Write spelling words from the box to complete the following news article.

Jon Arletta, a student at Adams Middle School, has been offered a scholarship to the Newport Summer Music Program. Jon, whose __14.__ is to play guitar in a rock band, says he will accept the award and __15.__ in the program. Jon has been taking lessons for five years, but he says he needs to __16.__ his technique if he wants to achieve __17.__ fame. Summer classes will be held in an __18.__ mansion on oceanfront __19.__. Jon will enjoy the __20.__ and beauty of a spacious, oceanside room.

enroll
property
improve
ambition
comfort
elegant
extreme

Spelling ^{And} Writing

Proofread a News Story

Six words are not spelled correctly in this news story. Write the words correctly.

A new parashute club is prepared to inroll its first students this Saturday. From his rustick office in a small building next to Stanton Airport, Apollo Skydive Club founder Lewis Daniels said, "My ambitshun is to have a campas in the sky where people can experience the extreme joy of skydiving." Daniels speaks with the wizdom that comes from twenty-five years of experience as a skydiver. Anyone interested in taking lessons can call Daniels at 555-1234 or visit his Web site at www.apolloskydiveclub.com.

Proofreading Marks

☰ Make a capital.

╱ Make a small letter.

∧ Add something.

℮ Take out something.

⊙ Add a period.

⌗ New paragraph

ⓢⓟ Spelling error

Write a News Story

Expository Writing

Write a news story about an actual upcoming or recent event in your school or community.

- Include details that answer the 5 W's: Who, What, When, Where, and Why (or How).
- Be sure the facts you present are accurate.
- Follow the form used in the proofreading sample.

Use as many spelling words as you can.

Proofread Your Writing During →

Proofread your writing for spelling errors as part of the editing stage in the writing process. Be sure to check each word carefully. Use a dictionary to check spelling if you are not sure.

Writing Process

Prewriting
⇩
Drafting
⇩
Revising
⇩
Editing
⇩
Publishing

Vocabulary

Strategy Words

Review Words: Short Vowels

Write a word from the box to complete each sentence.

advance	attic	contact
develop		research

1. Scientists hope to find a cure for certain types of cancer through _____.
2. For details about the revised contest rules, _____ Ms. O'Grady.
3. It takes time and effort to _____ a lasting friendship.
4. Theo asked for an _____ on his allowance.
5. I found Dad's journals in a trunk in the _____.

Preview Words: Short Vowels

Write a word from the box to complete each sentence.

agenda	criminal	dismal
eccentric		victim

6. A doctor treated the accident _____ in the hospital's emergency room.
7. The weather all last week was rainy and _____.
8. The _____ turned himself in to the police.
9. Because he refuses to put his money in a bank, you might think he is _____.
10. I printed and distributed the _____ for our weekly meeting on Wednesday.

Connections

Content Words

Social Studies: Exploration

Write the words from the box to complete the paragraph.

conquer	expansion	expedition
explorers	territorial	

Cabeza de Vaca was one of the Spanish __1.__ who attempted to __2.__ Florida in the early 1500s. The __3.__, sponsored by the King of Spain, was led by Pánfilo de Narváez. However, when attempts to occupy the __4.__ regions of Florida failed, Spain's __5.__ in the New World suffered a setback.

Language Arts: Persuasion

Write the words from the box to complete the paragraph.

display	distinguish	endorse
propaganda	testimonial	

As campaign manager for Mia Wang, I will ask each class officer to __6.__ Mia for president and give a __7.__ about Mia at a rally. I plan to __8.__ photos of Mia to show that she is a caring, involved student. Through my efforts, voters will be able to __9.__ between the truth and the __10.__ that is being spread by our opponents.

Apply the Spelling Strategy

Circle the content words you wrote that have the short vowel sound.

Spelling and Thinking

READ THE SPELLING WORDS

1.	notify	*notify*	When will they **notify** the contest winners?
2.	raven	*raven*	Is that large black bird a **raven** or a crow?
3.	climate	*climate*	Our grandmother has moved to a warm **climate**.
4.	vehicle	*vehicle*	We need a large **vehicle** to transport all of us.
5.	alien	*alien*	Dishonesty is **alien** to her nature.
6.	idol	*idol*	My uncle, a successful actor, is my **idol**.
7.	trial	*trial*	Lawyers prepared evidence for the **trial**.
8.	basis	*basis*	He picked players on the **basis** of their talent.
9.	creature	*creature*	Every **creature** in nature has different traits.
10.	motivate	*motivate*	A cheering crowd can **motivate** a team to win.
11.	species	*species*	There are thousands of **species** of ants.
12.	notion	*notion*	It was my **notion** that Lee should be captain.
13.	prior	*prior*	Do you have **prior** experience as a lifeguard?
14.	reality	*reality*	He would rather dream than face **reality**.
15.	noble	*noble*	Knights performed **noble** deeds for their king.
16.	idle	*idle*	While we worked hard, he was **idle**.
17.	trophy	*trophy*	The winner of the tournament received a **trophy**.
18.	premium	*premium*	My teacher puts a high **premium** on hard work.
19.	oval	*oval*	An **oval** mirror hung over the fireplace.
20.	mutual	*mutual*	They share a **mutual** respect for the environment.

SORT THE SPELLING WORDS

Write the words whose first syllable contains the following sound.

1.–3.	long a	**14.–19.**	long o
4.–8.	long e	**20.**	long u
9.–13.	long i		

Draw a line between the syllables of each word. Use the **Spelling Dictionary** for help.

REMEMBER THE SPELLING STRATEGY

Remember that long vowel sounds may be spelled in a variety of ways.

Word Groups

Write a spelling word that is related in meaning to complete each group.

1. square, circle, triangle, _____
2. adored object, model, hero, _____
3. class, family, genus, _____
4. past, preceding, former, _____
5. crow, magpie, cowbird, _____
6. award, prize, blue ribbon, _____
7. opinion, idea, belief, _____
8. weather, atmospheric conditions, _____
9. tell, proclaim, announce, _____

Word Structure

Write a spelling word by changing the ending of each of the following base words.

10. create
11. try
12. motive
13. base
14. real

USING THE Dictionary

When an entry word has more than one meaning, the **multiple definitions** are listed in order, from most common to least common. Write a spelling word for each underlined word or phrase. Then use the **Spelling Dictionary** to write the letter of the definition that best fits the context.

15. Friends often have <u>common</u> interests.
16. Democracy is a <u>lofty</u> ideal.
17. He has been <u>unemployed</u> since January.
18. I put a <u>high value</u> on honesty.
19. Laziness is <u>strange</u> to him.
20. Writing is a <u>means</u> of personal expression.

Spelling ^{and} Reading

notify	raven	climate	vehicle	alien
idol	trial	basis	creature	motivate
species	notion	prior	reality	noble
idle	trophy	premium	oval	mutual

Replace the Words Replace each underlined word or phrase by writing a spelling word.

1.–2. Rashad won the <u>prize</u> in our neighborhood derby for the most original <u>structure for transporting things</u>.

3. His <u>egg-shaped</u> wagon rolled easily around the track.

4.–5. We should <u>inform</u> the newspaper about the award for this unusual <u>type</u> of transportation!

Solve the Analogies Write the spelling word that best completes each analogy.

6. **Exciting** is to **dull** as **busy** is to _____.

7. **Hilly** is to **landscape** as **hot** is to _____.

8. **Friend** is to **compassionate** as **knight** is to _____.

9. **Red** is to **cardinal** as **black** is to _____.

10. **Familiar** is to **usual** as **unfamiliar** is to _____.

Complete the Paragraph Write spelling words from the box to complete the paragraph.

Last week, Tino wrote a feature story about Ms. Cali, our social studies teacher. Ms. Cali, who is our __11.__ , places a __12.__ on education and knows how to __13.__ us to learn. For example, last month we held a mock __14.__ to decide whether President Andrew Jackson should have been impeached for forcing Native Americans to leave their homes in the 1830s. Ms. Cali appointed a judge, two teams of lawyers, and a jury. During the week __15.__ to the mock trial, each team prepared its argument. In __16.__ , we all shared the __17.__ __18.__ that Jackson was guilty, but some of us had to support Jackson. Ms. Cali reminded us to document the facts that formed the __19.__ of our arguments. In the end, the jury declared that Jackson was a heartless __20.__ and that he was guilty.

> notion
> mutual
> creature
> basis
> reality
> idol
> trial
> premium
> motivate
> prior

Spelling and Writing

Proofread a Paragraph

Six words are not spelled correctly in this lead paragraph of a feature article. Write the words correctly.

Standing beside her nobil horse Night Wind, Pamela Hightower waited for her name to be called. As she waited, she remembered watching her idal, Joe Fargis, win the Equestrian Gold Medal at the 1984 Olympics. Soon she would have a chance to prove whether she and the majestic creeture beside her could also perform with excellence. Hightower, who has a contagious smile and an upbeat personality, has always placed a premium on doing her best, even in difficult times. When she suffered a serious fall during a tryal competition last month, the noshen of giving up never entered her mind. "Quitting is allien to me," she said.

Write a Paragraph

Expository Writing

A feature article informs, interests, and entertains readers. Write the lead paragraph for a feature article.

- Select a person or an event from sports.
- Use the opening to arouse your reader's curiosity.
- Include feelings and thoughts about the subject as well as facts.
- Follow the form used in the proofreading sample.

Use as many spelling words as you can.

Proofread Your Writing During

Writing Process

Prewriting
⇩
Drafting
⇩
Revising
⇩
Editing
⇩
Publishing

Proofread your writing for spelling errors as part of the editing stage in the writing process. Be sure to check each word carefully. Use a dictionary to check spelling if you are not sure.

Vocabulary

Strategy Words

Review Words: Long Vowels

Write a word from the box to complete each sentence.

bugle	encyclopedia	labor
protect	require	

1. Bike helmets help _____ people from serious head injuries in accidents.
2. Cleaning the garage was hard _____.
3. The camp counselor played a _____ to awaken the sleeping campers.
4. Making the team will _____ long hours of practice and complete dedication.
5. Look in an _____ to find an article about Spain.

Preview Words: Long Vowels

Write words from the box to complete the paragraph.

chaos	retrace	typhoon
utilize	violent	

A __6.__ struck a small island in the Pacific. With extremely high winds and heavy rains, the __7.__ storm created __8.__ when it destroyed hundreds of homes and businesses. The power went out during the storm and was not restored for days. People had to __9.__ candles for light and barbecue grills for cooking. Afterward, it was easy to __10.__ the trail the storm had taken. Islanders just followed the path of destruction.

Connections

Content Words

Social Studies: Elections

Write words from the box to complete the paragraph.

poll	predict	sampling
tabulate		trend

The __1.__ in recent school elections has been to elect the most popular student. Ian wants voters to elect him because of his ideas. His campaign is going well, but his committee cannot __2.__ who will win. Therefore, committee members will conduct a __3.__ to find out how students plan to vote. After that, they will take a __4.__ from among their findings and __5.__ the results. Ian can then decide if he wants to change his campaign strategy.

Language Arts: Story Structure

Write words from the box to match each definition.

climax	conflict	crisis
resolve		signify

6. a struggle between two opposing forces or characters in a story
7. the most intense point
8. a crucial turning point
9. to have meaning or importance
10. to find a solution to

Apply the Spelling Strategy

Circle the five content words you wrote that have long vowel sounds.

Spelling and Thinking

READ THE SPELLING WORDS

1.	keyboard	*keyboard*	Type on the **keyboard**.
2.	self-esteem	*self-esteem*	Everyone needs **self-esteem**.
3.	dining room	*dining room*	We ate in the **dining room**.
4.	classmate	*classmate*	Greet your new **classmate**.
5.	far-fetched	*far-fetched*	He told a **far-fetched** tale.
6.	granddaughter	*granddaughter*	Mr. An has a **granddaughter**.
7.	briefcase	*briefcase*	Put the pen in my **briefcase**.
8.	self-taught	*self-taught*	My French is **self-taught**.
9.	four-fifths	*four-fifths*	What is **four-fifths** of 20?
10.	word processing	*word processing*	Sid teaches **word processing**.
11.	newsstand	*newsstand*	Buy papers at the **newsstand**.
12.	quick-witted	*quick-witted*	I gave **quick-witted** answers.
13.	pencil sharpener	*pencil sharpener*	Use my **pencil sharpener**.
14.	well-known	*well-known*	That actor is **well-known**.
15.	thirteen-year-olds	*thirteen-year-olds*	We are **thirteen-year-olds**.
16.	textbook	*textbook*	Read the **textbook** carefully.
17.	self-employed	*self-employed*	I'm a **self-employed** writer.
18.	study hall	*study hall*	Meet me in the **study hall**.
19.	brother-in-law	*brother-in-law*	Dan is my **brother-in-law**.
20.	three-fourths	*three-fourths*	Nine is **three-fourths** of 12.

SORT THE SPELLING WORDS

1.–6. Write the compounds that are written as one word. Draw a line between the two words that form each compound.

7.–10. Write the compounds that are written as two words.

11.–20. Write the compounds that are hyphenated.

REMEMBER THE SPELLING STRATEGY

Remember that a compound word may be written as one word, two words, or a hyphenated word.

Word Meanings

Write the spelling word that matches each definition.

1. a book used for studying a subject
2. someone in the same class at school
3. pride in oneself
4. a device for putting a point on a writing instrument
5. young teenagers
6. part of a typewriter or a computer
7. a portable carrier for books and papers
8. a schoolroom or a period of time devoted to study
9. 75%

Word Replacements

Write a spelling word that could replace the underlined words in each sentence.

10. Nadia got eighty percent of the answers correct.
11. I am going fishing with my sister's husband.
12. Her son's daughter is now two years old.
13. Our new home has a large place for eating dinner.
14. They gave a very unlikely and unbelievable reason for being late.
15. The recognized and famous ballplayer will sign baseballs after the game.

USING THE Dictionary

Dictionaries use abbreviations to indicate the parts of speech of entry words. Look at page 266 in the **Spelling Dictionary** for a list of part-of-speech abbreviations. Write the following words. Next to each word, write its part-of-speech label.

16. word processing
17. quick-witted
18. self-employed
19. self-taught
20. newsstand

Spelling and Reading

keyboard	far-fetched	dining room	classmate	pencil sharpener
briefcase	granddaughter	self-taught	four-fifths	word processing
newsstand	quick-witted	self-esteem	well-known	thirteen-year-olds
textbook	self-employed	study hall	three-fourths	brother-in-law

Answer the Questions   Write the spelling word that best answers each question.

1. Where might you purchase today's paper?
2. What do you call the man married to your sister?
3. What do you study to get information on a particular subject?
4. What do you call people who learn a skill on their own?
5. What kind of worker is his or her own boss?
6. What helps people respect themselves?
7. What does a lawyer use to carry papers to court?

Complete the Sentences   Write the spelling word that best completes each sentence.

8. We painted the walls in the kitchen, bedroom, and _____.
9. This computer comes with a modem, a monitor, and a _____.
10. At work he uses an electric stapler, calculator, and _____.
11. The answer is either two-fifths, three-fifths, or _____.
12. I looked for her in the cafeteria, gym, and _____.
13. We accept eleven-year-olds, twelve-year-olds, and _____.

Complete the Paragraph   Write spelling words from the box to complete the paragraph.

My grandmother was born in Italy and moved here as a baby. She grew up in a community where __14.__ of the people were immigrants. Nana married right out of high school. Going to college then seemed like a __15.__ idea. Recently, Nana went back to school. First, she took a course in __16.__. Then she enrolled in college. As the oldest student on campus, she was soon __17.__ by all. A __18.__ of Nana's told me that younger students like Nana because she's funny and __19.__. I am proud to be her __20.__.

word processing
quick-witted
classmate
granddaughter
three-fourths
well-known
far-fetched

28

Spelling and Writing

Proofread a Biographical Sketch

Six words are not spelled correctly in this biographical sketch. Write the words correctly.

> Over the years I have grown to greatly admire my brotherinlaw, Don. Don is a self taught man. Born in New York City in 1969, he worked at a newstand when he was a teenager and learned about the stock market by asking questions of businesspeople who bought papers from him every day. Naturally intelligent and quikwitted, Don wanted to learn more about finance. He couldn't afford to go to college, so he borrowed an economics text book from a former high school classmate. This may sound farfeched, but Don is now a well-known TV personality who hosts a weekly program called "Pennies Matter."

Proofreading Marks

≡ Make a capital.

/ Make a small letter.

∧ Add something.

ℓ Take out something.

⊙ Add a period.

⌗ New paragraph

(SP) Spelling error

Write a Biographical Sketch

 Expository Writing

A **biographical sketch** is a brief summary of a person's life. Write a biographical sketch of an older person you know or know of.

- Choose someone who has done something new or who has approached life in an unusual way.
- Identify the person and give details about his or her birth, education, misfortunes, goals, and accomplishments.
- Follow the form used in the proofreading sample.

Use as many spelling words as you can.

Proofread Your Writing During

Writing Process

Prewriting
⇩
Drafting
⇩
Revising
⇩
Editing
⇩
Publishing

Proofread your writing for spelling errors as part of the editing stage in the writing process. Be sure to check each word carefully. Use a dictionary to check spelling if you are not sure.

Strategy Words

Review Words: Compound Words

Write a word from the box to match each clue.

| all right | campfire | daydream |
| post office | | self-addressed |

1. Go to this place to mail a letter or package.
2. You can cook over it, and it can keep you warm outdoors on cold nights.
3. You might do this if you let your mind wander.
4. You might say this instead of "yes" or "okay."
5. If you want someone to reply to your letter, you might enclose this kind of envelope.

Preview Words: Compound Words

Write the word from the box that best completes each sentence.

| best-selling | mastermind | old-fashioned |
| out-of-date | | postmaster general |

6. The _____ has announced an increase in the price of first-class stamps.
7. Who was the _____ who thought up this clever plan for raising money?
8. The bank will not accept this _____ check.
9. Kara wants an _____ wedding.
10. He is the _____ author of several books and articles for young adults.

Connections

Content Words

Science: Endangered Species

Write a word from the box to match each definition.

ecology	endangered	sanctuary
wilderness	wildlife	

1. an uncultivated region left in its natural condition
2. the science of the relationships between living things and their environments
3. an area in which animals are protected
4. animals living in their natural surroundings
5. faced with the possibility of extinction

Math: Geometry

Write a word from the box to complete each sentence.

formula	hypotenuse	square root
symbol	theorem	

6. A _____ is the side of a right triangle opposite the right angle.
7. The Pythagorean _____ states that the sum of the squares of the lengths of the sides of a right triangle is equal to the square of the length of the hypotenuse.
8. The _____ of 4 is 2. ($\sqrt{4} = 2$)
9. A _____ is a mathematical statement, often written in equation form, of a principle, an answer, or a rule.
10. A _____ is a printed or written sign for a mathematical operation. ($+, -, \times, \div$)

Apply the Spelling Strategy

Circle the two content words you wrote that are compound words.

Spelling ^{and} Thinking

(Spelling and Thinking)

READ THE SPELLING WORDS

1.	challenge	*challenge*	First, **challenge** them to a rematch.
2.	embarrass	*embarrass*	If I act silly, will I **embarrass** you?
3.	apparent	*apparent*	It was **apparent** that he had been ill.
4.	exaggerate	*exaggerate*	Ina tends to **exaggerate** her skills.
5.	communicate	*communicate*	We **communicate** by e-mail once a week.
6.	accompany	*accompany*	Will you **accompany** Maria to the dance?
7.	unnecessary	*unnecessary*	That comment was **unnecessary.**
8.	surrender	*surrender*	They agreed to **surrender** to end the war.
9.	impression	*impression*	What is your **impression** of that movie?
10.	allegiance	*allegiance*	The knight swore **allegiance** to the king.
11.	immense	*immense*	The **immense** ship had a golf course!
12.	accomplish	*accomplish*	How much can you **accomplish** in a day?
13.	procession	*procession*	The bride and groom led the **procession**.
14.	interrupt	*interrupt*	I did not mean to **interrupt** your talk.
15.	equipped	*equipped*	The car is **equipped** with air bags.
16.	assess	*assess*	We will **assess** the damage to your home.
17.	warrant	*warrant*	We need a **warrant** to arrest the suspect.
18.	possibility	*possibility*	There is a **possibility** of rain tonight.
19.	alliance	*alliance*	The two nations formed an **alliance**.
20.	professional	*professional*	Hector is a **professional** tennis player.

SORT THE SPELLING WORDS

1.–3. Write the words that have two sets of double consonants. Circle the double consonants.

4.–15. Write the words that have one set of double consonants and two or three syllables. Circle the double consonants.

16.–20. Write the words that have one set of double consonants and four or more syllables. Circle the double consonants.

REMEMBER THE SPELLING STRATEGY

Remember that a consonant sound may be spelled with two consonant letters together.

Word Meanings

Write the spelling word that matches each clue.

1. loyalty
2. a group moving in a line
3. not needed
4. a person who earns money as an actress
5. to justify or call for
6. huge
7. connection, union
8. readily seen, obvious
9. a feeling that remains following an experience
10. to give up
11. supplied with tools or provisions

Word Structure

Change each of these nouns into a verb to write a spelling word.

12. interruption
13. exaggeration
14. assessment

USING THE Dictionary

The **inflected forms** of an entry word in a dictionary appear after the part-of-speech label and include the irregular plurals of nouns and the principal parts of verbs. Write the entry word for each inflected form below. Use the **Spelling Dictionary** if you need help.

15. communicating
16. accompanied
17. embarrassing
18. possibilities
19. accomplished
20. challenging

Spelling *and* Reading

challenge	communicate	impression	procession	warrant
embarrass	accompany	allegiance	interrupt	possibility
apparent	unnecessary	immense	equipped	alliance
exaggerate	surrender	accomplish	assess	professional

Solve the Analogies   Write a spelling word to complete each analogy.

1. **Untrained** is to **expert** as **amateur** is to _____.
2. **Face** is to **confront** as **dare** is to _____.
3. **Partners** are to **contract** as **nations** are to _____.
4. **Simile** is to **compare** as **hyperbole** is to _____.
5. **Frown** is to **smile** as **betrayal** is to _____.
6. **Continue** is to **proceed** as **stop** is to _____.
7. **Intrusion** is to **intrude** as **embarrassment** is to _____.

Complete the Advertisements   Write a spelling word to replace the underlined word or words in each advertisement.

8. **For Sale:** Used car, fully <u>furnished</u> (except motor).
9.–10. **Wanted:** Tuba player for <u>huge</u> Labor Day <u>parade</u>; must have own instrument.
11. **Wanted:** Experienced tutor; <u>chance</u> of travel with family.
12. **Buy Sanitize-It!** Watch germs <u>abandon</u> all hope!
13.–14. **Order now!** You can <u>achieve</u> the impossible with no <u>visible</u> effort. Read whole books overnight with Sleep Tapes!

Complete the Paragraph   Write spelling words from the box to complete the paragraph.

Advertisements that sound too good to be true probably __15.__ a closer look. You need to __16.__ the offer. Is it true and honest? Do restrictions or hidden costs __17.__ the offer? Unless you read the fine print, you may get the wrong __18.__. You may find yourself paying for __19.__ extras or signing up for something you neither want nor need. A smart consumer asks questions before making a purchase. And if you are not satisfied with a product, __20.__ your dissatisfaction to the company promptly.

accompany
unnecessary
assess
communicate
impression
warrant

Spelling and Writing

Proofread an Advertisement

Six words are not spelled correctly in this advertisement. Write the words correctly.

Are you a profesionnal with a busy schedule? Do you find it a challange to acomplish all your daily chores? Does the possability of unexpected guests send you into a frenzy? Don't panic! Call Harry's Helping Hands today. Tell us your needs. We'll arrive at your door, aquipped to clean, cook, mow the lawn, and do whatever other chores you need to have done. Don't let a messy house embarrass you ever again! Call Harry's Helping Hands at 555-1534. We'll help you make a good impresion!

Proofreading Marks

≡	Make a capital.
/	Make a small letter.
∧	Add something.
ℓ	Take out something.
⊙	Add a period.
⌗	New paragraph
SP	Spelling error

Write an Advertisement

Select a product or service you have enjoyed, for example, a movie, book, restaurant, or arcade. Write an ad to promote that product or service.

- Begin with a question, startling fact, or endorsement by a famous person.
- Use language that will make consumers feel that they can't live without the product or service.
- Follow the form used in the proofreading sample. Use as many spelling words as you can.

Proofread Your Writing During

Proofread your writing for spelling errors as part of the editing stage in the writing process. Be sure to check each word carefully. Use a dictionary to check spelling if you are not sure.

Writing Process

Prewriting
⇩
Drafting
⇩
Revising
⇩
Editing
⇩
Publishing

Vocabulary

Strategy Words

Review Words: Double Consonants

Write a word from the box to match each clue.

banner	error	horrible	innocent	tissue

1. It means "not guilty."
2. This would spoil a perfect score on a test.
3. It can be a group of cells or thin paper.
4. This is a sign displayed for a special event.
5. It is a synonym for **terrible** and **shocking**.

Preview Words: Double Consonants

Write a word from the box to complete each sentence.

accommodate	bookkeeping	occasional
questionnaire		successor

6. She responded honestly to all the items on the _____.
7. According to my _____, we need $100 more to cover our trip expenses.

8. The ship can _____ five hundred passengers safely and comfortably.
9. When he retired, the president of the company appointed his daughter as his _____.
10. According to the forecast, the weather will be mostly sunny with an _____ shower.

Connections

Content Words

Math: Properties

Write a word from the box to match each clue.

associative	commutative	distributive
identity	properties	

1. a (b + c) = (a × b) + (a × c)
2. (a + b) + c = a + (b + c)
3. a × b = b × a **or** a + b = b + a
4. a × 1 = a **or** a + 0 = a
5. illustrated by the equations in 1.–4.

Language Arts: Genres

Write words from the box to complete the paragraph.

anecdote	autobiographical	narrative
sequel	successive	

James Herriot's novels are __6.__ , based on his experiences as a country veterinarian. Herriot, a master of the brief, humorous __7.__ , wrote the novels in rough chronological order. Each __8.__ book is therefore a __9.__ to the previous works and continues the __10.__ of Herriot's life as a veterinarian, husband, and father.

Apply the Spelling Strategy

Circle all the double consonants in four of the content words you wrote.

Assessment and Review

Assessment   Units 1–5

Each Assessment Word in the box fits one of the spelling strategies you have studied over the past five weeks. Read the spelling strategies. Then write each Assessment Word under the unit number it fits.

Unit 1 _____

1. Remember that the English language includes many words that relate to the media.

Unit 2 _____

2.–5. Remember that short vowel sounds may be spelled in a variety of ways.

Unit 3 _____

6.–11. Remember that long vowel sounds may be spelled in a variety of ways.

Unit 4 _____

12.–16. Remember that compound words may be written as one word, two words, or a hyphenated word.

Unit 5 _____

17.–20. Remember that a consonant sound may be spelled with two consonant letters.

patron
arrest
excess
wheelbarrow
harass
lifeguard
radiate
ammonia
expense
wholesale
stable
appendix
wash-and-wear
appraise
confess
cable
native
consent
turnpike
vanilla

Review — Unit 1: Media Words

edition	media	headline	copy	editorial
verify	deliver	masthead	exclusive	coverage

Write the spelling word that completes each sentence.

1. Newspaper and television are popular news _____.
2. The early _____ of the newspaper comes in the morning.
3. My brother helps to _____ papers in our neighborhood.
4. Mom reads the _____ page first.
5. Her opinion is that the *Post* has the best news _____.
6. Often the *Post* has _____ coverage.
7. Today's _____ is this: TEST SCORES ARE UP 20 PERCENT.
8. The reporter had to _____ that the information was correct.
9. Ms. Farmer sent in two pages of _____ for the article.
10. The editor and publisher are listed on the paper's _____.

Review — Unit 2: Syllabication Patterns: Short Vowels

indicate	culprit	parachute	elegant	mistake
campus	property	support	improve	wisdom

Write the spelling word that matches the clue.

11. The first and second syllables have **short i**.
12. In the first syllable, **e** spells **short e,** but in the second syllable, **e** spells **short i**.
13.–15. The first syllable of these two-syllable words has **short i**.
16. The first syllable has a **short u** sound. The second syllable has a **short i** sound.
17. The first syllable has a **short a** sound. The second syllable has a **short u** sound.
18. It has three syllables. The first syllable has a **short a** sound.
19. The first syllable has **short o**.
20. The first of the two syllables has **short u**. There is a double consonant in its spelling.

39

climate	vehicle	idol	trial	basis
creature	species	reality	noble	idle

Write the word that fits the meaning.

1. conditions that include wind, temperature, and rain
2. an image that is the object of adoration
3. the examination of evidence in court
4. grand or stately, as an idea
5. not busy; not in use
6. the quality of being actual or true
7. a device, as a car, for carrying people or goods
8. a living being
9. a group of similar animals or plants
10. foundation or supporting principle

Review   Unit 4: Compound Words

keyboard	self-esteem	classmate	granddaughter
self-taught	word processing	well-known	textbook
	brother-in-law	three-fourths	

Write spelling words to complete the paragraph.

Elizabeth's __11.__ , Ken, thought Elizabeth, his new relative, would enjoy using a computer. So, he bought Elizabeth a __12.__ to study. First, Elizabeth learned how to place her hands properly on the __13.__ . Then she learned __14.__ so she could write a letter to Jill, her __15.__ who lives in Germany. When Elizabeth was __16.__ of the way through the book, she realized that she was truly __17.__ . Knowing that raised her __18.__ a great deal. After all, it is a __19.__ fact that computers are here to stay. Now she can even send e-mail to Jill and Margot, Jill's __20.__ and friend.

Review   **Unit 5: Double Consonants**

challenge	embarrass	apparent	exaggerate
communicate	accompany	unnecessary	equipped
	possibility	professional	

Change the underlined part of these words to write spelling words.

1. equip<u>ment</u>
2. embas<u>sy</u>
3. appar<u>ition</u>
4. cap<u>ability</u>
5. exact<u>ly</u>

6. <u>a</u>viary
7. acc<u>urate</u>
8. profess<u>or</u>
9. cham<u>pion</u>
10. comm<u>unity</u>

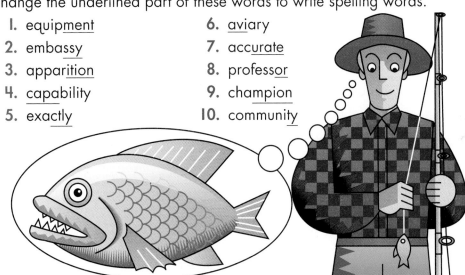

GAME   **Spelling Study Strategy**

Word Swap

Write words you want to study on cards—one word to a card. Put your initials on each card. Give your cards to a partner. Your partner will give you a similar set of cards.

1. Read aloud a word from your partner's stack.

2. Your partner spells the word aloud. Check to see that the word is spelled correctly. If it is, give the card back to your partner. If it is not, give the spelling and keep the card.

3. Your partner will then say one of the cards from your stack for you to spell. If you spell it correctly, you get the card. If you don't, your partner keeps the card.

4. Continue taking turns until each of you has all of your own stack of cards back.

Grammar, Usage, and Mechanics

Parts of a Sentence

Every sentence has a subject and a predicate. The **simple subject** is the one noun or pronoun that tells what or whom the sentence is about. The **simple predicate** is the verb or verb phrase of the sentence—the word or words telling what the subject is, has, or does.

Some <u>workers</u> on the farm <u>have used</u> a large wheelbarrow.
      ↑   ↑

simple subject   simple predicate

Practice
Activity

A. Write the simple subject of each sentence.

1. Our favorite teacher will deliver the address.
2. Was the coverage of the event fair?
3. The ripcord on the parachute opened slowly.
4. These arrows indicate where to set the boxes.
5. José supports our position.
6. This old television set is the property of our class.
7. We listed every species of plant.
8. The sad reality is that we lost the game by one point.

B. Write the simple predicate of each sentence.

9. Chicago's climate is cooler than San Antonio's.
10. Two well-known dancers will perform tonight.
11. Marlene ate three-fourths of the pie herself.
12. She challenged us to a game of chess.
13. Please accompany me to the office now.
14. Good letter writers communicate clearly.
15. I have given you all the directions you need.

WORKSHOP

Proofreading Strategy

Circle and Check

Good writers always proofread their writing for spelling errors. Here's a strategy you can use to proofread your papers.

Instead of trying to proofread everything in one reading, look at just three or four words at a time. Check to see that they are spelled correctly. If you are sure those words are correct, go to the next three or four words. If you have a question about any word, circle it and keep going. Continue to check a few words at a time until you have checked your whole paper. Then use a dictionary to look up all of the circled words. This way you can stay focused on your proofreading and then save time by checking all the words you are unsure about. Try it!

Electronic Spelling

New Technology—New Words

The use of computers has brought new terms into our language. It has also brought new meanings to familiar words. For example, when your grandparents were young, they would not have known what it means to "**click** a **mouse**"!

Some words have taken on new meaning because of new media, such as computers. Some words that have been around a long time now have new meanings in the electronic medium.

Write each misspelled computer term correctly.

1. A dasktop is found on the computer screen's background.
2. A netwurk is a system of connecting several computers so that they work together.
3. You log on to the Internet by entering your pasword.
4. Some screansavers have moving animals.
5. A liptop computer is portable.

Spelling and Thinking

READ THE SPELLING WORDS

1.	fearlessness	fearlessness	Her **fearlessness** was legendary.
2.	requirement	requirement	Some experience is a **requirement**.
3.	extremely	extremely	I was **extremely** happy to see him.
4.	reconsider	reconsider	They will **reconsider** the theory.
5.	thoughtfulness	thoughtfulness	We appreciate your **thoughtfulness**.
6.	inability	inability	I inherited an **inability** to whistle.
7.	disappointment	disappointment	I understood her **disappointment**.
8.	unexpected	unexpected	Her **unexpected** news startled us.
9.	surname	surname	His **surname** is Johnson.
10.	alphabetical	alphabetical	Are these in **alphabetical** order?
11.	reappearance	reappearance	We waited for his **reappearance**.
12.	surprisingly	surprisingly	The day was **surprisingly** cool.
13.	agreeable	agreeable	Is the decision **agreeable** to you?
14.	regardless	regardless	I will go **regardless** of the weather.
15.	unemotional	unemotional	Her reaction was **unemotional**.
16.	adventuresome	adventuresome	Skydivers are **adventuresome**.
17.	thoughtlessness	thoughtlessness	His **thoughtlessness** hurt me.
18.	underestimate	underestimate	Do not **underestimate** her strength.
19.	improvement	improvement	My grades show **improvement**.
20.	emotional	emotional	A wedding is an **emotional** event.

SORT THE SPELLING WORDS

1.–10. Write the words that have both a prefix and a suffix. Circle all the prefixes and suffixes.

11.–13. Write the words that have prefixes but not suffixes. Circle all the prefixes.

14.–20. Write the words that have suffixes but not prefixes. Circle all the suffixes.

REMEMBER THE SPELLING STRATEGY

Remember that words such as **inability, unexpected,** and **fearlessness** contain affixes.

Word Meanings

Write the spelling word that matches each definition.

1. lack of skill or talent
2. a family name
3. reemergence
4. advancement
5. think over again
6. without feeling
7. in spite of everything

Word Structure

Add one or more suffixes to each word to write a spelling word.

8. alphabet
9. agree
10. fear
11. emotion
12. surprise
13. adventure
14. extreme
15.–16. thought

USING THE Thesaurus

A thesaurus provides synonyms and antonyms for words. When you use a thesaurus, be sure that the word you choose is used in the way that you intend. Write a spelling word that is a synonym for each word below. Use the **Writing Thesaurus** if you need help.

17. undervalue
18. surprising
19. necessity
20. frustration

Spelling and Reading

Solve the Analogies   Write a spelling word to complete each analogy.

1. **Correct** is to **incorrect** as **ability** is to _____.
2. **Unevenly** is to **uneven** as **unexpectedly** is to _____.
3. **Dislike** is to **like** as **disagreeable** is to _____.
4. **Class** is to **classical** as **alphabet** is to _____.
5. **Count** is to **discount** as **appointment** is to _____.
6. **Care** is to **carelessness** as **thought** is to _____.
7. **Awe** is to **awesome** as **adventure** is to _____.

Complete the Sentences   Write a spelling word to complete each sentence.

8. The only _____ for joining our bike club is a love of bike riding.
9. He showed his _____ by remembering her birthday.
10. I waited quietly for the _____ of the rare bird.
11. Even though he had won, he seemed _____.
12. Never _____ the strength of a tornado's winds.
13. After hearing the facts, I had to _____ my opinion.
14. It seemed early, but it was _____ late.

Complete the Paragraph   Write spelling words from the box to complete the paragraph.

My neighbor told me how she came to the United States. Her parents wanted a better life for the family. They thought there would be an __15.__ in their lives if they emigrated to the United States. It was an __16.__ dangerous journey, but they decided to set sail __17.__. I was impressed by their __18.__ and bravery. Soon after they arrived, they changed their __19.__ from Johannison to Johnson. As my neighbor spoke of friends she had left behind, she became __20.__ and began to cry. Although she loved her life here, she yearned to see some of those old faces once again.

> surname
> fearlessness
> improvement
> emotional
> extremely
> regardless

46

Spelling and Writing

Proofread a Journal Entry

Six words are not spelled correctly in this journal entry. Write the words correctly.

June 10, 1807. The stagecoach bumped westward. The reapearrance of a huge cloud I had noticed earlier convinced me that a rainstorm was approaching. I drained my canteen, but I regretted drinking all my water when the cloud turned out to be a dust storm. I began to doubt my ability to survive in this new world. I slumped in my seat with a feeling of dissappointment and began to reconsider my decision to travel west. My companions, who earlier had seemed unamotional, came alive in the rush to close the stagecoach windows and secure the baggage. Their adventursome spirits seemed strengthened by the unexpected storm, regardless of the dangers it posed. I silently admired their fearlisness. I was learning never to underestamate the West or its people.

Proofreading Marks

≡ Make a capital.

/ Make a small letter.

∧ Add something.

ℓ Take out something.

⊙ Add a period.

New paragraph

SP Spelling error

Write a Journal Entry

Expository Writing

Imagine that you are a pioneer in the Old West. Write a journal entry.

- Begin with the date to set the scene.
- Use specific details to describe your surroundings.
- Include your thoughts, opinions, and feelings.
- Follow the form used in the proofreading sample. Use as many spelling words as you can.

Writing Process

Prewriting
⇩
Drafting
⇩
Revising
⇩
Editing
⇩
Publishing

Proofread Your Writing During

Proofread your writing for spelling errors as part of the editing stage in the writing process. Be sure to check each word carefully. Use a dictionary to check spelling if you are not sure.

Vocabulary

Strategy Words

Review Words: Affixes

Write a word from the box to complete each sentence. Use the underlined words as clues.

amendment	disagreement	inheritance
probable	replacement	

1. I inherited the money. How will I spend my _____?
2. I don't agree with you. Let's settle our _____.
3. The Constitution was amended. One _____ gives the right to free speech.
4. I replaced the broken dish. Unfortunately, the _____ was not exactly the same as the original.
5. You will probably like the movie. It is _____ that I will like it, too.

Preview Words: Affixes

Write the word from the box that matches each clue.

disappearance	disprove	recycle
surcharge	unprecedented	

6. to show for certain to be false
7. a sum added to the original cost or amount
8. the act of passing out of sight
9. occurring with no previous example; unexpected
10. to reuse in some form

Connections

Science: Radioactivity

Write a word from the box to complete each sentence.

disintegrate	half-life	isotope
radioactive	sensitive	

1. An _____ of carbon is present in all organic compounds.
2. Carbon 14 is _____; therefore, it emits radiation.
3. Scientists can use _____ instruments to measure the levels of radioactivity in an organic object.
4. Time causes many substances to _____.
5. Carbon 14 has a _____ of 5,780 years.

Social Studies: Exploration

Write the word from the box to complete each sentence.

destination	discovery	English
navigation	seafaring	

6. Sir Francis Drake was the first _____ explorer to sail around the world (1577–1580).
7. He grew up in a _____ community and became a sailor while he was still a young boy.
8. Drake's chief _____ was America.
9. Queen Elizabeth I recognized Drake's _____ skills when she supported his voyage around the world.
10. One _____ that Drake made was from land rather than sea; he got his first view of the Pacific Ocean from the top of a high tree!

Apply the Spelling Strategy

Circle the content words you wrote that contain affixes.

READ THE SPELLING WORDS

1.	encouragement	*encouragement*	Thanks for your **encouragement**.
2.	idleness	*idleness*	Wasting time shows **idleness**.
3.	canoe	*canoe*	Be careful not to tip the **canoe**!
4.	manage	*manage*	He will **manage** the entire project.
5.	forgiveness	*forgiveness*	Is **forgiveness** always easy?
6.	acreage	*acreage*	What is the **acreage** of this farm?
7.	outrageous	*outrageous*	His **outrageous** speech shocked us.
8.	management	*management*	I admire her **management** skills.
9.	forgive	*forgive*	He will **forgive** me for my mistake.
10.	canoeing	*canoeing*	I think **canoeing** is fun!
11.	inventiveness	*inventiveness*	Her solution showed **inventiveness**.
12.	encourage	*encourage*	We **encourage** teamwork.
13.	acre	*acre*	My house sits on one **acre** of land.
14.	commencement	*commencement*	She got a degree at **commencement**.
15.	advantageous	*advantageous*	The offer was **advantageous**.
16.	commence	*commence*	When will the parade **commence**?
17.	fierceness	*fierceness*	A lion's **fierceness** is well known.
18.	amazement	*amazement*	I view his magic with **amazement**.
19.	awareness	*awareness*	His **awareness** of the issue is clear.
20.	announcement	*announcement*	Her **announcement** was a surprise.

SORT THE SPELLING WORDS

1.–6. Write the base words that end in a silent final **e**.

7.–11. Write the words with the **-ment** suffix.

12.–16. Write the words with the **-ness** suffix.

17.–18. Write the words with the **-ous** suffix.

19.–20. Write the words with the **-age** or **-ing** suffix.

REMEMBER THE SPELLING STRATEGY

Remember that some base words retain a final silent **e** when certain suffixes are added.

Spelling and Vocabulary

Word Meanings

Write a spelling word for each definition.

1. state of being fierce
2. state of being aware
3. traveling by canoe
4. state of being idle
5. causing outrage
6. area of land measured in acres
7. bringing or giving advantage
8. state of being inventive

Word Structure

Add a suffix to each verb to write a noun that is a spelling word.

9. manage
10. encourage
11. announce
12. forgive
13. commence
14. amaze

USING THE Dictionary

An **etymology** explains the origin and history of a word. Etymologies appear in brackets at the end of entries (following the definitions). The abbreviation **Obs.** (for "obsolete") means that the entry originated from a spelling no longer in use.

Abbreviations of Languages Used in Etymologies

<	comes from	VLat.	Vulgar Latin	OFr.	Old French
Lat.	Latin	Gk.	Greek	ME	Middle English
LLat.	Late Latin	Fr.	French	OE	Old English

Use the **Spelling Dictionary** to find the etymology of each spelling word below. Write the spelling words with the specified origins.

acre   canoe   commence   encourage   forgive   manage

15.–17. These words come from Latin.

18.–19. These words come from Old English.

20. This word has an origin that is now obsolete.

Spelling and Reading

encouragement	idleness	canoe	manage
forgiveness	acreage	outrageous	management
forgive	canoeing	inventiveness	encourage
acre	commencement	advantageous	commence
fierceness	amazement	awareness	announcement

Answer the Questions   Write the spelling word that best answers each question.

1. What characteristic are tigers known for?
2. What is a formal way in which news or information can be spread?
3. With what might someone react to an unusually spectacular sight?
4. What method of travel requires paddles?
5. How might you describe someone who causes chaos and misery?
6. In what state of activity would you accomplish nothing?
7. What do you need so that you know what is going on around you?
8. What can you give someone to show your support?
9. What quality do people like Thomas Edison have?
10. What can you offer to someone who has hurt you?

Complete the Sentences   Write a spelling word to complete each sentence.

11. What is the _____ of the Zippety Ranch?
12. I hope she can _____ me for losing her sweater.
13. When you are busy, it is important to _____ your time well.
14. The fireworks display will _____ as soon as it gets dark.

Complete the Paragraph   Write spelling words from the box to complete the paragraph.

> canoe
> acre
> commencement
> advantageous
> management
> encourage

    Attention, shoppers. The __15.__ of Chuck's Superstore is excited to announce the __16.__ of its biggest sale ever! We __17.__ you to look for __18.__ bargains in every department. For example, in our yard and garden department, we have a special sale on lawn mowers. One of our models can cut an entire __19.__ of grass in less than an hour! In our sporting goods department, we have a brand-new __20.__ for half price. Included are life vests and paddles. For fabulous bargains, Chuck's Superstore is a shopper's dream come true.

Spelling *and* Writing

Proofread a Speech

Six words are not spelled correctly in this speech. Write the words correctly.

Ladies and gentlemen, I will comence my speech with one simple statement. Our environment needs better managment. We are ruining acre after acre of forest by cutting down trees. We are polluting the beautiful, clear waters of our rivers. The number of plants and animals that have become extinct is outragous. We need to raise our awearness and consider the dangers of idilness. We must encourage our local and federal governments and industries to take more responsibility for the environment. I will conclude my speech with another simple statement: We need to earn Mother Nature's forgivness.

Proofreading Marks

≡ Make a capital.

/ Make a small letter.

∧ Add something.

℮ Take out something.

⊙ Add a period.

⌗ New paragraph

ⓢⓟ Spelling error

Write a Speech — *Persuasive Writing*

Choose something in your neighborhood or town that requires better management. Write a speech to persuade others.

- Begin by stating your position.
- Use facts and details to support your opinion.
- Follow the form used in the proofreading sample. Use as many spelling words as you can.

Writing Process

Prewriting
⇩
Drafting
⇩
Revising
⇩
Editing
⇩
Publishing

Proofread Your Writing During ➤

Proofread your writing for spelling errors as part of the editing stage in the writing process. Be sure to check each word carefully. Use a dictionary to check spelling if you are not sure.

53

Vocabulary

Strategy Words

Review Words:
Adding Suffixes to Words Ending in Silent e

Write a word from the box to complete each sentence.

advancement	excitement	measurement
mileage	wholesome	

1. We took a _____ to find the length of the hall.
2. The discovery of vaccines was an important _____ in medicine.
3. Eating _____ foods can help you stay healthy.
4. I could hardly contain my _____ on my thirteenth birthday.
5. We used a road map to determine the _____ between the two cities.

Preview Words:
Adding Suffixes to Words Ending in Silent e

Write the word from the box that matches each clue.

definitely	entirely	interchangeable
leisurely	peaceable	

6. able to be switched or exchanged
7. in an unhurried manner
8. certainly
9. calm or quiet; not aggressive
10. completely

54

Connections

Content Words

Social Studies: Economics

Write a word from the box to complete each sentence.

endorsement	depositor	countersign
withdrawal	reconcile	

1. The teller checked my signature, or my _____.
2. Mom had to _____ Mike's check by adding her signature on the back.
3. A _____ puts money into a bank.
4. If you want to make a _____, you have to show identification.
5. Each month, I _____ my account by comparing my records with the bank's records.

Science: Computers

Write a word from the box to match each clue.

compile	execute	format
generate	interpret	

6. to explain what the report means
7. to produce a brand-new program
8. to carry out a particular computer function
9. to gather together all the data to write a report
10. to set up the data in an attractive form or style

Apply the Spelling Strategy

Circle the content word you wrote that retained its final silent **e** when a suffix was added.

Spelling and Thinking

READ THE SPELLING WORDS

1.	recognize	*recognize*	I did not **recognize** you in that mask.
2.	recognition	*recognition*	The medal is in **recognition** of bravery.
3.	decoration	*decoration*	A banner is a great party **decoration**.
4.	decorate	*decorate*	Let's **decorate** the room with flags.
5.	combine	*combine*	Red and blue **combine** to make purple.
6.	combination	*combination*	I know the **combination** of the safe.
7.	determination	*determination*	Her **determination** showed in her eyes.
8.	determine	*determine*	Can you **determine** the type of insect?
9.	graduation	*graduation*	I wore a blue robe on **graduation** day.
10.	graduate	*graduate*	He will **graduate** from college soon.
11.	hesitate	*hesitate*	Do not **hesitate** before diving in.
12.	hesitation	*hesitation*	Her **hesitation** indicated her fear.
13.	education	*education*	A good **education** is important in life.
14.	educate	*educate*	A teacher's job is to **educate** students.
15.	compete	*compete*	They will **compete** to see who is faster.
16.	competition	*competition*	We watched a swimming **competition**.
17.	eliminate	*eliminate*	Can I **eliminate** bugs from the garden?
18.	elimination	*elimination*	We hope for the **elimination** of poverty.
19.	admiration	*admiration*	A hero is worthy of **admiration**.
20.	admire	*admire*	I **admire** people who do kind deeds.

SORT THE SPELLING WORDS

1.–10. Write the words that do not have a suffix.

11.–17. Write the words with the **-tion** suffix.

18.–20. Write the words with the **-ation** suffix.

REMEMBER THE SPELLING STRATEGY

Remember that the final **te** or silent **e** is dropped in words like **hesitate** and **determine** before attaching the noun-forming suffix **-tion** or **-ation**.

Word Groups

Write a spelling word related in meaning to complete each group.

1. remove, cancel, _____
2. adorn, garnish, _____
3. decide, figure out, _____
4. battle, oppose, _____
5. identify, notice, _____
6. like, respect, _____

Word Analysis

Add a suffix to each verb to write a noun that is a spelling word.

7. decorate
8. admire
9. eliminate
10. determine
11. compete
12. recognize

USING THE Dictionary

The **primary stress** (′) marks the syllable in a word that receives the greatest stress. The **secondary stress** (′) marks a moderate, or lesser, stress. Write the spelling word for each phonetic spelling. Circle the syllable that has the primary stress. Underline the syllable that has a secondary stress. Use the **Spelling Dictionary** if you need help.

13. /grăj′ o͞o āt′/
14. /grăj′o͞o ā′ shən/
15. /kəm bīn′/
16. /kŏm′bə nā′ shən/
17. /ĕj′ ə kāt′/
18. /ĕj′ə kā′ shən/
19. /hĕz′ ĭ tāt′/
20. /hĕz′ĭ tā′ shən/

recognize	recognition	decoration	decorate	combine
combination	determination	determine	graduation	graduate
hesitate	hesitation	education	educate	compete
competition	eliminate	elimination	admiration	admire

Replace the Words   Write a spelling word to replace the underlined word or words in each sentence.

1. I have a high opinion of people who help others.
2. Students can help instruct other students.
3. Scientists work toward the complete removal of disease.
4. A doctor tries to figure out what a person's symptoms mean.
5. I want to receive a degree from college someday.
6. When I had a chance to help others, I did not act reluctantly.
7. I helped furnish a senior center.
8. My sister trained a Special Olympics athlete for a gymnastics contest of skill or ability.
9. When asked to help, she agreed without pausing.
10. It is easy to join together hard work and good deeds.
11. People who enjoy helping others do not contend with one another.
12. They enjoy helping others and are not looking for approval and esteem.

Complete the Paragraph   Write spelling words from the box to complete the paragraph.

Before the 1800s, society did not __13.__ the need for women to receive an __14.__. Women were appreciated for their domestic skills or their beauty, but Mary Lyon was one woman who refused to be treated as a mere __15.__. She put herself through school. After her __16.__, Lyon dedicated herself to educating other young women. Through a __17.__ of stubbornness and __18.__, she realized her dream. In 1837, she founded Mount Holyoke, the first women's college in America. Today, Mary Lyon receives the __19.__ she deserves for helping to __20.__ an old prejudice.

recognition
combination
decoration
eliminate
recognize
determination
graduation
education

58

Spelling and Writing

Proofread a Paragraph

Six words are not spelled correctly in this paragraph. Write the words correctly.

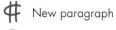
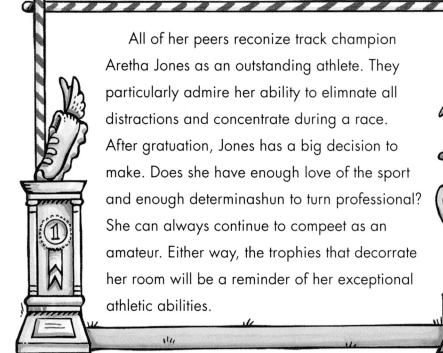

All of her peers reconize track champion Aretha Jones as an outstanding athlete. They particularly admire her ability to elimnate all distractions and concentrate during a race. After gratuation, Jones has a big decision to make. Does she have enough love of the sport and enough determinashun to turn professional? She can always continue to compeet as an amateur. Either way, the trophies that decorrate her room will be a reminder of her exceptional athletic abilities.

Write a Paragraph

Narrative Writing

Choose a decision that you or someone else had to make. Write a paragraph about it.

- Describe the decision that had to be made.
- Explain the choices that were involved and the reasons for choosing one side or the other.
- Follow the form used in the proofreading sample. Use as many spelling words as you can.

Proofread Your Writing During

Writing Process

Prewriting
⇩
Drafting
⇩
Revising
⇩
Editing
⇩
Publishing

Proofread your writing for spelling errors as part of the editing stage in the writing process. Be sure to check each word carefully. Use a dictionary to check spelling if you are not sure.

Vocabulary

Strategy Words

Review Words: Suffixes -tion, -ation

Write a word from the box that matches each definition.

completion	introduction	location
operation	population	

1. the place where something is
2. all of the people living in a certain area
3. a surgical procedure
4. the act of finishing a certain process
5. the first part, as of a book

Preview Words: Suffixes -tion, -ation

Write a word from the box to complete each sentence. Use the underlined words as clues.

aspiration	defamation	expiration
inclination	revelation	

6. We do not tolerate slander, abuse, or _____ of any kind.

7. The reasons behind their behavior came as a disclosure, discovery, or _____.

8. Measure the slant, slope, or _____ of the angle.

9. What is your goal, dream, or _____ in life?

10. Dad checked the termination, end, or _____ date on the milk carton.

Connections

Content Words

Language Arts: Story Elements

Write a word from the box to match each definition.

atmosphere	backdrop	duration
setting	situation	

1. the time and place of a story
2. the circumstances in which a character finds himself or herself
3. the background or setting of a story
4. the tone or mood of a story
5. the length of time during which a story situation exists

Social Studies: Economy

Write a word from the box to replace each word or phrase in parentheses.

deficit	economy	federal
inflation	maintain	

The careful management of our __6.__ (income, materials, or labor) is an important priority for the members of the __7.__ (central, not state) government. They must try to __8.__ (keep) a balance by limiting both __9.__ (a surplus of money leading to high prices) and a budget __10.__ (shortage of money caused by heavy borrowing and spending).

Apply the Spelling Strategy

Circle the three content words you wrote that have the suffix **-tion**.

61

Spelling and Thinking

READ THE SPELLING WORDS

1. demonstration — *demonstration* — We saw a cooking **demonstration**.
2. concentrate — *concentrate* — He will try harder to **concentrate**.
3. issuing — *issuing* — The Treasury is **issuing** new coins.
4. believable — *believable* — His books have **believable** characters.
5. excuse — *excuse* — What is your **excuse** for being late?
6. communication — *communication* — I received a **communication** by mail.
7. comparable — *comparable* — These shirts are **comparable** in price.
8. endure — *endure* — He can **endure** the heat better than I.
9. appreciation — *appreciation* — She smiled to show her **appreciation**.
10. ignorance — *ignorance* — My **ignorance** of the area got us lost.
11. concentrating — *concentrating* — I am **concentrating** on my math.
12. examination — *examination* — Our final **examination** was difficult.
13. likable — *likable* — Anita is a sweet and **likable** child.
14. concentration — *concentration* — Batting a ball takes **concentration**.
15. excusable — *excusable* — Illness made her absence **excusable**.
16. receiving — *receiving* — He will be **receiving** an award.
17. organization — *organization* — Who founded that **organization**?
18. endurance — *endurance* — It takes **endurance** to swim a mile.
19. celebration — *celebration* — We attended his birthday **celebration**.
20. achieving — *achieving* — Are you **achieving** your goals?

SORT THE SPELLING WORDS

1.–3. Write the spelling words that do not end in a suffix.

4.–10. Write the spelling words that end in the suffix **-tion** or **-ation**.

11.–14. Write the spelling words that end in the suffix **-able**.

15.–16. Write the spelling words that end in the suffix **-ance**.

17.–20. Write the spelling words that end in the suffix **-ing**.

REMEMBER THE SPELLING STRATEGY

Remember that the final silent **e** is dropped in words like **concentrate** before attaching a suffix that begins with a vowel.

Spelling and Vocabulary

Word Meanings

Write a spelling word for each definition.

1. uneducated, uninformed state
2. attaining; accomplishing
3. focusing on; paying attention
4. the act of paying close attention
5. the act of celebrating
6. able to be compared
7. the result of being orderly
8. producing; distributing
9. deserving of pardon
10. can be believed

Word Replacements

Write the spelling word that could best replace each underlined word.

11. Jorge expressed his gratitude by sending us a thank-you note.
12. Only the sturdiest trees were able to withstand the storm's fury.
13.–14. We should be getting a formal message about the outcome of the election any minute now.
15. Despite the conversations going on around her, she can focus easily.

USING THE Thesaurus

Write a spelling word that is a synonym for each series of words. Use the **Writing Thesaurus** to check your answers.

16. agreeable, attractive, congenial, pleasing, popular
17. inquiry, inspection, investigation, scrutiny
18. display, exhibition, presentation
19. remove the blame from, forgive, overlook
20. perseverance, persistence, stamina, tenacity

Spelling and Reading

demonstration	concentrate	issuing	believable	excuse
communication	comparable	endure	appreciation	ignorance
concentrating	examination	likable	concentration	excusable
receiving	organization	endurance	celebration	achieving

Solve the Analogies   Write a spelling word to complete each analogy.

1. **Reach** is to **reaching** as **achieve** is to _____.
2. **Enjoyment** is to **displeasure** as **knowledge** is to _____.
3. **Eating** is to **dining** as **distributing** is to _____.
4. **Unlikely** is to **improbable** as **credible** is to _____.

Complete the Sentences   Write the spelling word that best completes each sentence.

5. We will not disturb you if you are _____ on your mathematics homework.
6. Because of the storm, their delay was _____.
7. Please accept this token of _____ for a job well done.
8. She applied all her powers of _____ to learn her lines.
9. I am _____ your signal loud and clear.
10. A victory _____ was held after the game.
11. You are the most pleasant and _____ person I have ever met!
12. After a careful _____, we concluded that the refrigerator was filled with delicious leftovers.

Complete the Paragraph   Write spelling words from the box to complete the paragraph.

The destruction wrought by the hurricane was _13._ to nothing we had ever seen. Few of the trees and plants had been able to _14._ the storm intact. We could not in good conscience _15._ ourselves from helping out. We decided to _16._ on picking up the debris first. Working so hard all day took a lot of _17._, but our efficient _18._ made the job much easier. A formal _19._ from the mayor a few days later mentioned our _20._ of outstanding teamwork during this emergency.

> endurance
> concentrate
> excuse
> demonstration
> communication
> comparable
> endure
> organization

Spelling and Writing

Proofread a Folktale

Six words are not spelled correctly in this retelling of an African folktale. Write the words correctly.

> Anansi, a likabel spider with six sons, fell into a river far from home. His first son, One Who Sees Trouble, was concentrateing when he began recieving mental images of Anansi in the river. He told his brothers; and Anansi's second son, Road Builder, built roads so that they could get to their father. Anansi's third son, River Dryer, gave a demonstration of his power by drying up the river, but all they found was a fish. After an examinetion of the fish, they realized it had eaten Anansi. Game Skinner then cut open the fish to get his father. They were about to have a cellebration for acheiving success when a bird swooped down and grabbed Anansi. Stone Thrower hurled a stone at the bird, making it drop Anansi to the ground. Then Soft-As-a-Cushion dashed to the ground to soften Anansi's fall.

Proofreading Marks

 Make a capital.

 Make a small letter.

 Add something.

 Take out something.

 Add a period.

⌗ New paragraph

SP Spelling error

Write a Folktale

Narrative Writing

Retell a folktale or a fable.

- Rewrite the story in your own words.
- Add a new setting and new characters if you wish.
- Follow the form used in the proofreading sample.

Use as many spelling words as you can.

Proofread Your Writing During

Proofread your writing for spelling errors as part of the editing stage in the writing process. Be sure to check each word carefully. Use a dictionary to check spelling if you are not sure.

Writing Process

Prewriting
⇩
Drafting
⇩
Revising
⇩
Editing
⇩
Publishing

Vocabulary

Strategy Words

Review Words: Adding Suffixes

Write words from the box to complete the letter.

adorable	continuous	imaginary
quotation	sensible	

Dear Editor,

The __1.__ from the police chief in today's paper about the number of dogs hit by cars each year was startling. Obviously, this problem is real, not __2.__. A __3.__ solution is to keep dogs on leashes. Dog owners must take responsibility for their __4.__ pets! I hope you will have __5.__ coverage of this important issue.

Sincerely,

Myra Jones

Preview Words: Adding Suffixes

Write the word from the box that best completes each item.

consolation	observant	proposal
proposition	respiration	

6. a marriage _____
7. alert, watchful, _____
8. a _____ prize
9. inhaling + exhaling = _____
10. a difficult _____

Connections

Content Words

Math: Numbers

Write a word from the box to match each definition.

cardinal	computational	numeration
	ordinal	twentieth

1. a number such as **first** or **third** that indicates a position in a series
2. a number such as **3** or **27** that does not indicate a position in a series
3. related to determining an amount or a number
4. the ordinal version of the cardinal number **20**
5. the process of counting or numbering

Social Studies: Building

Write words from the box to complete the paragraph.

construct	expensive	fabric
	materials	painstaking

Last week, Ms. Amos chose a team of students to __6.__ the set for our school play. She told us not to choose any __7.__ that were too __8.__ for our budget. We just learned that we can get __9.__ for all the curtains for free. We are off to a good start, but creating a set turns out to be a __10.__, though challenging and creative, task.

Apply the Spelling Strategy

Circle the four content words you wrote in which the final silent **e** was dropped from the base word before the suffix was added.

Spelling and Thinking

1. wrestle	*wrestle*	I had to **wrestle** the tight lid off the jar.
2. scenic	*scenic*	The **scenic** view from the top floor is lovely.
3. guarantee	*guarantee*	I **guarantee** that you will enjoy this book.
4. descendant	*descendant*	He is a **descendant** of the former president.
5. knoll	*knoll*	We climbed the **knoll** to pick some flowers.
6. align	*align*	Please **align** the books along the shelf.
7. spaghetti	*spaghetti*	We had **spaghetti** and meatballs for dinner.
8. herb	*herb*	Her secret recipe called for a rare **herb**.
9. sought	*sought*	I **sought** them out in the crowded room.
10. honesty	*honesty*	People respect him for his **honesty**.
11. schedule	*schedule*	The **schedule** tells when the show will begin.
12. thoroughly	*thoroughly*	I was **thoroughly** pleased with the results.
13. gnarled	*gnarled*	The branches were **gnarled** and knotty.
14. hustle	*hustle*	We had to **hustle** through the crowded shop.
15. descend	*descend*	The stairs **descend** to the basement.
16. scenery	*scenery*	I watched the **scenery** from my window seat.
17. exhibition	*exhibition*	Her painting was shown at an **exhibition**.
18. resign	*resign*	The letter explained her wish to **resign**.
19. gauge	*gauge*	There is no way to **gauge** the damage done.
20. jostle	*jostle*	I apologize when I **jostle** someone.

1.–5. Write the spelling words with a silent **h**.

6.–9. Write the spelling words with a silent **k** or **g**.

10.–12. Write the spelling words with a silent **t**.

13.–16. Write the spelling words with a silent **c**.

17.–19. Write the spelling words with a silent **u**.

20. Write the spelling word with a silent **gh**.

REMEMBER THE SPELLING STRATEGY

Remember that some words contain more letters than sounds.

Spelling **and** Vocabulary

Word Meanings

Write a spelling word for each definition.

1. a small, rounded hill
2. to collide, push, or elbow
3. to arrange in a line
4. an instrument for testing or measuring
5. knotty; twisted; misshapen
6. a promise or assurance; something that ensures a particular outcome or condition

Word Groups

Write a spelling word to complete each group.

7. grandchild, offspring, _____
8. hurry, bustle, _____
9. searched, hunted, _____
10. completely, extensively, _____
11. demonstration, show, _____
12. breathtaking, picturesque, _____

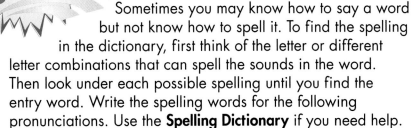

USING THE Dictionary

Sometimes you may know how to say a word but not know how to spell it. To find the spelling in the dictionary, first think of the letter or different letter combinations that can spell the sounds in the word. Then look under each possible spelling until you find the entry word. Write the spelling words for the following pronunciations. Use the **Spelling Dictionary** if you need help.

13. /sē′ nə rē/
14. /dĭ sĕnd′/
15. /ûrb/
16. /ŏn′ ĭ stē/

17. /spə gĕt′ ē/
18. /rĭ zīn′/
19. /skĕj′ o͞ol/
20. /rĕs′ əl/

Spelling and Reading

wrestle	scenic	guarantee	descendant	knoll
align	spaghetti	herb	sought	honesty
schedule	thoroughly	gnarled	hustle	descend
scenery	exhibition	resign	gauge	jostle

Complete the Sentences   Write spelling words to complete the sentences.

1.–2. We have to _____ through the crowd if we want to get to the boat _____.

3.–4. Carl wants to see the _____ along the coastline, so he plans to drive on the _____ route during his vacation.

5.–6. For her research paper, Abby _____ facts about a direct _____ of Washington Irving.

7.–8. If your new stereo came with a written _____ from the manufacturer, be sure to read it _____.

9. I have to check my _____ to see if I am busy on that day.

10. Scientists use seismographs to _____ the intensity of earthquakes.

11. I will _____ from the presidency of the debating club.

12. It is an amazing sight when the planets _____.

Complete the Paragraph   Write spelling words from the box to complete the paragraph.

There once was an old woman who lived on a __13.__ near a village. The townsfolk often came to her for help. With her __14.__ hands, she would apply an __15.__ to a wound, and the wound would heal. One day, she hired a boy from the town as an assistant. She made him promise that he would never use her cooking pot. That night, the boy heard the woman chanting a poem. Curious, he peeked through the door. The pot was magically filling with __16.__ as she spoke! When the woman went out the next day, the boy, forgetting about __17.__, repeated the poem. The pot began to fill with pasta! Word spread and the house filled with curious townsfolk. They began to __18.__ each other in a rush to eat. Soon, they were all stuffed. The pot, however, continued to cook. The boy tried to __19.__ the lid on while waves of pasta began to __20.__ on the town.

wrestle
herb
jostle
knoll
honesty
descend
gnarled
spaghetti

Proofread a Tall Tale

Six words are not spelled correctly in this tall tale. Write the words correctly.

Have you ever heard of Pete Bunkin? He was a direct desendent of the giant lumberjack, Paul Bunyan. Pete Bunkin was so big that when he lay down in the countryside, he used a nole as a pillow. He was so thoroly remorseful for the trees his great-great-grandfather had chopped down that he sought to replace each and every one. Pete carried bundles of trees on his shoulder the way we might carry small piles of sticks. The trees looked like pieces of spagetti in his giant narled hands. He would poke them directly into the ground. Pete spent his life putting trees anywhere he could. Thanks to Pete Bunkin, there are senic forests all over the country.

Proofreading Marks

≡ Make a capital.

/ Make a small letter.

∧ Add something.

℮ Take out something.

⊙ Add a period.

⌗ New paragraph

SP Spelling error

Write a Tall Tale

Narrative Writing

The **tall tale,** a form of humorous "brag" that grew out of the American frontier of the early 1800s, exaggerates elements of truth for humorous effect.

- Select a story from a newspaper or magazine.
- Retell the story as a tall tale.
- Follow the form used in the proofreading sample. Use as many spelling words as you can.

Writing Process

Prewriting
⇩
Drafting
⇩
Revising
⇩
Editing
⇩
Publishing

Proofread Your Writing During

Proofread your writing for spelling errors as part of the editing stage in the writing process. Be sure to check each word carefully. Use a dictionary to check spelling if you are not sure.

Vocabulary

Strategy Words

Review Words:
Words With More Letters Than Sounds

Write the word from the box that matches each definition.

crumb	kneel	knob
plumber	solemn	

1. a rounded handle, usually found on a drawer or door
2. serious; somber; grave
3. a small scrap or morsel of food
4. someone who installs and repairs pipes and plumbing
5. to assume a position of resting on one or both knees

Preview Words:
Words With More Letters Than Sounds

Write a word from the box to complete each sentence.

campaign	mortgage	pneumonia
raspberry	subtle	

6. The doctor gave me medicine to clear up my _____.
7. Shelley likes strawberry ice cream, but I prefer _____.
8. I tried to be _____, but I ended up being completely obvious.
9. The politicians posted _____ signs all over town.
10. You get a _____ when you borrow money from a bank to buy a house.

Connections

Content Words

Public Speaking: Debate

Write words from the box to complete the paragraph.

convince	extemporaneous	informative
	orator	rhetoric

An effective __1.__ is a master of __2.__. A good speech is usually __3.__, introducing an audience to new facts or opinions. Whether a speech is rehearsed or __4.__, an experienced speaker knows how to use words and tone to __5.__ an audience that his or her argument is valid.

Science: Gems

Write a word from the box to match each definition.

crystalline	emerald	gemstone
	homogeneous	sapphire

6. uniform throughout
7. of or like crystal; clear or transparent
8. a precious or semiprecious stone that may be used as a jewel when it is cut and polished
9. a blue variety of corundum; deep blue
10. a rare green variety of beryl; a brilliant shade of green

Apply the Spelling Strategy

Circle the three content words you wrote that contain more consonant letters than consonant sounds.

Assessment and Review

Assessment — Units 7–11

Each Assessment Word in the box fits one of the spelling strategies you have studied over the past five weeks. Read the spelling strategies. Then write each Assessment Word under the unit number it fits.

Unit 7

1.–5. Remember that words such as **inability, unexpected,** and **fearlessness** contain affixes.

Unit 8

6.–7. Remember that some base words retain a final silent **e** when a suffix is added.

Unit 9

8.–11. Remember that the final **te** or silent **e** is dropped in words like **hesitate** and **determine** before attaching the noun-forming suffix **-tion** or **-ation**.

Unit 10

12.–16. Remember that the final silent **e** is dropped in words like **concentrate** before attaching suffixes that begin with a vowel.

Unit 11

17.–20. Remember that some words contain more letters than sounds.

> indefinite
> grateful
> exploration
> curable
> consign
> hesitating
> prearrangement
> isolation
> received
> gnash
> spiteful
> indifferent
> shepherd
> evaporation
> uselessness
> severely
> bristle
> sincerity
> evaporate
> freezing

requirement	extremely	unexpected	improvement
alphabetical	surprisingly	regardless	disappointment
	emotional	agreeable	

Write the spelling word that is an affixed form for each of these words.

1. extreme
2. agree
3. appoint
4. require
5. prove

6. surprise
7. regard
8. expect
9. emotion
10. alphabet

Review Unit 8: Adding Suffixes to Words Ending in Silent e

encouragement	canoe	manage	acreage
management	canoeing	encourage	acre
	advantageous	announcement	

Write the word that completes the sentence.

11. Please paddle the _____ from the left side.

12. I can _____ the paddling from the right side by myself.

13. Please don't talk while we are _____ down the rapids.

14. During the race, our coach shouted words of _____ from the shore.

15. It will certainly be _____ if we practice before we begin the race.

16. We will start as soon as we hear the _____ that everything is ready.

17. I _____ you to work on your technique.

18. Ms. Amiri's style of _____ is to support everyone who tries to succeed.

19. The survey accounts for every _____ of land.

20. How much _____ has been planted in corn?

recognize	combine	determination	hesitate
recognition	compete	hesitation	competition
	determine	combination	

Write the spelling word and its affixed form for each sentence.

1.–2. In a one-on-one basketball _____, two players _____ against each other.

3.–4. If you _____ too long in helping someone, that _____ might result in danger.

5.–6. The committee can clearly _____ that you would like _____ for your hard work.

7.–8. It was the judge's _____ that the jury could _____ the damages in the court case.

9.–10. If you _____ two odd numbers, the _____ will always be an even number.

 **Review** Unit 10: Adding Suffixes to Words Ending in Silent e

concentrate	issuing	excuse	communication
comparable	likable	concentration	excusable
	organization	celebration	

Write the word that fits the clue.

11. to apologize for

12. to focus

13. forgivable

14. sending out

15. an organized group

Write the spelling word that is the suffixed form of each word.

16. communicate

17. concentrate

18. celebrate

19. like

20. compare

 **Unit 11: Words With More Letters Than Sounds**

scenic	guarantee	spaghetti	sought
honesty	schedule	thoroughly	scenery
	exhibition	gauge	

Write a spelling word that goes with each set.

1. pretty, picturesque
2. macaroni, linguini
3. completely, fully
4. truthfulness, integrity
5. promise, pledge

6. view, landscape
7. timetable, plan
8. display, show
9. measure, check
10. asked, requested

Spelling Study Strategy

Sorting by Parts of Speech

Sorting words is a good way to master their meaning and spelling. Here is a way to work with a partner to sort the spelling words:

1. Make a four-column chart with the headings **Noun, Verb, Adjective, Adverb**.

2. Choose a partner and take turns writing a spelling word in the proper columns.

3. Use the word in a sentence to demonstrate its part of speech.

4. If you can think of how the word might be used as a different part of speech, list it in that column, too.

For example, you might put **excuse** in the Noun column and also in the Verb column by giving the sentence, "I can **excuse** (verb) you for giving that poor **excuse** (noun) for being absent."

Grammar, Usage, and Mechanics

Identifying Modifiers: Adverbs

An adverb is a word that modifies a verb, an adjective, or another adverb. Many adverbs end in **-ly** and tell how, when, or to what extent something is done.

> Fido looked up **indifferently,** although Marge spoke **loudly.**
> New York has **very** tall buildings.
> We reviewed the lesson **quite thoroughly**.

A. Write the adverb in each sentence below.

1. We are postponing the game indefinitely.
2. "We'll win next year," Marcus said hopefully.
3. The captains shook hands agreeably.
4. Juana tapped the empty piggy bank uselessly.
5. Ali glared severely at his opponent.
6. Carly called encouragingly to her teammates.
7. I sincerely hope that I am ready for the test.
8. Sue has completely finished the quilt.

B. Write the adverb form of the word in parentheses by adding **-ly**.

9. Please answer every question (honest).
10. I have (thorough) examined the evidence.
11. He cried out (emotional) at the sight.
12. The test was (surprising) easy.
13. Mr. DeNardo showed up (unexpected).
14. He handled the problem (professional).
15. The small boy ran (fearless) into the game.

WORKSHOP

Proofreading Strategy

One at a Time

Good writers always proofread their writing for spelling errors. Here's a strategy you can use to proofread your papers.

Go through your paper looking for just one kind of error at a time. You might first look for word endings, such as **-ing** or **-able**. Then you could look for contractions. Then check for words that have silent consonants.

Although this might seem like a lot of extra work, each go-through takes only a few minutes. It will be worth the trouble. Try it!

Electronic Spelling

Internet Addresses: "You Have E-mail!"

When you send or receive e-mail, you use an Internet address. The computer user has to be sure to type in the address exactly, or the mail won't be delivered.

One part of an Internet address follows a period, or "dot." There should not be any space before or after the dot. Here are some examples of the dot part of an Internet address:

.com   a company
.edu   an educational institution
.gov   some part of the government, probably the United States federal government
.org   an organization

Look for misspellings in the dot part of these addresses that would prevent the e-mail from being delivered. Write the address correctly from @.

1. SubScripts@aol.com
2. jmjd_root@indstate.eud
3. ncmc@loc.gov
4. BLOR@newways.ogr
5. JimA@juno.omc

Spelling and Thinking

1.	absolutely	*absolutely*	He is **absolutely** my favorite actor.
2.	briefly	*briefly*	Since time is short, explain **briefly**.
3.	vague	*vague*	He gave us only a **vague** description.
4.	fortunately	*fortunately*	I was wearing a seat belt, **fortunately**.
5.	urgent	*urgent*	Move fast if it is **urgent**.
6.	particular	*particular*	I do not like that **particular** color.
7.	instantly	*instantly*	She **instantly** knew the answer.
8.	necessarily	*necessarily*	This is not **necessarily** bad news.
9.	deliberate	*deliberate*	His actions were slow and **deliberate**.
10.	particularly	*particularly*	I am not **particularly** fond of beets.
11.	immediately	*immediately*	Please give her this note **immediately**.
12.	urgently	*urgently*	We **urgently** need new uniforms.
13.	accurately	*accurately*	She will relay the message **accurately**.
14.	deliberately	*deliberately*	Did you **deliberately** let me win?
15.	presently	*presently*	Dinner will be ready **presently**.
16.	readily	*readily*	I will **readily** attend the dance.
17.	approximately	*approximately*	He is **approximately** six feet tall.
18.	vaguely	*vaguely*	I remember my dreams only **vaguely**.
19.	positively	*positively*	He is **positively** my best friend ever!
20.	absolute	*absolute*	The president's power is not **absolute**.

SORT THE SPELLING WORDS

1.–5. Write the spelling words that are adjectives.

6.–13. Write the words that are adverbs ending in silent **e** + **-ly**.

14.–18. Write the words that are adverbs ending in **consonant** + **-ly**.

19.–20. Write the adverbs that were made by changing **y** to **i** and adding **-ly**.

REMEMBER THE SPELLING STRATEGY

Remember that the suffix **-ly** may be added to adjectives like **urgent** to form adverbs.

Word Meanings ▬ ▬ ▬ ▬ ▬ ▬ ▬ ▬

Write a spelling word to complete each sentence. Use the underlined words to help you.

1. We will _____ get the children <u>ready</u> for the party.

2. Just add water to the <u>instant</u> soup, and we can eat it _____!

3. She will not _____ remember to bring the <u>necessary</u> items.

4. The young man inherited a <u>fortune</u>, and _____ he is using it wisely.

Word Replacements ▬ ▬ ▬ ▬ ▬ ▬ ▬ ▬

Write a spelling word that best replaces the underlined words in each sentence.

5. Will you finish your homework <u>soon after the present time</u>?

6. He spoke <u>in a positive way</u> about his teacher.

7. She will talk <u>in a brief manner</u> and then answer questions.

8. Can you tell me <u>in an approximate way</u> what time it is?

9. When a tornado comes, find shelter <u>in an immediate way</u>.

10. It is important to answer the questions <u>in an accurate way</u>.

USING THE Dictionary

Write pairs of spelling words for each Latin etymology given below. Use the **Spelling Dictionary** if you need help.

11.–12. **vagus,** wandering

13.–14. **urgens,** pressing

15.–16. **deliberatus,** considered

17.–18. **absolutus,** ended

19.–20. **particularis,** part

absolutely	briefly	vague	fortunately
urgent	particular	instantly	necessarily
deliberate	particularly	immediately	urgently
accurately	deliberately	presently	readily
approximately	vaguely	positively	absolute

Answer the Questions Write the spelling words that best answer the questions.

   1.–2. Which two spelling words are synonyms for **definitely**?
   3. Which spelling word is a synonym for **soon**?
   4.–5. Which two spelling words are synonyms for **now**?
   6.–7. Which two spelling words are antonyms for **exactly**?
   8. Which spelling word is a synonym for **unclear**?

Complete the Dialogue Write spelling words from the box that best complete the dialogue.

readily
fortunately
deliberately
particularly
accurately
absolute
necessarily
urgent
particular
urgently
briefly
deliberate

Moderator: The subject for our debate is how to meet the __9.__ need for new energy sources. Are there any questions before we begin?

Carlos: Would you please fill us in on the rules of the debate? I am __10.__ curious about how much time we have to speak.

Moderator: You will have only two minutes to speak, so please present your views __11.__. This rule is __12.__; I must stop anyone from exceeding the time limit. Be sure to use supporting facts and details to state your position __13.__.

Michelle: What if the other team is __14.__ misleading the judges, and we __15.__ want to argue the point? May we interrupt?

Moderator: We will accept no __16.__ interruptions! But, __17.__, you will get time for a rebuttal.

Carlos: How is the winner chosen?

Moderator: At the end, the judges will confer and then announce the winner. The decision will not __18.__ be based on any __19.__ facts. It will include how carefully the research was prepared and how __20.__ the participants are able to respond to the opposing arguments.

Spelling and Writing

Proofread a Dialogue

Six words are not spelled correctly in this dialogue between an American colonist and a modern-day reporter. Write the words correctly.

Colonist: Do people still read the newspaper?

Reporter: Many do, but it's not neccesarily the way they get news. They get news from television, too.

Colonist: That's absolutely intriguing. How does it work?

Reporter: I'll explain breifly. Sounds and images are converted to digital signals, which are sent to satellites, returned to Earth, translated back to sounds and images, and sent to television sets. Urgent news is delivered instently.

Colonist: I do not have even a vage idea of what you mean. Digital? Satellites? I am posatively confused by such words!

Proofreading Marks

≡ Make a capital.

/ Make a small letter.

∧ Add something.

℮ Take out something.

⊙ Add a period.

⌗ New paragraph

SP Spelling error

Write a Dialogue

Narrative Writing

Write a dialogue between two imaginary characters, one from the past and one from the present.

- Before you begin, decide what your characters might discuss, for example, politics, entertainment, transportation, or technology.
- Follow the form used in the proofreading sample. Use as many spelling words as you can.

Proofread Your Writing During

Writing Process

Prewriting
⇩
Drafting
⇩
Revising
⇩
Editing
⇩
Publishing

Proofread your writing for spelling errors as part of the editing stage in the writing process. Be sure to check each word carefully. Use a dictionary to check spelling if you are not sure.

Vocabulary

Review Words: Suffix -ly

Write a word from the box to complete each sentence.

additionally	barely	carefully
certainly	exactly	

1. I thought the store would be crowded, but it had _____ any people in it.
2. That is _____ not my hat; mine is blue, and that one is red.
3. Please carry the tray _____ so that you do not drop it.
4. You have three telephone messages; _____, your neighbor stopped by to say hello.
5. I counted the books, and there were _____ forty-seven on the top shelf.

Preview Words: Suffix -ly

Write the word from the box that matches each definition.

coincidentally	diagonally	patiently
strictly	voicelessly	

6. in a tolerant or understanding way
7. in a mute or speechless way
8. across, from corner to corner
9. happening at the same time, seemingly accidentally
10. with firm discipline or control

Connections

Content Words

Language Arts: Transitions

Write a word from the box to complete each group.

complex	consequently	furthermore
nevertheless		thesis

1. so, therefore, _____
2. in spite of, however, _____
3. theory, opinion, _____
4. complicated, detailed, _____
5. additionally, also, _____

Science: Computers

Write words from the box to complete the paragraph.

configuration	interactive	network
password	simultaneously	

A school or office may have a chain, or __6.__, of computers. A __7.__, or arrangement, in which many computers connect to one central computer can provide workers __8.__ use of a shared database. From their individual stations, many workers can feed information __9.__ into one memory bank. To gain access to the system, each worker must type in a __10.__, or personal secret code.

Apply the Spelling Strategy

Circle the two content words you wrote that have the suffix **-ly**.

Spelling and Thinking

READ THE SPELLING WORDS

1. compatible — *compatible* — I have very **compatible** friends.
2. questionable — *questionable* — Were the test results **questionable**?
3. uncomfortable — *uncomfortable* — How **uncomfortable** these shoes feel!
4. eligible — *eligible* — All **eligible** voters may enter now.
5. unavoidable — *unavoidable* — We made an **unavoidable** detour.
6. accessible — *accessible* — The attic is **accessible** by ladder.
7. reasonable — *reasonable* — Make a **reasonable** offer for my bike.
8. unacceptable — *unacceptable* — Most sloppy work is **unacceptable**.
9. permissible — *permissible* — Is it **permissible** to leave early?
10. incredible — *incredible* — Her story was **incredible** but true.
11. unreasonable — *unreasonable* — Ignore any **unreasonable** requests.
12. remarkable — *remarkable* — She has had a **remarkable** career.
13. unmistakable — *unmistakable* — He speaks with **unmistakable** dignity.
14. ineligible — *ineligible* — You are **ineligible** to run for mayor.
15. considerable — *considerable* — Anna displayed **considerable** courage.
16. recognizable — *recognizable* — A duck is **recognizable** by its bill.
17. suitable — *suitable* — You have many **suitable** hats to wear.
18. admirable — *admirable* — Generosity is an **admirable** quality.
19. noticeable — *noticeable* — I made **noticeable** improvement!
20. disagreeable — *disagreeable* — The cranky child was **disagreeable**.

SORT THE SPELLING WORDS

1.–6. Write the spelling words that end in **-ible**.

7.–9. Write the spelling words in which the silent **e** is dropped from the base word when **-able** is added.

10.–14. Write the spelling words that contain a prefix and a base word and **-able**.

15.–20. Write the spelling words that contain only a base word and **-able**.

REMEMBER THE SPELLING STRATEGY

Remember that the suffixes **-able** and **-ible** may be added to base words or word roots to form adjectives.

Spelling and Vocabulary

Word Meanings

Write the spelling word that could best replace the underlined word
or words.

1. The notion that dogs and cats are not <u>capable of getting along</u> is false.

2. Will is shy and <u>ill at ease</u> around strangers.

3. Only I was <u>capable of being identified</u> in the picture.

4. It was <u>doubtful and debatable</u> whether he would stay in the race
after he fell.

5. Budding trees and flowering crocuses are <u>sure and undeniable</u>
signs of spring.

6. The flight delay was <u>impossible to escape</u> because of the dense fog.

7. Two fans were asked to leave the stadium because their behavior
was rude and <u>not allowable</u>.

Word Analysis

Change the underlined affixes in the words to write spelling words.

8. <u>ad</u>miss<u>ion</u>   9. disagree<u>ment</u>   10. <u>dis</u>credit   11. notic<u>ing</u>

Antonyms

Write a spelling word that is an antonym for each word.

12. The antonym is **unqualified,** and the word ends in **-ible**.

13. The antonym is **sensible,** and the word begins with **un-**.

14. The antonym is **qualified,** and the word begins with **in-**.

15. The antonym is **illogical,** and the word ends in **-able**.

USING THE Dictionary

To save space, some forms of an entry word
appear before the definition of the main entry.
Such **run-on entries** usually have a different part of
speech from that of the entry word. Write the entry word
(a spelling word) and its part of speech for each of the run-on
entries below. Use the **Spelling Dictionary** if you need help.

16. considerably, *adv.*   19. admirably, *adv.*

17. suitability, *n.*   20. accessibility, *n.*

18. remarkably, *adv.*

Spelling and Reading

compatible	eligible	uncomfortable	questionable	unavoidable
reasonable	accessible	unacceptable	permissible	recognizable
admirable	ineligible	unmistakable	remarkable	considerable
incredible	suitable	unreasonable	noticeable	disagreeable

Complete the Sentences Write spelling words to complete the sentences. Use the base words indicated in parentheses.

1. Is it _____ to swim with no lifeguard present? (permit)
2. Dan's report was _____ to Ms. Lee, so he rewrote it. (accept)
3. Trahn has a _____ talent for drawing landscapes. (remark)
4. It is _____ to expect us to pay attention to a dull speech. (reason)
5.–6. Because Amy was in such an unpleasant, _____ mood, it was _____ whether anyone would volunteer to be her partner. (agree, question)

Draw Conclusions Use the clue in each sentence to write a spelling word that best concludes each statement.

7. If your argument makes sense, then your argument is _____.
8. If you would never mistake your friend's voice for someone else's, then your friend's voice is _____.
9. If everyone who sees the sign notices it, then the sign must be _____.
10. If a teacher is easy to approach, then the teacher is _____.
11. If a story could not possibly be true, then the story is _____.
12. If a dance is formal, then jeans are not _____ to wear.
13. If a room is hot and stuffy, then you may feel _____ in it.

Complete the Paragraph Write spelling words from the box to complete the paragraph.

The harsh taxes imposed by England on American colonists were not __14.__ with the colonists' way of life. By 1774, war seemed __15.__. In April 1775, the Revolutionary War began. Every __16.__ man was recruited into the colonial army. Even though women were __17.__, a few __18.__ female patriots disguised themselves as men so that they would not be __19.__ as they fought in the Revolutionary Army. One of those women was Deborah Sampson, who displayed __20.__ courage as she fought alongside her compatriots.

ineligible
considerable
unavoidable
recognizable
eligible
compatible
admirable

88

Spelling and Writing

Proofread a Paragraph

Six words are not spelled correctly in this paragraph. Write the words correctly.

Recently, school officials sectioned off a portion of the cafeteria for band practice. This might be a reasnable solution for the band's problem, but many students find it unaceptable. While there has been conciderable improvement in the quality of cafeteria food, the cafeteria is no longer suitible for the number of students who eat there. The space is crowded and uncomftable. The tables are so close together that they are barely axcessible to students in wheelchairs. I suggest that the band use part of the old gym for practice. It is incredible that no one else has suggested this solution. The new gym and part of the old gym will still be available for sports and physical education.

Proofreading Marks

≡   Make a capital.

/   Make a small letter.

∧   Add something.

℮   Take out something.

⊙   Add a period.

⌗   New paragraph

(SP)   Spelling error

Write a Paragraph

Persuasive Writing

Think about a problem in your school or community that has more than one solution. Write a paragraph about the problem.

- Define the problem and offer two solutions.
- Evaluate the pros and cons of each solution, and explain which solution you think is most reasonable.
- Follow the form used in the proofreading sample. Use as many spelling words as you can.

Writing Process

Prewriting
⇩
Drafting
⇩
Revising
⇩
Editing
⇩
Publishing

Proofread Your Writing During

Proofread your writing for spelling errors as part of the editing stage in the writing process. Be sure to check each word carefully. Use a dictionary to check spelling if you are not sure.

Vocabulary

Strategy Words

Review Words: Suffixes -able, -ible

Write a word from the box to complete each sentence.

edible	favorable	flexible
notable	profitable	

1. The artist is worthy of note. Her work is _____.
2. These mushrooms can be eaten. They are _____.
3. I can bend and flex this wire. The wire is _____.
4. His business made a large profit. His business is _____.
5. The winds are in our favor for sailing. The winds are _____.

Preview Words: Suffixes -able, -ible

Write words from the box to complete the paragraph.

disposable	hospitable	inadvisable
irresponsible	sociable	

My cousins, who often have parties, are warm and __6.__ to their guests. I enjoy their parties because I can visit with friends, talk, and be __7.__. I have one problem though. At most of the parties, beverages and food are served in __8.__ paper cups and plates. I have come to believe that this practice is __9.__ and __10.__. Paper is made from trees. If we switch to real dishes and cups, we can stop adding to the earth's trash, and we might save some trees from destruction.

Connections

Content Words

Science: Pollution

Write words from the box to complete the paragraph.

biodegradable	detergent	phosphates
pollutants	toxic	

Does your laundry __1.__ contain any poisonous or __2.__ chemical compounds such as __3.__? When those __4.__ are washed into rivers and streams, they can do great damage to animals, fish, and plants. Because these harmful products are not __5.__, they remain in the environment indefinitely.

Social Studies: Productivity

Write words from the box to complete the paragraph.

desirable	inexpensive	quality
synthetic	technology	

What could be more __6.__ than clothes that never get dirty? Advances in science and __7.__ will soon make that idea a reality. One of the country's major clothing manufacturers plans to introduce a line of clothing made of a __8.__ material that repels dirt and does not stain. According to a company spokesperson, the clothing will be of high __9.__. It also will be __10.__ and affordable.

Apply the Spelling Strategy

Circle the two content words you wrote that end in the suffix **-able**.

Spelling and Thinking

READ THE SPELLING WORDS

1.	breathe	*breathe*	To **breathe** fresh air is a pleasure.
2.	usually	*usually*	I **usually** eat a big meal at lunch.
3.	vacuum	*vacuum*	Please **vacuum** the rug in your room.
4.	picnicking	*picnicking*	We enjoy **picnicking** by the lake.
5.	bouquet	*bouquet*	Joe brought Mom a **bouquet** of wildflowers.
6.	annually	*annually*	The company reports its earnings **annually**.
7.	pursuit	*pursuit*	She is in **pursuit** of a gold medal.
8.	bouillon	*bouillon*	Eli had a bowl of beef **bouillon** for lunch.
9.	actual	*actual*	Is that an **actual** account of the event?
10.	league	*league*	Sasha is a member of a softball **league**.
11.	mimicking	*mimicking*	The monkey is **mimicking** human behavior.
12.	variety	*variety*	Sentence **variety** adds interest to a story.
13.	coupon	*coupon*	She has a **coupon** for a free CD.
14.	maneuver	*maneuver*	Can he **maneuver** the boat past the dock?
15.	curiosity	*curiosity*	The mysterious note aroused his **curiosity**.
16.	peculiar	*peculiar*	What is the source of that **peculiar** odor?
17.	visually	*visually*	Soft, pastel colors are **visually** soothing.
18.	courtesy	*courtesy*	It shows **courtesy** not to interrupt.
19.	initial	*initial*	He scored on the **initial** play of the game.
20.	pursue	*pursue*	Val hopes to **pursue** a career as an actress.

SORT THE SPELLING WORDS

1.–8. Write the spelling words that have one or two syllables. Remember that there is a syllable for every vowel sound in a word.

9.–15. Write the spelling words that have three syllables.

16.–20. Write the spelling words that have four or five syllables.

REMEMBER THE SPELLING STRATEGY

Remember that it is important to know the spelling of words that are frequently misspelled.

Word Meanings

Write a spelling word with the same meaning as each group of words.

1. real, true, factual
2. first, beginning, introductory
3. diversity, assortment, different kinds
4. club, association, organization
5. exploration, hobby, activity
6. graciousness, politeness, refinement
7. odd, strange, different

Word Structure

Add a suffix to each word to write a spelling word. You may have to change the spelling of the word before adding the suffix.

8. usual
9. picnic
10. annual
11. visual
12. mimic
13. curious

USING THE Dictionary

For entry words with more than one acceptable pronunciation, the phonetic spelling of the preferred pronunciation appears first. The alternative phonetic spelling shows only those syllables that differ from the preferred pronunciation. Look up each of the following words in the **Spelling Dictionary**. Write the word and the number (1, 2, or 3) of acceptable pronunciations given.

14. vacuum
15. coupon
16. breathe
17. bouillon
18. pursue
19. maneuver
20. bouquet

Spelling ᵃⁿᵈ Reading

breathe	usually	vacuum	picnicking	bouquet
annually	pursuit	bouillon	actual	league
mimicking	variety	coupon	maneuver	curiosity
peculiar	visually	courtesy	initial	pursue

Complete the Sentences Write the spelling word that best completes each sentence.

1. Please _____ this receipt to show that you got your money back.
2. People who ask a lot of questions are often rewarded for their _____.
3. Do you understand the expression "to operate in a _____"?
4. Mountaineers find it hard to _____ above certain altitudes.
5. Adding _____ to the stew will give it the liquid it needs.
6. Thank you for remembering my birthday with this _____.
7. People became suspicious of his _____ behavior.
8. Is this the _____ cost, or are there hidden fees?
9. The dog officer is in _____ of a stray dog.
10. He _____ walks in the park, but today he walked downtown.
11. Looking at the bright bold colors was _____ stimulating.

Complete the Announcement Write spelling words from the box to complete the announcement.

> league
> coupon
> annually
> mimicking
> pursue
> variety
> maneuver
> picnicking
> courtesy

Join us this Saturday for Field Day, which is held __12.__ at Roland Park. Enjoy a __13.__ of games and activities. There will be __14.__ by the pond, with box lunches, __15.__ of Armond's Delicatessen. The town's soccer __16.__ and the softball club will sponsor several competitions. You can also enter a lip sync contest and have fun __17.__ your favorite singers. Younger children can __18.__ their bikes through an obstacle course as they __19.__ prizes, including a __20.__ for six free admissions to the See-It-Now Moviehouse. Be sure to come on Saturday!

Spelling and Writing

Proofread a Paragraph

Six words are not spelled correctly in this paragraph. Write the words correctly.

> Mr. Morris, our English teacher, explained that many people like to play with language. He said that although they often use words in peculyer ways, people who create puns and other plays on words usully have a good understanding of grammar and vocabulary. Then he gave us a veriety of examples of language play. His inishal one was a poem title and author: "Ode to Darkness," by Son E. Day. Another example was an actual sign he had seen in a tailor's shop: "For those in persute of the perfect fitting suit, I charge $40 per suit." His final example was a line from a book: "At court I see they lack kertesy."

POETRY

Proofreading Marks

≡ Make a capital.

/ Make a small letter.

∧ Add something.

ℓ Take out something.

⊙ Add a period.

⌗ New paragraph

ⓢⓟ Spelling error

Write a Paragraph

Narrative Writing

Choose a topic that has to do with language—puns, metaphors, similes, alliteration, and so on. Write a paragraph about it.

- Explain the topic or term you have chosen.
- Give specific examples of the topic or term.
- Follow the form used in the proofreading sample. Use as many spelling words as you can.

Proofread Your Writing During

Proofread your writing for spelling errors as part of the editing stage in the writing process. Be sure to check each word carefully. Use a dictionary to check spelling if you are not sure.

Writing Process

Prewriting
⇩
Drafting
⇩
Revising
⇩
Editing
⇩
Publishing

Vocabulary

Strategy Words

Review Words: Frequently Misspelled Words

Write the word from the box that matches each clue.

jewelry	probably	restaurant
rhythm	surely	

1. This is a synonym for **certainly**.
2. Rings, bracelets, and earrings are examples of this.
3. This is a good thing for drummers to have.
4. It is not your kitchen, but you can eat there.
5. This is not for sure, but it is most likely.

Preview Words: Frequently Misspelled Words

Write words from the box to complete the paragraph.

committee	exhaust	genuine
liaison	numerous	

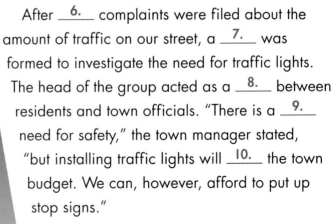

After ___6.___ complaints were filed about the amount of traffic on our street, a ___7.___ was formed to investigate the need for traffic lights. The head of the group acted as a ___8.___ between residents and town officials. "There is a ___9.___ need for safety," the town manager stated, "but installing traffic lights will ___10.___ the town budget. We can, however, afford to put up stop signs."

Connections

Content Words

Social Studies: Archaeology

Write words from the box to complete the paragraph.

archaeology	artifact	dwelling
excavate	primitive	

I have always been interested in the study of __1.__ cultures and plan to pursue a career in __2.__ . I dream about being part of a team sent to __3.__ an ancient site. I imagine being the first person to enter a prehistoric __4.__ , where I find a rock painting, a hand-crafted tool, or another priceless __5.__ .

Science: Engines

Write a word from the box to match each definition.

carburetor	combustion	crankshaft
diesel	piston	

6. a shaft that is turned by a handle or crank
7. the process of burning
8. a type of engine
9. a solid cylinder that fits snugly into a larger cylinder and moves under pressure
10. a device used in engines to produce an efficient explosive vapor of fuel and air

Apply the Spelling Strategy

Circle the two content words you wrote that have the most unexpected spellings.

Spelling and Thinking

READ THE SPELLING WORDS

1. confer   *confer*   Krista will **confer** with her math teacher.
2. conferred   *conferred*   The President **conferred** with his advisers.
3. conference   *conference*   When is the parent-teacher **conference**?
4. occur   *occur*   What time will the solar eclipse **occur**?
5. occurred   *occurred*   The hailstorm **occurred** on our way home.
6. occurrence   *occurrence*   Lightning is a common **occurrence** in summer.
7. omit   *omit*   Do not **omit** your name from your test paper.
8. omitted   *omitted*   Part of the tour was **omitted** to save time.
9. omitting   *omitting*   He is **omitting** two chapters from his book.
10. prefer   *prefer*   I **prefer** e-mail to handwritten notes.
11. preferred   *preferred*   Otis **preferred** soccer to any other sport.
12. preference   *preference*   Do you have a **preference** for red socks?
13. infer   *infer*   I **infer** from his letter that he is homesick.
14. inferred   *inferred*   Dad **inferred** that I did not want to leave.
15. refer   *refer*   You may **refer** to your notes during the test.
16. reference   *reference*   Use more than one atlas for **reference**.
17. referring   *referring*   He is **referring** to a news article he read.
18. compel   *compel*   What could **compel** you to wear a pink hat?
19. compelled   *compelled*   Such kindness **compelled** us to give thanks.
20. compelling   *compelling*   I was absorbed in a **compelling** mystery.

SORT THE SPELLING WORDS

1.–7. Write the spelling words that are base words.

8.–17. Write the spelling words in which the final consonant of the base word is doubled when the suffix is added.

18.–20. Write the spelling words in which the stress shifts to the first syllable when the suffix is added.

REMEMBER THE SPELLING STRATEGY

Remember that a final consonant preceded by a single vowel is doubled when adding a suffix that begins with a vowel except when the accent is on or shifts to the first syllable.

Word Meanings ━ ▬ ▬ ▬ ▬ ▬ ▬ ▬ ▬ ▬ ▬ ▬

Write a spelling word for each definition.

1. to draw a conclusion on the basis of evidence
2. to take place
3. a first choice or favorite; partiality or liking
4. bestowed or consulted with
5. pressing or persuasive
6. a written statement about qualifications
7. a discussion, meeting, or session

Word Replacements ━ ▬ ▬ ▬ ▬ ▬ ▬ ▬ ▬ ▬ ▬

Write the spelling word that best replaces the underlined word or words.

8. Why are you <u>leaving out</u> the most exciting part of the story?
9. Do you know what actually <u>happened</u> on July 4, 1776?
10. I have always <u>favored</u> pizza over hamburgers.
11. From the early returns, the reporter <u>concluded</u> that the candidate would win the election by a landslide.
12. Was the principal <u>alluding</u> to our class in her announcement?
13. Lani's name was accidentally <u>dropped</u> from the drama club list.
14. If you do not understand the concept of flight, I can <u>direct</u> you to a good book on the subject.
15. Juana's curiosity <u>drove</u> her to ask one more question.

USING THE Thesaurus

Write a spelling word that is a synonym for each group of words. Check your answers in the **Writing Thesaurus.**

16. choose, pick, select
17. eliminate, fail to include, leave out
18. coerce, force, constrain
19. advise, deliberate, discuss
20. circumstance, event, incident

Spelling and Reading

confer	conferred	conference	occur	occurred
occurrence	omit	omitted	omitting	prefer
preferred	preference	infer	inferred	refer
reference	referring	compel	compelled	compelling

Complete the Sentences Write a spelling word to complete each sentence.

1. We could not find a _____ to that author.
2. The five judges will _____ before choosing a winner.
3. Ruby has always _____ the mountains to the ocean.
4. What celebrity was that writer _____ to in her article?
5. I suspect that he is _____ several facts from the story.
6. Mom enjoys baseball, but Dad has a _____ for football.
7. When did that excellent idea _____ to you?
8. It can be _____ from the wet floor that the pipe leaks.
9. The county fair is an annual summer _____.
10. We did not mean to _____ Cal's name from the guest list.
11. What can you _____ from her refusal to take the test?

Complete the Debate Write spelling words from the box to complete the debate.

prefer
occurred
conferred
compelling
refer
compel
conference
compelled
omitted

Topic: Should the minimum wage be lowered for persons under eighteen years of age?

Pro: We feel there should be legislation to __12.__ states to lower the minimum wage for those under eighteen. To support this view, we __13.__ to testimony given at a recent __14.__ on unemployment, indicating that there is __15.__ evidence that many small businesses would __16.__ to hire additional help but cannot afford to pay minimum wage.

Con: We are __17.__ to disagree with our colleagues. They may have __18.__ with experts, but they have __19.__ historic facts. Mistreatment of young workers __20.__ frequently in the past. By lowering wages for young persons, we would encourage similar behavior.

Spelling and Writing

Proofread a Paragraph

Six words are not spelled correctly in this persuasive paragraph. Write the words correctly.

At a recent safety confrence, students were asked if they thought that bicycle riders should be compeled by law to wear helmets. Many students said that they would preffer that the decision be left to them. I disagree. I strongly support a law that would compell bicyclists to wear helmets. According to research, thousands of people suffer serious head injuries from bicycle accidents each year. You can infer, therefore, that if people wear helmets, the occurance of death and disabling injuries from bicycle accidents will decline. In fact, research has shown that wearing safety helmets reduces the chance of serious head injuries by more than 75 percent. That is a comppeling statistic!

Proofreading Marks

≡ Make a capital.

/ Make a small letter.

∧ Add something.

℘ Take out something.

⊙ Add a period.

⌗ New paragraph

🆂🅿 Spelling error

Write a Paragraph

Persuasive Writing

Write a paragraph supporting or challenging an issue.

- Choose an issue about which you have a strong opinion.
- State the issue and present your opinion.
- Support your opinion with facts.
- Follow the form used in the proofreading sample. Use as many spelling words as you can.

Proofread Your Writing During →

Writing Process

Prewriting
⬇
Drafting
⬇
Revising
⬇
Editing
⬇
Publishing

Proofread your writing for spelling errors as part of the editing stage in the writing process. Be sure to check each word carefully. Use a dictionary to check spelling if you are not sure.

Vocabulary

Strategy Words

Review Words:
Adding Suffixes That Change Stress

Write a word from the box to complete each sentence.

assume	autumn	autumnal
practice	practical	

1. His ideas for making money are not particularly exciting or creative, but they are _____.

2. The _____ equinox, when the length of day and night is almost equal all over the earth, occurs around September 22.

3. Do not _____ that the story is true until you check all of the facts.

4. When the leaves change colors, it is a sure sign that _____ has arrived in New England.

5. Becoming a musician takes some talent and lots of _____.

Preview Words:
Adding Suffixes That Change Stress

Write a word from the box to match each clue.

condemn	condemnation	malign
malignant	resignation	

6. It is the withdrawal from a job or position.

7. This can mean "to judge critically" or "to denounce."

8. To do this is to slander.

9. This describes something that is diseased.

10. This is an expression of strong disapproval.

Connections

Content Words

Write words from the box to complete the paragraph.

competitive	feud	friendship
resolution		rivalry

A certain amount of healthy __1.__ among countries can spur progress. If the __2.__ spirit is carried too far, though, a bitter quarrel or __3.__ may arise. The prompt __4.__ of minor differences can help preserve __5.__ among nations and prevent major conflicts.

Language Arts: Humor

Write a word from the box to match each definition.

entertain	instructive	ridiculous
sarcasm		satire

6. a written work that uses irony, sarcasm, or ridicule to expose human folly
7. a sharply mocking remark
8. absurd; laughable
9. enlightening; conveying information
10. to amuse

Apply the Spelling Strategy

Circle the two content words you wrote with suffixes that created an accent shift in the base word.

READ THE SPELLING WORDS

1.	avocado	*avocado*	We added slices of ripe **avocado** to the salad.
2.	stampede	*stampede*	Lightning caused the cattle to **stampede**.
3.	cafeteria	*cafeteria*	Our friends eat lunch in the **cafeteria**.
4.	rodeo	*rodeo*	Dad took us to a Western **rodeo**.
5.	mustang	*mustang*	The wild **mustang** reared on its hind legs.
6.	iguana	*iguana*	An **iguana** moved slowly across the rocks.
7.	lariat	*lariat*	The cowhand used a **lariat** to rescue the calf.
8.	sierra	*sierra*	They hiked and camped in the **sierra**.
9.	tornado	*tornado*	That dark funnel cloud looks like a **tornado**.
10.	cinch	*cinch*	The **cinch** on the horse's saddle came loose.
11.	fiesta	*fiesta*	We danced and ate Spanish food at the **fiesta**.
12.	mosquito	*mosquito*	A **mosquito** was buzzing in my ear.
13.	cabana	*cabana*	You can change clothes in the beach **cabana**.
14.	bravado	*bravado*	That show of **bravado** covered up his terror.
15.	mesa	*mesa*	From afar, the **mesa** looked like a huge table.
16.	canyon	*canyon*	A stream ran along the bottom of the **canyon**.
17.	pronto	*pronto*	Please take your muddy shoes off **pronto**!
18.	siesta	*siesta*	After a short **siesta,** Jack felt rested.
19.	patio	*patio*	She sits outside on the brick **patio** to read.
20.	tortilla	*tortilla*	He wrapped the chicken mixture in a **tortilla**.

SORT THE SPELLING WORDS

1.–7. Write the spelling words that end with a **long o** sound.

8.–15. Write the spelling words that end with a **schwa** sound.

16. Write the spelling word that ends in **e-consonant-e**.

17.–20. Write the spelling words that end in a consonant.

REMEMBER THE SPELLING STRATEGY

Remember that the English language includes many words from Spanish.

Spelling and Vocabulary

Word Meanings

Write a spelling word related in meaning to complete each group.

1. festival, holiday, _____
2. plateau, tableland, _____
3. reptile, lizard, _____
4. windstorm, cyclone, _____
5. insect, bug, _____
6. courtyard, deck, _____
7. bathhouse, shelter, _____
8. restaurant, coffee shop, _____

Spelling Patterns

Write a spelling word to complete each sentence. The underlined words in the sentences are contained in the spelling words.

9. I am <u>ill</u> and do not feel like eating my soup <u>or</u> my _____.

10. You <u>must</u> have gotten that <u>tan</u> while you were watching the _____ race across the prairie.

11. When we all <u>stamp</u> our feet, the noise sounds like a _____ of wild horses.

12. I <u>can</u> see there is not <u>any</u> way to climb into the _____ on horseback.

13. Paul wrote an <u>ode</u> to those who <u>rode</u> in the _____.

14. Here is an <u>ad</u> for the _____ sale at the fruit market.

USING THE Dictionary

In a dictionary, words that are acceptable in conversation but unsuitable for formal writing are labeled *Informal* or *Slang*. The definitions below appear in the **Spelling Dictionary**. Write a spelling word for each definition.

15. *Slang*. Something easy to accomplish.
16. *Informal*. Without delay.
17. A long rope with a running noose for catching livestock.
18. A rest or nap.
19. False bravery.
20. A rugged range of mountains.

avocado	stampede	cafeteria	rodeo	mustang
iguana	lariat	sierra	tornado	cinch
fiesta	mosquito	cabana	bravado	mesa
canyon	pronto	siesta	patio	tortilla

Solve the Analogies Write the spelling word that best completes each analogy.

1. **Red** is to **tomato** as **green** is to _____.
2. **Woods** is to **cabin** as **beach** is to _____.
3. **Chirp** is to **cricket** as **buzz** is to _____.
4. **Clown** is to **circus** as **cattle roper** is to _____.
5. **Bird** is to **hawk** as **lizard** is to _____.

Complete the Sentences Write the spelling word that best completes each sentence.

6. We often grill chicken outside and eat it on our _____.
7. As he prepared to rope the calf, Jim checked his _____ to be sure it was not twisted.
8. They descended into the _____ on donkeys.
9. Mom said to clean up the mess _____!
10. A leather _____ held the saddle securely.
11. We all sometimes disguise our fear with _____.
12. Our school _____ serves breakfast, lunch, and dinner.
13. Their camp is sponsoring a _____ with activities that will go on all weekend.

Complete the Paragraph Write spelling words from the box to complete the paragraph.

Our hiking club trekked along the jagged peaks of the
_14._ . After a strenuous climb, we each ate a corn _15._
with chili and cheese. Then we settled down for a _16._ .
As we rested, our guide told us about the first time he saw
a _17._ of horses. He had been traveling across a flat
_18._ when he spied a lone _19._ . It was eerily quiet.
Moments later he heard the thunderous sound of galloping
horses. He said the dust they kicked up looked like a
swirling _20._ .

> **stampede**
> **mesa**
> **tornado**
> **sierra**
> **siesta**
> **mustang**
> **tortilla**

Spelling and Writing

Proofread a Paragraph

Six words are not spelled correctly in this paragraph. Write the words correctly.

Proofreading Marks

≡ Make a capital.

／ Make a small letter.

∧ Add something.

ℓ Take out something.

⊙ Add a period.

⌗ New paragraph

(SP) Spelling error

I support the laws Congress has passed to protect wild horses. To me, nothing symbolizes the American spirit better than wild horses. Last year, I was in New Mexico, where I saw stallions and mares stampeed across a messa. I also was able to watch a mustang climb out of a steep canion. Our guide tried to use a lariet to pull the horse to safety, but that magnificent animal did not need help. It climbed free on its own and raced away. I knew that its spirit should never be broken with a saddle and tightly fastened sinch. That horse reminded me of the American pioneer spirit that valued independent strength, not mere bravadoe.

Write a Paragraph

Narrative Writing

Write a paragraph about something that symbolizes the American spirit for you.

- Choose an animal or object and explain why you chose it.
- Explain why you think it should be protected.
- Follow the form used in the proofreading sample.

Use as many spelling words as you can.

Proofread Your Writing During

Writing Process

Prewriting

⇩

Drafting

⇩

Revising

⇩

Editing

⇩

Publishing

Proofread your writing for spelling errors as part of the editing stage in the writing process. Be sure to check each word carefully. Use a dictionary to check spelling if you are not sure.

Vocabulary

Strategy Words

Review Words: Words From Spanish

Write the words from the box that best complete the paragraph.

alligator	burro	guitar
hammock	plaza	

I had a strange dream as I dozed in the __1.__ in our back yard. In my dream, I was traveling across Mexico on the back of a __2.__ . Tired and thirsty, I stopped to get a drink at a fountain in an open __3.__ in the center of town. A man was leaning against the fountain, strumming his __4.__ . He sang a song about a sad __5.__ that lived in a swamp!

Preview Words: Words From Spanish

Write a word from the box to complete each sentence.

armadillo	bonanza	embargo
guerrilla	vigilante	

6. If a country wants to forbid ships from leaving or entering its ports, it may order an _____.

7. A person in a frontier town who was a member of a vigilance committee was known as a _____.

8. A person who belongs to a band of fighters who are not part of a regular army is called a _____.

9. If you visit Texas, you might see an _____, an animal covered with a hard, plated shell.

10. If miners strike gold, they have found a _____.

Connections

Content Words

Social Studies: China

Write the word from the box that matches each clue.

abacus	bamboo	dynasty
	emperor	pagoda

1. This person is similar in ranking to a king.
2. Think of it as an ancient calculator.
3. This building may be a shrine or a memorial.
4. You can get lost in this tall, woody grass.
5. It is a family or group that rules for generations.

Language Arts: Poetry

Write a word from the box to match each definition.

lyrical	metrical	refrain
	sonnet	stanza

6. a fourteen-line poem
7. of, pertaining to, or composed in rhythmic meter
8. one of the divisions of a poem
9. a verse repeated throughout a poem or song
10. expressing deep personal feeling or emotion

Apply the Spelling Strategy

Circle the one content word that comes from Portuguese. Underline the two content words that come from Italian. Look in a dictionary if you are not sure.

Assessment and Review

Assessment   Units 13–17

Each Assessment Word in the box fits one of the spelling strategies you have studied over the past five weeks. Read the spelling strategies. Then write each Assessment Word under the unit number it fits.

Unit 13 _____

1.–5. Remember that the suffix **-ly** may be added to adjectives like **urgent** to form adverbs.

Unit 14 _____

6.–10. Remember that the suffixes **-able** and **-ible** may be added to base words or word roots to form adjectives.

Unit 15 _____

Remember that it is important to know the spellings of words that are frequently misspelled.

Unit 16 _____

11.–17. Remember that a final consonant preceded by a single vowel is doubled when adding a suffix that begins with a vowel except when the accent is on or shifts to the first syllable.

Unit 17 _____

18.–20. Remember that the English language includes many words from Spanish.

defer
presentable
beautifully
enchilada
inedible
likely
preferring
referred
predictable
palomino
stirring
enormously
rapidly
guitarist
deferred
unforgivable
controllable
stirred
slightly
convertible

absolutely	fortunately	particular	necessarily
particularly	immediately	accurately	readily
	approximately	absolute	

Write the spelling words that complete the paragraph.

On one ___1.___ day last October, Mario wanted to try a new chocolate cake recipe. Mario ___2.___ liked chocolate cake. Since he ___3.___ had everything he needed, he began ___4.___ after lunch. He knew he must measure each ingredient ___5.___ in order to have good results. Although Mario did not ___6.___ need two cakes, he made two anyway. Then he would be able to have a party. The two cakes would be enough for ___7.___ twenty friends. When the cakes were ready, Mario thought they were ___8.___ delicious. He thought his friends would ___9.___ agree. These cakes would be the ___10.___ top of Mario's baking career.

 **Review** Unit 14: Suffixes -able, -ible

uncomfortable	eligible	permissible	remarkable
unmistakable	considerable	recognizable	suitable
	noticeable	disagreeable	

Write a spelling word that is formed from each of these words.

11. comfort
12. consider
13. mistake
14. remark
15. notice
16. suit

Write a spelling word for each clue.

17. unpleasant
18. easily identified
19. qualified; worthy
20. allowable

breathe	usually	vacuum	actual	variety
coupon	maneuver	curiosity	peculiar	courtesy

Write a spelling word to complete each analogy.

1. **Mouth** is to **taste** as **nose** is to _____.
2. **Unnecessary** is to **necessary** as **unusually** is to _____.
3. **Really** is to **real** as **actually** is to _____.
4. **Push** is to **shove** as **move** is to _____.
5. **Cotton** is to **shirt** as **paper** is to _____.
6. **Wonderful** is to **marvelous** as **strange** is to _____.
7. **Broom** is to **sweep** as **electric appliance** is to _____.
8. **Thoughtfulness** is to **consideration** as **politeness** is to _____.
9. **Generous** is to **generosity** as **curious** is to _____.
10. **Heavy** is to **light** as **sameness** is to _____.

occur	preference	infer	occurrence	prefer
conference	preferred	occurred	confer	inferred

Write the spelling words that fit each sentence.

11.–12. We will _____ at the 10:00 A.M. _____.

13.–14. The agent entered my seating _____. I have always _____ to sit on the aisle.

15.–16. As a daily _____, we used to watch the programs that _____ between 4:30 and 5:30 P.M.

17.–18. Did it ever _____ to you that I _____ not to be disturbed while I study?

19.–20. Shall I _____ from the pleased look on your face that you have _____ the correct answer?

avocado	stampede	cafeteria	rodeo	mustang
sierra	tornado	fiesta	mosquito	canyon

Write the spelling word that replaces each underlined word or words.

1. An annoying <u>insect</u> buzzed around noisily.
2. That is a beautiful <u>wild horse</u>.
3. The building was blown down in the <u>storm</u>.
4. My salad includes a sliced <u>fruit</u>.
5. Rusty will rope a horse in the <u>western show</u>.
6. Thunder echoed through the <u>gorge</u>.
7. Everyone had a great time at the <u>festival</u>.
8. We will get to camp in the high <u>rugged mountains</u>.
9. What's for lunch today in the <u>lunchroom</u>?
10. We were afraid that the cattle would <u>suddenly rush</u>.

GAME Spelling Study Strategy

Spelling Tic-Tac-Toe

Practicing spelling words can be fun if you make it into a game. Play this game with a partner.

1. Both you and your partner write a list of spelling words. Trade lists.

2. Draw a tic-tac-toe board on a piece of paper. Decide who will use **O** and who will use **X**.

3. Ask your partner to call the first word on your spelling list to you. Spell it out loud. If you spell it correctly, make an **X** or an **O** on the tic-tac-toe board. If you misspell the word, ask your partner to spell it out loud for you. You miss your turn.

4. Now you call a word from your partner's spelling list.

5. Keep playing until one of you makes tic-tac-toe. Keep starting over until you both have practiced all your spelling words.

WRITER'S

Grammar, Usage, and Mechanics

Identifying Modifiers: Adjectives

An adjective is a word that modifies a noun or pronoun. Some adjectives tell what kind. Others, such as **many** and **few,** tell how many. The adjectives **this, that, these,** and **those** tell which ones. The articles **a, an,** and **the** are also adjectives.

These **twenty** contestants will compete for **the grand** prize.
The clever leader showed **remarkable** courage.
Some poets use **unexpected** rhymes.

Practice **Activity**

A. Decide which boldfaced word is an adjective. Then write the word.

1. We **calmly** endured an **uncomfortable** silence.

2. Douye showed his **considerable** skill as he **vaulted** over the pole.

3. We thought the **movie** had a **peculiar** ending.

4. There isn't any **noticeable** difference **between** the positions of the two candidates.

5. Nellima **usually** finds a **suitable** solution.

6. Let's share this **delicious avocado**.

7. **She** is from the **great** state of Texas.

8. Her **enormous** smile made **everyone** happy.

9. What is the **approximate** distance **between** the rows?

10. Ms. Pullon **needs** an **immediate** response.

B. Write the noun that is modified by the underlined adjective.

11. Who is the <u>fortunate</u> winner of the free tickets?

12. The guests will sleep on the <u>convertible</u> sofa.

13. His rude behavior was an <u>unforgivable</u> mistake.

14. Have you found a <u>suitable</u> site for the picnic?

15. We took many pictures of the <u>beautiful</u> canyon.

WORKSHOP

Proofreading Strategy

Read It Backwards

Good writers always proofread their writing for spelling errors. Here's a strategy you can use to proofread your papers.

Instead of reading from the first word to the last, try reading from the last to the first. You won't be thinking about the meaning because it won't make any sense at all. For example, you would read **This is a great idea!** as **idea! great a is This** instead.

This might seem peculiar, but it will help you focus on the spelling of each word. Try it!

Electronic Spelling

Spell Checkers

Computers have many programs and tools that help you proofread. Many have spell checkers that signal misspelled words. But sometimes you have to be smarter than the computer!

If your misspelled word is the correct spelling of another word but not of the word you wanted, the computer won't know the difference. Maybe you have left off the ending of a similar word. For example, you might have put in **cloth** instead of **clothe** or **considerably** instead of **considerable**. The spell checker wouldn't catch those kinds of mistakes.

Show how much smarter you are than the computer spell checker that checked these sentences. Find the words it missed and spell them correctly.

1. I go to the museum often to see that particle painting.
2. Without the windows open, we could hardly breath.
3. Plan to meet hear in the morning.
4. When the audience was comfortable seated, the concert began.
5. Are you sure you know where your going?
6. We hope to go horseback riding in the high siesta.

Spelling and Thinking

READ THE SPELLING WORDS

1.	activities	*activities*	We like to do craft **activities**.
2.	potatoes	*potatoes*	I love **potatoes** and gravy.
3.	mix-ups	*mix-ups*	A few **mix-ups** ruined the plan.
4.	copies	*copies*	I made four **copies** of the letter.
5.	shelves	*shelves*	We put your books on the **shelves**.
6.	spoonfuls	*spoonfuls*	I ate several **spoonfuls** of soup.
7.	mothers-in-law	*mothers-in-law*	The **mothers-in-law** sat in front.
8.	echoes	*echoes*	I yelled and listened for **echoes**.
9.	knives	*knives*	Please dry the **knives** and forks.
10.	opportunities	*opportunities*	I had two **opportunities** to play.
11.	tomatoes	*tomatoes*	He sliced **tomatoes** for the salad.
12.	cupfuls	*cupfuls*	Next, add two **cupfuls** of flour.
13.	fathers-in-law	*fathers-in-law*	The **fathers-in-law** may sit here.
14.	thieves	*thieves*	The police arrested the **thieves**.
15.	boundaries	*boundaries*	Play in the **boundaries** of our yard.
16.	volcanoes	*volcanoes*	Hawaii was formed by **volcanoes**.
17.	passersby	*passersby*	We handed the fliers to **passersby**.
18.	teaspoonfuls	*teaspoonfuls*	I added two **teaspoonfuls** of sugar.
19.	companies	*companies*	Several **companies** sell mustard.
20.	mosquitoes	*mosquitoes*	I can hear **mosquitoes** buzzing.

SORT THE SPELLING WORDS

1.–5. Write the spelling words that end with **consonant + o + es**.

6.–8. Write the spelling words in which the final **f** was changed to **v** before adding **es**.

9.–13. Write the spelling words in which the final **y** was changed to **i** before adding **es**.

14.–20. Write the spelling words that are compound words.

REMEMBER THE SPELLING STRATEGY

Remember that plural nouns are formed in a variety of ways.

Spelling and Vocabulary

Word Meanings

Write a spelling word to match each definition.

1. more than one of a plant that is a starchy, edible tuber
2. more than one of a plant that has an edible, fleshy, usually red fruit
3. more than one of a geological formation that is a crack or hole in the earth's crust through which molten lava and gases can erupt

Word Groups

Write a spelling word to complete each group.

4. reproductions, duplicates, _____
5. businesses, groups, _____
6. mayflies, gnats, _____
7. events, tasks, _____
8. robbers, burglars, _____
9. daughters, mothers, _____
10. sons, fathers, _____
11. foul-ups, mistakes, _____
12. edges, limits, _____

USING THE Dictionary

An entry shows the plural form of a noun (labeled *pl.*) when the plural is **irregular** (formed other than by adding **s** or **es**). An entry also shows a regular plural when the spelling might pose a problem. Write the plural forms of the following nouns. Use the **Spelling Dictionary** if you need help.

13. passerby
14. echo
15. opportunity
16. shelf
17. spoonful
18. cupful
19. knife
20. teaspoonful

Spelling and Reading

activities	potatoes	mix-ups	copies
shelves	spoonfuls	mothers-in-law	echoes
knives	opportunities	tomatoes	cupfuls
fathers-in-law	thieves	boundaries	volcanoes
passersby	teaspoonfuls	companies	mosquitoes

Solve the Analogies Write the spelling word that best completes each analogy.

1. **Father** is to **father-in-law** as **fathers** is to _____.
2. **Leaf** is to **leaves** as **knife** is to _____.
3. **Pocket** is to **pocketfuls** as **spoon** is to _____.
4. **Sister** is to **sisters-in-law** as **mother** is to _____.
5. **Jelly** is to **grapes** as **ketchup** is to _____.
6. **Hobo** is to **hoboes** as **volcano** is to _____.
7. **Hero** is to **heroes** as **echo** is to _____.
8. **Wife** is to **wives** as **thief** is to _____.
9. **Party** is to **parties** as **copy** is to _____.
10. **Chin-up** is to **chin-ups** as **mix-up** is to _____.

Complete the Sentences Write the spelling word that best completes each sentence.

11. Which after-school _____ did you sign up for?
12. We will have many _____ to take pictures along the scenic drive.
13. This bug repellent will keep the _____ from biting you.
14. He worked for three different _____ before he started his own business.
15. We used the trees and bushes as _____ for our soccer game.

Complete the Paragraph Write spelling words from the box to complete the paragraph.

The voices of farmers calling out their wares ring through the open-air market. Strolling __16.__ are tempted by the colorful produce piled high on __17.__ and in bins. There are green and red peppers, __18.__, melons, and oranges. As we wander, we sample __19.__ of homemade jam and buy __20.__ of fresh-squeezed juice.

> shelves
> teaspoonfuls
> cupfuls
> passersby
> potatoes

Spelling **and** Writing

Proofread a Short Story in Process

Six words are not spelled correctly in this unfinished short story.
Write the words correctly.

> Dr. Kim Su recently developed a new concentrated plant food to be used by farms and other agricultural companies. Always looking for oppertunitys to get rich without working, a local band of theefs plotted to steal the miraculous plant food from the laboratory. However, through a series of mix-ups, the burglars took the wrong boxes from the shellfs.
>
> Alongside a nearby farm, the getaway truck suddenly overturned, and the concoction spilled into several rows of pottatos and tomatose. The crooks and several passerbys began to notice some strange activities in the field.

Proofreading Marks

≡	Make a capital.
/	Make a small letter.
∧	Add something.
℮	Take out something.
⊙	Add a period.
⌗	New paragraph
ⓈⓅ	Spelling error

Complete a Short Story

Narrative Writing

What happens next? Use your imagination to complete the short story.

- Before you begin, think about what will happen next. You may choose to complete the mystery by explaining exactly what was happening in the field and why.
- Follow the form used in the proofreading sample. Use as many spelling words as you can.

Writing Process

Prewriting
⇩
Drafting
⇩
Revising
⇩
Editing
⇩
Publishing

Proofread Your Writing During

Proofread your writing for spelling errors as part of the editing stage in the writing process. Be sure to check each word carefully. Use a dictionary to check spelling if you are not sure.

Vocabulary

Strategy Words

Review Words: Plural Nouns

Write words from the box to complete the sentences.

groceries	heroes	latches
loaves		treaties

1. Please buy two _____ of bread at the store.
2. Our country signs peace _____ with many other nations.
3. The clerk helped carry the heavy bags of _____ to our car.
4. As soon as we unfasten these _____, we can open this old-fashioned trunk and see what is inside.
5. Zeus and Hercules are _____ of Greek mythology.

Preview Words: Plural Nouns

Write a word from the box to match each definition.

analyses	criteria	data
indices		stimuli

6. measures, rules, or standards on which a judgment or decision is based
7. things that cause responses
8. systematic, careful examinations, usually of information
9. alphabetized lists of words that give the page numbers on which the words can be found in a book
10. facts or pieces of information

Connections

Content Words

Write the word from the box that matches each symbol and definition.

asterisk	bracket	hyphen
parentheses		parenthesis

1. - often used in a compound word; also used to break a word at the end of a line
2. * directs the reader to a footnote
3. (half of a pair; signals a less important idea
4. [half of a pair; signals a lesser idea within a parenthetical statement
5. ( ) sets off a less important idea; may appear within a sentence or may enclose a complete sentence

Science: Biology

Write a word from the box to match each definition.

amoeba	bacteria	bacterium
fungus		microorganism

6. a specific type of microorganism with an indefinite shape
7. a plantlike organism, such as a mushroom
8. any animal or plant of microscopic size
9. a one-celled organism with a well-defined shape; can cause disease
10. more than one bacterium

Apply the Spelling Strategy

Circle the two content words you wrote that are plural nouns.

Spelling and Thinking

READ THE SPELLING WORDS

1.	application	*application*	I filled out an **application** for a job.
2.	asset	*asset*	His experience is an **asset** to our company.
3.	affirm	*affirm*	Can you **affirm** your good intentions?
4.	according	*according*	We prepared it **according** to the recipe.
5.	attain	*attain*	Studying hard can help you **attain** success.
6.	applaud	*applaud*	The audience began to **applaud** loudly.
7.	assurance	*assurance*	I give you my **assurance** that I will attend.
8.	account	*account*	We opened a savings **account** at the bank.
9.	assortment	*assortment*	The box contained an **assortment** of nails.
10.	affix	*affix*	Please **affix** an address label to the box.
11.	appetite	*appetite*	This meal should satisfy your **appetite**.
12.	attempt	*attempt*	We will **attempt** to climb to the top.
13.	accustomed	*accustomed*	I am not yet **accustomed** to my new boots.
14.	approval	*approval*	I hope our choice meets with your **approval**.
15.	attire	*attire*	His holiday **attire** included a plaid tie.
16.	assemble	*assemble*	We need some tools to **assemble** the bike.
17.	appliance	*appliance*	A toaster is a useful **appliance** to have.
18.	afford	*afford*	If I save, I can **afford** to buy it myself.
19.	assert	*assert*	I will **assert** his right to a fair decision.
20.	attentive	*attentive*	She was **attentive** while I told my story.

SORT THE SPELLING WORDS

1.–3. Write the words with the prefix **ad-** spelled **af**.

4.–8. Write the words with the prefix **ad-** spelled **as**.

9.–11. Write the words with the prefix **ad-** spelled **ac**.

12.–15. Write the words with the prefix **ad-** spelled **at**.

16.–20. Write the words with the prefix **ad-** spelled **ap**.

REMEMBER THE SPELLING STRATEGY

Remember that the prefix **ad-,** meaning "to" or "toward," may be assimilated into the spelling of the base word or word root.

Spelling ᵃⁿᵈ Vocabulary

Word Meanings ▬ ▬ ▬ ▬ ▬ ▬ ▬ ▬ ▬ ▬ ▬ ▬

Write a spelling word to match each definition.

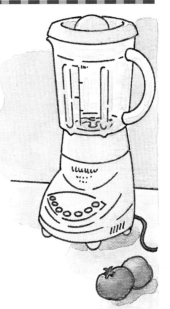

1. paying attention; observant
2. usual; in the habit of
3. to clothe; one's clothing
4. to gain, reach, or accomplish
5. a useful or valuable quality
6.–7. to declare positively; to state
8. to fasten or attach; a word part that is attached to a base word or a word root
9. a collection of various things
10. a statement that inspires confidence; a guarantee
11. to be able to meet the expense of
12. a device, usually operated by electricity and meant for household use

Word Structure ▬ ▬ ▬ ▬ ▬ ▬ ▬ ▬ ▬ ▬ ▬ ▬

Add the missing prefixes to write spelling words.

13. -plication
14. -semble
15. -cording
16. -count

USING THE Dictionary

Write a spelling word for each etymology.
Use the **Spelling Dictionary** if you need help.

17. Lat. *applaudere: ad-*, to + *plaudere*, to clap
18. Lat. *appetitus*, strong desire < *appetere*, to strive after: *ad-*, toward + *petere*, to seek
19. Lat. *approbare: ad-*, to + *probare*, to test < *probus*, good
20. Lat. *attemptare: ad-*, to + *temptare*, to test

application	asset	affirm	according	attain
applaud	assurance	account	assortment	affix
appetite	attempt	accustomed	approval	attire
assemble	appliance	afford	assert	attentive

Replace the Words   Write a spelling word to replace the underlined word or words in each sentence.

1. What level of schooling do you plan to <u>reach</u>?
2. Give a brief <u>record</u> of your job experience.
3. Are you <u>used</u> to studying hard for tests?
4. Are you willing to <u>try</u> new tasks?
5. What is the most useful <u>valuable quality</u> you would bring to this job?
6. Are you aware that our dress code requires you to wear company <u>clothing</u> every day?
7. If you receive our <u>recommendation</u>, when would you be able to start?
8. Please provide an <u>array or collection</u> of references from teachers and former employers.
9. Sign at the bottom to <u>assert</u> that the information you have given is true.
10.–11. You will have to <u>put together</u> the job <u>request form</u>, your references, and a cover letter.
12. Please <u>attach</u> a stamp to your envelope before mailing it.

Complete the Advertisement   Write spelling words from the box to complete the advertisement.

Can you __13.__ to buy new items when the old ones break? Do you have an __14.__ for greater self-reliance? Sign up for our "Repair It Right" course! We __15.__ that you will learn how to repair any small __16.__ as easily as a professional can. All of our graduates __17.__ the program, giving their __18.__ that they are now capable of making all sorts of small repairs. The only requirement for the course is an __19.__ mind; __20.__ to our satisfied graduates, you will never have to throw away a broken clock or radio again!

appetite
appliance
according
assert
attentive
afford
assurance
applaud

Spelling <small>and</small> Writing

Proofread a Letter

Six words are not spelled correctly in this letter. Write the words correctly.

Frank Lee, Manager
Ed's Electronics
47 Sham Rock Ave.
Paducah, KY 42003

Dear Mr. Lee:

I would like to apply for a position at your store. Although I have an asortment of skills, my most useful asset is that I can asemble or repair any small aplience. I also am an atentave, helpful salesperson, and I am accustomed to working efficiently under pressure. After filling out an aplication, I would be happy to come in for an interview. I hope my request meets with your aprovel. Please call me at 413-555-1717.

Yours truly,

Sam Lorenzo

Proofreading Marks

≡ Make a capital.

/ Make a small letter.

∧ Add something.

℘ Take out something.

⊙ Add a period.

⌗ New paragraph

ⓢⓟ Spelling error

Write a Letter

Expository Writing

Imagine that you have just invented something useful (perhaps a new appliance or a piece of sports equipment). Write a letter to the U.S. Patent Office applying for a patent.

- Explain what your invention is, why you think there is a use for it, and the ways in which it is unique.
- Follow the form used in the proofreading sample. Use as many spelling words as you can.

Writing Process

Prewriting
⇩
Drafting
⇩
Revising
⇩
Editing
⇩
Publishing

Proofread Your Writing During

Proofread your writing for spelling errors as part of the editing stage in the writing process. Be sure to check each word carefully. Use a dictionary to check spelling if you are not sure.

Vocabulary

Strategy Words

Review Words: Assimilated Prefix ad-

Write words from the box to complete the sentences.

accident	accurate	appointment
assistant		attendance

1. Are you sure that this information is _____?
2. He was so busy he had to hire an _____ to help him in the office.
3. Since I have never missed a day of school, I have a perfect _____ record.
4. She was wearing a seat belt, so she was not hurt in the _____.
5. Can we schedule an _____ for tomorrow?

Preview Words: Assimilated Prefix ad-

Write the word from the box that matches each definition.

accelerate	accountability	accumulate
appropriate		assistance

6. responsibility
7. the act of helping; help or aid
8. to increase the speed of
9. proper or suitable
10. to gather; to increase

Connections

Content Words

Science: Scientific Method

Write the word from the box that matches each definition.

apparatus	experimental	hypothesis
	propose	theory

1. undergoing a test
2. an explanation that must be tested; a theory
3. to put forward for consideration or discussion
4. a group of machines used to accomplish a task
5. an assumption based on limited information

Social Studies: Contracts

Write the words from the box to complete the paragraph.

bargaining	dissatisfied	labor union
	security	assembly

In the early days of industrialization, workers labored long hours on __6.__ lines. The conditions were unpleasant and often dangerous. With the formation of the __7.__, however, __8.__ workers could use collective __9.__ to reach agreements with management. This practice led to improved working conditions and increased job __10.__.

Apply the Spelling Strategy

Circle the two content words you wrote that have the assimilated prefix **ad-**.

Spelling *and* **Thinking**

READ THE SPELLING WORDS

1.	tangerine	*tangerine*	I peeled the **tangerine** and ate it.
2.	suede	*suede*	Have you seen my **suede** gloves?
3.	gardenia	*gardenia*	I placed the **gardenia** in water.
4.	calico	*calico*	The apron was made of red and blue **calico**.
5.	frankfurter	*frankfurter*	I would like mustard on my **frankfurter**.
6.	tuxedo	*tuxedo*	He wore a **tuxedo** to the wedding.
7.	angora	*angora*	My sister has a pink **angora** sweater.
8.	cardigan	*cardigan*	I got chilly, so I buttoned my **cardigan**.
9.	damask	*damask*	She bought beautiful silk **damask** curtains.
10.	cheddar	*cheddar*	I like cream cheese and **cheddar** cheese.
11.	magnolia	*magnolia*	I can smell the **magnolia** tree from here.
12.	denim	*denim*	He wore a pair of **denim** overalls.
13.	hamburger	*hamburger*	Who wants this well-done **hamburger**?
14.	cantaloupe	*cantaloupe*	My favorite melon is **cantaloupe**.
15.	satin	*satin*	The dancers wore glamorous **satin** dresses.
16.	currant	*currant*	We made homemade **currant** jelly.
17.	leotard	*leotard*	I need a new **leotard** for gymnastics class.
18.	cashmere	*cashmere*	The **cashmere** scarf kept my neck warm.
19.	hyacinth	*hyacinth*	The garden overflowed with **hyacinth** plants.
20.	camellia	*camellia*	This **camellia** looks a lot like a rose.

SORT THE SPELLING WORDS

1.–6. Write the spelling words that name foods.

7.–16. Write the spelling words that name textiles or clothing.

17.–20. Write the spelling words that name flowers.

REMEMBER THE SPELLING STRATEGY

Remember that the English language includes many words taken from names and places.

Word Meanings

Write a spelling word to match each description.

1. a citrus fruit from Tangier
2. an elastic garment named after Jules Léotard
3. a patterned fabric first produced in Damascus in the Middle Ages
4. fur of a goat or a rabbit from Ankara, Turkey
5. wool from a goat; originally produced in Kashmir, India
6. a sweater that opens in the front, originally named after the Seventh Earl of Cardigan
7. a durable fabric originally from Nîmes, France (the French word for "from" is **de**)
8. a formal suit; named after Tuxedo Park, New York
9. a napped leather; from the French term **gants de Suède,** meaning "gloves from Sweden"
10. a fragrant, usually white, flower; named for Alexander Garden
11. a flower named for Hyacinthus, a figure in Greek mythology
12. a small, sour fruit; from the Middle English **raysons of coraunte,** meaning "raisins of Corinth"
13. a flower named for Pierre Magnol
14. a patterned fabric, originally from Calicut, India
15. a flower named for Georg Josef Kamel

USING THE Dictionary

Write the spelling word for each of these respellings. In each word, circle the syllable with the primary stress. Use the **Spelling Dictionary** if you need help.

16. /**kăn′** tl ōp′/
17. /**chĕd′** ər/
18. /**frăngk′** fər tər/
19. /**hăm′** bûr′ gər/
20. /**săt′** n/

Spelling and Reading

tangerine	suede	gardenia	calico	frankfurter
tuxedo	angora	cardigan	damask	cheddar
magnolia	denim	hamburger	cantaloupe	satin
currant	leotard	cashmere	hyacinth	camellia

Complete the Sentences   Write the spelling word that best completes each sentence.

1. I bought a new pair of _____ shoes for the party.
2. The dancer wore a _____, tights, and ballet slippers.
3. The elegant _____ tablecloth provided the perfect background for the fine china dishes.
4. The _____ is a close relative of the orange.
5. The bottom button on her _____ was missing.
6. Camella was named after her mother's favorite flower, the _____.
7.–9. She carried a bouquet of _____, _____, and _____ flowers.
10. The long fibers in her _____ sweater made her neck itch.

Complete the Restaurant Review   Write spelling words from the box to complete the restaurant review.

The Cat's Meow offers a delightful array of sights, smells, and tastes. We were greeted at the door by a friendly hostess who showed us to a table set with a cheery _11._ tablecloth. As we read the menu, a waiter brought us a basket of fresh bread and jellies. Our favorite was the oatmeal bread with _12._ jelly. The fruit salad of _13._, grapes, and bananas was delicious. The addition of a thick slice of sharp _14._ cheese made an ordinary _15._ extraordinary. A common _16._ was complemented by a side order of baked beans. The restaurant offers a variety of beverages, including blended fruit juices as smooth as _17._. The setting is informal. Diners' attire ranged from _18._ sweaters to _19._ jeans. You certainly don't need a _20._ to eat here!

calico
cantaloupe
cashmere
cheddar
currant
denim
frankfurter
hamburger
satin
tuxedo

Spelling and Writing

Proofread a Paragraph

Six words are not spelled correctly in this descriptive paragraph. Write the words correctly.

Proofreading Marks

≡ Make a capital.

/ Make a small letter.

∧ Add something.

ℓ Take out something.

⊙ Add a period.

⌗ New paragraph

(SP) Spelling error

The sun hung low in the sky, glowing like a fiery tangiarine. As it slipped below the horizon, colors splashed across the clouds. It looked as if someone had thrown a piece of richly colored demask over the sea. From hyasinth purple to magnolia pink to camelia red, the colors reached as far as I could see. Bits of white flecked the edges of the magnificent sunset like tiny gardinia petals. A soft wind blew across the sand, rustling my denim skirt and rippling the water like a giant satin sheet. Savory odors drifted toward me from the food vendors. I could smell the French fries from the frankfurter stand. At another stand, a vendor called to passersby, tempting them to feast on a hamberger. I tasted the salt air and decided there was no place else I would rather be.

Write a Paragraph

Descriptive Writing

Choose a memorable scene, person, or event and write a descriptive paragraph.

- Make your writing vivid by using precise words that appeal to the five senses.
- Follow the form used in the proofreading sample. Use as many spelling words as you can.

Proofread Your Writing During

Proofread your writing for spelling errors as part of the editing stage in the writing process. Be sure to check each word carefully. Use a dictionary to check spelling if you are not sure.

Writing Process

Prewriting

⇩

Drafting

⇩

Revising

⇩

Editing

⇩

Publishing

Vocabulary

Strategy Words

Review Words: Words From Names and Places

Write the word from the box that matches each clue.

bayonet	ampere	sardine	valentine	sandwich

1. This fish can be found around Sardinia, a Mediterranean island.

2. This gift or greeting card is named for Saint Valentine.

3. The Earl of Sandwich, who invented a convenient way of eating meat, gave us this word.

4. The name of this weapon comes from the name of the town where it was first used, Bayonne, France.

5. You may be shocked to know that André Ampère gave us this term for measuring electrical current.

Preview Words: Words From Names and Places

Write the word from the box that matches each clue.

badminton	cologne	marathon
tarantula	vandalism	

6. This spider was named after the Italian town Taranto.

7. This type of destruction is named after the Vandals, who sacked Rome in 455.

8. This scented liquid is named after the French name for a city in Germany.

9. This game was named after the Duke of Beaufort's country estate in western England.

10. A Greek city gave its name to this kind of race; a messenger ran there from Athens in 490 B.C. to announce a victory over the Persians.

Connections

Content Words

Math: Geometry

Write the word from the box that matches each definition.

cylinder	polyhedron	pyramid
sphere	symmetry	

1. the exact match of the two halves of a figure
2. a three-dimensional figure with a polygonal base and triangular sides that meet at the top
3. a three-dimensional figure with faces that are polygons
4. a figure with a circle at each end, like a tube
5. a ball-shaped figure

Social Studies: Geography

Write the words from the box to complete the paragraph.

aerial	cartography	contour
surveyor	topography	

Mapmaking, or __6.__, requires preparation and research. First, a __7.__ determines the features of the land. This is often done by __8.__ observation. Once the __9.__ of the area has been determined, a map is drawn to show each __10.__ of the land.

Apply the Spelling Strategy

Circle the content word that names a person's occupation. Underline the word that describes what that person might carefully study.

Spelling and Thinking

1. laboratory	*laboratory*	Chemicals are stored in the **laboratory**.
2. auxiliary	*auxiliary*	She is an **auxiliary** firefighter.
3. mischievous	*mischievous*	A **mischievous** kitten can be amusing.
4. salary	*salary*	His new job included a raise in **salary**.
5. temperature	*temperature*	The **temperature** fell below freezing.
6. accidentally	*accidentally*	Tina **accidentally** stepped on my glasses.
7. remembrance	*remembrance*	Joe saved the shell as a **remembrance**.
8. veterinarian	*veterinarian*	Dr. Franco is our dog's **veterinarian**.
9. disastrous	*disastrous*	A drought can be **disastrous** for farmers.
10. athletic	*athletic*	That gymnast has great **athletic** ability.
11. separately	*separately*	We arrived together but left **separately**.
12. laundry	*laundry*	We put **laundry** in the washing machine.
13. temperament	*temperament*	His new turtle has a calm **temperament**.
14. principally	*principally*	She works **principally** to pay off a loan.
15. miniature	*miniature*	Bonsai are **miniature** trees.
16. partially	*partially*	The lake is only **partially** frozen.
17. hindrance	*hindrance*	Icy roads are a **hindrance** to drivers.
18. incidentally	*incidentally*	We discovered the truth **incidentally**.
19. privilege	*privilege*	Being team captain is a **privilege**.
20. maintenance	*maintenance*	A **maintenance** crew groomed the field.

SORT THE SPELLING WORDS

1.–2. Write the spelling words with two syllables.

3.–10. Write the spelling words with three syllables.

11.–16. Write the spelling words with four syllables.

17.–20. Write the spelling words with five or more syllables.

Draw a vertical line between the syllables.

REMEMBER THE SPELLING STRATEGY

Remember that it is important to know the spellings of words that are frequently misspelled.

Spelling and Vocabulary

Word Meanings

Write the spelling word that is the best antonym for each word.

1. together
2. intentionally
3. oversized
4. well-behaved
5. completely
6. help
7. successful

Word Replacements

Write the spelling word that best replaces the underlined word or words.

8. Every member of that family enjoys muscle-strengthening and intellectual activities.
9. The coach is chiefly interested in improving the team's speed and stamina.
10. We performed the experiment under sterile conditions in the room equipped for scientific experimentation.
11. Bring your bike in for upkeep to keep it in good condition at least three times a year.
12. As a memento of the winning season, the coach gave each team member an engraved plaque.
13. Oh, parenthetically, I met your cousin Sue yesterday.
14. My brother left his dirty clothing overnight at Suds and Bubbles.

USING THE Dictionary

Write a spelling word for each etymology. Use the **Spelling Dictionary** if you need help.

15. ME *salarie* < Lat. *salarium*, money given to Roman soldiers to buy salt
16. Lat. *veterinarius*, pertaining to beasts of burden
17. ME < OFr. < Lat. *privilegium*, a law affecting one person: *privus*, single + *lex*, law
18. Lat. *auxiliarius* < *auxilium*, help
19. Lat. *temperatura*, composition < *temperare*, to mix
20. ME < Lat. *temperamentum* < *temperare*, to temper

135

Spelling and Reading

laboratory	auxiliary	mischievous	accidentally	temperature
laundry	athletic	remembrance	veterinarian	disastrous
separately	salary	temperament	principally	miniature
partially	privilege	incidentally	hindrance	maintenance

Solve the Analogies Write the spelling word that best completes each analogy.

1. **Brain** is to **intellectual** as **muscles** are to ____.
2. **Weekly** is to **annual** as **paycheck** is to ____.
3. **Normally** is to **usually** as **mainly** is to ____.
4. **All** is to **some** as **totally** is to ____.
5. **Baby** is to **pediatrician** as **cat** is to ____.
6. **Copy** is to **reproduction** as **advantage** is to ____.
7. **Rival** is to **opponent** as **helper** is to ____.
8. **Baker** is to **kitchen** as **scientist** is to ____.
9. **Snapshot** is to **photograph** as **souvenir** is to ____.

Draw Conclusions Write a spelling word that is related to the underlined word.

10. If she tends to lose her <u>temper</u>, she may have an irritable ____.
11. If he <u>maintains</u> his car, his car gets regular ____.
12. If snow <u>hinders</u> travel, snow is a ____.
13. If I trip by <u>accident</u>, I trip ____.
14. If your puppy gets into <u>mischief</u>, your puppy is ____.

Complete the Paragraph Write spelling words from the box to complete the paragraph.

The first time I did my own __15.__ was __16.__! Dad told me to wash colors and whites __17.__, but I threw everything in together, including my red socks and my favorite white sweatshirt. I also neglected to turn the water __18.__ down to cold. Did you know that hot water can make colors run together and can make clothes shrink to __19.__ size? My favorite white sweatshirt, which, __20.__, is now bright pink, is small enough for my baby sister!

> temperature
> incidentally
> laundry
> miniature
> disastrous
> separately

Spelling **and** Writing

Proofread a Paragraph

Six words are not spelled correctly in this paragraph. Write the words correctly.

My first day of work at Dr. Mendez's animal hospital was disasterous. Dr. Mendez, the vetrinarian, was called away on an emergency. While he was gone, the heating system went haywire. We were waiting for maintainence personnel to arrive when a mischivous monkey escaped from its cage and partially destroyed the washroom. Then a small poodle with a nervous temprament knocked down a shelf of supplies. I know it is a privlidge to work for Dr. Mendez, but I hope we never have a day like that again! Even so, I took a picture of the monkey covered with toilet tissue as a remembrance.

Proofreading Marks

≡	Make a capital.
/	Make a small letter.
∧	Add something.
ℓ	Take out something.
⊙	Add a period.
⌗	New paragraph
SP	Spelling error

Write a Paragraph

Narrative Writing

Write a paragraph describing how humor helped you get through a difficult day at school.

- Describe in detail what went wrong.
- Explain how humor helped you put events in perspective.
- Follow the form used in the proofreading sample. Use as many spelling words as you can.

Writing Process

Prewriting
⇩
Drafting
⇩
Revising
⇩
Editing
⇩
Publishing

Proofread Your Writing During ▶

Proofread your writing for spelling errors as part of the editing stage in the writing process. Be sure to check each word carefully. Use a dictionary to check spelling if you are not sure.

Vocabulary

Strategy Words

Review Words: Frequently Misspelled Words

Write words from the box to complete the paragraph.

amateur	athlete	muscle
	pigeon	villain

I enjoy cartoons, especially ones in which the evil __1.__ is defeated by a sweet, noble character. My favorite cartoon is about a dove, or __2.__ . The dove wants to be the star __3.__ in an __4.__ athletic competition. He works out to build __5.__ so that he can compete. A sly, nasty crow, meanwhile, tries every trick he can think of to keep the dove out of the competition. In the end, the crow is caught in one of his own traps. The dove triumphs!

Preview Words: Frequently Misspelled Words

Write a word from the box to match each clue.

aluminum	lightning	luxury
	prejudice	spontaneous

6. This is another word for **bigotry** or **intolerance**.
7. This describes something that is not planned.
8. This is usually accompanied by thunder.
9. This metal is a good conductor of heat.
10. This is something that can be expensive but is not necessary.

Connections

Content Words

Language Arts: Point of View

Write words from the box to complete the paragraph.

assumption	first-person	narrator
perspective	third-person	

In literature, **point of view** is the ___1.___ from which a story is told. The use of **I** in a ___2.___ account makes the story seem more immediate and realistic. In an omniscient, or ___3.___, account, the ___4.___ is that the storyteller, or ___5.___, knows everything.

Science: Genealogy

Write a word from the box to replace each word or phrase in parentheses to finish the paragraph.

ancestors	ethnic	genealogy
genetics	hereditary	

On the one hand, ___6.___ (the study of family history) provides facts about a person's ___7.___ (racial, religious, national, or cultural) background and ___8.___ (forebears). On the other hand, ___9.___ (the biological science of heredity) supplies information about the ___10.___ (inborn) traits of a person, such as blood type.

Apply the Spelling Strategy

Circle the two content words you wrote that may be misspelled because a double consonant spelling has a single consonant sound.

Spelling and Thinking

READ THE SPELLING WORDS

1. abstract	abstract	An **abstract** idea may need explanation.
2. complicate	complicate	Her absence will **complicate** our plans.
3. persist	persist	Children may **persist** in questioning.
4. attractive	attractive	That is an **attractive** pair of boots.
5. strict	strict	He had **strict** orders to be on time.
6. replica	replica	I bought a tiny **replica** of that statue.
7. distract	distract	Will loud music **distract** the students?
8. consist	consist	Dinner will **consist** of three courses.
9. restrict	restrict	Will they **restrict** traffic on that road?
10. insistence	insistence	At our **insistence,** prices were lowered.
11. duplicate	duplicate	Keep a **duplicate** of your application.
12. resist	resist	Such a generous offer is hard to **resist**.
13. constrict	constrict	This cast will **constrict** arm movement.
14. detract	detract	Those trash cans **detract** from the view.
15. resistance	resistance	We wore down his **resistance** to hiking.
16. complication	complication	The plan succeeded without **complication**.
17. attract	attract	Your perfume may **attract** bees.
18. insist	insist	I **insist** that you stay for supper.
19. retract	retract	The paper refused to **retract** the story.
20. consistent	consistent	Lee's ideas are **consistent** with ours.

SORT THE SPELLING WORDS

1.–6. Write the spelling words with the Latin root **tract,** meaning "to pull or draw."

7.–10. Write the spelling words with the Latin root **plic,** meaning "to fold."

11.–17. Write the spelling words with the Latin root **sist,** meaning "to stand still."

18.–20. Write the spelling words with the Latin root **strict,** meaning "to bind tightly."

REMEMBER THE SPELLING STRATEGY

Remember that knowing Latin roots like **tract, plic, sist,** and **strict** can give clues to the meaning and spelling of certain words.

Spelling and Vocabulary

Word Meanings

Write a spelling word to match each description.

1. to be made up of or composed of
2. a reproduction of a work of art
3. apart from concrete existence; a genre of painting
4. to draw back or take back
5. to make smaller or narrower; to restrict
6. to take away a desirable part; to diminish
7. a force that tends to oppose or retard motion
8. a firmness in a demand or a refusal to yield
9. pleasing to the eye or mind; charming
10. a factor, condition, or element that complicates

Word Structure

Write the spelling word that is derived from each Latin word and prefix.

11. **tractus** meaning "pull" + **ad-** meaning "toward"
12. **strictus** meaning "bind" + **re-** meaning "back"
13. **plicare** meaning "to fold" + **du-** meaning "twice"
14. **plicare** meaning "to fold" + **com-** meaning "together"
15. **sistere** meaning "to stand" + **per-** meaning "intensely"
16. **tractus** meaning "pull" + **dis-** meaning "apart"

USING THE Thesaurus

Write spelling words that could replace the underlined words. Use the **Writing Thesaurus** to check your answers.

17. That organization has <u>inflexible</u> rules.
18. Such an adorable puppy was impossible to <u>rebuff</u>.
19. Team coaches <u>demand</u> that the athletes attend all practices.
20. Her loyalty to the team has been <u>constant</u>.

Spelling and Reading

> | abstract | complicate | persist | attractive | strict |
> |----------|-----------|---------|-----------|--------|
> | replica | distract | consist | restrict | insistence |
> | duplicate | resist | constrict | detract | resistance |
> | complication | attract | insist | retract | consistent |

Complete the Sentences Write a spelling word to complete each sentence.

1. Which photocopier should I use to _____ these documents?
2. Billboards would _____ from the beauty of the landscape.
3. Will the editor _____ the statement she made about him?
4. My cousin bought a bronze _____ of an Egyptian sphinx.
5. What does the Korean dish kimchee _____ of?
6. Tie a tourniquet above the wound to _____ the blood vessels and restrict the flow of blood.
7. A _____ slowed my progress.
8. Rain will _____ all weekend, so let's rent a movie.
9. I tried, but I could not _____ a third slice of pie.
10. Try to _____ the baby's attention with this rattle.
11. I am finally beginning to understand this _____ art.
12. The smell of freshly baked bread will _____ customers to the store.

Complete the Journal Entries Write spelling words from the box to complete each journal entry.

March 10. My parents have worked out a __13.__ schedule for our trip west. However, my grandparents are showing great __14.__ to traveling on superhighways. They want to __15.__ our driving to back roads. Their __16.__ that we take back roads is going to __17.__ our plans. It's not __18.__ with our desire to reach the coast by Monday.

March 15. If we had not listened to my grandparents, think of all the __19.__ sights we would have missed. For our trip next year, I too will __20.__ on driving the back-roads, scenic route!

> insistence
> attractive
> strict
> insist
> consistent
> resistance
> restrict
> complicate

Spelling and Writing

Proofread a Passage

Six words are not spelled correctly in this passage. Write the words correctly.

> On a visit to an exhibit of abstrack art, I overheard a conversation between an art critic and an eager new artist.
>
> "I ensist that you review my work," the artist said. The critic tried to resist giving an opinion. "Must I percist? I never give up, you know," continued the artist.
>
> Finally, the critic's resistence was worn down. "It's atractive," she said, obviously trying to restrict her comments.
>
> "Can't you see the symbolism?" the artist asked.
>
> "I prefer the strickt interpretation of the realists," the critic said. Feeling trapped, she turned to me, a total stranger, and said, "Where have you been?" Then she took my arm and escorted me around the museum.

Proofreading Marks

- ≡ Make a capital.
- / Make a small letter.
- ∧ Add something.
- ℓ Take out something.
- ⊙ Add a period.
- ⌗ New paragraph
- ⑤⑫ Spelling error

Write a Passage

Narrative Writing

Imagine that you have overheard a conversation between an artist and an art critic at an art exhibit.

- Describe the incident from your perspective.
- Use vivid verbs and adjectives, along with concrete details, to add meaning and interest to your account.
- Follow the form used in the proofreading sample.

Use as many spelling words as you can.

Proofread Your Writing During

Writing Process

Prewriting
⇩
Drafting
⇩
Revising
⇩
Editing
⇩
Publishing

Proofread your writing for spelling errors as part of the editing stage in the writing process. Be sure to check each word carefully. Use a dictionary to check spelling if you are not sure.

Unit 23 enrichment

Strategy Words

Review Words: Latin Roots tract, plic, sist, strict

Write words from the box to complete the advertisement.

applicant	assist	contract
district	extract	

The local school __1.__ is looking for help in the superintendent's office. The person seeking this position will be required to __2.__ the superintendent's office manager with data entry. This __3.__ should also be able to __4.__ information from completed teacher forms. The position is temporary and does not require the new employee to sign a __5.__.

Preview Words: Latin Roots tract, plic, sist, strict

Write a word from the box to match each clue.

contractor	distraction	inconsistency
persistence	stricture	

6. This shows an unwillingness to give up.
7. This person makes an agreement to do a job.
8. This can mean either "a restriction" or "criticism."
9. This characteristic makes people unpredictable.
10. This may cause you to lose focus.

Connections

Content Words

Math: Geometry

Write words from the box to complete the paragraph.

| compass | concentric | ellipse | protractor | straightedge |

A __1.__ is an ideal tool for drawing __2.__ circles. A __3.__ may be used to draw straight lines. A __4.__ is used for measuring and constructing angles. An __5.__, however, is not easily measured with simple tools. It is composed of all the points that have the sum of their distances from two fixed points equal to a constant.

Language Arts: Persuasion

Write words from the box to replace the word or words in parentheses to complete the paragraph.

| association | context | explicit | implicit | inference |

By making a careful __6.__ (conclusion based on clues), you can often predict what will happen next in a story. Look for two kinds of clues to meaning as you read: __7.__ (direct) and __8.__ (indirect) [unstated but understood from the __9.__ (surrounding words)]. Use __10.__ (mental connection) to figure out what symbols represent. Symbols are often an important clue to the theme of a story.

Apply the Spelling Strategy

Circle the three content words you wrote that contain the Latin roots **tract** or **plic**.

145

Assessment and Review

Assessment   Units 19–23

Each Assessment Word in the box fits one of the spelling strategies you have studied over the past five weeks. Read the spelling strategies. Then write each Assessment Word under the unit number it fits.

Unit 19
1.–6. Remember that plural nouns are formed in a variety of ways.

Unit 20
7.–14. Remember that the prefix **ad-,** meaning *to* or *toward,* may be assimilated into the spelling of the base word or word root.

Unit 21
Remember that the English language includes many words taken from names and places.

Unit 22
Remember that it is important to know the spellings of words that are frequently misspelled.

Unit 23
15.–20. Remember that knowing Latin roots like **tract, plic, sist,** and **strict** can give clues to the meaning and spelling of certain words.

restriction
brothers-in-law
accidental
utilities
desist
appall
appropriate
agencies
consistency
torpedoes
insistent
retractable
assessment
communities
resistor
authorities
attitude
attraction
accommodate
affair

Review — Unit 19: Plural Nouns

activities	potatoes	shelves	knives	opportunities
tomatoes	volcanoes	passersby	companies	mosquitoes

Write the spelling word that is the plural form of the word in parentheses.

1. How many (activity) have you completed?
2. I have written to the presidents of five (company).
3. The billboard caught the attention of all the (passerby).
4. Jim sharpened all the kitchen (knife).
5. You will have many (opportunity) to see that movie.
6. Put the glasses on the (shelf).
7. Hawaii has several (volcano).
8. A swarm of (mosquito) gathered around the pond.
9. Please peel these (potato) for the stew.
10. Carol picked five ripe (tomato) from the vine.

Review — Unit 20: Assimilated Prefix: ad-

application	according	attain	account	appetite
attempt	accustomed	approval	assemble	afford

Write the spelling word that contains each of these word parts.

11. count
12. tempt
13. custom
14. ford
15. plic

16. sem
17. prov
18. tain
19. tite
20. cord

Review Unit 21: Words From Names and Places

tangerine	suede	calico	frankfurter	cheddar
denim	hamburger	cantaloupe	cashmere	camellia

Write a spelling word that rhymes with each of these words.

1. tambourine
2. interim
3. cedar
4. reindeer

5. Mexico
6. shade
7. Amelia
8. antelope

Write the spelling word that fits the clue.

9. meat usually served on a round bun
10. meat usually served on a long bun

Review Unit 22: Frequently Misspelled Words

laboratory	salary	temperature	accidentally
remembrance	athletic	separately	laundry
	hindrance	privilege	

Write the spelling words that solve the analogies.

11. **Pound** is to **weight** as **degree** is to _____.
12. **Artist** is to **studio** as **scientist** is to _____.
13. **Free** is to **expensive** as **purposefully** is to _____.
14. **Disharmony** is to **musical** as **clumsy** is to _____.
15. **Vegetable** is to **stew** as **soap** is to _____.
16. **Fair** is to **just** as **advantage** is to _____.
17. **Attached** is to **together** as **apart** is to _____.
18. **Award** is to **prize** as **pay** is to _____.
19. **Vow** is to **promise** as **keepsake** is to _____.
20. **Greeting** is to **welcome** as **obstacle** is to _____.

Unit 23: Latin Roots: tract, plic, sist, strict

complicate	attractive	strict	insistence	duplicate
resist	resistance	attract	insist	consistent

Write a spelling word to replace the underlined word or words in each sentence.

1. The secretary had to <u>make copies of</u> the report.
2. All of the puppies are <u>good-looking</u>.
3. We agreed to go at the <u>firm suggestion</u> of Ms. Matthews.
4. Having to get to a noon meeting will <u>make difficult</u> my plans.
5. The athletes had to follow a <u>rigid</u> diet.
6. How can you <u>keep away from</u> that delicious pie?
7. Is there much <u>opposition</u> to the new plans?
8. We will try to plan dates that are <u>agreeable</u> with your schedule.
9. We have to think of ways to <u>draw in</u> new members.
10. I really must <u>strongly urge</u> that you pay close attention.

 **Spelling Study Strategy**

Sorting by Plural Forms of Nouns

One way to practice your spelling words is to place them into groups according to some spelling rule. Here is a way to organize the spelling words to practice with a partner.

1. Make columns for the plural endings: **s, es, ies, ves**.
2. Have a partner choose a spelling word from Units 19 through 23 that can be a noun.
3. Agree on whether the word is singular or plural.
4. Write the plural form of the word in the proper column.

Grammar, Usage, and Mechanics

Identifying Conjunctions

Coordinating conjunctions, such as **and, but,** and **or,** connect words or groups of words (including independent clauses) that are similar.

Donisha **and** Kenneth will not sing, **but** they will recite poems.

Subordinating conjunctions, such as **although, as, when, because, if,** and **before,** show how one clause is related to another.

Although we were late, we didn't miss the first act.

Practice Activity

A. Write the conjunction in each sentence below. Circle each subordinating conjunction.

    1. We can work together, or we can work separately.

    2. Please put tomatoes and avocados on my sandwich.

    3. If you come early, you can help give out programs.

    4. I have asked you to help because you are so good at this.

    5. Put your ballots in the box as you come in the door.

    6. If you will wait a few minutes, I will go with you.

    7. I wanted to get up early, but I overslept.

    8. Although Jennie is accustomed to being the leader, she will give someone else the opportunity.

B. Complete each sentence with a conjunction. Circle it if it is a subordinating conjunction.

    9. Set the table with knives, forks, _____ spoons.

    10. Choose the red team _____ the blue team.

    11. We'll watch that program _____ we get home in time.

    12. I can't reach the shelves _____ I am not tall enough.

    13. Turn in your papers _____ you leave the room.

    14. We will finish working _____ the clock strikes six.

    15. You could order two hamburgers, _____ it's not a good idea.

Proofreading Strategy

Share in a Pair

Good writers always proofread their writing for spelling errors. Here's a strategy you can use to proofread your papers.

You can share the proofreading task by pairing up with a partner. Ask your partner to read your work aloud slowly. While your partner reads, listen to each word in your work. Check to see that each word you hear is the word you meant to write and that it is spelled correctly.

Then you can return the favor by reading aloud to your partner. Both you and your partner will be able to focus carefully on every word. Try it!

Electronic Spelling

Search Engines

One way in which a computer can be especially helpful is in searching for information. You might search on the Internet, on a CD-ROM, or on an online library. A search engine helps you find the information. The search engine searches through a great many sources very quickly.

To get the search engine to find what you want, you have to provide clues that the search engine can use. You need to spell the search words correctly—or you might be surprised at what you get! If you type in **mesquite** when you mean **mosquito,** you'll get information about a tree instead of an insect.

Choose the word the computer user should use as a search word. The meaning of the subject wanted is in parentheses. Write the words correctly.

1. commuters, communities (neighborhoods)
2. voltage, volcanoes (forces of nature)
3. denim, dentist (clothing material)
4. hockey, hobby (athletics)
5. camellia, chameleon (flowers)
6. knaves, knives (cutting utensils)

READ THE SPELLING WORDS

1.	monopoly	*monopoly*	The company has a **monopoly** on red bread.
2.	dual	*dual*	The **dual** speakers provide stereo sound.
3.	unique	*unique*	The sand and silk collage was **unique**.
4.	biennial	*biennial*	Is this the year of the **biennial** sale?
5.	monotony	*monotony*	I cannot stand the **monotony** of that song.
6.	duplication	*duplication*	We want no **duplication** of photographs.
7.	unite	*unite*	The rival teams will **unite** for a party.
8.	monocle	*monocle*	He wore a **monocle** over his left eye.
9.	unify	*unify*	How will we **unify** the arguing parties?
10.	duo	*duo*	My dachshund and I make a great **duo**.
11.	binoculars	*binoculars*	With **binoculars** I see two distant ducks.
12.	university	*university*	My ambition is to go to a **university**.
13.	monorail	*monorail*	A **monorail** may replace the subway.
14.	duplex	*duplex*	In which half of the **duplex** do you live?
15.	unison	*unison*	The members of the choir sang in **unison**.
16.	monotonous	*monotonous*	Repeating the same task is **monotonous**.
17.	biannual	*biannual*	We attend the **biannual** town meetings.
18.	monotone	*monotone*	The lecturer spoke in a droning **monotone**.
19.	universe	*universe*	Is the **universe** really expanding?
20.	monogram	*monogram*	His **monogram** was sewn onto his towel.

SORT THE SPELLING WORDS

1.–6. Write the words that are derived from the Latin **unus**, meaning "one."

7.–13. Write the words that are derived from the Greek **monos**, meaning "one" or "single."

14.–17. Write the words that are derived from the Latin **duo**, meaning "two."

18.–20. Write the words that are derived from the Latin **bis**, meaning "twice."

REMEMBER THE SPELLING STRATEGY

Remember that the prefixes **uni-**, **mono-**, **duo-**, and **bi-** indicate number.

Word Meanings

Write a spelling word for each phrase.

1. a twosome
2. field glasses designed for use by both eyes at once
3. every two years
4. all existing things regarded as a single whole
5. singular in nature; unlike anything else
6. composed of two parts; having two uses or purposes
7. occurring twice each year
8. an institute of higher learning; a college with graduate schools
9. to become unified, to consolidate, to make into a unit
10. to bring people together

Word Structure

Write the spelling word for each etymology.

11. from the Latin **unus,** "one," and **sonus,** "sound"
12. from the Latin **duo,** "two," and **-plex,** "fold"
13. from the Latin **duplicare,** "to double," and **-ion,** "the process of"

USING THE Dictionary

Guidewords appear at the top of each dictionary page. They indicate the first entry word and the last entry word on the page.

14.–20. Imagine that the guidewords on a dictionary page are **monkey** and **monsoon**. In alphabetical order, write the spelling words that would appear between those guidewords.

153

monopoly	dual	unique	biennial	monotony
duplication	unite	monocle	unify	duo
binoculars	university	monorail	duplex	unison
monotonous	biannual	monotone	universe	monogram

Complete the Sentences   Write the spelling word that best completes each sentence.

1. Twice a year, we march in our city's _____ parade.

2. It is often illegal in the United States for one company to have a _____ on a particular service.

3. She raised her _____ to her right eye, closed the other, and peered down at the opera singers.

4. You are able to _____ enthusiasm with good sense.

5. The twins seemed to read each other's mind when they gave the same response in _____.

6. People sometimes wish their birthday could be a _____ event!

7. Batman is one-half of a famous superhero _____.

8. They bought a _____ so that they could live in one side and rent out the other side.

9. The _____ on the tie was so ornate that we could not make out the initials.

10.–11. I tried to pay attention, but she spoke in a _____ that was so _____ I fell asleep.

Complete the Paragraph   Write spelling words from the box to complete the paragraph.

The architects of the miniature "City of the Future" had a __12.__ vision: one was to __13.__ every aspect of their city into a seamless whole; the second was to steer clear of any possible boring __14.__ by avoiding all __15.__ of color, shape, or texture. The buildings were all connected by a tiny, operating __16.__. When I peered through my __17.__, I could see lifelike people inside every building, including students and teachers in classrooms in the __18.__. The __19.__ that the planners had created was both diverse and unified: a __20.__ accomplishment!

dual
university
monorail
unique
duplication
universe
monotony
binoculars
unify

154

Spelling and Writing

Proofread a Paragraph

Six words are not spelled correctly in this paragraph.
Write the words correctly.

The bianual skating competition at the univercity was about to begin. In silence, the first skating duo glided gracefully onto the ice, moving in perfect unason. The lights dimmed, the spotlight went on, and the music began. The first figure, a triple axel, was followed by a brilliant and unike series of spins and turns. Each skater's movements were a perfect duplecation of the other's. For the finale, the skaters astonished the crowd by tracing their dool monograms on the ice. At the end of their performance, the skaters bowed to the audience, whose applause sounded as loud as thunder.

Proofreading Marks

≡ Make a capital.

/ Make a small letter.

∧ Add something.

℮ Take out something.

⊙ Add a period.

⌗ New paragraph

(SP) Spelling error

Write a Paragraph

Expository Writing

Choose an event that you saw or in which you participated. Write a paragraph describing the event.

- Make sure your paragraph follows a logical sequence.
- Use words such as **first, next, then,** or **finally** to clearly indicate the sequence.
- Follow the form used in the proofreading sample.

Use as many spelling words as you can.

Proofread Your Writing During ▶ Editing

Proofread your writing for spelling errors as part of the editing stage in the writing process. Be sure to check each word carefully. Use a dictionary to check spelling if you are not sure.

Writing Process

Prewriting
⇩
Drafting
⇩
Revising
⇩
Editing
⇩
Publishing

Vocabulary

Strategy Words

Review Words: Prefixes uni-, mono-, duo-, bi-

Write a word from the box to complete each sentence.

biplane	bisect	duet
bimonthly	uniform	

1. The word _____ can mean "happening every two months," or it can mean "happening twice a month."
2. Draw a line to _____ the circle.
3. The pilot flew the _____ in a series of acrobatic moves.
4. We mixed the paint well so that the color was _____ throughout.
5. The two singers performed a _____.

Preview Words: Prefixes uni-, mono-, duo-, bi-

Write the word from the box that matches each clue.

bicoastal	duplicity	monologue
monopolize	unilateral	

6. deceitfulness or dishonesty
7. involving one side only
8. a dramatic speech by one character
9. referring to two coasts
10. to exclude others and dominate

Connections

Content Words

Math: Geometry

Write the word from the box that fits each meaning.

bisector	collinear	equidistant
midpoint	skew	

1. existing on the same line
2. neither parallel nor intersecting
3. a line that divides an angle into two smaller equal angles
4. equally distant
5. the center position on a line

Math: Geometry

Write the words from the box to identify the features on the graph.

axis	coordinates	grid
origin	quadrant	

6. AB or CD
7. E and I
8. F
9. G
10. H

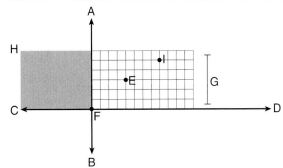

Apply the Spelling Strategy

Another Latin prefix that indicates number is **quad-,** meaning "four." Circle the two content words you wrote that have a prefix indicating a number.

READ THE SPELLING WORDS

1.	phonics	*phonics*	My little brother has **phonics** homework.
2.	telescope	*telescope*	We looked at stars through the **telescope**.
3.	chronology	*chronology*	What was the **chronology** of the events?
4.	diagram	*diagram*	I drew a **diagram** of the machine.
5.	microphone	*microphone*	The mayor spoke into the **microphone**.
6.	stethoscope	*stethoscope*	A nurse brought a **stethoscope** with him.
7.	headphones	*headphones*	She listens with the **headphones** on.
8.	telegram	*telegram*	Can you still send a **telegram** to someone?
9.	chronic	*chronic*	She has a **chronic** need to tell jokes.
10.	anagram	*anagram*	I can make an **anagram** with this word.
11.	symphonic	*symphonic*	I enjoyed the **symphonic** performance.
12.	grammatical	*grammatical*	Please correct any **grammatical** mistakes.
13.	synchronize	*synchronize*	I **synchronize** my watch with the clock.
14.	telephone	*telephone*	Did you get your **telephone** messages yet?
15.	periscope	*periscope*	A tube and mirrors can make a **periscope**.
16.	chronicle	*chronicle*	His diary is a **chronicle** of his life.
17.	megaphone	*megaphone*	The coach yelled into a **megaphone**.
18.	earphones	*earphones*	I cannot find the **earphones** for my radio.
19.	microscope	*microscope*	The science lab needs a new **microscope**.
20.	saxophone	*saxophone*	I practice my **saxophone** every day.

SORT THE SPELLING WORDS

1.–4. Write the words that contain **gram,** from the Greek "letter."

5.–8. Write the words that contain **chron,** from the Greek "time."

9.–16. Write the words that contain **phon(e),** from the Greek "sound."

17.–20. Write the words that contain **scope,** from the Greek "see."

REMEMBER THE SPELLING STRATEGY

Remember that the Greek word parts **gram, chron, phon(e),** and **scope** combine with other word parts to form new words.

Spelling and Vocabulary

Word Meanings

Write the spelling word that best completes each sentence.

1. What is the _____ of events that led to World War I?
2. At the health fair, I used a _____ to listen to my heart.
3. My brother plays the _____ in a jazz band.
4. "Between you and I" is an example of a _____ error.
5. The crew on the submarine used the _____ to scan the ocean surface from below the water.
6. We looked through the _____ to see the tiny organisms swimming in the pond water.
7. The word **stop** is an _____ of **tops**.
8. In the past, a quick way to send a printed message was by _____.
9. One rule of _____ is that the letters **ph** stand for the **f** sound.
10. If you look through this _____, you can see the craters on the moon.
11.–12. When you listen to the radio, you can use _____ or _____ so you do not disturb others.
13. I heard the _____ ringing, so I answered it.
14. The cheerleader yelled into the cone-shaped _____ so that the crowd could hear her.
15. The singer's _____ was not turned on, and the audience in the back row could not hear the song.
16. The choreographer will _____ the dance movements with the music.
17. Many of Beethoven's musical works are _____.

USING THE Thesaurus

Write a spelling word that is a synonym for each word below. Use the **Writing Thesaurus** if you need help.

18. habitual
19. chart
20. record

Spelling and Reading

phonics	telescope	chronology	diagram	microphone
stethoscope	headphones	telegram	chronic	anagram
symphonic	grammatical	synchronize	telephone	periscope
chronicle	megaphone	earphones	microscope	saxophone

Replace the Phrases   Write the spelling word that best replaces each underlined phrase.

1. a sequence of events in the history of communications tools

2. 1590: Invention of the instrument for viewing small objects.

3. 1668: Isaac Newton proposes design for the instrument for viewing faraway objects.

4. 1816: R. T. H. Laënnec constructs the instrument for listening to sounds within the body.

5. 1844: First message sent by telegraph sent in Morse code.

6. 1846: Adolphe Sax patents the single-reed wind instrument.

7. 1854: E. H. Marie-Davy invents the first "submarine sight tube."

8. 1876: Invention of the instrument that converts sound into electric current.

9. 1876: First successful use of the instrument that transmits spoken words over a distance.

10. 1912: First attempts to operate together sound on disks and action on film.

Complete the Paragraph   Write spelling words from the box to complete the paragraph.

When Sarah, our foreign exchange student from Poland, studies English tapes at school, she uses __11.__ or __12.__ . That way, she does not disturb anyone in study hall. Her English has improved tremendously. She never makes __13.__ mistakes. She even uses the __14.__ at soccer games and helps the pep squad. Sarah loves music. She wants to conduct __15.__ music someday. Sarah is also a __16.__ puzzle maker who is always rearranging the letters in words. For example, she told me that **Chopin's** is almost an __17.__ for __18.__ . She is writing a __19.__ of her visit. She even drew a __20.__ of our neighborhood to show to her family back in Warsaw.

symphonic
anagram
earphones
diagram
megaphone
headphones
chronicle
phonics
chronic
grammatical

160

Spelling and Writing

Proofread an Outline

Six words are not spelled correctly in this outline. Write the words correctly.

The Telephone

I. Brief description
   A. Handsets
      1. Speech converted to electrical signals by micraphone
      2. Signals converted back into sound through earphoans
   B. Other parts [Note to myself: Include a diogram.]
      1. Ringers   2. Switch hooks   3. Dialers
II. History and development
   A. Early telecommunications cronology
      1. Telegraph invented, 1837; first Morse code tellegram, 1844
      2. Alexander Graham Bell's first demonstration of telephone apparatus, 1876
   B. Modern advances
      1. Digital phone lines and modems; the Internet
      2. New technologies syncranize transmission of sound and data

Proofreading Marks

≡ Make a capital.

/ Make a small letter.

∧ Add something.

℘ Take out something.

⊙ Add a period.

⌗ New paragraph

Ⓢ🅿 Spelling error

Write an Outline and Paragraph

Expository Writing

Choose a communications device from the spelling words to research. Write an outline of your findings and then write a paragraph.

- Divide your outline into major topics, subtopics, and details.
- Follow the form used in the proofreading sample.
- Write a well-organized paragraph.

Use as many spelling words as you can.

Proofread Your Writing During

Proofread your writing for spelling errors as part of the editing stage in the writing process. Be sure to check each word carefully. Use a dictionary to check spelling if you are not sure.

Writing Process

Prewriting
⇩
Drafting
⇩
Revising
⇩
Editing
⇩
Publishing

Vocabulary

Strategy Words

Review Words: Greek Forms

Write a word from the box to complete each sentence.

grammar	gramophone	microscopic
parallelogram		telescopic

1. A record player used to be called a _____.
2. With _____ vision, we can see very distant objects.
3. A square is a _____; a rectangle is one also.
4. "It is I" is an example of correct _____.
5. A skin cell is so small that it is _____.

Preview Words: Greek Forms

Write a word from the box to match each definition.

chronogram	gyroscope	phonetic
polyphonic		symphonious

6. harmonious
7. having two or more melodies played or sung at the same time
8. representing the sounds of speech with letters that indicate single sounds
9. the record produced by an instrument that measures the passing of time
10. a device with an axis that can turn or spin in one or more directions

Connections

Content Words

Fine Arts: Music

Write words from the box to complete the paragraph.

ovation	instrumental	orchestral
stereophonic	symphony	

I am listening to my favorite __1.__ sound recording. Zubin Mehta is conducting a large __2.__ work known as a __3.__. Vladimir Horowitz is playing an __4.__ solo for piano. At the end, the __5.__ is deafening. I feel as if I am in the middle of the concert hall!

Science: Geology

Write words from the box to complete the paragraph.

geological	intense	seismic
seismograph	tremor	

One well-known __6.__ fact is that the earth's crust moves beneath us all the time. This movement causes the trembling we know as earthquakes. Sometimes an earthquake is large and destructive. At other times, though, a __7.__ is so slight that we do not notice it. A __8.__ measures the intensity of __9.__ activity. Depending on how __10.__ the release of energy is, the earthquake is assigned a number on the Richter scale.

Apply the Spelling Strategy

Circle the two content words you wrote that contain the Greek word part **phon**.

Spelling and Thinking

READ THE SPELLING WORDS

1. adapt	*adapt*	Did he **adapt** his play for television?
2. adopt	*adopt*	They want to **adopt** the stray kitten.
3. personnel	*personnel*	He is the director of **personnel**.
4. personal	*personal*	The message was private and **personal**.
5. stationary	*stationary*	That old train engine is **stationary**.
6. stationery	*stationery*	She wrote to us on fancy **stationery**.
7. advise	*advise*	I **advise** you to study for the test.
8. advice	*advice*	Fran offered me some friendly **advice**.
9. formally	*formally*	We have not been **formally** introduced.
10. formerly	*formerly*	Ennis was **formerly** a Senate page.
11. complement	*complement*	This hat will **complement** your coat.
12. compliment	*compliment*	Thank you for your kind **compliment**.
13. affect	*affect*	How will the news **affect** your family?
14. effect	*effect*	That speech had no **effect** on me.
15. device	*device*	Use this **device** to pry open the lid.
16. devise	*devise*	Who wants to **devise** a better plan?
17. conscious	*conscious*	I was not **conscious** during surgery.
18. conscience	*conscience*	His **conscience** told him it was wrong.
19. disinterested	*disinterested*	She offered a **disinterested** opinion.
20. uninterested	*uninterested*	You seem **uninterested** in that book.

SORT THE SPELLING WORDS

1.–3. Write the words that can be both nouns and verbs.

4.–8. Write the words that are nouns.

9.–13. Write the words that are verbs.

14.–18. Write the words that are adjectives.

19.–20. Write the words that are adverbs.

REMEMBER THE SPELLING STRATEGY

Remember that when words sound similar to each other or when they are homophones, their spellings can be easily confused.

Spelling and Vocabulary

Word Meanings

Write a spelling word that is related in meaning to complete each group.

1. influence, sway, _____
2. adaptation, adaptable, _____
3. suggest, recommend, _____
4. informal, formality, _____
5. awake, alert, _____
6. still, motionless, _____
7. opinion, recommendation, _____
8. arrange, contrive, _____
9. incomplete, completion, _____
10. business, employer, _____
11. desk, pen, _____

Antonyms

Write the spelling word that is an antonym for each word.

12. intrigued
13. reject
14. ridicule
15. afterward
16. biased
17. public

USING THE Dictionary

An **idiomatic phrase** has a meaning as a whole that may not be suggested by its parts. In a dictionary, the phrase and its meaning can be found in the entry for the main word, before the etymology. Write the spelling word that completes each idiom. Use the **Spelling Dictionary** if you need help.

18. —*idiom.* **in (all)** _____. in all truth or fairness.
19. —*idiom.* **leave to (one's) own** _____s. to allow to do as one pleases.
20. —*idiom.* **in** _____. in fact; actually; in operation.

adapt	adopt	personnel	personal
stationary	stationery	advise	advice
formally	formerly	complement	compliment
affect	effect	device	devise
conscious	conscience	disinterested	uninterested

Complete the Pairs Write pairs of spelling words to complete each sentence.

1.–2. The woman who _____ had been ambassador to England _____ addressed our graduating class.

3.–4. A _____ party has no stake in a dispute; an _____ party is indifferent to its outcome.

5.–6. Did that amazing special _____ in the movie _____ you in any special way?

7.–8. We received a nice _____ from our art instructor for finding the full _____ of missing sketches.

9.–10. My _____ has made me _____ of the fact that I should always be honest.

Complete the Paragraph Write spelling words from the box to complete the paragraph.

Our English project last term was to __11.__ a scene from a book to videotape. We wrote to a production company in California for __12.__. (The principal's secretary was nice enough to type our letter on school __13.__.) "I __14.__ you," a studio producer replied, "to first __15.__ a professional, rather than a __16.__, approach. Next, make up a list of __17.__. Then __18.__ a plan and a recording schedule. Cast the show carefully. Also, include as much action as you can. There's nothing worse than a movie that is __19.__. Remember that the camera is just a __20.__ you use to capture the action—and the hearts and minds of your audience."

> advice
> advise
> devise
> device
> adapt
> adopt
> personnel
> personal
> stationary
> stationery

Spelling *and* Writing

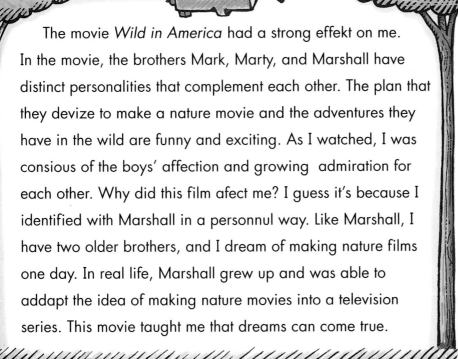

Proofread a Paragraph

Six words are not spelled correctly in this paragraph. Write the words correctly.

The movie *Wild in America* had a strong effekt on me. In the movie, the brothers Mark, Marty, and Marshall have distinct personalities that complement each other. The plan that they devize to make a nature movie and the adventures they have in the wild are funny and exciting. As I watched, I was consious of the boys' affection and growing admiration for each other. Why did this film afect me? I guess it's because I identified with Marshall in a personnul way. Like Marshall, I have two older brothers, and I dream of making nature films one day. In real life, Marshall grew up and was able to addapt the idea of making nature movies into a television series. This movie taught me that dreams can come true.

Proofreading Marks

≡	Make a capital.
/	Make a small letter.
∧	Add something.
ℓ	Take out something.
⊙	Add a period.
⌗	New paragraph
⑤⑫	Spelling error

Write a Paragraph

Narrative Writing

Think of a movie, play, or television program that affected you strongly. Write a paragraph about the experience.

- Briefly describe the movie, play, or TV program.
- Explain how and why it affected you.
- Follow the form used in the proofreading sample.

Use as many spelling words as you can.

Writing Process

Prewriting
⇩
Drafting
⇩
Revising
⇩
Editing
⇩
Publishing

Proofread Your Writing During ▶

Proofread your writing for spelling errors as part of the editing stage in the writing process. Be sure to check each word carefully. Use a dictionary to check spelling if you are not sure.

Vocabulary

Strategy Words

Review Words: Commonly Confused Words

Write words from the box to complete the paragraph.

colonel	their	there
they're	kernel	

The __1.__ stood before the troops. Rumors had been spreading that he had shirked his duties as an officer. Now he was prepared to inform those he commanded that __2.__ leader was an honest, upright soldier. "I am here to tell you," he said, "that __3.__ is not a __4.__ of truth to the rumors that I neglected my duties as an officer. If you encounter people who accuse me of being an irresponsible leader, tell them that __5.__ absolutely wrong."

Preview Words: Commonly Confused Words

Write a word from the box to match each definition.

assent	bazaar	bizarre
eminent	imminent	

6. high in rank; greater than others
7. extremely odd or unusual in appearance
8. about to happen; near at hand
9. agree or concur
10. a marketplace where various goods are sold

Connections

Content Words

Math: Statistics

Write a word from the box to match each description.

frequency	median	mode
statistician	statistics	

1. This is a person who compiles numerical facts.
2. If you have two 6's, one 5, and four 7's, this is four 7's.
3. This describes how often something occurs.
4. This is something in the middle.
5. These are collections of numerical facts.

Science: Geography

Write words from the box to complete the paragraph.

equator	hemisphere	latitude
longitude	rotate	

Do you know how to read a globe of the earth? The horizontal line around the middle is the __6.__. The lines parallel to the equator are lines of __7.__, and the lines perpendicular to the equator are lines of __8.__. The top half of the earth is the northern __9.__, in which North America lies. You can __10.__ the globe to show how the earth spins on its axis.

Apply the Spelling Strategy

Circle the word you wrote that may be confused with the word **medium**. Underline the two words that may be confused because of similar endings and related meanings.

READ THE SPELLING WORDS

1.	deluxe	*deluxe*	We stayed in a **deluxe** two-bedroom suite.
2.	carousel	*carousel*	The **carousel** turned while music played.
3.	mirage	*mirage*	Do I see water in the desert or a **mirage**?
4.	fiancé	*fiancé*	My sister will marry her **fiancé** in June.
5.	picturesque	*picturesque*	That mountain inn is very **picturesque**.
6.	masquerade	*masquerade*	Your costume for the **masquerade** is ready.
7.	corsage	*corsage*	The rose **corsage** complemented her gown.
8.	fatigue	*fatigue*	Extreme **fatigue** made him fall asleep.
9.	impasse	*impasse*	We are at an **impasse** and cannot continue.
10.	chaperone	*chaperone*	Raina's parents will **chaperone** the party.
11.	intrigue	*intrigue*	The mystery play was filled with **intrigue**.
12.	fiancée	*fiancée*	His **fiancée** will plan the entire wedding.
13.	boutique	*boutique*	I bought Mom's pin at a jewelry **boutique**.
14.	camouflage	*camouflage*	The tree branches will **camouflage** the car.
15.	expertise	*expertise*	We rely on Dr. Wing's medical **expertise**.
16.	silhouette	*silhouette*	Our art teacher cut out my **silhouette**.
17.	résumé	*résumé*	List all previous jobs on your **résumé**.
18.	souvenir	*souvenir*	We kept the ticket stub as a **souvenir**.
19.	menagerie	*menagerie*	The circus had a **menagerie** of animals.
20.	gourmet	*gourmet*	The hotel chef prepared a **gourmet** meal.

SORT THE SPELLING WORDS

1.–4. Write the words that end in /ā/.

5.–7. Write the words that end in /ēg/ or /ĕl/.

8.–10. Write the words that begin with **de-, ex-,** or **im-**.

11.–13. Write the words that begin with /**s**/ or /**sh**/.

14.–17. Write the words in which /**zh**/ or /**j**/ is spelled **ge**.

18.–20. Write the words in which /**k**/ is spelled **que**.

REMEMBER THE SPELLING STRATEGY

Remember that the English language includes many words from French.

Spelling and Vocabulary

Word Meanings

Write a spelling word for each description.

1. a summary of one's job experiences
2. one who appreciates fine food
3. luxurious, elegant
4. to conceal something by making it look like its natural surroundings
5. a collection of wild animals on exhibition
6. exhaustion, weariness
7. a dead end

Word Replacements

Write the spelling word that best replaces the underlined word or words.

8. He would soon reveal his true identity because he could not keep up the pretense much longer.
9. We rode up and down on the wooden merry-go-round horses.
10. Cal's older sister will be a supervisor on the seventh-grade trip to the science museum.
11. They moved to a charming town by the seashore.
12. At their fiftieth anniversary party, Grandfather pinned a small flower bouquet on Grandmother's suit jacket.
13. They could use a chef with your ability in their restaurant.

USING THE Dictionary

Write a spelling word for each etymology. Use the **Spelling Dictionary** if you need help.

14. Fr., memory < *souvenir,* to recall < Lat. *subvenire,* to come to mind
15. Fr. < OProv. *botica* < Lat. *apotheca,* storehouse
16. Fr. < *mirer,* to look at < Lat. *mirari,* to wonder at
17. Fr., p.part. of *fiancer,* to betroth < *fier,* to trust
18. Fr., fem. of *fiancé,* fiancé
19. Fr. < Etienne de *Silhouette* (1709–1767)
20. Fr. < Ital. *intrigo* < *intrigare,* to perplex < Lat. *intricare*

deluxe	carousel	mirage	fiancé	picturesque
masquerade	corsage	fatigue	impasse	chaperone
intrigue	fiancée	boutique	camouflage	expertise
silhouette	résumé	souvenir	menagerie	gourmet

Solve the Analogies   Write the spelling word that best completes each analogy.

1. **Trophy** is to **plaque** as **memento** is to _____.
2. **Vegetables** are to **salad** as **flowers** are to _____.
3. **Storm** is to **hurricane** as **fantasy** is to _____.
4. **Shark** is to **aquarium** as **zebra** is to _____.
5. **Comedy** is to **humor** as **mystery** is to _____.
6. **Sunlight** is to **darkness** as **energy** is to _____.
7. **Milk** is to **supermarket** as **dress** is to _____.

Complete the Questions   Write the spelling word that best completes each question.

8. Will the artist cut out your _____ from black paper?
9. Can you afford such expensive _____ accommodations?
10. When do your sister and her _____ plan to get married?
11. Which animal's _____ makes the animal look like a log in water?
12. What information should I put on my _____?
13. How will they get over this _____ in their discussion and find a solution to the problem?
14. Is she a _____, or does she prefer fast food?

Complete the Paragraph   Write spelling words from the box to complete the paragraph.

We attended the opening of *Romeo and Juliet* at the community theater last night. My brother's __15.__, who is in the cast, got us tickets. The production was lovely! The __16.__ ball was my favorite scene. The set designer had built a __17.__ that rotated the sets, and the painted backdrops were charming and __18.__. The designer's __19.__ showed in the detail of the period costumes. The actress who played Juliet's __20.__ stole the show!

carousel
chaperone
masquerade
picturesque
fiancée
expertise

Spelling and Writing

Proofread a Paragraph

Six words are not spelled correctly in this first paragraph of a mystery story. Write the words correctly.

My partner and I were about to lock the doors to our detective agency when suddenly a stranger appeared. He told us he was a goormé chef who had catered a fancy maskerade ball the night before. He and his fiancée had set up serving tables near a menajerie of exotic animals. At midnight, his beloved had disappeared. He thought he had seen her silooette against one of the dining room walls, but it turned out to be a mirage. Now he wanted us to use our expertese as detectives to locate her. We enjoy intreeg, so we took the case.

Write a Paragraph

Narrative Writing

Write the next paragraph of this mystery story, or write the first paragraph of your own story.

- If you continue the story above, begin by describing your actions the next day.
- If you start your own story, include the setting, the characters, and the mysterious conflict.
- Follow the form used in the proofreading sample.

Use as many spelling words as you can.

Proofread Your Writing During

Proofread your writing for spelling errors as part of the editing stage in the writing process. Be sure to check each word carefully. Use a dictionary to check spelling if you are not sure.

Proofreading Marks

≡ Make a capital.

/ Make a small letter.

∧ Add something.

℘ Take out something.

⊙ Add a period.

⌗ New paragraph

SP Spelling error

Writing Process

Prewriting
⇩
Drafting
⇩
Revising
⇩
Editing
⇩
Publishing

Vocabulary

Strategy Words

Review Words: Words From French

Write a word from the box to match each clue.

beret	brochure	crochet
garage	amateur	

1. a craft performed with a hooked needle and yarn
2. describes an athlete who does not get paid for playing a sport
3. a flat, round cap, usually made of wool
4. a place for one or more cars, although people often store bikes, lawn mowers, and other items in it
5. a pamphlet, often used to describe or advertise a product or a service

Preview Words: Words From French

Write a word from the box to complete each sentence.

antique	etiquette	finesse
rendezvous	reservoir	

6. We planned to ____ in the park after the game.
7. Do you know the proper ____ to use in the presence of royalty?
8. That hundred-year-old table is a valuable ____.
9. Our water comes directly from the town ____.
10. The diplomat handled the hostile leaders with great ____ and avoided an angry confrontation.

Connections

Content Words

Write words from the box to complete the paragraph.

applause	encore	matinee
premiere	rehearsal	

The ___1.___, or first, performance of the musical was at the 2 o'clock ___2.___ on Saturday, May 1. As film and theater critic for the school newspaper, Elena was invited to attend the dress ___3.___. The opening number was so moving that Elena and the rest of the audience responded with thunderous ___4.___. Hoping to hear the song again, they shouted for an ___5.___.

Science: Sound

Write words from the box to complete the paragraph.

chamber	larynx	mechanics
resonate	vibration	

To understand how we speak, you first have to understand the ___6.___ of the human voice, or how the voice works. In human beings, sound is produced by the ___7.___ of the vocal cords. These are found in the ___8.___, a boxlike ___9.___ in the throat, sometimes called the voice box. When we speak, sounds produced in the voice box ___10.___ through the air and are heard.

Apply the Spelling Strategy

Circle the four content words you wrote that come from French.

READ THE SPELLING WORDS

1.	fluctuate	*fluctuate*	Her moods **fluctuate** from glad to sad.
2.	mannerism	*mannerism*	Blinking rapidly is a **mannerism**.
3.	missive	*missive*	Admiral Orr sent a **missive** to the ship.
4.	fluent	*fluent*	Diana is **fluent** in Spanish and Italian.
5.	magnanimous	*magnanimous*	It is **magnanimous** of you to pardon us.
6.	admission	*admission*	I applied for **admission** to music camp.
7.	influence	*influence*	A clever lawyer can **influence** a jury.
8.	inanimate	*inanimate*	An **inanimate** object lacks life.
9.	manicure	*manicure*	Does she **manicure** her nails often?
10.	remiss	*remiss*	It would be **remiss** of me not to help.
11.	manipulate	*manipulate*	I cannot **manipulate** the kite strings.
12.	fluency	*fluency*	His **fluency** in Chinese was a surprise.
13.	transmission	*transmission*	The old van needs a new **transmission**.
14.	emancipate	*emancipate*	Please **emancipate** me from this duty.
15.	unanimous	*unanimous*	The decision to rest was **unanimous**.
16.	manual	*manual*	The **manual** says to twist the two wires.
17.	dismiss	*dismiss*	Mr. Curtis will **dismiss** class early.
18.	animate	*animate*	An **animate** object has life.
19.	fluorescent	*fluorescent*	Dad put **fluorescent** lights in the den.
20.	intermission	*intermission*	We will now take a brief **intermission**.

SORT THE SPELLING WORDS

Write the spelling words that come from the following Latin words:

1.–6. miss, from **missus,** past participle of **mittere,** meaning "to send" or "let go"

7.–11. man, from **manus,** meaning "hand"

12.–16. flu, from **fluere,** meaning "to flow"

17.–20. anim, from **animus** or **anima,** meaning "soul" or "spirit"

REMEMBER THE SPELLING STRATEGY

Remember that knowing Latin roots like **miss, manus, fluere,** and **animus** can give clues to the meaning and spelling of certain words.

Spelling and Vocabulary

Word Meanings

Write a spelling word related in meaning to complete each group.

1. careless, neglectful, _____

2. undulate, sway, _____

3. ultraviolet, incandescent, _____

4. ease, ability, _____

5. characteristic, trait, _____

6. letter, note, _____

Word Structure

Write the spelling words that are formed from the following Latin words and prefixes.

7. **unus,** meaning "one" + **animus,** meaning "mind"

8. **trans-,** meaning "across" + **mittere,** meaning "to send"

9. **in-,** meaning "in" + **fluere,** meaning "to flow"

10. **in-,** meaning "not" + **anima,** meaning "spirit"

11. **ex-,** meaning "out of" + **mancipium,** meaning "ownership"

12. **inter-,** meaning "between" + **missus,** meaning "let go"

13. **magnus,** meaning "great" + **animus,** meaning "soul"

USING THE Dictionary

Write a spelling word to complete each sentence. Then look up the word in the **Spelling Dictionary** and write the letter of the definition that best suits the way the word is used in the sentence.

14. Before you try to assemble the bike, read the instruction _____ carefully.

15. Tanya is _____ in French.

16. How much is the _____ fee to the planetarium?

17. Paco is getting paid to _____ his neighbor's lawn and hedges.

18. Will the principal _____ all the classes right after lunch today?

19. To land the plane in these circumstances, the pilot will have to _____ the controls skillfully.

20. Someday, she hopes to _____ her own cartoons.

Spelling and Reading

fluctuate	mannerism	missive	fluent	magnanimous
admission	fluorescent	inanimate	manicure	transmission
manipulate	fluency	remiss	emancipate	unanimous
manual	dismiss	animate	influence	intermission

Solve the Analogies   Write a spelling word to complete each analogy.

1. **School** is to **recess** as **theater** is to _____.
2. **Window shade** is to **fabric** as **lamp** is to _____.
3. **Notable** is to **remarkable** as **generous** is to _____.
4. **Refusal** is to **acceptance** as **denial** is to _____.
5. **Bicycle** is to **gear** as **car** is to _____.
6. **Article** is to **editorial** as **letter** is to _____.
7. **Leave out** is to **omit** as **release** is to _____.

Complete the Sentences   Write a spelling word to complete each sentence.

8. Our summer temperatures _____ between 80 and 90 degrees.
9. Her _____ of tossing back her hair makes her seem dramatic.
10. The vote to adopt new club rules must be _____.
11. Emilio has a positive _____ on his brother's behavior.
12. I glued tiny gold hearts on my nails after my _____.
13. We would be _____ if we did not congratulate the winners.
14. The translator's job requires _____ in Spanish.

Complete the Paragraph   Write spelling words from the box to complete the paragraph.

Animation gives the illusion of life to __15.__ objects. Today, filmmakers __16.__, or bring to life, everything from packages and clothes to maps and diagrams. The smooth, __17.__ movement in a cartoon is not easy to achieve. Each frame requires a new drawing or model. In a sense, computers have served to __18.__ filmmakers. With computers, they are now able to __19.__ images in ways that were impossible when animation was a totally __20.__ skill.

> animate
> emancipate
> manual
> inanimate
> manipulate
> fluent

Spelling and Writing

Proofread a Paragraph

Six words are not spelled correctly in this paragraph. Write the words correctly.

In discussing animation, it would be rimiss not to mention Walt Disney, a man who had a tremendous influence in this field. Before Disney, the quality of animation would often fluctuait from film to film. Then in 1937, Disney produced the first full-length animated feature, *Snow White and the Seven Dwarfs*. Critics were unannimus in hailing Disney as a pioneer in the use of fluint motion. Disney knew how to minipulate his characters. He often gave each character a peculiar manerizm that made him or her unique. An example is the dwarf Dopey, whose absolute silence endeared him to audiences of all ages.

Write a Paragraph

Expository Writing

Write a paragraph about a person who has had a great impact on movies, television, or some other field of entertainment.

- Write a clear topic sentence that identifies the main idea of the paragraph.
- Include details that support the main idea stated in your topic sentence.
- Follow the form used in the proofreading sample.

Use as many spelling words as you can.

Proofread Your Writing During

Writing Process

Prewriting
⇩
Drafting
⇩
Revising
⇩
Editing
⇩
Publishing

Proofread your writing for spelling errors as part of the editing stage in the writing process. Be sure to check each word carefully. Use a dictionary to check spelling if you are not sure.

Vocabulary

Review Words: Latin Forms

Write words from the box to complete the paragraph.

admitted	affluent	manner
mission	permission	

Uncle George told me that his main ___1.___ in life is to educate people about threats to our environment. Uncle George plans to launch his own "Protect the World" campaign, but he ___2.___ to me that he needs the financial backing of the more ___3.___ members of our community to support his campaign. Uncle George has a persuasive ___4.___, so he should be able to raise all the funds he needs. In fact, he just got the mayor's ___5.___ to hold a fundraising rally on the steps of City Hall.

Preview Words: Latin Forms

Write a word from the box to match each clue.

animosity	commissary	confluence
emancipation	unanimity	

6. It is where two streams flow together.
7. This is what people who share the same views or opinions about an issue have.
8. Here is where military personnel buy groceries.
9. This is what any enslaved group desires most.
10. It describes intense hostile feelings.

Connections

Content Words

Language Arts: Literature

Write a word from the box to match each definition.

anonymous	by-line	copyright
manuscript	pseudonym	

1. alias; pen name
2. a typewritten or handwritten version of a book
3. unknown or withheld authorship
4. author credit appearing at the head of an article
5. the legal right to exclusive publication of a book, article, song, play, or other written work

Math: Whole Numbers

Write words from the box to complete the paragraph.

absolute value	consecutive	integer
mathematics	numerical	

The number line is used in __6.__ to illustrate relationships between __7.__ values and __8.__ whole numbers. (A whole number is also known as an __9.__ .) The __10.__ is indicated by a point on the number line and its relation to the origin.

Apply the Spelling Strategy

Circle the content word you wrote that contains the Latin combining form **manus**.

Assessment and Review

Assessment Units 25–29

Each Assessment Word in the box fits one of the spelling strategies you have studied over the past five weeks. Read the spelling strategies. Then write each Assessment Word under the unit number it fits.

Unit 25

1.–6. Remember that the prefixes **uni-, mono-, duo-,** and **bi-** indicate number.

Unit 26

7.–10. Remember that the Greek word parts **gram, chron, phon(e),** and **scope** combine with other word parts to form new words.

Unit 27

11.–12. Remember that when words sound similar to each other or when they are homophones, their spellings can be easily confused.

Unit 28

13.–16. Remember that the English language includes many words from French.

Unit 29

17.–20. Remember that knowing Latin roots like **miss, manus, fluere,** and **animus** can give clues to the meaning and spelling of certain words.

unified
disposition
phonograph
admissible
morality
milligram
mortality
fluorescence
triplane
biyearly
microscopically
fillet
entourage
universal
chronometer
mandatory
mystique
animosity
monopolizing
monogrammed

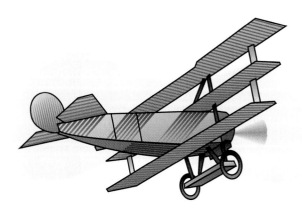

Unit 25: Prefixes: uni-, mono-, duo-, bi-

monopoly	dual	unique	monotony	duplication
binoculars	unite	university	monotonous	universe

Write the spelling word that completes the sentence.

1. Each person's fingerprints are _____.

2. After hearing the same song ten times, I felt it was getting _____.

3. If the only two widget makers join, they will have a _____ on the widget market.

4. The hoozit makers do not want the widget makers to _____.

5. This clock radio has a _____ purpose, which is that of both a clock and a radio.

6. Here's a new CD to relieve the _____ of listening to the old one over and over.

7. There are many solar systems in the _____.

8. You may look through my _____ to watch the birds.

9. Check to see that there is no _____ of efforts.

10. Dr. Schnable is a professor at the _____.

Unit 26: Greek Forms: gram, chron, phon(e), scope

telescope	grammatical	earphones	stethoscope	telegram
diagram	synchronize	telephone	microphone	microscope

Write a spelling word that goes with each occupation. Use the Greek word part given in parentheses.

11. doctor (scope)

12. secretary (phone)

13. architect (gram)

14. astronomer (scope)

15. radio announcer (phone)

16. airline pilot (phones)

17. research scientist (scope)

18. telegraph operator (gram)

Write the spelling word that completes the sentence.

19. Proofread your sentences to see that they are _____.

20. We'll _____ our swimming strokes for the show.

Unit 27: Commonly Confused Words

personnel	stationary	advise	affect	devise
effect	device	advice	personal	stationery

Write two spelling words for each sentence.

Jermaine is writing on __1.__ that is on a __2.__ desk.

Wait until I __3.__ you that I want your __4.__ .

All the company's __5.__ have filled out __6.__ reports.

Let's __7.__ a clever __8.__ for saving old papers.

The fireworks will __9.__ the overall __10.__ of the celebration.

 **Review**

Unit 28: Words From French

mirage	masquerade	picturesque	fiancé	fatigue
intrigue	camouflage	silhouette	résumé	souvenir

Write the spelling words for these clues.

11. a dark outline
12. betrothed
13. pretty as a picture
14. desert illusion
15. protective coloring
16. secret plotting

Write each spelling word by adding the missing letters.

17. fat_ _ _ _
18. s_ _venir
19. ré_ _mé
20. masq_ _ _ade

magnanimous	dismiss	influence	inanimate	transmission
unanimous	manual	admission	fluorescent	intermission

Write the spelling word that completes each sentence.

1. There was one short _____ between acts.
2. A violent storm interrupted the radio _____.
3. A teacher has a lasting _____ on students.
4. The proposal received the _____ support of the committee.
5. The principal decided to _____ the classes early on Friday.
6. The geologist studied the rocks and other _____ objects.
7. Anyone seeking _____ to this school must pass a test.
8. The new classroom will have _____ lights in the ceiling.
9. Before operating the new computer, be sure to read the _____.
10. The charity received a generous gift from a _____ citizen.

GAME Spelling Study Strategy

What's My Word?

Practicing spelling words can be fun if you make it into a game. Prepare a list of words you want to study. Trade lists with a partner. Play "What's My Word?" with your partner.

1. Ask your partner, "What's my word?" Your partner reads one of the words from your list.

2. Write the word and then spell the word aloud. If you have spelled it correctly, your partner will say, "That's your word!" and you get two points. If you did not spell it correctly, your partner will say, "That's not your word!" and give you a clue, such as "It ends with a silent **e**." If you get the word right the second time, you get one point. If not, you get no points.

3. Then it's your partner's turn to ask, "What's my word?" Continue until you've gone through both lists of words.

Grammar, Usage, and Mechanics

Prepositions

A **preposition** relates a word in a sentence to a noun or pronoun called the **object of the preposition**. The preposition, its object, and the words in between make up a prepositional phrase.

The pilot placed the earphones <u>over</u> his <u>ears</u>.

          ↑   ↑

    preposition   object

Here are some common prepositions:

above	around	between	from	near	over	into
among	behind	for	in	on	with	of

A. Write the preposition in each sentence below.

   1. Ming-Shian enrolled in the university.

   2. I wore my binoculars around my neck.

   3. Speak clearly into the microphone.

   4. What is the difference between the candidates?

   5. Place the manual on the tallest stack.

   6. Is that an admission of guilt?

   7. We bought several souvenirs from the vendor.

   8. Let's meet here during intermission.

B. Write the object of the preposition in each sentence below.

   9. Climb carefully up the ladder.

  10. You might not like the effect of that advice.

  11. We noticed a familiar silhouette on the wall.

  12. The class all looked toward the teacher.

  13. The children were quiet throughout the program.

  14. The team ran twice around the track.

  15. The little mouse scurried down the hole.

WORKSHOP

Window Reading

Good writers always proofread their writing for spelling errors. Here's a strategy you can use to proofread your papers.

Cut a small hole or window in a piece of paper. Use it to slide along your written work so that you can inspect one or two words at a time through the window. Using such a paper on the first sentence in this paragraph, you might see just **Cut a small** and then **hole or window** instead of the whole sentence.

Reading your work this way lets you focus on the spelling of the words instead of the sense of the sentences. Try it!

Electronic Spelling

Graphics

Computers allow you to make graphics quickly and easily. You can make a chart or a diagram in just a few seconds, and it will look good and help to explain your ideas clearly.

You will need to proofread carefully the copy in the graphics because many graphics programs do not have spell checkers.

Jeff made a chart of his CDs. The list below has the titles. Find the words Jeff misspelled. Write them correctly.

1. Sincronized Sounds
2. Personnal Listening
3. Misty's Miraje
4. The Soovenir Album
5. Entrigue
6. Cole Unaversity Choir

Spelling ^{and} Thinking

READ THE SPELLING WORDS

1.	specific	specific	Please give a **specific** description.
2.	classically	classically	The music was **classically** composed.
3.	mechanical	mechanical	His actions are **mechanical** and stiff.
4.	scientific	scientific	Her **scientific** research was famous.
5.	artistically	artistically	The image was depicted **artistically**.
6.	dynamic	dynamic	People like his **dynamic** personality.
7.	historical	historical	This is a **historical** document.
8.	drastically	drastically	She has changed **drastically**.
9.	heroic	heroic	The brave knight's deed was **heroic**.
10.	scientifically	scientifically	I approach a problem **scientifically**.
11.	artistic	artistic	His **artistic** talents are well-known.
12.	mechanically	mechanically	The robot moved **mechanically**.
13.	classic	classic	It is a **classic** piece of literature.
14.	historically	historically	This chart is **historically** incorrect.
15.	economic	economic	It was a time of **economic** prosperity.
16.	heroically	heroically	She acted **heroically** during a crisis.
17.	dynamically	dynamically	The actor performed **dynamically**.
18.	drastic	drastic	These **drastic** measures are necessary.
19.	specifically	specifically	Tell me **specifically** what happened.
20.	economically	economically	It was an **economically** unwise choice.

SORT THE SPELLING WORDS

1.–10. Write the spelling words that are adjectives ending with **ic** or **ical**.

11.–20. Write the spelling words that are adverbs ending with **-ly**.

REMEMBER THE SPELLING STRATEGY

Remember that you must add **al** to words ending with **ic** before adding the suffix **-ly**.

Word Meanings

Write the spelling word that matches each definition, using the part of speech in parentheses as an additional clue.

1. with great energy or force (adverb)
2. in a way that leaves no uncertainty (adverb)
3. relating to the study of natural phenomena (adjective)
4. showing imagination or creativity (adverb)
5. having existed in the past (adjective)
6. in an automatic or machinelike way (adverb)

Synonyms

Write the spelling word that is a synonym for each of the following words.

7. courageously
8. energetic
9. severe
10. logically
11. particular

12. cheaply
13. timeless
14. creative
15. thrifty

USING THE Dictionary

Look up each of the following spelling words in the **Spelling Dictionary**.

mechanical	drastically	heroic
classically	historically	

16.–17. Write the words that have an individual or **separate entry**.

18.–20. Write the words that have a joined or **run-on entry**.

specific	classically	mechanical	scientific
artistically	dynamic	historical	drastically
heroic	scientifically	artistic	mechanically
classic	historically	economic	heroically
dynamically	drastic	specifically	economically

Replace the Words Write the spelling word that best replaces the underlined word or phrase in each sentence.

1.–2. Many inventors do not pursue their goals <u>traditionally</u>; however, by going about their work in an innovative way, they may endure <u>monetary</u> hardships.

3. Such inventors face the challenge of poverty <u>gallantly</u>, always believing in their goals.

4.–5. Inventions do not always result in <u>radical</u> changes. Often, they are <u>financially</u> impossible or impractical.

6.–8. Archimedes, a citizen of ancient Greece, was one of the first inventors. His <u>lasting, significant</u> ideas changed the world <u>radically</u>. A true genius, he invented the <u>automatic</u> pulley.

9.–10. A king once challenged him with the <u>exact</u> task of raising water from a ship's hold. The <u>noble</u> Archimedes invented a crank and screw that successfully raised the water.

Complete the Sentences Write the spelling word that completes each sentence.

11. He decorated the room _____ with paintings and sculptures.

12. To complete this experiment _____, we should take exact measurements, observe carefully, and keep track of all details.

13. The year 1776 is _____ important for Americans.

14. The teacher was so _____ that she never sat at her desk.

Choose the Modifiers Write the spelling word from each adjective-adverb pair in parentheses that correctly completes each sentence.

15. Have you read any of James Michener's (**historical, historically**) novels?

16. Considerable (**scientific, scientifically**) research went into each of his books.

17.–18. Michener portrayed history (**dynamic, dynamically**), not (**mechanical, mechanically**).

19.–20. He described times and places very (**specific, specifically**); he directed his (**artistic, artistically**) talent into breathing life into the past.

Spelling and Writing

Proofread a Biographical Sketch

Six words are not spelled correctly in this biographical sketch. Write the words correctly.

Leonardo da Vinci was perhaps one of the most historicly important artists of all time. Not only was he a talented painter, but he devised many inventions, including a flying machine, a parachute, and a diving bell. He succeeded in his work by carefully observing and interpreting natural and mechanicle phenomena. Amazingly, da Vinci sketched his design of a helicopter hundreds of years before the first airplane was built! He based the dynamics of his invention on spesific observations of birds in flight.

This artistic genius was a product of the Italian Renaissance. To aid his painting, da Vinci scientificaly researched human anatomy. He then used his understanding of the human body to convey his subjects on canvas dinamically and artistickly.

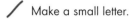

Proofreading Marks

≡ Make a capital.

/ Make a small letter.

∧ Add something.

ℓ Take out something.

⊙ Add a period.

⌗ New paragraph

(SP) Spelling error

Write a Biographical Sketch

Expository Writing

Choose a famous artist, inventor, or scientist. Write a biographical sketch.

- Use both print and on-line sources to do your research.
- Include a specific incident, fascinating detail, or interesting story about your subject.
- Follow the form used in the proofreading sample.

Use as many spelling words as you can.

Proofread Your Writing During

Writing Process

Prewriting
⇩
Drafting
⇩
Revising
⇩
Editing
⇩
Publishing

Proofread your writing for spelling errors as part of the editing stage in the writing process. Be sure to check each word carefully. Use a dictionary to check spelling if you are not sure.

Vocabulary

Strategy Words

Review Words: Adding -ly to Words Ending in ic

Write a word from the box to complete each sentence.

poetic	poetically	synthetically
tropic	tropically	

1. This material was created _____ in a laboratory.
2. We enjoyed the warm _____ weather of the island.
3. If you added music to those _____ words, you would have a beautiful song.
4. The adverbial form of the word **tropic** is _____.
5. He related the event _____, using vivid imagery and even some metaphors.

Preview Words: Adding -ly to Words Ending in ic

Write a word from the box to match each definition.

epidemically	laconically	melodic
melodically	mythically	

6. in a way that uses few words; concisely
7. in an imaginary or fictional way
8. spreading rapidly
9. musically
10. musical

Connections

Content Words

Social Studies: Crafts

Write a word from the box to replace each underlined word or phrase.

embroidery	illustrate	nostalgia
realistic	tradition	

1. In her seventies, when her hands became too stiff to do <u>needlework</u>, Grandma Moses began painting.

2.–3. Her paintings are simple and <u>true to life</u>, revealing her strong sense of <u>custom</u>.

4.–5. They also <u>show</u> the <u>longing</u> she felt for the rural setting of her childhood in the late 1800s.

Science: Biology

Write words from the box to complete the paragraph.

anatomy	medical	physical
physiology	structure	

A __6.__ student studies many branches of biology. The study of the normal functions of living things is called __7.__. The study of the shapes and parts of the body is called __8.__. The first deals with __9.__ processes while the second deals with form and __10.__.

Apply the Spelling Strategy

Circle the content word you wrote that ends in **ic**.

Spelling and Thinking

READ THE SPELLING WORDS

1.	conscientious	*conscientious*	A **conscientious** student works hard.
2.	crucial	*crucial*	The data are **crucial** to our research.
3.	substantial	*substantial*	A **substantial** amount is needed.
4.	spacious	*spacious*	Is the bedroom closet **spacious**?
5.	repetitious	*repetitious*	The boring speech was **repetitious**.
6.	spatial	*spatial*	I like the new **spatial** arrangement.
7.	confidential	*confidential*	The information is **confidential**.
8.	ferocious	*ferocious*	This tiny puppy is hardly **ferocious**.
9.	residential	*residential*	Drive slowly in a **residential** area.
10.	financial	*financial*	The **financial** impact was minimal.
11.	gracious	*gracious*	He was **gracious** even when he declined.
12.	impartial	*impartial*	A judge should be **impartial**.
13.	vicious	*vicious*	A hungry lion can be **vicious**.
14.	facial	*facial*	He has unusual **facial** features.
15.	influential	*influential*	She is quite an **influential** citizen.
16.	ambitious	*ambitious*	The **ambitious** students worked hard.
17.	glacial	*glacial*	The **glacial** ice melted very slowly.
18.	suspicious	*suspicious*	His obvious disguise was **suspicious**.
19.	potential	*potential*	You have **potential** for great success!
20.	superficial	*superficial*	The **superficial** cuts healed quickly.

SORT THE SPELLING WORDS

1.–7. Write the words in which /shəl/ is spelled **tial**.

8.–12. Write the words in which /shəl/ is spelled **cial**.

13.–17. Write the words in which /shəs/ is spelled **cious**.

18.–20. Write the words in which /shəs/ is spelled **tious**.

REMEMBER THE SPELLING STRATEGY

Remember that a final /shəs/ may be spelled **cious** or **tious** and a final /shəl/ may be spelled **tial** or **cial**.

Word Meanings ━━━━━━━━━━━━━━━━━━━━━━━━━━━━

Write the spelling word that best completes each sentence.

1. Our softball team has the _____ to win the championship again this year.

2. My mother works for a bank in the _____ district.

3. The _____ relationship between the floor and the ceiling is parallel.

4. We had already heard the lecture, so hearing it again was _____.

5. Our family has just recently moved to a new home in a quiet _____ area.

6. The police artist drew a sketch based on the witness's description of the suspect's eyes, nose, and other _____ features.

7. These boulders were left here when a _____ formation moved through the area during the last ice age.

Antonyms ━━━━━━━━━━━━━━━━━━━━━━━━━━━━

Write the spelling words that are antonyms for the following words.

8.–10. unimportant (three antonyms)

11. biased

12. cramped

13. trustful

14. deep

15. ill-mannered

16.–17. gentle (two antonyms)

18. publicized

USING THE Thesaurus

Write a spelling word that is a synonym for each given word. Check your answers in the **Writing Thesaurus**.

19. eager

20. careful

conscientious	crucial	substantial	spacious	repetitious
spatial	confidential	ferocious	residential	financial
gracious	impartial	vicious	facial	influential
ambitious	glacial	suspicious	potential	superficial

Solve the Analogies   Write spelling words to complete the analogies.

1. **Algebra** is to **numerical** as **geometry** is to _____.
2. **Boorish** is to **charming** as **surly** is to _____.
3. **Loving** is to **hating** as **trusting** is to _____.
4. **Lazy** is to **idle** as **fair** is to _____.
5. **Narrow** is to **wide** as **crowded** is to _____.
6. **Widespread** is to **public** as **secret** is to _____.
7. **Speech** is to **vocal** as **smile** is to _____.
8. **Exciting** is to **original** as **boring** is to _____.
9.–10. **Pet** is to **gentle** as **beast** is to _____ or _____.
11. **Real** is to **actual** as **possible** is to _____.

Complete the Paragraph   Write the spelling words from the box to complete the paragraph.

The earth is constantly changing. Over many centuries, such seemingly __12.__ changes as minor land shifts can cause __13.__ changes in the earth's crust. Earthquakes, __14.__ movement, volcanic eruptions, and erosion are all __15.__ in the alteration of geography. Some natural forces have an immediate social and __16.__ impact on business and __17.__ areas. For example, the San Francisco earthquake of 1906 destroyed more than 28,000 buildings and caused 400 million dollars' worth of fire damage. It is __18.__ that we continue to study the sometimes harsh, sometimes gentle forces of nature. We need to be prepared for geological changes. The __19.__ and __20.__ study of scientific data is a good start.

ambitious
conscientious
crucial
financial
glacial
influential
residential
substantial
superficial

Spelling and Writing

Proofread a Paragraph

Six words are not spelled correctly in this paragraph. Write the words correctly.

It is the year 1,002,000. A feroshus sandstorm rages. It happens daily since the rain stopped. Who would have thought it would never rain again? A million years ago, humans ruined the environment. After eons of planetary drought, the earth is one giant desert. Oceans, lakes, and rivers are dry. Even glashal formations have melted and dried up. All wild plants have died. In spashious domes, scientists now create water, but there is not enough of the crucial substance for everyone. Some people left the earth to live in resadential colonies in space, but only influencial people who had the finantial means could afford the trip. For those who remain, the earth is a dismal place.

Proofreading Marks

≡ Make a capital.

/ Make a small letter.

∧ Add something.

℮ Take out something.

⊙ Add a period.

⌗ New paragraph

⟨SP⟩ Spelling error

Write a Paragraph

Descriptive Writing

What will the earth be like in a million years? Imagine the changes or find out what experts predict. Write a paragraph describing what you think the world will look like a million years from now.

- Include specific details to make your description vivid.
- Compare and contrast features of the earth today with features of the earth a million years from now. What will the climate be like? What living things will populate the earth? What geological changes will occur?
- Follow the form used in the proofreading sample.

Use as many spelling words as you can.

Proofread Your Writing During ➤

Writing Process

Prewriting
⇩
Drafting
⇩
Revising
⇩
Editing
⇩
Publishing

Proofread your writing for spelling errors as part of the editing stage in the writing process. Be sure to check each word carefully. Use a dictionary to check spelling if you are not sure.

Vocabulary

Strategy Words

Review Words: Endings tial, cial, cious, tious

Write a word from the box to match each definition.

antisocial	cautious	nutritious
	partial	precious

1. not whole; incomplete
2. providing nourishment
3. of high value; cherished or beloved
4. avoiding others; unfriendly
5. careful

Preview Words: Endings tial, cial, cious, tious

Write a word from the box to complete each sentence.

beneficial	circumstantial	confidentially
	essential	malicious

6. Oxygen is _____ for human beings.
7. Judge Gaines freed the suspect because the prosecuting attorney presented only _____ evidence.
8. I am telling you this _____, so please keep it a secret.
9. She said that she meant no harm, but her actions appeared _____.
10. A nap is sometimes _____ if you are tired in the afternoon.

Connections

Content Words

Science: Ecology

Write the words from the box to complete the paragraph.

decompose	ecological	environmental
nutrients	predator	

The lion is a fierce __1.__ . It hunts other animals to get the __2.__ it needs. After a lion has eaten, what remains rarely gets a chance to __3.__ . Instead, a scavenger feasts on the leftover meat. Lions face many __4.__ and __5.__ threats, mainly from humans who destroy their natural habitats.

Social Studies: Human Society

Write the words from the box to complete the paragraph.

anthropology	cultural	sociology
vegetarian	weapons	

Both __6.__ , the study of human development and culture, and __7.__ , the study of social behavior, often focus on isolated societies. Some tribes who live in jungles use __8.__ to hunt so that they can add meat to their mostly __9.__ diet. Researchers watch for signs of __10.__ change as these peoples come into contact with the modern world.

Apply the Spelling Strategy

Circle the content word you wrote that has a root to which **tious** can be added to form the word **nutritious**.

READ THE SPELLING WORDS

1.	involve	*involve*	I want to **involve** you in my plans.
2.	conversation	*conversation*	We had a long **conversation** about pets.
3.	extrovert	*extrovert*	A performer is usually an **extrovert**.
4.	prospect	*prospect*	The **prospect** of your visit excites me.
5.	revolution	*revolution*	When did the computer **revolution** begin?
6.	spectacular	*spectacular*	The sunset this evening is **spectacular**.
7.	anniversary	*anniversary*	Today is my parents' wedding **anniversary**.
8.	evolve	*evolve*	Did alligators **evolve** from dinosaurs?
9.	respect	*respect*	I **respect** kind and honest people.
10.	versatile	*versatile*	He displayed his **versatile** talents.
11.	expectation	*expectation*	Our **expectation** of success has come true!
12.	advertise	*advertise*	The shop will **advertise** on television.
13.	inspect	*inspect*	Closely **inspect** the item before buying it.
14.	spectator	*spectator*	He was the loudest **spectator** at the game.
15.	converse	*converse*	We should **converse** about this decision.
16.	revolve	*revolve*	Satellites **revolve** around a planet.
17.	spectacle	*spectacle*	The parade was quite a **spectacle**.
18.	controversy	*controversy*	The new rule has caused some **controversy**.
19.	suspect	*suspect*	I **suspect** we will learn the truth shortly.
20.	introvert	*introvert*	An **introvert** tends to keep silent.

SORT THE SPELLING WORDS

1.–4. Write the words that contain the Latin root **volv,** from the Latin verb **volvere,** meaning "to roll."

5.–12. Write the words that contain the Latin root **spec,** from the Latin verb **spectare,** "to watch," and from **specere,** "to look at," "to see."

13.–20. Write the words that contain the Latin root **ver,** from the Latin verb **vertere,** meaning "to turn."

REMEMBER THE SPELLING STRATEGY

Remember that knowing Latin roots like **spec, volv,** and **ver** can give clues to the meaning and spelling of certain words.

Word Meanings

Write the spelling words that best complete the sentences.

1.–2. Every _____ at a tennis match ought to refrain from carrying on a loud _____ during play.

3.–5. Though many citizens joined in the celebration of the third _____ of the _____, others did not want to _____ themselves.

6.–7. I auditioned for the play, but the _____ of a starring role was far beyond my wildest _____.

8.–10. If those salespeople do not start to _____ instead of jumping up and down, I _____ that people will begin to stare at such a _____.

Word Structure

Write the spelling word that comes from each Latin prefix and verb.

11. **ex-,** out + **volvere,** to roll

12. **ad-,** toward + **vertere,** to turn

13. **intro-,** to the inside + **vertere,** to turn

14. **extro-,** outside + **vertere,** to turn

15. **contra-,** against + **versus,** to turn

USING THE Thesaurus

Write a spelling word that is a synonym for each word. Check your answers in the **Writing Thesaurus.**

16. magnificent

17. skillful

18. turn

19. examine

20. admire

201

Spelling and Reading

involve	conversation	extrovert	prospect	revolution
spectacular	anniversary	evolve	respect	versatile
expectation	advertise	inspect	spectator	converse
revolve	spectacle	controversy	suspect	introvert

Complete the Sentences Write the spelling word that best completes each sentence.

1. The _____ of a nonstop, around-the-world airplane flight did not become probable until 1981.

2. Before 1981, there was _____ among aerospace experts as to whether such a flight was possible and how to accomplish it.

3. That was when Dick Rutan and Jeana Yeager had a _____ over lunch during which they discussed the notion.

4. As they considered new, lightweight, strong materials, they began to _____ that the idea was possible.

5. Their idea started to _____ into an actual probability.

6. Soon businesses wanted to _____ themselves in the project and donated equipment and services.

7. At the 1984 test flight of the *Voyager*, the sight of the aircraft slowly rising from the runway was quite a _____ .

8. The success of the test flight boosted the _____ that the *Voyager* would indeed succeed in an around-the-world flight.

9. The _____ record-breaking flight took place in 1986.

Complete the Paragraph Write spelling words from the box to complete the paragraph.

Don't be just a __10.__! Be a part of the fitness __11.__! We are getting ready to celebrate our first __12.__! We don't usually __13.__, but we want everyone to know about our special offer. Come and __14.__ our facility. If you are an __15.__, you might like to work out by yourself. If you are an __16.__, join an aerobics class, and you will meet plenty of people with whom to __17.__. Our __18.__ instructors offer many other workout options. Bring a friend, and we will give you two memberships for the price of one! We __19.__ all levels of ability, and we will design a regimen to __20.__ around your needs!

revolution
extrovert
revolve
inspect
converse
advertise
versatile
spectator
introvert
respect
anniversary

Spelling and Writing

Proofread a Paragraph

Six words are not spelled correctly in this paragraph. Write the words correctly.

> Do you take the moon for granted? Most people do not notice how specktaculer the moon is. Take some time to inspect its fascinating craters and mountains. A contraversy once raged about whether water was present on the moon, and then ice was discovered. That led scientists to suspekt that water was, and still might be, present. Thus, the prospeck of living on the moon exists. No one has been to the moon in many years, but science and technology will one day avolve so that a weekend trip to the moon may be a common occurrence. Keep in mind that the white disk in the night sky is not just a spectackle; it is a future vacation spot!

Proofreading Marks

≡ Make a capital.

/ Make a small letter.

∧ Add something.

ℓ Take out something.

⊙ Add a period.

⌗ New paragraph

(SP) Spelling error

Write a Paragraph

Persuasive Writing

Choose an item, object, or event that is generally considered common or familiar. Write a paragraph about why it is extraordinary rather than commonplace.

- Use facts and details to hold the reader's attention and to support your opinion.
- Follow the form used in the proofreading sample.

Use as many spelling words as you can.

Proofread Your Writing During

Proofread your writing for spelling errors as part of the editing stage in the writing process. Be sure to check each word carefully. Use a dictionary to check spelling if you are not sure.

Writing Process

Prewriting
⇩
Drafting
⇩
Revising
⇩
Editing
⇩
Publishing

Vocabulary

Strategy Words

Review Words: Latin Roots spec, volv, ver

Write a word from the box to complete each sentence.

convert	expect	respectable
reversible		suspected

1. The office of mayor is a _____ position.
2. Long ago, people tried to _____ metals into gold.
3. The _____ blanket is red on one side and blue on the other.
4. I am calling to say that you can _____ us to arrive by six.
5. I have long _____ that you are the best friend anyone could have.

Preview Words: Latin Roots spec, volv, ver

Write a word from the box to match each definition.

controversial	diversity	introspection
irreversible		revolutionary

6. variety
7. resulting in a radical change or new idea
8. impossible to return to an original state
9. causing conflict or disagreement
10. reflection on one's own thoughts and feelings

Connections

Content Words

Math: Geometry

Write a word from the box to label each illustration.

equilateral	isosceles	proportional	scalene	vertices

1. each side a different length

2. all sides of equal length

3. two sides of equal length

4. points at which the sides of each angle intersect

5. a/b = c/d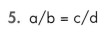

Language Arts: Revising

Write a word from the box to match each clue.

abridged	condense	excerpt	paraphrase	version

6. This is a passage quoted directly from a book.
7. This means that the text (of a novel, for example) has been shortened.
8. You can do this to language to make it more concise.
9. This is an account or description from a particular point of view.
10. If you reword a paragraph from a book, you do this.

Apply the Spelling Strategy

Circle the two content words you wrote that have the Latin root **ver**.

205

Spelling and Thinking

READ THE SPELLING WORDS

1.	commercial	*commercial*	Gina is in that pizza **commercial**.
2.	colleague	*colleague*	A **colleague** of mine is in charge.
3.	correlate	*correlate*	His plans **correlate** with my plans.
4.	cooperation	*cooperation*	I am relying on your **cooperation**.
5.	commend	*commend*	We **commend** you for your generosity.
6.	correspondence	*correspondence*	They shared a long **correspondence**.
7.	coordinate	*coordinate*	I will **coordinate** their arrival.
8.	commuter	*commuter*	Does the **commuter** train stop here?
9.	collaborate	*collaborate*	We will **collaborate** on a new song.
10.	corruption	*corruption*	He rid city hall of **corruption**.
11.	collide	*collide*	What happens when atoms **collide**?
12.	correction	*correction*	She made a spelling **correction**.
13.	commute	*commute*	How long is her **commute** to work?
14.	correspond	*correspond*	They **correspond** daily by e-mail.
15.	commemorate	*commemorate*	We will **commemorate** the victory.
16.	coordination	*coordination*	Party planning takes **coordination**.
17.	commodity	*commodity*	One valuable **commodity** is wheat.
18.	corrode	*corrode*	What caused the pipes to **corrode**?
19.	collapse	*collapse*	Heavy snow made the roof **collapse**.
20.	collision	*collision*	My car was damaged in a **collision**.

SORT THE SPELLING WORDS

1.–3. Write the words in which the assimilated prefix is spelled **co-**.

4.–8. Write the words in which the assimilated prefix is spelled **col-**.

9.–14. Write the words in which the assimilated prefix is spelled **cor-**.

15.–20. Write the words in which the assimilated prefix is spelled **com-**.

REMEMBER THE SPELLING STRATEGY

Remember that the prefix **com-,** meaning "together" or "with," may be assimilated into the spelling of a base word or a root.

Spelling ^{and} Vocabulary

Word Meanings

Write a spelling word for each definition.

1. to honor the memory of
2. similarity; communication by the exchange of letters
3. having profit as a chief aim; an advertisement on radio or television
4. to be similar, parallel, equivalent, or equal; to communicate by letter, usually over a period of time
5. an article of trade or commerce, especially an agricultural or mining product
6. to substitute (one thing for another); to travel from one place to another
7. to have or to make a parallel or complementary relationship to something

Word Structure

Replace the underlined affixes with different affixes to write spelling words.

8. <u>e</u>laborate
9. <u>directed</u>
10. <u>e</u>rup<u>ted</u>
11. <u>e</u>rode

12. <u>a</u>mend
13. <u>re</u>lapse
14. <u>per</u>mut<u>ation</u>

USING THE Dictionary

Write a spelling word for each etymology.
Use the **Spelling Dictionary** if you need help.

15.–16. Lat. **co(m),** same + **ordinatio,** arrangement < **ordinare,** to arrange in order < **ordo,** order.

17. Lat. **collega: co(m),** together + **legare,** to depute (to appoint).

18. Lat. **co(m),** same + **operari,** to work < **opus,** work.

19.–20. Lat. **collidere: co(m),** together + **laedere,** to strike.

Spelling and Reading

commercial	colleague	correlate	cooperation	commend
correspondence	coordinate	commuter	collaborate	corruption
commemorate	correction	commute	correspond	collide
coordination	commodity	corrode	collapse	collision

Replace the Words   Write spelling words to replace the words in the sentences.

1.–2. They <u>travel</u> to work on the <u>traveler's</u> train.

3. Players wear padding to keep them safe if they <u>clash</u>.

4.–6. Widespread <u>dishonesty</u> among employees can <u>wear away</u> a company from within and cause its <u>breakdown</u>.

7. Does his sudden popularity <u>have a direct relationship</u> with his winning the lottery?

8. We made a radio <u>advertisement</u> to promote our school play.

9. A gymnast needs excellent <u>balanced interaction of muscles</u>.

Complete the Letter   Write spelling words from the box to complete the letter to the editor of a newspaper.

To the Editor:

   Certain groups in our community are on a __10.__ course because of town planning. Some want to __11.__ our historical heritage by saving old buildings, while others want to erect skyscrapers. If these groups would __12.__ their efforts in a spirit of __13.__, they should be able to __14.__ on town planning to link old and new. The old brownstones in our town are a precious __15.__. I, for one, __16.__ the effort many have made to preserve them. I also recognize the need for new facilities, such as the bus terminal. I learned through written __17.__ with a former __18.__ that a major __19.__ has been made to the design of the terminal. The structure will now __20.__ to the old architecture of the town.

colleague
cooperation
commend
correspondence
coordinate
collaborate
correction
correspond
commemorate
commodity
collision

                    Angelina Perez, President
                    Neighborhood Associations

Spelling and Writing

Proofread a Paragraph

Six words are not spelled correctly in this paragraph. Write the words correctly.

Fairborough is only a short commute by comutor train to a major city, but the town is miles away from the city in character. In the city, it is easy to colide with people on the crowded sidewalks. In Fairborough, open space is a valued commodaty, and residents treasure the town's slow pace. As you enter Fairborough from the east, you see a stone statue of a Colonial soldier. It was erected to comemerate the brave people who fought in the Revolutionary War. Just beyond the statue is our new town hall, where officials collaberate on resolving issues, such as whether to allow big companies to build commercial properties in town. Because Fairborough residents care so much, town meetings are always packed.

Proofreading Marks

≡ Make a capital.
/ Make a small letter.
∧ Add something.
ℓ Take out something.
⊙ Add a period.
⌗ New paragraph
(SP) Spelling error

Write a Paragraph

Descriptive Writing

Every city or town has unique qualities and characteristics. Write a paragraph describing your city or town.

- Think about the buildings, parks, monuments, or natural landmarks that make your hometown special.
- Use vivid details to describe your hometown and what makes it attractive to you and others.
- Follow the form used in the proofreading sample.

Use as many spelling words as you can.

Proofread Your Writing During ➤

Writing Process

Prewriting
⇩
Drafting
⇩
Revising
⇩
Editing
⇩
Publishing

Proofread your writing for spelling errors as part of the editing stage in the writing process. Be sure to check each word carefully. Use a dictionary to check spelling if you are not sure.

Vocabulary

Strategy Words

Review Words: Assimilated Prefix com-

Write a word from the box to complete each sentence.

college	commander	cooperate
correct	corruptible	

1. During World War II, the U.S. general George Patton was a tank _____.
2. The new judge is honest and known for not being _____.
3. If you two cannot _____, you will never finish putting together that desk.
4. My brother is filling out _____ applications.
5. Please _____ the grammatical mistakes in your essay.

Preview Words: Assimilated Prefix com-

Write words from the box to complete the paragraph.

colloquial	commendable	committed
cooperative	correlation	

My friends refuse to be __6.__ when it comes to using proper language in formal situations. Some of them have __7.__ the grave error of using slang when it is totally inappropriate. I believe that knowing when formal language is required is __8.__. I think there is a direct __9.__ between the way people speak and what others think of them. People who use __10.__ expressions are not taken as seriously as people who use formal language. My friends think I am too serious!

Connections

Content Words

Science: Geology

Write a word from the box to match each clue.

conglomerate	igneous	metamorphic
sedimentary		subterranean

1. This word means "underground."
2. This rock is formed from molten lava.
3. This rock is formed by water action.
4. This rock is formed by heat and pressure.
5. This rock is formed from cementing material.

Social Studies: Government

Write words from the box to complete the paragraph.

coalition	legislation	lobbyist
publicity		representative

If you are concerned about a national issue, you should first contact your state __6.__. If he or she cannot help, you may wish to form a __7.__ with citizens who share your opinion. You may even be able to afford to hire a __8.__ to press your case. You will gain __9.__ for your cause and may even influence lawmakers to enact special __10.__ to solve the problem.

Apply the Spelling Strategy

Circle the two content words you wrote that have the prefix **con-** or **co-**.

READ THE SPELLING WORDS

1. beautify	*beautify*	We planted flowers to **beautify** the park.
2. sufficient	*sufficient*	Is there a **sufficient** amount for everyone?
3. defective	*defective*	I returned the **defective** lamp to the store.
4. clarify	*clarify*	I want to **clarify** what I said earlier.
5. facsimile	*facsimile*	This is a good **facsimile** of the original.
6. perfection	*perfection*	She always strives for **perfection**.
7. liquefy	*liquefy*	At what temperature will ice **liquefy**?
8. certificate	*certificate*	I asked for a copy of my birth **certificate**.
9. defect	*defect*	Can you see the **defect** in this sweater?
10. artificial	*artificial*	I prefer sugar to **artificial** sweeteners.
11. effective	*effective*	This new rule is **effective** immediately.
12. identify	*identify*	He can **identify** any bird by its call.
13. faction	*faction*	Each **faction** argued for its own ideas.
14. efficient	*efficient*	The new light bulb is bright and **efficient**.
15. infection	*infection*	The doctor said I had a throat **infection**.
16. magnify	*magnify*	A telescope can **magnify** distant objects.
17. faculty	*faculty*	Teachers eat in the **faculty** dining room.
18. magnificent	*magnificent*	It was a truly **magnificent** painting.
19. certify	*certify*	Can you **certify** that the diamond is real?
20. manufacture	*manufacture*	Does this company **manufacture** radios?

SORT THE SPELLING WORDS

1.–5. Write the spelling words that contain the Latin root **fic**.

6.–10. Write the spelling words that contain the Latin root **fec**.

11.–14. Write the spelling words that contain the Latin root **fac**.

15.–20. Write the spelling words that contain the Latin word part **fy**.

REMEMBER THE SPELLING STRATEGY

Remember that knowing Latin roots like **fic, fec, fac,** and word parts like **fy** can give clues to the meaning and spelling of certain words.

Word Meanings ━ ━ ━ ━ ━ ━ ━ ━ ━ ━ ━ ━ ━ ━ ━ ━

Write a spelling word to replace the underlined words in each sentence.

1. Cleaning a wound can prevent an <u>invasion of microorganisms</u>.

2. We cannot hear the radio because it has a <u>faulty</u> speaker.

3. Which type of heat is more <u>able to produce a result with a minimum of waste or expense</u>, solar or electric?

4. My older brother just received his teaching <u>document confirming that he is competent to practice a profession</u>.

5. A mediator might succeed in getting the members of each <u>group of people with similar opinions</u> to come to an agreement.

6. To apply for a passport, I need a notarized <u>exact copy</u> of my birth certificate.

7. Could you please <u>make clearer</u> what you said?

8. It is almost impossible to achieve <u>the condition of being entirely without flaws</u> on the first try.

9. The "Keep Off" sign was not <u>having the intended effect</u> in stopping people from walking on the grass.

Word Groups ━ ━ ━ ━ ━ ━ ━ ━ ━ ━ ━ ━ ━ ━ ━ ━ ━ ━

Write a spelling word to complete each group.

10. melt, dissolve, _____

11. decorate, enhance, _____

12. assemble, build, _____

13. fake, phony, _____

14. prove, confirm, _____

15. define, label, _____

USING THE Thesaurus

Write a spelling word that is a synonym for each word below. Check your answers in the **Writing Thesaurus**.

16. flaw
17. ability
18. exquisite

19. enlarge
20. adequate

Spelling and Reading

beautify	sufficient	defective	clarify	facsimile
perfection	liquefy	certificate	defect	artificial
effective	identify	faction	efficient	infection
magnify	faculty	magnificent	certify	manufacture

Complete the Sentences   Write the spelling words that best complete the sentences.

1.–2. Everyone should help _____ the United States by preserving its _____ trees and forests.

3.–4. To get your life-saving _____, you have to be able to perform _____ respiration.

5.–6. A member of one political _____ asked the senator to _____ her complex statement on nuclear disarmament.

7.–8. The office copy machine can make a _____ of an original document, and it also can _____ a document to a larger size.

9.–10. To fix the problem, we have to _____ the source and then repair the _____.

11.–12. Ten days is usually a _____ amount of time for antibiotics to cure an ear _____.

13.–14. As soon as we _____ that you have completed the training program, you will become a member of the _____ of this school.

Complete the Paragraph   Write spelling words from the box to complete the paragraph.

Rubber is a commodity that is both __15.__ and __16.__. Yet it took Charles Goodyear many years and all of his money to find a way to make rubber usable. In the early 1800s, the rubber used to __17.__ various goods was __18.__. In the heat, it would __19.__. In the cold, it would become brittle and crack. Goodyear decided to experiment. Despite repeated failures, he continued to strive for __20.__. One day, he accidentally dropped a mixture of rubber and sulfur on a hot stove. As he cleaned it, he noticed that the rubber was firm and pliable. The heat had hardened the mixture, not melted it. In 1844, Goodyear received his patent for rubber.

> liquefy
> perfection
> manufacture
> effective
> defective
> efficient

Spelling and Writing

Proofread a Paragraph

Six words are not spelled correctly in this paragraph. Write the words correctly.

> If you follow these steps, you will make more afficient use of your time. First, identify a problem area. For example, do you have trouble getting your homework done? Next, clarafy your goal or desired outcome. Perhaps you want to finish your homework and still have time for after-school activities. Define the deffect in your present system. Maybe you waste your study periods by talking to friends instead of working. If so, you need to take steps toward more efective time management. You might decide to complete at least one-half of your homework during your study period. You will be able to certafy your improvement when you have used your study period to complete half your homework and you still have suficiant time for after-school activities.

Proofreading Marks

- ≡   Make a capital.
- /   Make a small letter.
- ∧   Add something.
- ℒ   Take out something.
- ⊙   Add a period.
- ⌗   New paragraph
- ⓢⓟ   Spelling error

Write a Paragraph

Expository Writing

Think of another circumstance in which someone might need advice on managing time. Write a paragraph describing a solution.

- When you give directions or describe a process, remember to give the steps in order.
- Follow the form used in the proofreading sample.

Use as many spelling words as you can.

Proofread Your Writing During ➤

Writing Process

Prewriting
⇩
Drafting
⇩
Revising
⇩
Editing
⇩
Publishing

Proofread your writing for spelling errors as part of the editing stage in the writing process. Be sure to check each word carefully. Use a dictionary to check spelling if you are not sure.

Vocabulary

Strategy Words

Review Words: Latin Roots: fic, fec, fac, fy

Write a word from the box to complete each sentence.

classify	factor	factory
imperfect		satisfy

1. Your level of experience will be a major _____ in determining your hourly pay.
2. The sketch was _____, but it was clearly a drawing of our house.
3. To keep track of these artifacts, we should _____ them according to the dates on which they were found.
4. A large meal should _____ your hunger.
5. My uncle worked on the assembly line in a _____.

Preview Words: Latin Roots: fic, fec, fac, fy

Write the word from the box that matches each definition.

affection	beneficiary	deface
efficiency		proficiency

6. to spoil the appearance of
7. the quality of producing a result with a minimum of waste or expense
8. a feeling of fondness toward someone or something
9. competence; the state of having mastered a particular skill or process
10. one who receives a benefit

Connections

Content Words

Science: Psychology

Write a word from the box to match each definition.

| behavior | characteristic | factual |
| imaginative | perception | |

1. a specific feature or quality; a trait
2. creative; original
3. the act of becoming aware through the senses, especially sight or hearing
4. a person's actions in response to certain stimuli
5. real or true; based on truth

Social Studies: Philosophy

Write words from the box to complete the paragraph.

| concrete | expedient | idealist |
| justify | pragmatism | |

The concept of ___6.___ is often contrasted with idealism. A pragmatist considers ___7.___ facts and short-term effects. An ___8.___ ponders abstract concepts of right and wrong and the long-term effects of actions. A pragmatist may argue that the end can ___9.___ the means. An idealist, however, would choose a moral approach over an ___10.___ one.

Apply the Spelling Strategy

Circle the two content words you wrote that contain the Latin root **fac** or the word part **fy**.

Assessment Units 31–35

Each Assessment Word in the box fits one of the spelling strategies you have studied over the past five weeks. Read the spelling strategies. Then write each Assessment Word under the unit number it fits.

Unit 31 ——————

1.–4. Remember that you must add **al** to words ending with **ic** before adding the suffix **-ly.**

Unit 32 ——————

5.–8. Remember that a final **/shəs/** may be spelled **cious** or **tious** and a final **/shəl/** may be spelled **tial** or **cial.**

Unit 33 ——————

9.–12. Remember that knowing Latin roots like **spec, volv,** and **ver** can give clues to the meaning and spelling of certain words.

Unit 34 ——————

13.–17. Remember that the prefix **com-,** meaning *together* or *with,* may be assimilated into the spelling of the base word or word root.

Unit 35 ——————

18.–20. Remember that knowing Latin roots like **fic, fec, fac,** and word parts like **fy** can give clues to the meaning and spelling of certain words.

column
scholastic
complain
respectful
atrocious
basically
gratify
authentically
uncoordinated
insufficient
deferential
authentic
superstitious
inspection
solidify
collaboration
revolving
preferential
speculation
corrosive

Unit 31: Adding -ly to Words Ending in ic

mechanical	scientific	historical	drastically
scientifically	mechanically	historically	economic
	drastic	economically	

Write the related spelling words that complete the sentences. First use the adjective form, then the adverb form.

1.–2. That so-called _____ account of the Civil War is not considered _____ accurate by historians.

3.–4. The emergency forced us to take _____ measures that were _____ different from those we had taken before.

5.–6. Because of our treasurer's smart _____ policies in the past, our company is now _____ sound.

7.–8. "Although I have some _____ skills, I am not _____ inclined," he said as he changed the light bulb.

9.–10. Although he claimed it was a _____ study of pollution, most scientists felt his methods were not _____ sound.

 **Review**

Unit 32: Endings: tial, cial, cious, tious

conscientious	substantial	confidential	financial
gracious	vicious	facial	ambitious
	suspicious	potential	

Change the underlined part of these words to write spelling words.

11. conten*tious*
12. conse*quential*
13. fac*tual*
14. ambi*dextrous*
15. *pre*tentious
16. substan*tive*
17. grav*ity*
18. victo*ry*
19. finan*ces*
20. suspici*on*

involve	conversation	prospect	revolution
spectacular	anniversary	respect	advertise
	controversy	suspect	

Write spelling words to complete the paragraph.

The Clover Club is planning a terrific fifth __1.__ celebration. It is to be a __2.__ event with music and delicious food. The planners have had a long phone __3.__ with __4.__ to the guest list and entertainment. They plan to __5__ the event through the newspaper and television. The many tasks to be done __6.__ such duties as making phone calls, decorating, collecting money, and printing programs. We __7.__ that this will be the biggest celebration ever. The __8.__ of such a successful event has everyone excited. It will truly be a __9.__ in the way Clover Club anniversaries are celebrated. The only problem so far is a little __10.__ over the location.

 **Review**   Unit 34: Assimilated Prefix com-

commercial	colleague	cooperation	correspondence
coordinate	corruption	collide	correspond
	collapse	collision	

Write the spelling word that rhymes with each word below.

11. intrigue
12. abide
13. relapse
14. precision
15. despondence
16. calibration

17. beyond
18. disruption
19. initial
20. subordinate

Unit 35: Latin Roots and Word Parts

sufficient	perfection	certificate	effective
identify	efficient	infection	magnify
	magnificent	manufacture	

Write the spelling word that belongs with each pair of words.

1. enough, adequate
2. document, award
3. sickness, disease
4. make, create
5. enlarge, increase
6. recognize, distinguish

Add the missing letters to write a spelling word.

7. p__rf____ion
8. magnif____nt
9. e____cient
10. ef__ct__ve

 **Spelling Study Strategy**

Sorting by Word Endings

Sorting words is a good way to help you practice your spelling words. Here is a way to sort the spelling words with a partner.

1. Make columns on a piece of paper and write these endings as column heads: **-fy, -ly, -ious,** and **-ial**. Write a sample word in each column. For example, you might write **magnify** under **-fy**, **drastically** under **-ly, gracious** under **-ious,** and **commercial** under **-ial**.

2. Ask a partner to write another spelling word in one of the columns. Work together to check the spelling.

3. Take turns filling the columns.

4. Place other words you want to study in a separate column.

WRITER'S

Grammar, Usage, and Mechanics

Subject-Verb Agreement

The subject of a sentence and the verb must agree in number. When the subject of a sentence is singular, it takes a singular verb. When the subject is plural, it takes a plural verb.

<u>Amy</u> <u>hopes</u> to join the softball team. (singular)

The <u>boys</u> <u>think</u> Amy will make a great player. (plural)

Practice Activity

A. Write the subject of each sentence. Write S if the subject is singular. Write P if the subject is plural.

  1. The fall leaves are spectacular this year.

  2. This building is in a commercial zone.

  3. The controversy revolves around the eligibility of players.

  4. That commercial shows a ridiculous situation.

  5. Potentially dangerous storms are on their way.

  6. Comic strips provide many laughs.

  7. Every word is spelled correctly.

B. Write the verb that agrees with the subject and correctly completes the sentence.

  8. The leaders (hope, hopes) for cooperation.

  9. Mom (respect, respects) our decision.

  10. Suddenly the speeding cars (collide, collides).

  11. Ms. Elizario (advertise, advertises) in our paper.

  12. Jean and a colleague (has, have) football tickets.

  13. Their wedding anniversary (was, were) last week.

  14. Your answer (affect, affects) our decision.

  15. If the boxes (collapse, collapses), the toys will be ruined.

WORKSHOP

First and Last

Good writers always proofread their writing for spelling errors. Here's a strategy you can use to proofread your papers.

Read just one sentence at a time. Look closely at the first word and the last word in each sentence. Check for a capital letter on the first word. Check for punctuation following the last word.

This proofreading idea helps you focus on details, such as capital letters and punctuation, instead of ideas. Try it!

Electronic Spelling

Computer Terms

Computers have brought about a new way of using words and abbreviations. Many people use shortened forms of words when sending e-mail.

The **e** in **e-mail** means "electronic," and the **e** is used in other terms as well. An **e-mail** user might attach **e-files,** meaning electronic files, or do **e-banking,** meaning electronic transfer of funds to or from a bank account.

In sending electronic transmissions, the words in the names of the files or transactions must be spelled correctly.

Which words in these e-file names are misspelled? Write the misspelled words correctly. Write **OK** if a file name is correct.

1. Histerical Data
2. Confidenchal Reports
3. Commercial Index
4. Ifficient Ideas
5. Cooperation Techniques
6. Annversary Dates and Addresses

Challenge Activities

folio	critique	pagination	photogenic
narrate	collate	journalism	frontispiece

A. Write the challenge word that goes with each definition.

1. the numbering of pages in a book
2. to tell a story
3. a review of a literary or artistic work
4. the illustration facing the title page of a book
5. to assemble pages of a book in the right order before they are bound
6. a page number in a book
7. the profession of newspaper reporters; the fourth estate
8. the quality of looking attractive in photographs

B. Write the challenge word that will correctly complete each sentence.

1. This machine will copy pages and _____ them so that they will be in the right order.
2. An actor will _____ the story of the ballet as the dancers perform.
3. Frank always looks good in pictures; he is very _____.
4. My sister wants to be a reporter, so she is taking courses in _____.
5. In his _____ of the play, the professor noted that the supporting actors were excellent.
6. The _____ of the book was sketched by a local artist.
7. The page with an even-numbered _____ always appears on the left.
8. The printer made a _____ chart to make sure all the book's pages were in the right place.

C. Imagine that you have been asked to critique one of the books you have read this year. In your review, you can make either favorable or unfavorable remarks, but be sure to comment on specific aspects of the book. Use some challenge words when you can.

Challenge Activities

trellis	selection	helicopter	crimson
penicillin	indigestion	reception	omelet

A. Read each group of words. Decide how they are related and what might happen next. Write the challenge word that could tell what will happen next.

    1. mixing bowl, milk, eggs, seasoning

    2. overeating of rich food, lots of excitement, heartburn

    3. wood strips, posts, climbing plants

    4. shopping, penny loafers, high-top basketball shoes

    5. formal attire, flowers, invitation

B. Write the challenge word that best completes each sentence.

    1. If you have an infection, your doctor may prescribe _____.

    2. If you eat a lot of spicy food, you might get _____.

    3. After a wedding, you might go to a _____.

    4. If you have grapevines, you might grow them on a _____.

    5. If you get embarrassed, you might turn _____.

    6. If a store has many items to choose from, it has a good _____.

    7. If you prepare a dish with eggs, you might make yourself an _____.

    8. If you want to travel a short distance by air, you might fly in a _____.

C. Write a challenge word to answer each question.

    1. Which challenge word is one kind of antibiotic?

    2. Which challenge word names a color?

D. Imagine you are at a fancy reception for a wedding or some other important event with two hundred guests. A helicopter from a large hospital lands not far from the guests. Use some of the challenge words to describe what happens next.

225

Challenge Activities

visa	vacancy	radiator	copious
agency	vial	meander	topiary

A. Write the challenge word you associate with each place.

1. a botanical garden
2. a chemist's lab
3. a foreign government office or agency
4. a hotel or an apartment building

B. Write the challenge word that completes the sentence correctly.

1. The _____ hissed as the steam came up.
2. The nurse carried a small _____ containing medicine.
3. We have harvested our garden, and we have a _____ supply of vegetables.
4. On Sunday afternoon, we like to _____ around our neighborhood.
5. We saw beautifully shaped shrubs in the _____ garden.
6. Carol went to a travel _____ to get information for her trip to Mexico.
7. There is a _____ in our teaching staff, and the principal would like to fill it as soon as possible.
8. In order to visit certain countries, you must apply for a _____.

C. Write the challenge word that . . .

1. is an adjective.
2. is a verb.

D. Imagine you were working in a real estate agency when a family came in. Each member wanted something different in a house. Write about how you successfully sold them a house that suited all of them. Use some of the challenge words.

Challenge Activities

> brainstorm   headquarters   stomachache   equal opportunity
> curling iron   radio broadcast   bulletin board   customer service

A. Write the challenge word that matches each definition.

1. a sudden inspiration
2. a pain in the stomach
3. a main office
4. a program on the radio
5. a board or wall on which notices or signs are put up
6. a department to deal with customers' problems, questions, complaints, etc.
7. a device used to style hair
8. the practice of providing the same opportunities for everyone without regard to race, gender, nationality, or religion

B. Write the challenge word that answers the question.

1. What is likely to be on the wall of a classroom?
2. What might you get after eating an unripe fruit?
3. What might you find in a hair salon?
4. To which department might you go to complain about faulty merchandise that you bought in a store?
5. To what might you listen to find out the latest news?
6. What kind of laws protect everyone's rights to jobs and housing?
7. What do people sometimes do to try to come up with ideas?
8. What do you call the main office of a company?

C. What kinds of notices might be posted on bulletin boards in your school, in a supermarket, or in a library? Decide on a specific place. Make up notices of your own. Use challenge words or forms of them in your notices.

Challenge Activities

A. Say each challenge word to yourself. Then answer each question.

   1.–3. Which challenge words have two syllables?

   4.–5. Which challenge words have three syllables?

   6.–7. Which challenge words have four syllables?

   8. Which challenge word has five syllables?

B. Write the challenge word that completes the sentence correctly.

   1. The manufacturer of a new product may try to get your attention with a clever _____.

   2. The builder's estimate gave an _____ of the cost of remodeling the house.

   3. The newspaper retracted an _____ statement that was printed in the last issue.

   4. His _____ and hostile behavior irritated many of his coworkers.

   5. The word **portly** has a more positive _____ than the word **obese**.

   6. The kindergarten classes are held in the _____ of the school.

   7. You should know how to use a card catalog in order to have _____ to all of the information in the library.

   8. The teacher _____ thirty minutes for the multiple-choice questions and one hour for the essay questions.

C. Imagine that you are a spokesperson for disabled people in your community. A new library has been proposed. You have seen the plans and sketches and you found certain things lacking. Write a letter to the city council explaining what is lacking and what you would suggest. For example, you might say that better access is needed for wheelchairs. Use some of the challenge words in your letter.

Challenge Activities

| canceling | unassisted | disconnected | misunderstanding |
| re-elected | quarrelsome | precautionary | resourcefulness |

A. Write the challenge word that can replace each underlined phrase.

1. The jigsaw puzzle was difficult, but Beth was determined to complete it without help from anyone.

2. My best friend is usually even-tempered, but when she is tired, she is ready to disagree, argue, and fight.

3. Because I no longer have an interest in stamp collecting, I am putting an end to my stamp magazine subscription.

4. Due to a failure to understand correctly, Jerry and Charlotte went to different theaters.

5. José was chosen again to be president of our class.

6. When we moved, the phone was taken out of our name and turned off and reconnected at our new address.

7. That medicine is strictly to guard against illness.

8. Your ability to come up with answers to problems and new ideas is amazing!

B. Write challenge words to complete the sentences.

1. The president has been _____ to a second term in office.

2. We will have our telephone service _____ before we move.

3. The parents watched proudly as their baby toddled _____ from the chair to the sofa.

4. Mr. Adams installed an alarm system as a _____ measure against burglary.

5. The pioneers' _____ enabled them to live under difficult conditions.

6. Tired children sometimes become _____ with each other.

7. Through a _____, Joanne arrived at the Chavez's house an hour later than they had expected her.

8. Joan said she is _____ her subscription to that magazine.

C. Imagine that you are campaigning for a second term as president of your class. Write the speech that you will deliver. Discuss plans you have for your next term. Be persuasive. Try to use as many challenge words as possible.

Challenge Activities

enforce	discourage	engagement	purposeful
enforcement	discouragement	distasteful	serviceable

A. Answer each question.

1.–3. Which three challenge words are nouns?

4.–5. Which challenge words are verbs?

6.–8. Which challenge words are adjectives?

B. Write the challenge word that will correctly complete each sentence.

1. Before a wedding, there is usually an _____.

2. If you don't want someone to do something, you might try to _____ that person.

3. If you don't succeed after trying hard, _____ may set in.

4. If something is very useful, you might say it is _____.

5. Members of the police force are sometimes referred to as law _____ officers.

6. When there is a state of emergency, officials will sometimes _____ a curfew.

7. If someone's behavior is rude or unpleasant, you will probably find it _____.

8. If you really want to achieve a goal, you must become _____.

C. Pretend it's 1820. You have been working on the construction of the Erie Canal for three long years. There's still a lot of work that must be done. Several things have caused you discouragement. For example, conditions in some of the camps have been rough and lawless. Write a letter to the company that employs you, with suggestions that will improve the conditions. Use as many challenge words as possible.

Challenge Activities

initiate	frustrate	contemplate	hibernation
initiation	frustration	contemplation	condensation

A. Write a challenge word or words to answer each question.

1.–2. Which challenge words have to do with beginning?

3. Which challenge word has to do with moisture?

4.–5. Which challenge words have to do with thinking?

6.–7. Which challenge words have to do with thwarting or preventing?

8. Which challenge word refers to a state that is something like sleep?

B. Write challenge words that will complete each paragraph.

1.–2. When a person wants to join a club, the people in the club may follow certain procedures to _____ that person. These procedures might be called an _____.

3.–4. Nina likes to go to museums. Sometimes she will stand in front of a painting and _____ it for a long time. People who see her might think that she is lost in _____.

5.–6. It was a long, cold winter, and the bear was in a period of _____ inside a cave. The vapor from the bear's breath produced _____ on the cave's walls.

7.–8. Suppose a family wants to go on a trip. The approach of a bad storm might _____ their plans. The family might feel the _____ of not being able to do what they had planned.

C. One day Jamaal announced, "I'm going into my own type of hibernation. I want to read a lot of books and get in touch with my thoughts."

Write about some things that might happen to Jamaal during his "hibernation." In your writing, use as many challenge words or forms of them as you can.

Challenge Activities

adverse	agile	captivate	congregate
adversity	agility	captivating	congregating

A. Look for a challenge word that is either a synonym or an antonym for the given word. Write the challenge word. Then write **s** if it is a synonym. Write **a** if it is an antonym.

1. assembling
2. stiffness
3. favorable
4. nimble
5. charming
6. repulse
7. misfortune
8. disperse

B. Write challenge words to complete the story.

   The audience was __1.__ in the theater for the debut of the new prima ballerina. There was excitement in the air. The audience knew that the ballerina had overcome a great deal of __2.__ to arrive at this night.

   As she performed her solo, the ballerina was graceful and __3.__ . Everyone especially admired the __4.__ with which she executed difficult leaps. Her performance was __5.__ .

   At the end of the evening many people stayed behind to __6.__ at the stage door. They congratulated her enthusiastically.

   There would be no __7.__ reviews—only praise from the critics. The ballerina had not failed to __8.__ them!

C. Imagine that you are a famous athlete describing a recent game or competition. Tell about the agility of some of the other athletes or your teammates. Describe what made their performances captivating to the spectators. Use as many challenge words or forms of challenge words as you can.

Challenge Activities

ghastly	rheumatism	rhythmic	answerable
rhapsody	rhododendron	reminisce	temptation

A. Write the challenge word that goes with each clue.

1. This is a condition that causes pain in the muscles or joints.
2. This is a shrub with large showy flowers.
3. This is a word you might use to describe something horrible.
4. This is meant to entice.
5. This is what you do when you call past events to mind.
6. This word is often used to describe a characteristic of music.
7. This is the name of a kind of musical composition.
8. This means the same as **responsible**.

B. Write the challenge word that will complete each sentence.

1. My grandmother likes to _____ and tell us stories about her childhood.
2. The _____ beat of the drums made me want to dance.
3. The distorting mirror in the fun house made everyone look _____.
4. As the treasurer of the club, Keiko is _____ for the use of all funds.
5. The violinist played an impassioned _____ as an encore.
6. A hot fudge sundae is a _____ that I resist.
7. The doctor prescribed exercise and rest to relieve her patient's _____.
8. The _____ is a beautiful flower, but its name is so long!

C. Imagine that you were on vacation for two weeks. You returned to find your yard and flower garden in need of a great deal of work. You have just spent most of the day working outside to remedy the situation, and you have many aches and pains. Write a diary entry. Express your immediate feelings. Try to use some of the challenge words.

Challenge Activities

intent	dubious	previous	gradually
intently	dubiously	previously	strenuously

A. Read each group of words. Write the challenge word whose meaning fits each group.

1. uncertainly, doubtfully
2. slowly, little by little
3. energetically, vigorously
4. before, earlier
5. fixedly, with concentration

B. Write the challenge words that are base words for three other challenge words.

C. Choose the correct challenge word to complete each sentence. Write the challenge word.

1. The scientist was _____ upon finding a cure for the rare disease. (intent, intently)
2. The scholar peered _____ at the old manuscript. (intent, intently)
3. Tim raised his eyebrows _____ as he listened to Betty's outlandish story. (dubious, dubiously)
4. The police found the suspect's alibi _____ and wanted to question him further. (dubious, dubiously)
5. Because Sara has a _____ engagement, she will not be able to come to our party tonight. (previous, previously)
6. Ms. Li is the new editor of our book reviews; _____, she was an editior at Bell Publishers. (previous, previously)
7. Little by little, Ms. Ames began to relinquish control over the project _____.
8. The suitcase was heavy, so George had to lift _____ to move it.

D. Pretend that a good friend of yours has broken a confidence and told someone else a secret you entrusted to your friend. You're trying to sort out in your mind whether your friend really intended to do you harm or not. You think through previous times you have shared with your friend. Write an imaginary paragraph in which you talk things over with yourself. Use as many challenge words as possible.

Challenge Activities

charitable	consumable	incapable	collectible
comfortable	improbable	inseparable	plausible

A. Read each group of words. Write the challenge word that describes each group.

    1. bread, water, fruit, vegetables

    2. stamps, coins, dolls, commemorative plates

    3. slippers, sweat pants, sneakers, pullovers

    4. kindly, generous, giving, unselfish

    5. believable, true, probable

B. Write the challenge words that have a prefix meaning "not."

C. Write a challenge word to complete each sentence.

    1. Someone who shows kindness to others is described as _____.

    2. An invasion of aliens from outer space is highly _____.

    3. Someone who is sitting in a big, soft armchair is probably very _____.

    4. To a museum curator, a rare Chinese vase may still be considered a _____.

    5. Best friends are often _____.

    6. The excuse that someone was late because of a traffic jam could be _____.

    7. The supermarket carries many items that are _____.

    8. Someone who is not fit for a job is _____ of doing it.

D. Imagine that you went to a flea market, yard sale, or craft show. Describe the booths and tables and the items on sale or on exhibition. Include displays for charitable causes. Use as many challenge words as you can in your description.

Challenge Activities

cynic	maestro	mistaken	gratitude
maximum	diminish	obliging	accordance

A. Read each definition. Write a challenge word that fits it.

1. wrong or incorrect
2. accommodating
3. the greatest amount
4. an eminent composer, conductor, or teacher of music
5. someone who believes that all people are selfish
6. thankfulness
7. agreement
8. to lessen

B. Write a challenge word to complete each sentence.

1. Lon always does favors for others. He is very _____.
2. The judge ordered the driver who had been caught speeding to pay the _____ fine.
3. Put an ice pack on your sprained ankle so the swelling will _____.
4. While we were away, our neighbors kept an eye on our house. We are showing our _____ by inviting them for dinner.
5. If you think I will give up before I finish this job, you are quite _____.
6. That woman never believes in the selflessness of others. She is a _____.
7. The orchestra prepared to play when the _____ raised her baton.
8. The new building is in _____ with the new zoning laws.

C. Try to make up wise sayings or proverbs using the challenge words. For example, you might use **maestro** in a saying such as: "Only one maestro is needed to conduct an orchestra." Try to use a challenge word in each saying. If you can't think of a way to use a challenge word, you may use another form of the word.

Challenge Activities

recur	recurrence	remittance	propel
recurring	remit	remitting	propelled

A. Write the challenge word that is the correct form of the word in parentheses and will complete each sentence.

1. Juan has a _____ dream in which he is a concert pianist. (recur)

2. The unexpected _____ of the patient's fever suggested to the doctor that she was treating an unusual virus. (recur)

3. Do you think the same questions may _____ on the semester test? (recur)

4. The landlord receives a _____ for the rent on the first of each month. (remit)

5. Jill is _____ her payment for the magazine subscription that she ordered. (remit)

6. The members would not _____ their dues until they were sure they had made their point with the club officers. (remit)

7. As we watched, the swimmer's strong kick _____ her rapidly through the water. (propel)

8. His great ambition will probably _____ him to a top post in the company. (propel)

B. Write the challenge word(s) that . . .

    1.–3. are in the present tense.

      4. is in the past tense.

    5.–6. are present participle forms.

    7.–8. are nouns.

C. As a prewriting activity, make lists of answers to the following questions:

    1. What could be recurring?

    2. To whom might you send a remittance? Why?

    3. What can propel an animal or an object?

After you have completed your lists, choose one of your answers as an idea starter and write a paragraph.

Challenge Activities

junta	gazpacho	serape	frijole
renegade	aficionado	bolero	palmetto

A. Write the challenge word that fits each definition.

1. a bean
2. a deserter who joins the other side
3. a woolen poncho
4. a short, open vest or jacket; a dance
5. a fan or devotee
6. a small palm tree with fan-shaped leaves
7. a group of persons controlling a government
8. a spicy soup

B. Complete each sentence with a challenge word.

1. Terrence has an extensive collection of jazz records; he is a true jazz _____.
2. The dictator of that country was overthrown; a military _____ has assumed power.
3. I put the tomatoes, peppers, cucumbers, and seasoning into a blender; a bowl of _____ is very refreshing on a hot day.
4. The dancers performed both the lively flamenco and a lovely _____.
5. In many countries a man as well as a woman might be seen wearing a _____ over the shoulders.
6. Andrea wove beautiful place mats from strips of leaves taken from a _____.
7. The _____ informed the enemy of the other side's plans.
8. The _____ is a versatile bean used in a number of tasty dishes.

C. Write an advertising brochure for a hotel in Spain, on a Latin American island, or in a Latin American country. Tell about the hotel itself—the accommodations, shops, restaurant, setting, and so on. Mention entertainment, such as sports and shows that are attractions in the area. Use some of the challenge words in your brochure.

Challenge Activities

glossaries	abilities	melodies	by-products
centuries	loyalties	wharves	cliffhangers

A. Write the challenge word that completes each series of words.

1. millennia, decades, _____
2. piers, docks, _____
3. mysteries, ghost stories, _____
4. songs, tunes, _____
5. dictionaries, thesauri, _____
6. skills, talents, _____
7. allegiances, devotions, _____
8. secondary results, bonuses, _____

B. Write a challenge word for each clue.

1. Each of these is a hundred years.
2. These can keep you in suspense.
3. These are often found at the end of textbooks.
4. Ships are often loaded at these places.
5. You probably have these toward your favorite teams.
6. These often result from the making of something.
7. These are things you do well.
8. You might hum these as you go about doing other things.

C. Imagine that Rip Van Winkle suddenly awoke in the present time. Invent a story in which he walks along a busy street, going in and out of stores. By observing people and by scanning books, he draws conclusions about this century and the people living at this time. Make your story as humorous as you wish. Use challenge words or forms of them where you can.

Challenge Activities

| acclaim | accompaniment | accordion | assimilate |
| accolade | accomplishment | affinity | attribute |

A. Write the challenge word that matches each definition.

1. a quality belonging to a particular person or thing
2. an expression of approval
3. an attraction
4. to take something in and cause it to blend indistinguishably
5. a hand-operated, portable keyboard instrument
6. achievement or performance
7. an instrumental or vocal part that supports or complements a principal voice or instrument
8. welcome with praise

B. Complete the story by writing the appropriate challenge words.

Raoul and Carmen are excellent musicians. Carmen is a singer; her voice is a wonderful __1.__. Raoul plays the __2.__. When they perform together, Carmen sings and Raoul provides the __3.__.

Both of them have an __4.__ for music. They learn new pieces easily and quickly. They __5.__ the music and make it their own.

Last year Raoul and Carmen gave a special recital. At that time, we were all able to see the high level of their __6.__. Their performance was received with great applause and __7.__. After the concert they were given an honorary award by their music school. This was an unexpected but well-deserved __8.__.

C. Describe a musical performance you have seen and heard. What instruments were played? Were there any particular attributes of the performers that you admired? How did the audience respond to the performance? Use some challenge words in your description.

Challenge Activities

| Melba toast | madras | forsythia | derby |
| mackintosh | begonia | paisley | milliner |

A. Write a challenge word or words to answer each question.

    1.–2. Which challenge words are names of flowers?

    3. Which challenge word is the name of a fine-textured cloth?

    4. Which challenge word describes a kind of design?

    5. Which challenge word names a kind of hat?

    6. Which challenge word is the name for a person who makes hats?

    7. Which challenge word names a kind of coat?

    8. Which challenge word names a kind of food?

B. Write the challenge word that will complete each sentence.

    1. If you like thin, crispy bread, have some _____ for breakfast.

    2. If you have to go out on a cold, rainy day, wear this _____ to keep you dry and warm.

    3. If you wore a scarf with pretty swirled shapes, someone might say to you, "Oh, what a beautiful _____ scarf!"

    4. If you like plaid and striped designs of bright colors, you might select a cotton _____ shirt.

    5. If you would like a houseplant with bright flowers and waxy leaves, you should buy a _____.

    6. If you see a man wearing a round felt hat with a small brim, you might say, "He's wearing a _____."

    7. You will know that spring has come if you see that the _____ bushes have blossomed with yellow flowers.

    8. If you like to design and make hats, you might become a _____.

C. Write a descriptive paragraph about a person sitting at the breakfast table one spring morning. The person looks out the window and observes the landscape and the people passing by. In your paragraph, use as many of the challenge words as you can.

Challenge Activities

menial	dachshund	facade	rigmarole
status	incognito	verbatim	ultimatum

A. Read each sentence. Write the challenge word that could replace the underlined word or words.

1. The agent was on a secret mission and had to travel in disguise.

2. Though Nora felt unhappy, she put on a cheerful false appearance at the party.

3. The mechanic tried to explain what was wrong with my car, but everything he said sounded like meaningless and foolish talk to me.

4. The newspaper published a word-for-word transcript of the President's State of the Union message.

5. Labor-saving devices have eliminated many slavish and for the benefit of others tasks in the home.

6. As a result of her promotion, Karen's rank and professional standing in the company has risen.

7. Lenny's small dog with a long body and droopy ears won first prize in the school pet show.

8. Throughout the difficult negotiations, the diplomat kept all doors open and avoided giving an order, proposition, or final demand to the other side.

B. Write the challenge words that . . .

1.–3. have two syllables.

4.–6. have three syllables.

7.–8. have four syllables.

C. Write a suspense story. Tell the story from the butler's viewpoint. Put yourself in that role, but pretend that you are really a detective in disguise. Mention all the rigmarole you must put up with from your employer and the other characters. What happens? Might the family dachshund play an important role? Use as many of the challenge words as you can.

Challenge Activities

restrictive	resistive	applicator	contraction
persistent	applicable	extraction	retraction

A. Write the challenge word that has the two meanings given.

1. **a.** confining or limiting; **b.** keeping within limits
2. **a.** refusing to give up; **b.** enduring
3. **a.** proper, appropriate; **b.** set apart for special use
4. **a.** ancestry, origin; **b.** pulling out or drawing out
5. **a.** shortened form; **b.** reduction in size
6. **a.** being drawn back in; **b.** withdrawal
7. **a.** actively opposing; **b.** impeding or retarding
8. **a.** tool, such as a brush; **b.** sponge-tipped device used for application

B. Complete each sentence with a challenge word. Then write **a** or **b** to tell which definition from Activity A is used in the sentence.

1. Gerald did not give up until he had sold his car for the price he wanted; he was _____.
2. When you exercise, don't wear _____ clothing.
3. The tooth _____ caused me very little discomfort.
4. Each bottle of shoe polish comes with an _____.
5. Mr. Wu demanded that the paper print a _____.
6. The lawyer studied earlier cases that were _____ to the case.
7. Vinyl is _____ to water.
8. **Don't** is a _____ for **do not**.

C. Pretend that you are an inventor. Describe your invention. What does it look like? What does it do? How does it work? Your invention can be funny or serious. Use as many challenge words as possible in describing your invention.

Unit 25

Challenge Activities

| biceps | biathlon | unicorn | monosyllable |
| binary | unicycle | duplicator | bicentennial |

A. Read each definition. Write the challenge word that matches each definition.

1. a machine that copies
2. relating to the 200th anniversary
3. a muscle having two points of origin
4. a word of one syllable
5. a mythical animal with one horn
6. made up of two things or parts
7. an athletic contest made up of two separate events
8. a vehicle with a single wheel propelled by pedals

B. Write a challenge word for each clue.

1. The United States had this type of celebration in 1976.
2. Dumbbells might be lifted to firm these.
3. This might appear in a fairy tale or as a stuffed animal.
4. There are only two digits in this number system.
5. Athletes who participate in this will require a lot of stamina.
6. A clown in a circus might get around on one of these.
7. Our conversation will be very dull if each word we speak is of this type.
8. This is another name for a "copy machine."

C. Imagine that you overheard a series of sentences that didn't make sense. In each sentence, either a challenge word was misused or a word sounding somewhat like a challenge word was substituted. Example: "The sailor looks handsome wearing his unicorn." Write eight sentences with misused words by using challenge words or words that sound somewhat like challenge words.

Challenge Activities

epigram	cacophony	kaleidoscope	chronological
cardiogram	xylophone	anachronism	synchronization

A. Write a challenge word to go with each word pair below to complete the series.

1. X-ray, sonogram
2. adage, proverb
3. telescope, periscope
4. sequential, successive
5. noise, racket
6. marimba, vibraphone
7. coordination, syncopation
8. outdated, misplaced

B. Write the challenge word that best completes each sentence.

1. A cave man in a movie that takes place in the twentieth century would be an _____.
2. Each chapter heading was followed by a two-line _____.
3. The noise of irate drivers blowing their horns in a traffic jam can create quite a _____.
4. To check a patient's heart, a doctor will often administer a _____.
5. We generally study historical events in _____ order.
6. I marveled at the beautiful patterns created by the _____.
7. The _____ of our watches will ensure that we meet at exactly the same time.
8. The percussionist used wooden mallets to play the _____.

C. Pick three or more of the challenge words that mean something special to you. Write about what you associate with each word. Write short, vivid descriptions.

Challenge Activities

caret	censor	marshal	persecute
carat	sensor	martial	prosecute

A. Write the challenge word for each clue.

1. This has to do with the weight of precious stones.
2. This person keeps law and order.
3. This has to do with taking legal action.
4. This person looks for objectionable material and deletes it.
5. This word might describe the rule of a military regime.
6. This mark is used in editing.
7. This word comes from a Latin word meaning "to pursue."
8. An electric eye is a type of this.

B. Choose the correct challenge word in parentheses to complete each sentence. Write the challenge word.

1. A diamond of one _____ is quite large. (caret, carat)
2. In proofreading, a _____ often shows where a word should be inserted. (caret, carat)
3. A repressive government may _____ what appears in the newspaper. (censor, sensor)
4. A smoke detector is equipped with a _____ that triggers an alarm when there is smoke in the air. (censor, sensor)
5. The band marched down the street to the strains of _____ music. (marshal, martial)
6. Our community will _____ all its energies for a big clean-up day. (marshal, martial)
7. The attorney was gathering evidence to _____ the suspect. (persecute, prosecute)
8. It is wrong to _____ people whose views are different from yours. (persecute, prosecute)

C. An imaginary young princess is fond of sending out royal decrees to her subjects. Unfortunately, she often confuses words that sound alike or almost alike. Set the scene by telling what the princess wanted to proclaim. Then write a humorous proclamation as the princess might have written it. Use the challenge words.

Challenge Activities

cuisine	flamboyant	hors d'oeuvre	à la carte
chandelier	connoisseur	carte blanche	pièce de résistance

A. Write a challenge word that goes with each definition.

1. a style of cooking
2. an appetizer
3. freedom to do whatever one wants
4. showy, elaborate
5. the outstanding dish of a meal
6. with a separate price for each item on the menu
7. an ornate lighting fixture
8. one who appreciates fine things

B. Complete the story by writing the challenge word that fits in each numbered space.

   Mr. Chambertin loves food. In fact, he is a ___1.___ of fine food. Last night he went to his favorite restaurant. The restaurant specializes in French ___2.___. The waiter greeted Mr. Chambertin at the door with a ___3.___ bow. Then he was seated at the best table, right under the crystal ___4.___.

   "Would you like to order our special complete dinner tonight?" asked the waiter.

   "No, thank you, René," replied Mr. Chambertin. "I will be ordering ___5.___. As an ___6.___, I would like to begin with the smoked mussels. Then I would like the rack of lamb."

   "Ah, you have chosen well," exclaimed René. "The lamb is the ___7.___ on tonight's menu!"

   "And since I'll be jogging and working off the calories tomorrow, I'm not holding back on dessert tonight," exulted Mr. Chambertin. "I'm going to give myself ___8.___."

C. Write a dialogue between a waiter and a customer in a French restaurant. Use as many of the challenge words as you can.

Challenge Activities

superfluous	influenza	manifest	animation
managerial	commission	omission	equanimity

A. Write the challenge word that is a synonym for each of the following words or phrases.

1. liveliness
2. executive
3. fee
4. viral illness

5. display
6. extra
7. composure
8. something left out

B. Complete the following paragraphs with challenge words.

Roxanne is in the sales department of a computer company. She gets a __1.__ for every sale she makes. Roxanne is an excellent salesperson, and she is enthusiastic about what she sells. She talks to prospective customers with great __2.__. In her explanation of how a product works, she covers every point with no __3.__. Roxanne is so good at her job that she will probably be promoted to a __4.__ position soon.

Jeff was sick in bed. The doctor came to see him and said, "You __5.__ symptoms such as a fever, a sore throat, and a headache. It looks as though you have a bad case of __6.__. I'm going to prescribe some medicine for you."

"Should I take aspirin, too?" asked Jeff.

"No," replied the doctor, "that would be __7.__."

Then he patted Jeff's hand and said, "Keep up your good spirits and don't lose your __8.__. You'll be over this in a few days."

C. Imagine that you are the president of a large company. You have an opening in the company at the managerial level. The personnel director has just stepped into your office. Think about what you might say regarding the type of person you want to fill the vacancy. Write your speech using some of the challenge words.

Challenge Activities

enthusiastic	automatic	apologetic	emphatic
enthusiastically	automatically	apologetically	emphatically

A. Write the challenge word that is a synonym or an antonym for each word below. Then write **s** if the challenge word is a synonym or **a** if it is an antonym.

1. regretful
2. eager
3. lackadaisically
4. forceful

5. defiantly
6. spontaneously
7. mechanical
8. vaguely

B. Write the challenge word that will best complete each sentence.

1.–2. When she was invited to the class picnic, Lashonda responded _____. She was very _____ about the picnic.

3.–4. Mrs. Frank's answering machine _____ takes all phone calls when she is out. Mrs. Frank finds her _____ answering machine very convenient.

5.–6. Kevin was _____ about the mess he and his friends had made in the kitchen while cooking spaghetti. He spoke _____ to his mother and promised to clean up.

7.–8. The ambassador spoke _____ about her country's needs. She was _____ in her demand for fairer trade practices.

C. The challenge words that are adverbs can be used to show different ways people might speak or act. Describe some situations in which a person might speak or act in each of these ways. Use the appropriate challenge words. Example: Because the students were given an interesting demonstration in the use of watercolors, they began their paintings enthusiastically.

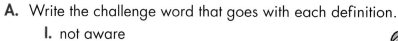

Unit 32

Challenge Activities

| sequential | provincial | tenacious | scrumptious |
| consequential | unconscious | vivacious | infectious |

A. Write the challenge word that goes with each definition.

1. not aware
2. important
3. delicious
4. animated
5. pertaining to a province; unsophisticated; limited in outlook
6. contaminated with disease-producing germs
7. in order of succession
8. stubborn, holding fast

B. Write the challenge word that will best complete each sentence.

1. Grandmother's cornbread tastes _____.
2. The _____ kitten would not let go of the ball of yarn.
3. The ambulance rushed the _____ man to the hospital.
4. Toronto is the _____ capital of Ontario, Canada.
5. Sandy is _____; everyone enjoys her lively personality.
6. Smallpox is an _____ disease that has now been eradicated worldwide.
7. The biography was published by a magazine in _____ parts.
8. Let us hope that our meeting will be both productive and _____.

C. Write a rhyme using one or more of the challenge words. You might use either of the lines below to begin your rhyme. Make it light and funny.

There once was a lad named Ignatius . . .

I met a young maid named Ms. Winchell . . .

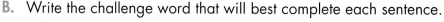

aspect	prospective	involvement	avert
aversion	speculate	evolvement	divert

A. Select the correct challenge word for each definition from the words in parentheses. Write the challenge word.

1. participation (involvement, evolvement)
2. development (involvement, evolvement)
3. turn from one course to another (avert, divert)
4. turn away; prevent (avert, divert)
5. expected (prospective, speculate)
6. ponder or reflect (prospective, speculate)
7. an element or facet (aversion, aspect)
8. extreme dislike (aversion, aspect)

B. Write the challenge word that will best complete each sentence.

1. Beavers' dams sometimes _____ streams into new courses.
2. The _____ of the scientist's theories took place over a number of years.
3. By swerving quickly out of the path of an oncoming car, the driver was able to _____ an accident.
4. People who _____ in the stock market sometimes lose money.
5. Beth's _____ in environmental issues led her to establish a recycling center.
6. The real estate broker showed the house to a _____ buyer.
7. I had not considered that _____ of the problem before.
8. Do you know anyone who has an _____ to cats?

C. Your class has decided to enter the stock market. However, you plan to plot your actions on paper only and not actually invest money at this time. Your "paper capital" is one thousand dollars. Tell how you plan to get started. For example, will you speculate on some stocks? What precautions will you take so you don't lose all your investment at once? Explain your plan, using some of the challenge words.

Challenge Activities

coincide	commiserate	compassion	corroborate
collateral	commissioner	compensate	corrosion

A. Write the challenge word that best completes each analogy.

1. **Enemy** is to **ruthlessness** as **friend** is to _____.
2. **Erosion** is to **rock** as _____ is to **metal**.
3. **Punish** is to **penalty** as _____ is to **payment**.
4. _____ is to **district** as **principal** is to **school**.
5. **Congratulate** is to **success** as _____ is to **loss**.
6. _____ is to **guarantee** as **word of honor** is to **promise**.
7. _____ is to a **fact** as **disavow** is to a **falsehood**.
8. _____ is to **coincidence** as **avoid** is to **avoidance**.

B. Write the challenge word that will correctly complete each sentence.

1. If you pay someone for a service, you _____ that person.
2. If you show sympathy for the problems of others, you have _____.
3. If you confirm someone else's story, you _____ it.
4. When iron rusts, it is undergoing a process of _____.
5. A person in charge of a governmental department is sometimes called a _____.
6. If two things occur at the same time, they _____.
7. If you express sorrow over someone's difficulties, you _____ with that person.
8. If you want to get a loan from a bank, you may have to put up _____.

C. You have purchased a faulty product. You want your money refunded. Write a letter of complaint in which you describe what is wrong with the product and how you expect to be compensated. In your letter, use as many of the challenge words as you can.

Challenge Activities

terrify	horrify	facilitate	affectionate
qualify	facility	disinfect	proficient

A. Write the challenge word that will best complete each sentence.

1. After an intense year of study and practice, Jack has become _____ at tennis.

2. Hospital workers _____ floors and beds by scrubbing them with special solutions.

3. Esther was the envy of all the piano students in the class because she could play difficult scales with great _____.

4. The main character in this movie is a horrible, ugly monster with long, sharp claws; the movie will _____ you!

5. Barking excitedly and wagging its tail, the _____ puppy rushed to meet me.

6. Riding roller coasters can sometimes _____ a young child.

7. It will _____ her job to know the procedures followed by her predecessor.

8. Dewan felt confident his education and experience would _____ him for the position.

B. Write the challenge word or words that . . .

    1.–5. are verbs.

    6.–7. are adjectives.

    8. is a noun.

C. Select two or three challenge words to use in a headline for a newspaper. Your headline can be serious or humorous. Then write a short lead story built around the headline. If you wish, write several headlines and news stories.

WRITER'S HANDBOOK
Contents

The first step in learning your spelling words is correcting your pretest. Follow these steps with your teacher.

These tips will help you do better on your spelling tests and remember how to spell words when you are writing.

Spelling is for writing. Learning these steps in the writing process will help you become a better writer.

These ideas will help you practice the four basic types of writing: descriptive, narrative, persuasive, and expository.

Spelling Strategy
When You Take a Test

1 **Get** ready for the test. Make sure your paper and pencil are ready.

2 **Listen** carefully as your teacher says each word and uses it in a sentence. Don't write before you hear the word **and** the sentence.

3 **Write** the word carefully. Make sure your handwriting is easy to read. If you want to print your words, ask your teacher.

6 **Circle** any misspelled parts of the word.

4 **Use** a pen to correct your test. Look at the word as your teacher says it.

7 **Look** at the correctly written word. Spell the word again. Say each letter out loud.

5 **Say** the word aloud. Listen carefully as your teacher spells the word. Say each letter aloud. Check the word one letter at a time.

8 **Write** any misspelled word correctly.

Spelling Strategy
When You Write a Paper

1. **Think** of the exact word you want to use.

2. **Write** the word, if you know how to spell it.

3. **Say** the word to yourself, if you are not sure how to spell it.

4. **Picture** what the word looks like when you see it written.

5. **Write** the word.

6. **Ask** yourself whether the word looks right.

7. **Check** the word in a dictionary if you are not sure.

SPELLING AND THE Writing Process

Writing anything—a friendly letter, a paper for school—usually follows a process. The writing process has five steps. It might look like this if you tried to draw a picture of it:

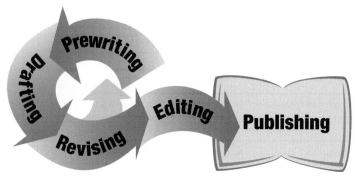

Notice that part of the writing process forms a loop. That is because not every writing task is the same. It is also because writers often jump back and forth between the steps as they change their minds and think of new ideas.

Here is a description of each step:

Prewriting This is thinking and planning ahead to help you write.

Drafting This means writing your paper for the first time. You usually just try to get your ideas down on paper. You can fix them later.

Revising This means fixing your final draft. Here is where you rewrite, change, and add words.

Editing This is where you feel you have said all you want to say. Now you proofread your paper for spelling errors and errors in grammar and punctuation.

Publishing This is making a copy of your writing and sharing it with your readers. Put your writing in a form that your readers will enjoy.

Confident spellers are better writers. Confident writers better understand their own writing process. Know the five steps. Know how they best fit the way you write.

SPELLING AND
Writing Ideas

Being a good speller can help make you a more confident writer. Writing more can make you a better writer. Here are some ideas to get you started.

Ideas for Descriptive Writing

You might…

- describe a profession you might be interested in or a career you might choose.
- describe a busy train station or airport. Choose details that involve all of your five senses.
- describe an extraordinary day you had recently. It could be extraordinarily awful or extraordinarily wonderful.
- select two fictional characters—or real people you know—and write two paragraphs: one describing similarities the characters share and one telling how the characters differ.

Ideas for Narrative Writing

You might…

- think of a real or imaginary experience that turned out better than expected and write a story about it.
- retell a familiar story or fairy tale in your own words. Change the story, adding fresh details, and give the story a surprise ending.
- write a letter to someone you have not seen for a long time, bringing that person up to date on what is happening in your life.
- think of a favorite object, plant, or animal. Pretend you are that thing and write a story about a day in your life.

Ideas for Persuasive Writing

You might…

- choose an issue and take a stand. Write about something you think should be changed. Give reasons to support your ideas.
- write an argument to persuade your parents to let you do something special, such as getting a new pet, or giving you a new privilege, such as a later weekend curfew.
- try to persuade a friend or family member to avoid an unhealthy or dangerous habit, such as smoking or eating mostly junk food.

Ideas for Expository Writing

You might…

- think of a saying or an expression you like or use frequently. Write the expression, tell what it means, and explain when and why people use it.
- choose an endangered animal or a serious environmental issue. Express your views and offer suggestions about how people can make a difference.
- design an invention that you think would help make life easier. Explain what it will look like, how it will help people, and who will use it.
- write instructions telling a classmate how to set up and care for a project, such as an aquarium or a terrarium.

Manuscript Handwriting Models

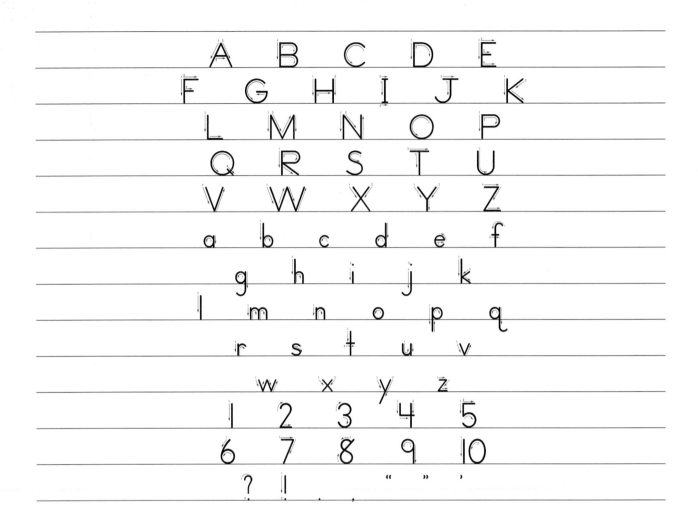

Cursive Handwriting Models

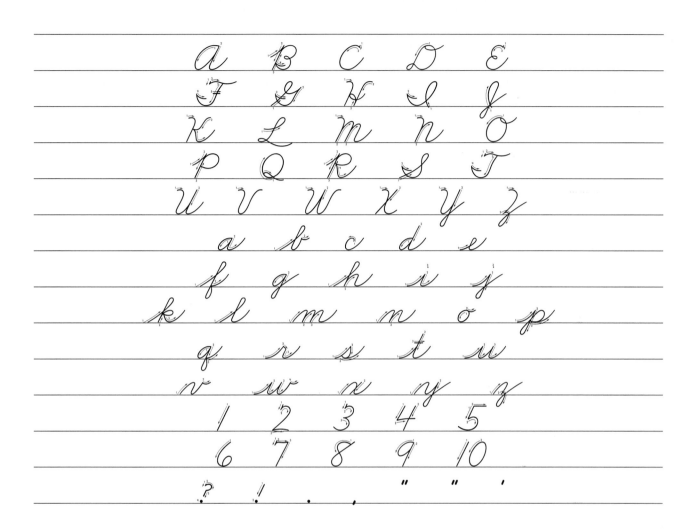

High Frequency Writing Words

A

a
about
afraid
after
again
air
all
almost
also
always
am
America
an
and
animal
animals
another
any
anything
are
around
as
ask
asked
at
ate
away

B

baby
back
bad
ball
balloons
baseball
basketball

be
bear
beautiful
because
become
bed
been
before
being
believe
best
better
big
bike
black
boat
book
books
both
boy
boys
bring
broke
brother
build
bus
but
buy
by

C

call
called
came
can
candy
can't
car
care

cars
cat
catch
caught
change
charge
children
Christmas
circus
city
class
clean
clothes
come
comes
coming
could
couldn't
country
cut

D

Dad
day
days
decided
did
didn't
died
different
dinner
do
does
doesn't
dog
dogs
doing
done

don't
door
down
dream

E

each
earth
eat
eighth
else
end
enough
even
every
everybody
everyone
everything
except
eyes

F

family
fast
father
favorite
feel
feet
fell
few
field
fight
finally
find
fire
first
fish
five

fix
food
football
for
found
four
free
Friday
friend
friends
from
front
fun
funny
future

G

game
games
gas
gave
get
gets
getting
girl
girls
give
go
God
goes
going
good
got
grade
grader
great
ground
grow

H

had
hair
half
happened
happy
hard
has
have
having
he
head
heard
help
her
here
he's
high
hill
him
his
hit
home
homework
hope
horse
horses
hot
hour
house
how
hurt

I

I
I'd
if
I'm
important
in
into
is
it
its
it's

J

job
jump
just

K

keep
kept
kids
killed
kind
knew
know

L

lady
land
last
later
learn
leave
left
let
let's
life
like
liked
likes
little
live
lived
lives
long
look
looked
looking
lost
lot
lots
love
lunch

M

mad
made
make
making
man
many
math
may
maybe
me
mean
men
might
miss
Mom
money
more
morning
most
mother
mouse
move
Mr.
Mrs.
much
music
must
my
myself

N

name
named
need
never
new
next
nice
night
no
not
nothing
now

O

of
off
oh
OK
old
on
once
one
only
or
other
our
out
outside
over
own

P

parents
park
party
people
person
pick
place
planet
play
played
playing
police
president
pretty
probably
problem
put

R

ran
read
ready
real
really
reason
red
responsibilities
rest
ride
riding
right
room
rules
run
running

High Frequency Writing Words (continued)

S

said
same
saw
say
scared
school
schools
sea
second
see
seen
set
seventh
she
ship
shot
should
show
sick
since
sister
sit
sleep
small
snow
so
some
someone
something
sometimes
soon
space
sport
sports
start
started

states
stay
still
stop
stopped
store
story
street
stuff
such
sudden
suddenly
summer
sure
swimming

T

take
talk
talking
teach
teacher
teachers
team
tell
than
Thanksgiving
that
that's
the
their
them
then
there
these
they
they're

thing
things
think
this
thought
three
through
throw
time
times
to
today
together
told
too
took
top
tree
trees
tried
trip
trouble
try
trying
turn
turned
TV
two

U

united
until
up
upon
us
use
used

V

very

W

walk
walked
walking
want
wanted
war
was
wasn't
watch
water
way
we
week
weeks
well
went
were
what
when
where
which
while
white
who
whole
why
will
win
winter
wish
with
without
woke

won
won't
work
world
would
wouldn't

Y

yard
year
years
yes
you
your
you're

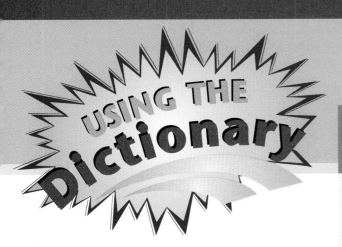

USING THE Dictionary

Tips for Finding a Word in a Dictionary

- The **guide words** at the top of each dictionary page show the first and last entries on the page. Think of words to spell. Practice using guide words to find each word's entry.

- Some spellings are listed with the base word. To find **calicoes,** look up **calico.** To find **occurring,** look up **occur.**

- If you do not know how to spell a word, guess the spelling and try to find the first three letters of the word. (Using just the first letter often takes too long.)

- If you can't find a word, think of alternative spellings. For example, if a word starts with the **/k/** sound, the spelling might begin with **k, c,** or even **ch.**

Information on page 266 provides additional explanation of terms and abbreviations in your Spelling Dictionary.

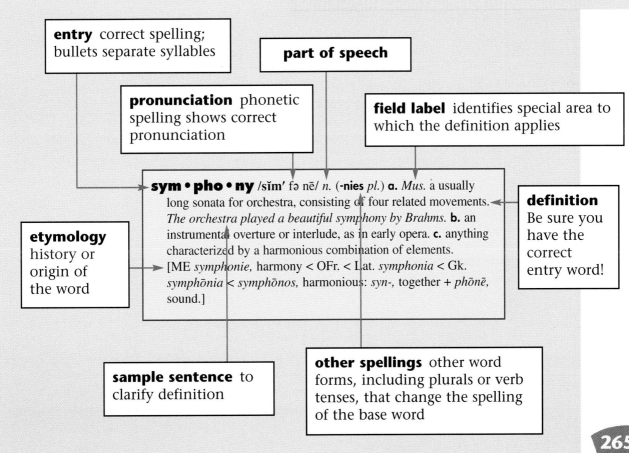

entry correct spelling; bullets separate syllables

part of speech

pronunciation phonetic spelling shows correct pronunciation

field label identifies special area to which the definition applies

sym•pho•ny /sĭm′ fə nē/ *n.* (**-nies** *pl.*) **a.** *Mus.* a usually long sonata for orchestra, consisting of four related movements. *The orchestra played a beautiful symphony by Brahms.* **b.** an instrumental overture or interlude, as in early opera. **c.** anything characterized by a harmonious combination of elements. [ME *symphonie,* harmony < OFr. < Lat. *symphonia* < Gk. *symphōnia* < *symphōnos,* harmonious: *syn-,* together + *phōnē,* sound.]

etymology history or origin of the word

definition Be sure you have the correct entry word!

sample sentence to clarify definition

other spellings other word forms, including plurals or verb tenses, that change the spelling of the base word

265

A pronunciation key appears on every right-hand page of your spelling dictionary.

The abbreviation for the **part of speech** of each entry word follows the phonetic spelling. These abbreviations include:

n.	noun	*adj.*	adjective	*conj.*	conjunction
pron.	pronoun	*prep.*	preposition	*interj.*	interjection
adv.	adverb	*pl.*	plural	*p.part.*	past participle
v.	verb	*sing.*	singular	*pr.part.*	present participle

Stylistic and geographic labels limit a definition to a particular level or style of usage. These labels include:

Nonstandard indicates a level of language usage that is not commonly accepted and is inappropriate for formal writing or speaking.

Slang indicates a style of language using figures of speech that are usually extravagant and overelaborate. Slang is often heard in informal conversation but is inappropriate for formal writing.

Obs. (Obsolete) indicates a term that is no longer in use.

Archaic indicates terms that were once common but are now rarely used. Archaic terms may be familiar, as they were once common in speaking and are still found in literature.

The following abbreviations also appear in your spelling dictionary.

aug. (augmentative—indicates an increase, as in size, force, or intensity, in the meaning of the original word)

comp. (comparative)

dim. (diminutive—denotes smallness, youth, or familiarity)

fem. (feminine)

freq. (frequentative—indicates that the meaning of a word is derived from the repetition of the action denoted by the original word)

perh. (perhaps)

prob. (probably)

var. (variant—indicates that a word differs slightly from the word that follows)

The **etymology,** or history of a word, appears in square brackets [ ] following the definitions. An etymology traces a word back to the language from which it is believed to have come. The symbol < means *derived from.* The abbreviations used to denote the original languages include:

AN	Anglo-Norman	*Ar.*	Arabic	*Canadian Fr.*	Canadian French
Du.	Dutch	*Fr.*	French	*MDu.*	Middle Dutch
Gk.	Greek	*Ital.*	Italian	*OProv.*	Old Provençal
G.	German	*OFr.*	Old French	*LLat.*	Late Latin
OE	Old English	*Sp.*	Spanish	*Med. Lat.*	Medieval Latin
Turk.	Turkish	*ON*	Old Norse	*Mex. Sp.*	Mexican Spanish
Lat.	Latin	*OSp.*	Old Spanish	*ME*	Middle English
Port.	Portuguese	*OItal.*	Old Italian	*MHG*	Middle High German
Prov.	Provençal	*NLat.*	New Latin	*Norman Fr.*	Norman French
OHG	Old High German			*VLat.*	Vulgar Latin

abacus

Pronunciation Key

ă	pat	ŏ	pot	th	**thin**
ā	pay	ō	toe	*th*	**this**
âr	care	ô	p**aw**, **for**	hw	**which**
ä	father	oi	n**oi**se	zh	vi**si**on
ĕ	pet	ou	**out**	ə	**a**bout,
ē	be	ŏŏ	t**oo**k		it**e**m,
ĭ	pit	ōō	b**oo**t		penc**i**l,
ī	pie	ŭ	c**u**t		gall**o**p,
îr	pier	ûr	**ur**ge		circ**u**s

ab•a•cus /ăb′ ə kəs, ə băk′ əs/ *n.* (**ab•a•cus•es** or **ab•a•ci** /ăb′ ə sī′, ə-băk′ ī/ *pl.*) a manual computing device consisting of a frame holding parallel rods strung with movable counters.

-able a suffix, used to form adjectives, that means: **a.** capable or worthy of: *eatable.* **b.** tending toward: *sizable.*

a•bridge /ə brĭj′/ *v.* (**a•bridg•es, a•bridged, a•bridg•ing**) **a.** to reduce the length of (a written text); condense. **b.** to curtail; cut short.

ab•so•lute¹ /ăb′ sə lōōt′/ *adj.* **a.** perfect in quality or nature; complete. **b.** not mixed; pure. **c.1.** not limited by restrictions or exceptions: *absolute trust;* **c.2.** unqualified in extent or degree; total: *absolute silence.* **d.** not to be doubted or questioned; positive: *absolute proof.* [ME *absolut* < Lat. *absolutus,* ended < *absoluere,* to finish: *ab,* from + *solvere,* to loose.]

ab•so•lute² /ăb′ sə lōōt′/ *n.* something that is absolute.

ab•so•lute•ly /ăb′ sə lōōt′ lē/ *adv.* definitely and completely; unquestionably.

ab•so•lute val•ue /ăb′ sə lōōt′ văl′ yōō/ *n.* the numerical value or magnitude of a quantity, as of a vector or of a negative integer, without regard to its sign.

ab•stract /ăb′străkt′, ăb′ străkt′/ *adj.* **a.** considered apart from concrete existence: *an abstract concept.* **b.** not applied or practical. **c.** thought of or stated without reference to a specific instance: *abstract words like "truth" and "justice."* **d.** designating a genre of painting or sculpture whose intellectual and affective content depends solely on intrinsic form. —*idiom.* **in the abstract.** apart from actual substance or experience. [ME < Lat. *abstractus,* p.part. of *abstrahere,* to draw away: *ab-,* away + *trahere,* to draw.]

ac•ces•si•ble /ăk sĕs′ ə bəl/ *adj.* (**ac•ces•si•bil•i•ty** *n.*) (**ac•ces•si•bly** *adv.*) **a.** easily approached or entered. **b.** easily obtained. **c.** easy to communicate or get along with. **d.** open to: *accessible to flattery.*

ac•ci•den•tal /ăk sĭ dĕn′ tl/ *adj.* (**ac•ci•den•tal•ly** *adv.*) **a.** occurring unexpectedly and unintentionally; by chance. **b.** not part of the real or essential nature of a thing.

ac•com•pa•ny /ə kŭm′ pə nē, ə kŭmp′ nē/ *v.* (**-nies, -nied, -ny•ing**) **a.** to go along with; join in company. **b.** to supplement; add to. **c.** to coexist or occur with. [ME *accompanien* < OFr. *acompagnier: a-,* to (< Lat. *ad-*) + *compaignon,* companion.]

ac•com•plish /ə kŏm′ plish/ *v.* **a.** to succeed in doing; bring to pass. **b.** to reach the end of; complete. [ME *accomplisshen* < OFr. *acomplir, accompliss-,* to complete: *a-,* to (< Lat. *ad-*) + *complir,* to complete < Lat. *complere,* to fill out.]

ac•cord¹ /ə kôrd′/ *v.* **a.** to cause to conform or agree; bring into harmony. **b.** to be in agreement, unity, or harmony.

ac•cord² /ə kôrd′/ *n.* agreement; harmony. —*idiom.* **of (one's) own accord.** voluntarily. [ME *accorden* < OFr. *acorder* < Med. Lat. *accordare:* Lat. *ad-,* to + Lat. *cor, cord,* heart.]

ac•cord•ing to *prep.* **a.** as stated or indicated by; on the authority of: *according to historians.* **b.** in keeping with; in agreement with: *according to instructions.* **c.** as determined by: *a list arranged according to the alphabet.*

ac•count /ə kount′/ *n.* **a.** a narrative or record of events; a written or oral explanation, as of blame or cause. **b.** a precise list or enumeration of monetary transactions. **c.** a business relationship involving the exchange of money or credit: *a charge account.* [ME < OFr. *acont* < *aconter,* to reckon: *a-,* to (< Lat. *ad-*) + *cunter,* to count (ult. < Lat. *computare,* to sum up).]

ac•cu•rate /ăk′ yər ĭt/ *adj.* (**ac•cu•rate•ly** *adv.*)
a. in exact conformity to fact; errorless.
b. deviating only slightly or within acceptable
limits from a standard.

ac•cus•tomed /ə kŭs′ təmd/ *adj.* **a.** usual, characteristic, or normal: *worked with her accustomed
thoroughness.* **b.** in the habit of: *accustomed to
sleeping late.* [ME *accustomen* < OFr. *acostumer:
a-,* to (< Lat. *ad-*) + *costume,* custom.]

a•chieve /ə chēv′/ *v.* (**a•chieves, a•chieved,
a•chiev•ing**) **a.** to do or finish with success.
b. to attain or get with effort: *finally achieved
mastery of the piano.*

a•cre /ā′ kər/ *n.* **a.** a unit of area used in land
measurement and equal to 160 square rods,
4,840 square yards, or 43,560 square feet.
b. *Archaic.* a field or plot of land. [ME *aker*
< OE *æcer.*]

a•cre•age /ā′ kər ĭj, ā′ krĭj/ *n.* area of land in
acres.

ac•tiv•i•ty /ăk tĭv′ ĭ tē/ *n.* (**-ties** *pl.*) **a.** energetic
action or movement. **b.** a specified form of
supervised action or field of action.

ac•tu•al /ăk′ chōō əl/ *adj.* **a.** existing in fact or
reality. **b.** current. **c.** based on fact: *an actual
account.*

ad- or **ac-** or **af-** or **ag-** or **al-** or **ap-** or **as-** or
at- a prefix that means toward, to: *adapt.*

a•dapt /ə dăpt′/ *v.* to adjust to a specified use or
situation.

ad•mi•ra•ble /ăd′ mər ə bəl/ *adj.* (**ad•mi•
ra•bly** *adv.*) deserving admiration; excellent.

ad•mi•ra•tion /ăd′ mə rā′ shən/ *n.* a feeling of
pleasure, wonder, and approval.

ad•mire /ăd mīr′/ *v.* (**-mires, -mired, -mir•ing**)
a. to regard with pleasure, wonder, and approval.
b. to have a high opinion of; esteem or respect.

ad•mis•sion /ăd mĭsh′ ən/ *n.* **a.1.** the act of
admitting or allowing to enter. **a.2.** the state of
being allowed to enter. **b.** the right to enter;
access. **c.** the price required or paid for entering;
entrance fee. **d.** a voluntary acknowledgment
that something is true. [ME < Lat. *admissio*
< *admittere: ad-,* + *mittere,* to send.]

a•dopt /ə dŏpt′/ *v.* (**a•dopt•a•ble** *adj.*) (**a•dop•
tion** *n.*) **a.** to take into one's family through legal
means and raise as one's own child. **b.** to take
and follow by choice: *adopt a new technique.*
c. to vote to accept: *adopt a resolution.*

ad•van•ta•geous /ăd′ văn tā′ jəs, -vən-/ *adj.*
affording benefit or gain; useful.

ad•ven•ture[1] /ăd věn′ chər/ *n.* (**ad•ven•ture•
some** *adj.*) **a.** an undertaking or enterprise of
a hazardous nature. **b.** an unusual experience
or course of events marked by excitement and
suspense. **c.** participation in hazardous or
exciting experiences.

ad•ven•ture[2] /ăd věn′ chər/ *v.* (**-tures, -tured,
-tur•ing**) to venture; risk; dare.

ad•ver•tise /ăd′ vər tīz′/ *v.* (**-tis•es, -tised,
-tis•ing**) (**ad•ver•tis•er** *n.*) **a.** to make public
announcement of, especially to proclaim the qualities or advantages of (a product or business) so as
to increase sales. **b.** to call the attention of the
public to a product or business. **c.** to inquire or
seek in a public notice, as in a newspaper: *advertise for an apartment.*
[ME *advertisen,* to
notify < OFr. *avertir,
avertiss-,* to notice <
Lat. *advertere,* to turn
toward: *ad-, toward* +
vertere, to turn.]

advertise

ad•vice /ăd vīs′/ *n.* opinion about what could or
should be done about a problem; counsel.

ad•vise /ăd vīz′/ *v.* (**-vis•es, -vised, -vis•ing**)
a. to offer advice to; counsel. **b.** to recommend;
suggest. **c.** to inform; notify: *advise a person of
a decision.*

aer•i•al[1] /âr′ ē əl, ā îr′ ē əl/ *adj.* **a.** of, in, or
caused by the air. **b.** living in the air. **c.** reaching
high into the air; lofty.

aer•i•al[2] /âr′ ē əl/ *n.* an antenna.

af•fect /ə fěct′/ *v.* **a.** to have an influence on;
bring about a change in. **b.** to touch or move the
emotions of.

af•firm /ə fûrm′/ *v.* (**af•fir•ma•tion** *n.*) **a.** to
declare positively or firmly; maintain to be true.
b. to confirm. [ME *affermen* < OFr. *afermer*
< Lat. *affirmare: ad-,* to + *firmare,* to strengthen
< *firmus,* strong.]

af•fix[1] /ə **fĭks**′/ *v.* **a.** to secure (an object) to another; attach: *affix a label to a package.* **b.** to attribute: *affix blame to him.* **c.** to place at the end; append: *affix a postscript.* [Med. Lat. *affiare,* freq. of Lat. *affigere: ad-,* to + *figere,* to fasten.]

af•fix[2] /**ăf**′ ĭks′/ *n.* **a.** something that is attached, joined, or added. **b.** a word element, such as a prefix or suffix, that can only occur attached to a base, stem, or root.

af•ford /ə **fôrd**′, ə **fōrd**′/ *v.* (**af•ford•a•ble** *adj.*) **a.** to have the financial means for; be able to meet the expense of. **b.** to be able to spare or give up: *could afford an hour for lunch.* **c.** to be able to do or perform (something) without incurring harm or criticism, or with benefit to oneself: *can afford to be tolerant.* [ME *aforthen* < OE *geforthian,* to carry out < *forthian,* to further < *forth,* forward.]

-age a suffix, used to form nouns, that means: **a.** collectively; in general: *mileage.* **b.** condition; state: *marriage.* **c.** charge or fee: *postage.* **d.** residence or place: *orphanage.* **e.** act or result: *spoilage.*

a•gree•a•ble /ə **grē**′ ə bəl/ *adj.* **a.** to one's liking; pleasing; pleasant. **b.** ready to consent or submit.

-al[1] a suffix that forms adjectives from nouns: *postal.*

-al[2] a suffix that forms nouns from verbs: *arrival.*

a•li•en[1] /**ā**′ lē ən, **āl**′ yən/ *adj.* **a.** owing political allegiance to another country or government; foreign. **b.** belonging to, characteristic of, or derived from another country, place, society, or person; strange. **c.** being inconsistent or opposed; repugnant: *Lying is alien to his nature.*

a•li•en[2] /**ā**′ lē ən, **āl**′ yən/ *n.* **a.** an unnaturalized foreign resident of a country. **b.** an outsider. **c.** *Slang.* a creature from outer space.

a•lign /ə **līn**′ / *v.* **a.** to arrange in a line. **b.** to adjust to produce a proper relationship or condition. **c.** to ally with one side of an argument or cause.

al•le•giance /ə **lē**′ jəns/ *n.* loyalty or the obligation of loyalty, as to nation, sovereign, or cause. [ME *alligeaunce* < OFr. *ligeance* < *lige,* liege.]

al•li•ance /ə **lī**′ əns/ *n.* **a.** a formal pact of union or confederation between nations in a common cause. **b.** a union, relationship, or connection by kinship, marriage, or common interest. [ME < OFr. *aliance* < *alier,* to ally < Lat. *alligare,* to bind to: *ad-,* to + *ligare,* to bind.]

Pronunciation Key

ă	pat	ŏ	pot	th	**th**in
ā	pay	ō	toe	*th*	**th**is
âr	care	ô	paw, for	hw	**wh**ich
ä	father	oi	n**oi**se	zh	vi**si**on
ĕ	pet	ou	**ou**t	ə	**a**bout,
ē	be	ŏŏ	t**oo**k		it**e**m,
ĭ	pit	ōō	b**oo**t		penc**i**l,
ī	pie	ŭ	c**u**t		gall**o**p,
îr	pier	ûr	**ur**ge		circ**u**s

al•pha•bet•i•cal /**ăl**′ fə **bĕt**′ ĭ kəl/ *adj.* (**al•pha•bet•i•cal•ly** *adv.*) **a.** arranged in the customary order of the letters of a language. **b.** of, pertaining to, or expressed by an alphabet.

a•maze•ment /ə **māz**′ mənt/ *n.* a state of extreme surprise or wonder; astonishment.

am•bi•tion /ăm **bĭsh**′ ən/ *n.* **a.** an eager or strong desire to achieve something. **b.** the object or goal desired.

am•bi•tious /ăm **bĭsh**′ əs/ *adj.* **a.** full of, characterized by, or motivated by ambition. **b.** greatly desirous; eager. **c.** showing or requiring much effort.

a•moe•ba /ə **mē**′ bə/ *n.* (**-bas** or **-bae** /-b ē/ *pl.*) a very small, one-celled organism that has an indefinite, changeable form.

amoeba

ana- a prefix that means: **a.** upward; up. **b.** backward; back. **c.** again; anew.

an•a•gram /**ăn**′ ə grăm′/ *n.* a word or phrase formed by reordering the letters of another word or phrase. [Fr. *anagramme:* Gk. *ana-,* from bottom to top + Gk. *gramma,* letter < *graphein,* to write.]

a•nat•o•my /ə **năt**′ ə mē/ *n.* (**-mies** *pl.*) **a.** the structure of a plant or animal, or of any of its parts. **b.** the science of the shape and structure of organisms and their parts.

-ance a suffix that forms nouns from verbs: *resemblance.*

an•ces•tor /ăn′ sĕs′ tər/ *n.* a person from whom one is descended, especially if more remote than a grandparent; forefather.

an•ec•dote /ăn′ ĭk dōt′/ *n.* a short account of some interesting or humorous incident.

An•go•ra /ăng gôr′ ə, -gōr′ ə/ *n.* (often **angora**) **a.** the long, silky hair of the Angora goat. **b.** the fine, light hair of the Angora rabbit, sometimes blended with wool in fabrics. **c.** a yarn or fabric made from either of these fibers. [after *Angora* (Ankara), Turkey.]

an•i•mate¹ /ăn′ ə māt′/ *v.* (**-mates, -mat•ed, -mat•ing**) **a.** to give life to; fill with life. **b.** to impart interest or zest to; enliven. **c.** to impart motion or activity to. **d.** to make, design, or produce (a cartoon, for example) so as to create the illusion of motion. [Lat. *animare, animat- < anima*, soul.]

an•i•mate² /ăn′ ə mĕt′/ *adj.* **a.** possessing life; living. **b.** of or relating to animal life as distinct from plant life.

an•ni•ver•sa•ry /ăn′ ə vûr′ sə rē/ *n.* (**-ries** *pl.*) the annual recurrence of an event that took place in some preceding year: *a wedding anniversary*. [ME *anniversarie* < Med. Lat. *anniversarium* < Lat. *anniversarius*, returning yearly: *annus*, year + *versus*, p.part. of *vertere*, to turn.]

an•nounce•ment /ə nouns′ mənt/ *n.* **a.** something that has been announced. **b.** a printed or published statement or notice.

an•nu•al /ăn′ yōō əl/ *adj.* (**an•nu•al•ly** *adv.*) **a.** recurring, done, or performed every year; yearly. **b.** of or pertaining to a year; determined by a year's time: *an annual income*.

a•non•y•mous /ə nŏn′ ə məs/ *adj.* having an unknown or withheld authorship.

-ant a suffix that forms nouns and adjectives: *resultant*.

an•thro•pol•o•gy /ăn′ thrə pŏl′ ə jē/ *n.* the scientific study of the origin and of the physical, social, and cultural development and behavior of man.

ap•pa•ra•tus /ăp′ ə rā′ təs, -răt′ əs/ *n.* (**apparatus** or **-tus•es** *pl.*) **a.** the means by which a specified function is performed. **b.1.** a machine. **b.2.** a group of machines used together or in succession to accomplish a task. [Lat., preparation < *apparare*, to prepare: *ad-*, to + *parare*, to prepare.]

ap•par•ent /ə păr′ ənt, ə pâr′-/ *adj.* **a.** readily seen; open to view; visible. **b.** readily understood or perceived; plain or obvious. **c.** appearing as such but not necessarily so: *an apparent advantage*. [ME *apparaunt* < OFr. *aparant*, pr.part. of *aparoir*, to appear.]

ap•pe•tite /ăp′ ĭ tīt′/ *n.* **a.** a desire for food or drink. **b.** a physical desire. **c.** a strong wish or urge: *an appetite for learning*. [ME *appetit* < OFr. < Lat. *appetitus*, strong desire < *appetere*, to strive after: *ad-*, toward + *petere*, to seek.]

ap•plaud /ə plôd′/ *v.* **a.** to express approval, especially by clapping the hands. **b.** to praise; approve. [Lat. *applaudere: ad-*, to + *plaudere*, to clap.]

ap•plause /ə plôz′/ *n.* **a.** approval expressed, especially by the clapping of hands. **b.** praise; commendation.

ap•pli•ance /ə plī′ əns/ *n.* a device or instrument, especially one operated by electricity and designed for household use. [ME *applien*, to apply < OFr. *aplier* < Lat. *applicare*, to affix: *ad-*, to + *plicare*, to fold together.]

appliance

ap•pli•ca•tion /ăp′ lĭ kā′ shən/ *n.* **a.** a request, as for assistance, employment, or admission to a school. **b.** the form or document upon which such a request is made. [ME *applicacioun* < Med. Lat. *applicatio* < Lat. *applicare*, to affix: *ad-*, to + *plicare*, to fold together.]

ap•pre•ci•a•tion /ə prē shē ā′ shən/ *n.* **a.** recognition of the quality, value, or significance of people and things. **b.** an expression of gratitude. **c.** a rise in value or price.

ap•prov•al /ə prōō′ vəl/ *n.* **a.** the act of approving. **b.** favorable regard; commendation. [ME *approven* < OFr. *aprover* < Lat. *approbare: ad-*, to + *probare*, to test < *probus*, good.]

ap•prove /ə prōōv′/ *v.* (**-proves, -proved, -prov•ing**) to consider right or good.

ap•prox•i•mate /ə prŏk′ sə mĭt/ *adj.* (**ap•prox•i•mate•ly** *adv.*) **a.** almost exact, correct, complete, or perfect. **b.** very similar; closely resembling.

ar•chae•ol•o•gy /är′ kē ŏl′ ə jē/ *n.* the systematic recovery and study of material evidence, such as graves, buildings, tools, and pottery, remaining from past human life and culture.

ar•ti•fact /är′ tə făkt′/ *n.* an object produced or shaped by human workmanship, especially, a tool, weapon, or ornament of archaeological or historical interest.

ar•ti•fi•cial /är′ tə fĭsh′ əl/ *adj.* **a.** made by man rather than occurring in nature: *an artificial sweetener.* **b.** made in imitation of something natural: *artificial flowers.* [ME < Lat. *artificialis* < *artificium*, craftsmanship: *ars*, art + *fex*, maker < *facere*, to make.]

ar•tis•tic /är tĭs′ tĭk/ *adj.* (**ar•tis•ti•cal•ly** *adv.*) **a.** of or relating to art or artists. **b.** appreciative of or sensitive to art or beauty.

as•sem•ble /ə sĕm′ bəl/ *v.* (**-bles, -bled, -bling**) **a.** to bring or gather together into a group or whole. **b.** to fit or join together the parts of. [ME *assemblen* < OFr. *assembler* < VLat. **assimulare*: Lat. *ad-*, to + Lat. *simul*, together.]

as•sem•bly /ə sĕm′ blē/ *n.* (**-blies** *pl.*) a group of persons gathered together for a common purpose.

as•sert /ə sûrt′/ *v.* **a.** to state or express positively; affirm. **b.** to defend or maintain. **c. assert oneself.** to express oneself forcefully or boldly. [Lat. *asserere*, assert-: *ad-*, to + *serere*, to join.]

as•sess /ə sĕs′/ *v.* to evaluate; appraise. [ME *assessen* < OFr. *assesser* < Lat. *assidere*, to sit by (as an assistant judge): *ad-*, near to + *sedere*, to sit.]

as•set /ăs′ ĕt′/ *n.* a useful or valuable quality or thing. [< OFr. *asez*, enough < VLat. **ad satis*, to sufficiency: Lat. *ad-*, to + *satis*, enough.]

as•so•ci•a•tion /ə sō′ sē ā′ shən, -shē-/ *n.* **a.** an organized body of people who have some interest, activity, or purpose in common; society; league. **b.** a mental connection or relation between thoughts, feelings, ideas, or sensations.

as•so•ci•a•tive /ə sō′ shē ā′ tĭv, -sē-, -shə tĭv/ *adj. Math.* independent of the grouping of elements. Used of mathematical operations: *If $a + (b + c) = (a + b) + c$, the operation indicated by + is associative.*

as•sort•ment /ə sôrt′ mənt/ *n.* a collection of various things; variety. [OFr. *assorter*: *a-*, to (< Lat. *ad-*) + *sorte*, kind < Lat. *sors*, chance, lot.]

Pronunciation Key

ă	pat	ŏ	pot	th	**th**in
ā	pay	ō	toe	*th*	**th**is
âr	care	ô	paw, for	hw	**wh**ich
ä	father	oi	n**oi**se	zh	vi**si**on
ĕ	pet	ou	**ou**t	ə	**a**bout,
ē	be	ŏŏ	t**oo**k		it**e**m,
ĭ	pit	ōō	b**oo**t		penc**i**l,
ī	pie	ŭ	c**u**t		gall**o**p,
îr	pier	ûr	**ur**ge		circ**u**s

as•sump•tion /ə sŭmp′ shən/ *n.* a statement accepted or supposed true without proof or demonstration.

as•sur•ance /ə shŏŏr′ əns/ *n.* **a.** a statement or indication that inspires confidence; guarantee. **b.1.** freedom from doubt; certainty. **b.2.** self-confidence. [ME *assuren* < OFr. *assurer* < Med. Lat. *assecurare*, to make sure: Lat. *ad-*, to + *securus*, secure.]

as•ter•isk /ăs′ tə rĭsk′/ *n.* a star-shaped figure (*) used in printing to indicate an omission or a reference to a footnote.

-ate¹ a suffix that forms adjectives: *affectionate.*

-ate² a suffix that forms verbs: *pollinate.*

ath•let•ic /ăth lĕt′ ĭk/ *adj.* **a.** of or for athletics or athletes. **b.** physically strong; muscular.

-ation a suffix that forms nouns from verbs: *civilization.*

at•mos•phere /ăt′ mə sfîr′/ *n.* **a.** the gaseous mass or envelope surrounding a celestial body, especially that surrounding the earth, and retained by the body's gravitational field. **b.** environment or surroundings regarded as having a psychological, physical, or other influence. **c.** the predominant tone or mood of a work of art.

atmosphere

at•tain /ə tān′/ *v.* to gain, reach, or accomplish by mental or physical effort. [ME *atteignen* < OFr. *ataindre*, to reach to < Lat. *attingere*: *ad-*, to + *tangere*, to touch.]

at•tempt[1] /ə tĕmpt′/ *v.* to try to do, make, or achieve. [ME *attempten* < OFr. *attempter* < Lat. *attemptare: ad-,* to + *temptare,* to test.]

at•tempt[2] /ə tĕmpt′/ *n.* **a.** an effort or try. **b.** an attack; assault: *an attempt on one's life.*

at•ten•tive /ə tĕn′ tĭv/ *adj.* **a.** paying attention; observant. **b.** mindful of the well-being of others; considerate. [ME *attenden* < OFr. *atendre* < Lat. *attendere,* to heed: *ad-,* to + *tendere,* to stretch.]

at•tire[1] /ə tīr′/ *v.* (**-tires, -tired, -tir•ing**) to dress or clothe, especially in elaborate or splendid garments. [ME *attiren* < OFr. *atirier,* to put in order: *a-* to (< Lat. *ad-*) + *tire,* order, rank.]

at•tire[2] /ə tīr′/ *n.* clothing; array.

at•tract /ə trăkt′/ *v.* **a.** to cause to draw near. **b.** to evoke by arousing interest or admiration; allure. [ME *attracten* < Lat. *attrahere: ad-,* to + *trahere,* to draw.]

at•trac•tive /ə trăk′ tĭv/ *adj.* **a.** having the power to attract. **b.** pleasing to the eye or mind; charming.

au•to•bi•og•ra•phy /ô′ tō bī ŏg′ rə fē, -bē ŏg′ rə fē/ *n.* (**-phies** *pl.*) (**au•to•bi•og•ra• pher** *n.*) (**au•to•bi•o•graph•ic, au•to•bi•o• graph•i•cal** *adj.*) the biography of a person written by that person.

aux•il•ia•ry[1] /ôg zĭl′ yə rē, -zĭl′ ə rē/ *adj.* **a.** giving assistance or support; helping. **b.** held in or used as a reserve: *auxiliary troops.*

aux•il•ia•ry[2] /ôg zĭl′ yə rē, -zĭl′ ə rē/ *n.* (**-ries** *pl.*) an individual or group that assists or functions in an auxiliary capacity. [Lat. *auxiliar- ius* < *auxilium,* help.]

av•o•ca•do /ăv′ ə kä′ dō, ä′ və-/ *n.* (**-dos** *pl.*) **a.** a tropical American tree, cultivated for its edible fruit. **b.** the oval or pear-shaped fruit of the avocado, having leathery green or blackish skin, a large seed, and bland, greenish-yellow pulp. [Mex. Sp. *aguacate* < Nahuatl *ahuactl.*]

avocado

a•ware /ə wâr′/ *adj.* (**a•ware•ness** *n.*) having knowledge or cognizance.

ax•is /ăk′ sĭs/ *n.* (**ax•es** *pl.*) **a.** a straight line about which a body or geometrical object rotates or may be imagined to rotate. **b.** *Math.* a reference line from which distances or angles are measured in a coordinate system.

back•drop /băk′ drŏp′/ *n.* **a.** a painted curtain hung at the back of a stage set. **b.** the setting, as of a historical event; background.

bac•te•ri•a /băk tîr′ ē ə/ *n.* plural of *bacterium.*

bac•te•ri•um /băk tîr′ ē əm/ *n.* (**-ri•a** *pl.*) a very small one-celled organism often considered to be a plant, although it lacks green coloring.

bam•boo /băm bōō′/ *n.* (**-boos** *pl.*) **a.** any of various mostly tropical grasses having hard-walled stems with ringed joints. **b.** the hollow woody stems of the bamboo, used in a variety of constructions, crafts, and manufactures.

bar•gain[1] /bär′ gĭn/ *n.* **a.** an agreement or con-tract, especially one involving the purchase and sale of goods or services; the terms or condi-tions of such an agreement. **b.** something offered or acquired at a price advantageous to the buyer.

bar•gain[2] /bär′ gĭn/ *v.* **a.** to negotiate the terms of a sale, exchange, or other agreement. **b.** to arrive at an agreement.

ba•sis /bā′ sĭs/ *n.* (**-ses** /-sēz/ *pl.*) **a.** a supporting element; foundation. **b.** the chief component of something. **c.** the essential principle. [Latin < Greek]

beau•ti•fy /byōō′ tə fī/ *v.* (**-fies, -fied, -fy•ing**) to make or become beautiful.

be•hav•ior /bĭ hāv′ yər/ *n.* **a.** the manner in which one behaves. **b.** the actions or reactions of persons or things under specified circumstances.

be•lieve /bĭ lēv′/ *v.* (**-lieves, -lieved, -liev•ing**) (**be•liev•a•ble** *adj.*) **a.** to accept as true or real. **b.** to expect or suppose; think: *I believe he will come shortly.*

bi- a prefix meaning two or twice: *bimonthly, bisect.*

bi•an•nu•al /bī ăn′ yōō əl/ *adj.* (**bi•an•nu•al•ly** *adv.*) happening twice each year; semiannual.

bi•en•ni•al[1] /bī ĕn′ ē əl/ *adj.* (**bi•en•ni•al•ly** *adv.*) **a.** lasting or living for two years. **b.** happening every second year.

bi•en•ni•al[2] /bī ĕn′ ē əl/ *n.* **a.** an event that occurs once every two years. **b.** a plant that normally requires two years to reach maturity, producing leaves in the first year, blooming and producing fruit in the second year, and then dying.

bin•oc•u•lar /bə nŏk′ yə lər, bī-/ *n.* (often **binoculars**) an optical device, especially a pair of field glasses, designed for use by both eyes at once.

binocular

bi•o•de•grad•a•ble /bī′ō dĭ grā′ də bəl/ *adj.* capable of being decomposed by natural biological processes: *a biodegradable detergent.*

bi•sec•tor /bī′ sĕk′ tər, bī sĕk′-/ *n.* something that bisects, especially a straight line that bisects an angle.

bleach•er /blē′ chər/ *n.* (often **bleachers**) an often unroofed outdoor grandstand for seating spectators.

bouil•lon /bōōl′ yŏn′, boo′ yŏn′, bōōl′-, -yən/ *n.* a clear, thin broth made typically by simmering beef or chicken in water with seasonings.

bound•a•ry /boun′ də rē, -drē/ *n.* (**-ries** *pl.*) something that indicates a border or limit.

bou•quet /bō kā′, bōō -/ *n.* a cluster of flowers; nosegay.

bou•tique /bōō tēk′/ *n.* a small retail shop that specializes in gifts, fashionable clothes, and accessories. [Fr. < OProv. *botica* < Lat. *apotheca*, storehouse.]

brack•et[1] /brăk′ ĭt/ *n.* **a.** a simple rigid structure in the shape of an L, one arm of which is fixed to a vertical surface, the other projecting horizontally to support a shelf or other weight. **b.** either of a pair of symbols, [ ], used to enclose written or printed material or to indicate a mathematical expression considered in some sense a single quantity.

Pronunciation Key

ă	pat	ŏ	pot	th	**th**in
ā	pay	ō	toe	*th*	**th**is
âr	care	ô	paw, for	hw	**wh**ich
ä	father	oi	noise	zh	vi**s**ion
ĕ	pet	ou	out	ə	**a**bout,
ē	be	ŏŏ	took		it**e**m,
ĭ	pit	ōō	boot		penc**i**l,
ī	pie	ŭ	cut		gall**o**p,
îr	pier	ûr	**ur**ge		circ**u**s

brack•et[2] /brăk′ ĭt/ *v.* **a.** to support with a bracket or brackets. **b.** to place within or as if within brackets. **c.** to classify or group together.

bra•va•do /brə vä′ dō/ *n.* (**-does** or **-dos** *pl.*) a pretense of courage; false bravery. [Sp. *bravada* < *bravo*, brave.]

breathe /brē*th*/ *v.* **a.** to inhale and exhale air. **b.** to be alive; live. **c.** to pause to rest or regain breath: *Give me a moment to breathe.*

brief /brēf/ *adj.* (**brief•ly** *adv.*) **a.** short in time or duration. **b.** short in length or extent.

brief•case /brēf′ kās′/ *n.* a portable rectangular case used for carrying books or papers.

broth•er•in•law /brŭ*th*′ ər ĭn lô′/ *n.* (**broth•ers•in•law** *pl.*) **a.** the brother of one's husband or wife. **b.** the husband of one's sister. **c.** the husband of the sister of one's husband or wife.

by-line also **by•line** /bī′ līn′/ *n.* a line at the head of a newspaper or magazine article with the author's name.

ca•ban•a also **ca•ba•ña** /kə băn′ ə, -băn′ yə/ *n.* a shelter on a beach or at a swimming pool used as a bathhouse. [Sp. *cabaña* < LLat. *capanna*, hut.]

caf•e•te•ri•a /kăf ĭ tîr′ ē ə/ *n.* a restaurant in which the customers are served at a counter and carry their meals on trays to tables. [Sp. *cafeteria*, coffee shop < *café*, coffee < Turk. *kahve*.]

Spelling Dictionary

Spelling Dictionary

cal•i•co /kăl′ ĭ kō′/ *n.* (**-coes** or **-cos** *pl.*) a coarse cloth, usually printed with bright designs. [after *Calicut* (Kozhikode), India.]

ca•mel•lia /kə mēl′ yə/ *n.* **a.** any of several shrubs or trees of the genus Camellia, native to Asia, having shiny evergreen leaves and showy, variously colored flowers. **b.** the flower of a camellia. [NLat. *Camellia*, genus name, after Georg Josef *Kamel* (1661–1706).]

cam•ou•flage¹ /kăm′ ə fläzh′, -fläj′/ *n.* the method or result of concealing personnel or material from an enemy by making them appear to be part of the natural surroundings. [Fr. < *camoufler*, to disguise < Ital. *camuffare*.]

cam•ou•flage² /kăm′ ə fläzh′, -fläj′/ *v.* (**-flag•es**, **-flaged**, **-flag•ing**) to conceal by or use camouflage.

cam•pus /kăm′ pəs/ *n.* (**-pus•es** *pl.*) the grounds of a school, college, or university.

ca•noe¹ /kə noo′/ *n.* a light, slender boat with pointed ends propelled by paddles.

ca•noe² /kə noo′ / *v.* (**-noes**, **-noed**, **-noe•ing**) (**ca•noe•ist** *n.*) **a.** to travel in a canoe. **b.** to propel a canoe. [Obs. *canoa* < Sp. of Cariban orig.]

can•ta•loupe /kăn′ tl ōp′/ *n.* **a.** a variety of melon, having fruit with a ribbed, rough rind and aromatic orange flesh. **b.** the fruit of a cantaloupe. [Fr. *cantaloup* < Ital. *cantalupo* < *Cantalupo*, a former papal villa near Rome.]

can•yon /kăn′ yən/ *n.* a narrow chasm with steep cliff walls, formed by running water; gorge. [Sp. *cañon*, aug. of *caña*, tube < Lat. *canna*, reed < Gk. *kanna*.]

canyon

cap•tion¹ /kăp′ shən/ *n.* a title, short explanation, or description accompanying an illustration or photograph.

cap•tion² /kăp′ shən/ *v.* to furnish a caption for.

car•bu•re•tor /kär′ bə rā′tər/ *n.* a device used in gasoline engines to produce an efficient explosive vapor of fuel and air.

car•di•gan /kär′ dĭ gən/ *n.* a sweater or knitted jacket opening down the front. [after the Seventh Earl of *Cardigan*; James Thomas Brudenell (1797–1868).]

car•di•nal num•ber /kär′ dn əl nŭm′ bər/ *n.* a number, such as 3 or 11 or 412, used to indicate quanitity but not order.

car•ou•sel /kăr′ ə sĕl′, -zĕl′/ *n.* a merry-go-round [Fr. *carrousel* < Ital. *carosello*, a kind of tournament.]

car•tog•ra•phy /kär tŏg′ rə fē/ *n.* the art or technique of making maps or charts.

cash•mere /kăzh′ mîr′, kăsh′/ *n.* a soft fabric made of wool from the Cashmere goat or of similar fibers. [after *Kashmir*, a region in India.]

cel•e•brate /sĕl′ ə brāt/ *v.* (**-brates**, **-brat•ed**, **-brat•ing**) (**cel•e•bra•tion** *n.*) **a.** to observe (a day or event) with ceremonies of respect, festivity, or rejoicing: *celebrated their anniversary.* **b.** to praise publicly; honor: *a sonnet that celebrates love.*

cer•tif•i•cate /sûr′ tĭf′ ĭ kĭt/ *n.* **a.** a document testifying to the factuality or truth of something: *a birth certificate.* **b.** a document certifying that a person may officially practice in certain professions. [ME *certificat* < Med. Lat. *certificatum* < LLat. *certificare*, to certify.]

cer•ti•fy /sûr′ tə fī′/ *v.* (**-fies**, **-fied**, **-fy•ing**) **a.** to confirm formally as true, accurate, or genuine, especially in writing. **b.** to guarantee as meeting a standard. [ME *certifien* < OFr. *certifier* < LLat. *certificare*: Lat. *certus*, certain + Lat. *facere*, to make.]

chal•lenge¹ /chăl′ ənj/ *n.* **a.** a demand for an explanation. **b.** the quality of requiring full use of one's abilities, energy, or resources: *a career that offers a challenge.* [ME *chalenge* < OFr. < *chalanger*, to accuse < Lat. *calumniari*, to accuse falsely < *calumnia*, calumny < *calvi*, to deceive.]

chal•lenge² /chăl′ ənj/ *v.* (**-leng•es**, **-lenged**, **-leng•ing**) **a.** to call to engage in a contest or fight. **b.** to take exception to; dispute: *challenged the statements.* **c.** to summon to action, effort, or use; stimulate: *a problem that challenges the imagination.*

cham•ber /chām′ bər/ *n.* **a.** a room in a house, especially a bedroom. **b.** an enclosed space or compartment; cavity. [ME *chaumbre* < OFr. < LLat. *camera*, chamber < Lat., vault < Gk. *kamara*.]

chap•er•one[1] also **chap•er•on** /shăp ə rōn'/ *n.* **a.** a person, especially an older or married woman, who accompanies a young unmarried woman in public. **b.** an older person who attends and supervises a social gathering for young people. [Fr. < *chaperon,* hood < OFr. < *chape,* covering.]

chap•er•one[2] also **chap•er•on** /shăp ə rōn'/ *v.* (**-ones, -oned, -on•ing**) to act as chaperone to or for.

char•ac•ter•is•tic /kăr′ ək tə rĭs′ tĭk/ *n.* (**char•ac•ter•is•ti•cal•ly** *adv.*) a distinguishing feature or attribute.

Ched•dar also **ched•dar** /chĕd′ ər/ *n.* any of several types of smooth, hard cheese varying in flavor from mild to extra sharp. [after *Cheddar,* England.]

Cheddar

cho•re•o•graph /kôr′ ē ə grăf′/ *v.* (**cho•re•og•ra•pher** *n.*) to specialize in choreography or create the choreography of.

cho•re•og•ra•phy /kôr′ē ŏg′ rə fē, kōr-/ *n.* the art of creating and arranging ballets or dances.

chron•ic /krŏn′ ĭk/ *adj.* **a.** of long duration; continuing; constant. **b.** prolonged; lingering, as certain diseases. **c.** subject to a disease or habit for a long time. [Fr. *chronique* < Lat. *chronicus* < Gk. < *khronos,* time.]

chron•i•cle[1] /krŏn′ ĭ kəl/ *n.* a chronological record of historical events. [ME *cronicle* < Norman Fr., var. of OFr. *cronique* < Lat. *chronica* < Gk. *khronika,* annals < *khronikos,* of time < *khronos,* time.]

chron•i•cle[2] /krŏn′ ĭ kəl/ *v.* (**-cles, -cled, -cling**) to record in or in the form of a chronicle.

chrono- or **chron-** a prefix meaning time: *chronometer.* [< Gk. *khronos,* time.]

chro•nol•o•gy /krə nŏl′ ə jē/ *n.* (**-gies** *pl.*) **a.** the determination of dates and the sequence of events. **b.** the arrangement of events in time. **c.** a chronological list or table.

cinch[1] /sĭnch/ *n.* **a.** a girth for a pack or saddle. **b.** *Slang.* something easy to accomplish. [Sp. *cincha* < Lat. *cingula* < *cingere,* to gird.]

cinch[2] /sĭnch/ *v.* **a.** to put a saddle girth on. **b.** *Slang.* to make certain of: *cinch a victory.*

clar•i•fy /klăr′ ə fī′/ *v.* (**-fies, -fied, -fy•ing**) to make clear or easier to understand. [ME *clarifien* < OFr. *clarifier* < LLat. *clarificare:* Lat. *clarus,* clear + Lat. *facere,* to make.]

clas•sic[1] /klăs′ ĭk/ *adj.* **a.** serving as an outstanding representative of its kind; model. **b.** having lasting significance or recognized worth. **c.** of or pertaining to ancient Greek or Roman literature or art; classical.

clas•sic[2] /klăs′ ĭk/ *n.* an artist, author, or work generally considered to be of the highest rank or excellence.

clas•si•cal /klăs′ ĭ kəl/ *adj.* (**clas•si•cal•ly** *adv.*) **a.** of or pertaining to the culture of ancient Greece and Rome, especially the art, architecture, and literature. **b.** standard and authoritative rather than new or experimental.

class•mate /klăs′ māt′/ *n.* a member of the same academic class.

cli•mate /klī′ mĭt/ *n.* **a.** the meteorological conditions, including temperature, precipitation, and wind, that characteristically prevail in a particular region. **b.** a prevailing condition or atmosphere: *a climate of hope.*

cli•max /klī′ măks′/ *n.* the point of greatest intensity in a series or progression of events; culmination.

co•a•li•tion /kō′ ə lĭsh′ ən/ *n.* an alliance, especially a temporary one, of factions, parties, or nations.

col•lab•o•rate /kə lăb′ ə rāt′/ *v.* (**-rates, -rat•ed, -rat•ing**) to work together, especially in a joint intellectual effort. [LLat. *collaborare, collaborat-:* Lat. *com-,* together + Lat. *laborare,* to work < *labor,* work.]

col•lapse[1] /kə lăps'/ *v.* (**-laps•es, -lapsed, -laps•ing**) **a.** to fall down or inward suddenly; cave in. **b.** to cease to function; break down suddenly in strength or health. **c.** to fold compactly. [Lat. *collabi, collaps-,* to fall together: *com-,* together + *labi,* to fall.]

col•lapse[2] /kə lăps'/ *n.* the act of falling down or inward, as from loss of supports.

col•league /kŏl' ēg'/ *n.* a fellow member of a profession, staff, or academic faculty; associate. [OFr. *collegue* < Lat. *collega: com-,* together + *legare,* to depute.]

col•lide /kə līd'/ *v.* (**-lides, -lid•ed, -lid•ing**) **a.** to come together with violent, direct impact. **b.** to meet in opposition; clash; conflict. [Lat. *collidere: com-,* together + *laedere,* to strike.]

col•lin•e•ar /kə lĭn' ē ər, kō-/ *adj.* lying on the same line.

col•li•sion /kə lĭzh' ən/ *n.* the act or process of colliding; crash. [ME < Lat. *collisio* < *collidere,* to strike: *com-,* together + *laedere,* to strike.]

com- a prefix meaning together, with, joint, or jointly: *compress.* Before **l** or **r, com-** becomes **col-** or **cor-**. Before vowels, **h,** or **gn,** it is reduced to **co-**. Before all other consonants except **p, b,** or **m,** it becomes **con-**. [ME < OFr. < Lat.]

com•bi•na•tion /kŏm' bə nā' shən/ *n.* **a.** the act of combining or state of being combined. **b.** something resulting from combining two or more things.

com•bine /kəm bīn'/ *v.* (**-bines, -bined, -bin•ing**) **a.** to bring into a state of unity. **b.** to join (two or more substances) to make a single substance; mix.

com•bus•tion /kəm bŭs' chən/ *n.* **a.** the process of burning. **b.** *Chem.* a chemical change, especially oxidation, accompanied by the production of heat and light.

com•fort[1] /kŭm' fərt/ *v.* **a.** to soothe in time of grief or fear; console. **b.** to ease physically; relieve.

com•fort[2] /kŭm' fərt/ *n.* **a.** a condition of ease or well-being. **b.** solace in time of grief or fear.

com•mem•o•rate /kə měm' ə rāt'/ *v.* (**-rates, -rat•ed, -rat•ing**) **a.** to honor the memory of with a ceremony. **b.** to serve as a memorial to. [Lat. *commemorare, commemorat-,* to remind: *com-* (intensive) + *memorare,* to remind *memor,* mindful.]

com•mence /kə měns'/ *v.* (**-menc•es, -menced, -menc•ing**) **a.** to begin; start. **b.** to come into existence; have a beginning. [ME *commencen* < OFr. *comencier* < VLat. **cominitiare:* Lat. *com-* (intensive) + LLat. *initiare,* to begin < Lat. *initium,* beginning.]

com•mence•ment /kə měns' mənt/ *n.* **a.** a beginning; start. **b.** a ceremony at which academic degrees or diplomas are conferred.

commencement

com•mend /kə měnd'/ *v.* **a.** to represent as worthy, qualified, or desirable; recommend. **b.** to express approval of; praise. [ME *commenden* < Lat. *commendare: com-* (intensive) + *mandare,* to entrust.]

com•men•tar•y /kŏm' ən tĕr' ē/ *n.* (**-ies** *pl.*) **a.** a series of explanations or interpretations. **b.** something that explains or illustrates.

com•mer•cial[1] /kə mûr' shəl/ *adj.* **a.** of or pertaining to commerce. **b.** having profit as a chief aim. **c.** sponsored by an advertiser or supported by advertising.

com•mer•cial[2] /kə mûr' shəl/ *n.* an advertisement on radio or television.

com•mod•i•ty /kə mŏd' ĭ tē/ *n.* (**-ties** *pl.*) **a.** something that is useful or can be turned to commercial or other advantage. **b.** an article of trade or commerce, especially an agricultural or mining product, that can be transported. [ME *commodite* < OFr., convenience < Lat. *commoditas* < *commodus,* convenient: *com-,* with + *modus,* measure.]

com•mu•ni•cate /kə myōō' nĭ kāt'/ *v.* (**-cates, -cat•ed, -cat•ing**) **a.** to have an interchange, as of ideas. **b.** to express oneself in such a way that one is readily and clearly understood. [Lat. *communicare, communicat-* < *communis,* common.]

com•mu•ni•ca•tion /kə myōō′ nĭ kā′ shən/ *n.* **a.** the act of communicating; transmission. **b.** the exchange of thoughts, messages, or information, as by speech, signals, or writing. **c.** something communicated; message.

com•mu•ta•tive /kŏm′ yə tā′ tĭv, kə myōō′ tə tĭv/ *adj.* independent of order; used of a logical or mathematical operation that combines objects two at a time.

com•mute[1] /kə myōōt′/ *v.* (**-mutes, -mut•ed, -mut•ing**) **a.** to substitute. **b.** to make substitution; exchange. **c.** to travel as a commuter. [ME *commuten,* to change < Lat. *commutare: com-,* together + *mutare,* to change.]

com•mute[2] /kə myōōt′/ *n. Informal.* the trip made by a commuter: *a 22-mile commute.*

com•mut•er /kə myōō′ tər/ *n.* a person who travels regularly from one place to another, as from suburb to city and back.

com•pa•ny /kŭm′ pə nē/ *n.* (**-nies** *pl.*) **a.** a group; gathering: *the whole company of Nobel Prize winners.* **b.** a business enterprise; firm.

com•pa•ra•ble /kŏm′ pər ə bəl/ *adj.* **a.** capable of being compared. **b.** similar or equivalent.

com•pass /kŭm′ pəs, kŏm′-/ *n.* **a.** a device used to determine geographical direction, usually consisting of a magnetic needle or needles horizontally mounted or suspended and free to pivot until aligned with the magnetic field of the earth. **b.** often **compasses.** a V-shaped device for drawing circles or circular arcs, consisting of a pair of rigid, end-hinged, and continuously separable arms, one of which is equipped with a pen or pencil and the other with a sharp point providing a central anchor or pivot about which the drawing arm is turned.

compass

com•pat•i•ble /kəm păt′ ə bəl/ *adj.* capable of living or performing in harmonious, agreeable, or congenial combination with another or others. [ME < Med. Lat. *compatibilis* < LLat. *compati,* to sympathize: Lat. *com-,* with + *pati,* to suffer.]

Pronunciation Key

ă	pat	ŏ	pot	th	**th**in
ā	pay	ō	toe	*th*	**th**is
âr	care	ô	paw, for	hw	**wh**ich
ä	father	oi	noise	zh	vision
ĕ	pet	ou	out	ə	about,
ē	be	ŏŏ	took		item,
ĭ	pit	ōō	boot		pencil,
ī	pie	ŭ	cut		gallop,
îr	pier	ûr	urge		circus

com•pel /kəm pĕl′/ *v.* (**-pels, -pelled, -pel•ling**) to force, drive, or constrain. [ME *compellen* < Lat. *compellere: com-,* together + *pellere,* to drive.]

com•pel•ling /kəm pĕl′ ĭng/ *adj.* pressing; persuasive; needing attention.

com•pete /kəm pēt′/ *v.* to strive or contend with another or others, as for profit or a prize; vie.

com•pe•ti•tion /kŏm′ pĭ tĭsh′ ən/ *n.* **a.** the act of competing, as for profit or a prize; rivalry. **b.** a contest or similar test of skill or ability.

com•pet•i•tive /kəm pĕt′ ĭ tĭv/ *adj.* **a.** of, involving, or determined by competition. **b.** liking or inclined to compete.

com•pile /kəm pīl′/ *v.* (**-piles, -piled, -pil•ing**) **a.** to put together or compose from materials gathered from several sources: *compile an encyclopedia.* **b.** to convert to machine language.

com•ple•ment[1] /kŏm′ plə mənt/ *n.* **a.** something that completes, makes up a whole, or brings to perfection. **b.** the quantity or number needed to make up a whole: *shelves with a full complement of books.* **c.** either of two parts that complete the whole or mutually complete each other. [ME < Lat. *complementum* < *complere,* to fill out: *com-*(intensive) + *plere,* to fill.]

com•ple•ment[2] /kŏm′ plə mĕnt′/ *v.* to add or serve as a complement to.

com•plex /kəm plĕks′, kŏm′ plĕks′/ *adj.* **a.** consisting of interconnected or interwoven parts; composite. **b.** involved or intricate, as in structure; complicated. **c.** pertaining to or designating a sentence consisting of an independent clause and one or more dependent clauses.

Spelling Dictionary

com•pli•cate /kŏm′ plĭ kāt′/ *v.* (**-cates, -cat•ed, -cat•ing**) **a.** to make or become complex, intricate, or perplexing. **b.** to twist or become twisted together. [Lat. *complicare, complicat-,* to fold up: *com-,* together + *plicare,* to fold.]

com•pli•ca•tion /kŏm′ plĭ **kā′** shən/ *n.* **a.** the act of complicating. **b.** a confused or intricate relationship of parts. **c.** a factor, condition, or element that complicates.

com•pli•ment[1] /kŏm′ plə mənt/ *n.* **a.** an expression of praise, admiration, or congratulation. **b.** a formal act of courtesy, or respect.

com•pli•ment[2] /kŏm′ plə mənt/ *v.* **a.** to pay a compliment to. **b.** to show fondness, regard, or respect for by giving a gift or performing a favor.

com•pu•ta•tion /kŏm′ pyŏŏ **tā′** shən/ *n.* (**com•pu•ta•tion•al** *adj.*) the act or process of computing.

com•pute /kəm pyŏŏt′/ *v.* to determine an amount or number.

con•cen•trate /kŏn′ sən trāt′/ *v.* (**-trates, -trat•ed, -trat•ing**) **a.** to direct or draw toward a common center; focus. **b.** to converge toward or meet in a common center. **c.** to direct one's thoughts or attention.

con•cen•tra•tion /kŏn′ sən **trā′** shən/ *n.* the act or process of concentrating, especially close, undivided attention.

con•cen•tric /kən **sĕn′** trĭk/ *adj.* having a common center.

con•crete /kŏn **krēt′,** kŏn′ krēt′/ *adj.* (**con•crete•ly** *adv.*) **a.** of or relating to an actual, specific thing or instance; particular. **b.** designating a thing or group of things as opposed to an obstraction.

con•dense /kən **dĕns′**/ *v.* (**-dens•es, -densed, -dens•ing**) **a.** to reduce the volume of; compress. **b.** to shorten or make more concise; abridge. **c.** to become more compact.

con•fer /kən **fûr′**/ *v.* (**-fers, -ferred, -fer•ring**) **a.** to bestow (an honor, for example): *conferred a medal on the hero.* **b.** to hold a conference; consult together. [Lat. *conferre: com-,* together + *ferre,* to bring.]

con•fer•ence /kŏn′ fər əns, -frəns/ *n.* **a.** a meeting for consultation or discussion. **b.** an exchange of views. **c.** a meeting of committees to settle differences between two legislative bodies. [OFr. < Med. Lat. *confernetia* < Lat. *conferrens,* pr.part. of *conferre,* to bring together: *com-,* together + *ferre,* to bring.]

conference

con•fi•den•tial /kŏn′ fĭ **dĕn′** shəl/ *adj.* done or communicated in confidence; secret.

con•fig•u•ra•tion /kən fĭg′ yə **rā′** shən/ *n.* **a.** the arrangement of the parts or elements of something. **b.** the form of a figure as determined by the arrangement of its parts; outline; contour.

con•flict[1] /kŏn′ flĭkt′/ *n.* a state of disagreement and disharmony; clash.

con•flict[2] /kən **flĭkt′**/ *v.* to be in or come into opposition; differ.

con•glom•er•ate[1] /kən **glŏm′** ə rāt′/ *v.* (**-ates, -at•ed, -at•ing**) to form or cause to form into an adhering or rounded mass.

con•glom•er•ate[2] /kən **glŏm′** ər ĭt/ *n. Geol.* a rock consisting of pebbles and gravel embedded in a loosely cemented material.

con•glom•er•ate[3] /kən **glŏm′** ər ĭt/ *adj.* **a.** gathered into a mass; clustered. **b.** *Geol.* made up of loosely cemented heterogeneous material.

con•quer /kŏng′ kər/ *v.* to be victorious; win.

con•science /kŏn′ shəns/ *n.* the faculty of recognizing the distinction between right and wrong in regard to one's conduct coupled with a sense that one should act accordingly. **—idiom. in (all) conscience.** in all truth or fairness.

con•sci•en•tious /kŏn′ shē **ĕn′** shəs/ *adj.* thorough and painstaking; careful: *a conscientious worker.*

con•scious /kŏn′ shəs/ *adj.* having an awareness of one's own existence, sensations, and thoughts and of one's environment.

con•sec•u•tive /kən **sĕk′** yə tĭv/ *adj.* **a.** following successively without interruption. **b.** marked by logical sequence.

con•se•quent•ly /kŏn′ sĭ kwĕnt′ lē/ *adv.* as a result; therefore.

con•sid•er•a•ble /kən sĭd′ ər ə bəl/ *adj.* (**con•sid•er•a•bly** *adv.*) **a.** large in amount, extent, or degree. **b.** worthy of consideration; important; significant.

con•sist /kən sĭst′/ *v.* to be made up or composed. [Lat. *consistere,* to stand still: *com-* (intensive) + *sistere,* to cause to stand.]

con•sis•tent /kən sĭs′ tənt/ *adj.* (**con•sis• tent•ly** *adv.*) in agreement; compatible. [Lat. *consistens, consistent-,* pr.part. of *consistere,* to stand still: *com-* (intensive) + *sistere,* to cause to stand.]

con•strict /kən strĭkt′/ *v.* **a.** to make smaller or narrower, as by shrinking or contracting. **b.** to squeeze or compress by or as if by narrowing or tightening. [Lat. *constringere, constrict-,* to compress: *com-,* together + *stringere,* to bind.]

con•struct /kən strŭkt′/ *v.* **a.** to form by assembling parts; build. **b.** to create by systematically arranging ideas or expressions.

con•text /kŏn′ tĕkst′/ *n.* the part of a written or spoken statement in which a word or passage at issue occurs and that often specifies its meaning.

con•tour¹ /kŏn′ tŏŏr′/ *n.* **a.** the outline of a figure, body, or mass. **b.** Often **contours.** a surface, especially of a curving form.

contour

con•tour² /kŏn′ tŏŏr′/ *adj.* following the contour of the land of uneven terrain to limit erosion of topsoil: *contour plowing.*

con•tro•ver•sy /kŏn′ trə vûr′ sē/ *n.* (**-sies** *pl.*) a dispute, especially a lengthy and public one, between sides holding opposing views. [ME *controversie* < Lat. *controversia* < *controversus,* disputed < *contro-,* against (var. of *contra-*) + *versus,* p.part. of *vertere,* to turn.]

con•ver•sa•tion /kŏn′ vər sā′ shən/ *n.* a spoken exchange of thoughts, opinions, and feelings; talk.

con•verse¹ /kən vûrs′/ *v.* (**-vers•es, -versed, -vers•ing**) to engage in spoken exchange of thoughts and feelings; talk. [ME *conversen,* to associate with < OFr. *converser* < Lat. *conversari: com-,* with + *versari,* to occupy oneself < *vertere,* to depend on: *com-* (intensive) + *vertere* to turn.]

con•verse² /kŏn′ vûrs′/ *n.* spoken interchange of thoughts and feelings; conversation.

con•verse³ /kən vûrs′, kŏn′ vûrs′/ *adj.* reversed, as in position, order, or action; contrary. [Lat. *conversus,* p.part. of *convertere,* to turn around: *com-* (intensive) + *vertere,* to turn.]

con•vince /kən vĭns′/ *v.* (**-vinc•es, -vinced, -vinc•ing**) to bring to belief by argument and evidence; cause to believe with certainty.

co•op•er•ate /kō ŏp′ ə rāt′/ *v.* (**-ates, -at•ed, -at•ing**) to work together toward a common end.

co•op•er•a•tion /kō ŏp′ ə rā′ shən/ *n.* an act of cooperating. [Lat. *co(m)-,* same + *operari,* to work < *opus,* work.]

co•or•di•nate¹ /kō ôr′ dn āt′, -ĭt/ *n.* **a.** one that is equal in importance, rank, or degree. **b.** *Math.* one of a set of numbers that determines the location of a point in a space of a given dimension.

co•or•di•nate² /kō ôr′ dn āt′/ *v.* (**-nates, -nat•ed, -nat•ing**) **a.** to place in the same rank. **b.** to work well together; to harmonize.

co•or•di•na•tion /kō ôr′ dn ā′ shən/ *n.* **a.** the state of being coordinate; harmonious interaction. **b.** *Physiol.* the coordinated functioning of muscles in the execution of a complex task. [Fr. or < LLat. *coordinatio: co(m)-,* same + *ordinatio,* arrangement < *ordinare,* to arrange in order < *ordo,* order.]

cop•y[1] /kŏp′ ē/ *n.* (**-ies** *pl.*) **a.** an imitation or reproduction of something original; duplicate. **b.** one specimen or example of a printed text or picture. **c.** a manuscript or other material to be set in type.

cop•y[2] /kŏp′ ē/ *v.* (**-ies, -ied, -y•ing**) **a.** to make a copy of. **b.** to follow as a model or pattern; imitate.

cop•y•right /kŏp′ ē rīt′/ *n.* the legal right granted to an author, composer, playwright, publisher, or distributor, to exclusive publication, production, sale, or distribution of a literary, musical, dramatic, or artistic work.

cor•rec•tion /kə rĕk′ shən/ *n.* **a.** the act or process of correcting. **b.** something offered or substituted for a mistake or fault.

cor•re•late /kôr′ ə lāt′, kŏr′-/ *v.* (**-lates, -lat•ed, -lat•ing**) **a.** to put or bring into complementary, parallel, or reciprocal relation. **b.** to establish or demonstrate as having a relationship. [CORRELATION: Med. Lat. *correlatio:* Lat. *com-,* together + *relatio,* relation < *referre,* to carry back.]

cor•re•spond /kôr′ ĭ spŏnd′, kŏr′-/ *v.* **a.** to be similar, parallel, equivalent, or equal in character, quantity, origin, structure, or function. **b.** to communicate by letter, usually over a period of time. [OFr. *correspondre* < Med. Lat. *correspondere:* Lat. *com-,* together + *respondere,* to respond.]

cor•re•spon•dence /kôr′ ĭ spŏn′ dəns, kŏr′-/ *n.* **a.** similarity. **b.1.** communication by the exchange of letters. **b.2.** the letters written or received.

cor•rode /kə rōd′/ *v.* (**-rodes, -rod•ed, -rod•ing**) **a.** to dissolve or wear away gradually, especially by chemical action. **b.** to be eaten or worn away; become corroded. [ME *corroden* < Lat. *corrodere,* to gnaw away: *com-,* (intensive) + *rodere,* to gnaw.]

cor•rupt /kə rŭpt′/ *adj.* **a.** lacking in moral restraint. **b.** dishonest.

cor•rup•tion /kə rŭp′ shən/ *n.* **a.** the act or result of corrupting. **b.** the state of being corrupt. [ME < Lat. *corruptus,* p.part. of *corrumpere,* to destroy: *com-,* together + *rumpere,* to break.]

cor•sage /kôr säzh′, -säj′/ *n.* a small bouquet of flowers worn by a woman at the shoulder or waist or on the wrist. [ME, torso < OFr. < *cors,* body < Lat. *corpus.*]

corsage

coun•ter•sign[1] /koun′ tər sīn′/ *v.* to sign (a previously signed document), as for authentication.

coun•ter•sign[2] /koun′ tər sīn′/ *n.* a second or confirming signature, as on a previously signed document.

cou•pon /kōō′ pŏn, kyōō′-/ *n.* **a.** a negotiable certificate attached to a bond that represents a sum of interest due. **b.** a detachable part, as of a ticket or advertisement, that entitles the bearer to certain benefits, such as a cash refund or a gift. [Fr. < OFr. *colpon,* piece cut off < *colper,* to cut < *coup,* blow.]

cour•te•sy /kûr′ tĭ sē/ *n.*(**-sies** *pl.*) **a.** polite behavior; gracious manner or manners. **b.** a polite gesture or remark.

cov•er•age /kŭv′ ər ĭj/ *n.* the extent or degree to which something is observed, analyzed, and reported.

crank•shaft /krăngk′ shăft′/ *n.* a shaft that turns or is turned by a crank.

crea•ture /krē′ chər/ *n.* **a.** something created. **b.** a living being, especially an animal. **c.** a human being.

cri•sis /krī′ sĭs/ *n.* (**-ses** /-sēz/ *pl.*) **a.** a crucial or decisive point or situation; turning point. **b.** the point in a story or drama at which hostile forces are in the most tense state of opposition.

cru•cial /krōō′ shəl/ *adj.* of supreme importance; critical: *a crucial election.*

crys•tal•line /krĭs′ tə lĭn, -līn′/ *adj.* **a.** pertaining to or made of crystal. **b.** resembling crystal; transparent.

cul•prit /kŭl′ prĭt/ *n.* **a.** one charged with an offense or crime. **b.** one guilty of a fault or crime.

cul•tur•al /kŭl′ chər əl/ *adj.* of or relating to culture.

cul•ture /kŭl′ chər/ *n.* **a.** the behavior patterns, arts, beliefs, and institutions characteristic of a community or population. **b.** intellectual and artistic activity, and the works produced by it.

cup•ful /kŭp' fŏol'/ *n.* (**-fuls** *pl.*) **a.** the amount a cup will hold. **b.** a measure of capacity equal to 1/2 pint, 8 ounces, or 16 tablespoons.

cu•ri•os•i•ty /kyŏor'ē ŏs' ĭ tē/ *n.* (**-ties** *pl.*) **a.** a desire to know or learn. **b.** a desire to know about people or things that do not concern one; nosiness. **c.** something that arouses interest, as by being novel or extraordinary. **d.** a strange or odd aspect.

cur•rant /kûr' ənt, kŭr'-/ *n.* **a.** the small, sour fruit of any of the currant plants, used chiefly for making jelly. **b.** a small, dried seedless grape of the Mediterranean region, used in cooking. [ME (*raysons of*) *coraunte,* (raisins of) Corinth.]

cyl•in•der /sĭl' ən dər/ *n.* **a.** *Math.* a surface generated by a straight line moving parallel to a fixed straight line and intersecting a plane curve. **b.** a cylindrical container or object.

dam•ask /dăm' əsk/ *n.* **a.** a rich patterned fabric of cotton, linen, silk, or wool. **b.** a fine, twilled table linen. [ME < Med. Lat. (*pannus de*) *damasco,* (cloth of) *Damascus.*]

date•line /dāt' līn'/ *n.* a phrase at the beginning of a newspaper or magazine article that gives the date and place of its origin.

de•com•pose /dē'kəm pōz'/ *v.* (**-pos•es, -posed, -pos•ing**) **a.** to break down into component parts; disintegrate. **b.** to decay; putrefy.

dec•o•rate /dĕk' ə rāt'/ *v.* (**-rates, -rat•ed, -rat•ing**) to furnish or adorn with fashionable or beautiful things.

dec•o•ra•tion /dĕk' ə rā' shən/ *n.* **a.** the act, process, technique, or art of decorating. **b.** an object or group of objects used to decorate. **c.** a medal, badge, or other emblem of honor.

de•fect /dē' fĕkt', dĭ fĕkt'/ *n.* **a.** the lack of something necessary or desirable for completion or perfection; deficiency. **b.** an imperfection; fault.

de•fec•tive /dĭ fĕk' tĭv/ *adj.* having a defect; faulty.

def•i•cit /dĕf' ĭ sĭt/ *n.* the amount by which something, as a sum of money, falls short of the required or expected amount; shortage.

de•lib•er•ate /dĭ lĭb' ər ĭt/ *adj.* (**de•lib•er•ate•ly** *adv.*) **a.** done or said on purpose; intentional. **b.** careful and thorough in deciding or determining: *a deliberate choice.* [Lat. *deliberatus,* resolved, p.part. of *deliberare,* to consider: *de-,* thoroughly + *librare,* to balance < *libra,* a balance, scales.]

de•liv•er /dĭ lĭv' ər/ *v.* to take to the intended recipient: *deliver groceries.*

deliver

de•luxe[1] also **de-luxe** /dĭ lŏoks', -lŭks'/ *adj.* particularly elegant and luxurious; sumptuous. [Fr., of luxury.]

de•luxe[2] also **de-luxe** /dĭ lŏoks', -lŭks'/ *adv.* in an elegant and luxurious manner; sumptuously.

dem•on•stra•tion /dĕm' ən strā' shən/ *n.* **a.** the act of making evident or proving. **b.** conclusive evidence; proof. **c.** an illustration or explanation, as of a theory or product, by practical application. **d.** a public display of group opinion, as by a rally or march.

den•im /dĕn' ĭm/ *n.* **a.** a coarse twilled cloth used for jeans, overalls, and work uniforms. **b.** **denims.** garments made of coarse denim. [Fr. (*serge*) *de Nîmes,* (serge) of Nîmes, a city in southern France.]

de•pos•it[1] /dĭ pŏz' ĭt/ *v.* **a.** to give as partial payment or security. **b.** to entrust (money) to a bank.

de•pos•it[2] /dĭ pŏz′ ĭt/ *n.* (**de•pos•i•tor** *n.*)
a. something entrusted for safekeeping, as money in a bank. **b.** a partial or initial payment of a cost or debt.

de•scend /dĭ sĕnd′/ *v.* **a.** to move from a higher to a lower place. **b.** to come down from a source; derive: *descended from an old New England family.*

de•scen•dant /dĭ sĕn′ dənt/ *n.* **a.** an individual descended from another. **b.** something derived from a prototype or earlier form.

de•sign[I] /dĭ zīn′/ *v.* **a.** to conceive in the mind; invent: *designed his dream vacation.* **b.** to plan by making a preliminary sketch, outline, or drawing. **c.** to create or execute in an artistic or highly skilled manner.

de•sign[2] /dĭ zīn′/ *n.* (**de•sign•er** *n.*) **a.** a drawing or sketch. **b.** the invention and disposition of the forms, parts, or details of something according to a plan. **c.** a decorative or artistic work.

de•sir•a•ble /dĭ zīr′ ə bəl/ *adj.* **a.** of such quality as to be worth seeking; pleasing. **b.** worth wanting or doing; advisable.

des•ti•na•tion /dĕs tə nā′ shən/ *n.* the place to which something or someone is going or directed.

de•ter•gent /dĭ tûr′ jənt/ *n.* a cleansing substance, especially a synthetic one that acts as a wetting agent and emulsifier and is made from chemical compounds rather than from fats and lye.

de•ter•mi•na•tion /dĭ tûr′mə nā′ shən/ *n.* **a.** the act of making or arriving at a decision. **b.** the quality of being resolute or firm in purpose; resoluteness.

de•ter•mine /dĭ tûr′ mĭn/ *v.* (**-mines, -mined, -min•ing**) **a.** to decide or settle (a dispute, for example) conclusively and authoritatively. **b.** to establish or ascertain definitely, as after consideration, investigation, or calculation.

de•tract /dĭ trăkt′/ *v.* **a.** to take away a desirable part; diminish. **b.** to distract. [ME *detracten* < Lat. *detractus,* p.part. of *detrahere,* to remove: *de-,* away + *trahere,* to pull.]

de•vice /dĭ vīs′/ *n.* **a.** something devised or constructed for a particular purpose, especially a machine used to perform one or more relatively simple tasks. —*idiom.* **leave to (one's) own devices.** to allow to do as one pleases.

de•vise /dĭ vīz′/ *v.* (**-vis•es, -vised, -vis•ing**) **a.** to form or arrange in the mind; contrive. **b.** Obs. to suppose; imagine.

dia- a prefix meaning through or across: *diagonal.*

di•a•gram /dī′ ə grăm′/ *n.* **a.** a plan, sketch, drawing, or outline designed to demonstrate or explain how something works or to clarify the relationship between the parts of a whole. **b.** a chart or graph. [Lat. *diagramma* < Gk. < *diagraphein,* to mark out: *dia-,* apart + *graphein,* to write.]

die•sel /dē′ zəl, -səl/ *n.* **a.** a diesel engine. **b.** a vehicle powered by a diesel engine.

dig•ni•ty /dĭg′ nĭ tē/ *n.* (**-ties** *pl.*) **a.** poise and self-respect. **b.** stateliness and reserve in deportment and appearance.

din•ing room /dī′ nĭng rōōm′/ *n.* a room in which meals are served.

dining room

dis- a prefix meaning: **a.** not: *dissimilar.* **b.1.** absence of: *disinterest.* **b.2.** opposite of: *disfavor.* **c.** undo; do the opposite of: *disarrange.* **d.** used as an intensive.

dis•a•gree•able /dĭs′ ə grē′ ə bəl/ *adj.* **a.** not to one's liking; unpleasant or offensive. **b.** characterized by a quarrelsome manner; bad-tempered.

dis•ap•point /dĭs′ ə point′/ *v.* to fail to satisfy the hope, desire, or expectation of.

dis•ap•point•ment /dĭs′ ə point′ mənt/ *n.* the act, condition, or feeling of being disappointed.

dis•as•ter /dĭ zăs′ tər, -săs′-/ *n.* **a.1.** an occurence causing widespread destruction and distress. **a.2.** a grave misfortune. **b.** a total failure.

dis•as•trous /dĭ zăs′ trəs, -săs′-/ *adj.* causing disaster.

dis•cov•er /dĭ skŭv′ ər/ *v.* **a.** to obtain knowledge of through observation, search, or study. **b.** to be the first to find, learn, or observe.

dis•cov•er•y /dĭ skŭv′ ə rē/ *n.* (**-ies** *pl.*)
a. the act or an instance of discovering.
b. something that has been discovered.

dis•in•te•grate /dĭs ĭn′ tĭ grāt′/ *v.*
(**-grates, -grat•ed, -grat•ing**) **a.** to fragment.
b. to decay or undergo a transformation, as
an atomic nucleus.

dis•in•ter•est•ed /dĭs ĭn′ trĭ stĭd,
-ĭn′ tə rĕs′ tĭd/ *adj.* free of bias and self-interest;
impartial.

dis•miss /dĭs mĭs′/ *v.* **a.** to discharge, as from
employment. **b.** to direct or allow to leave: *dismiss troops.* **c.** to discontinue consideration of;
drop. [ME *dismissen* < Med. Lat. *dismissus,*
p.part. of *dismittere,* alteration of Lat. *dimittere:
dis-,* apart + *mittere,* to send.]

dis•play¹ /dĭ splā′/ *v.* **a.** to hold up to view;
exhibit. **b.** to make noticeable.

dis•play² /dĭ splā′/ *n.* an advertisement
designed to catch the eye, as distinguished from
a classified advertisement.

dis•sat•is•fied /dĭs săt′ ĭs fīd′/ *adj.* feeling or
exhibiting a lack of contentment or satisfaction.

dis•tin•guish /dĭ stĭng′ gwĭsh/ *v.* **a.** to recognize as being different or distinct. **b.** to detect or
recognize; pick out. **c.** to make noticeable or
different; set apart.

dis•tract /dĭ străkt′/ *v.* to cause to turn away
from the original focus of attention or interest;
divert. [ME *distracten* < Lat. *distractus,* p.part.
of *distrahere,* to pull away: *dis-,* apart + *trahere,*
to draw.]

dis•trib•ute /dĭ strĭb′ yo͞ot/ *v.* (**-utes, -ut•ed,
-ut•ing**) **a.** to divide and dispense in portions.
b. to apply (multiplication by a given factor)
to each of the terms that make up a
mathematical expression.

dis•trib•u•tive /dĭ strĭb′ yə tĭv/ *adj.*
a. serving to distribute. **b.** of or pertaining to
the distributive property.

dras•tic /drăs′ tĭk/ *adj.* (**dras•ti•cal•ly** *adv.*)
a. taking effect violently or rapidly. **b.** quite
severe or radical in nature; extreme: *took
drastic steps.*

du•al /do͞o′ əl, dyo͞o′-/ *adj.* **a.** composed of
two parts; double; twofold. **b.** having a double
characater, nature, or purpose. [Lat. *dualis*
< *duo,* two.]

du•o /do͞o′ ō, dyo͞o′ ō/ *n.*
(**-os** *pl.*) **a.** *Mus.*
a.1. a duet. **a.2.** two
performers singing
or playing together.
b. two people in close
association. [Ital.
< Lat., two.]

duo

duo- a prefix meaning two.

du•plex¹ /do͞o′ plĕks′, dyo͞o′-/ *adj.* twofold or
double. [Lat. < *duplex,* twofold.]

du•plex² /do͞o′ plĕks′, dyo͞o′-/ *n.* a duplex apartment or house.

du•pli•cate¹ /do͞o′ plĭ kĭt, dyo͞o′-/ *adj.*
a. identically copied from an original.
b. existing or growing in two corresponding
parts; double. [ME < Lat. *duplicatus,* p.part. of
duplicare, to double < *duplex,* twofold.]

du•pli•cate² /do͞o′ plĭ kĭt, dyo͞o′-/ *n.* **a.** an
identical copy; facsimile. **b.** something that cor-
responds exactly to something else, especially
an original.

du•pli•cate³ /do͞o′ plĭ kāt′/ *v.* (**-cates, -cat•ed,
-cat•ing**) **a.** to make an identical copy of.
b. to double; make twofold.

du•pli•ca•tion /do͞o′ plĭ kā′ shən, dyo͞o′-/ *n.*
a. the act, procedure, or condition of being
duplicated. **b.** a duplicate; replica.

du•ra•tion /do͞o rā′ shən, dyo͞o-/ *n.* **a.** continu-
ance or persistence in time. **b.** the period of time
during which something exists or persists.

Spelling Dictionary

283

dwell•ing /dwĕl′ ĭng/ *n.*
a place to live in; abode.

dy•nam•ic /dī năm′ ĭk/
adj. (**dy•nam•i•cal•ly** *adv.*)
characterized by vigor
and energy; forceful:
a dynamic personality.

dwelling

dy•nas•ty /dī′ nə stē/ *n.* (**-ties** *pl.*) **a.** a succession of rulers from the same family or line.
b. a family or group that maintains power for several generations.

ear•phone /îr′ fōn′/ *n.* a device that converts electric signals, as from a telephone or radio receiver, to audible sound and that fits over or in the ear.

ech•o[1] /ĕk′ ō/ *n.* (**-oes** *pl.*) **a.** repetition of a sound by reflection of sound waves from a surface.
b. a repetition or imitation of something.

ech•o[2] /ĕk′ ō/ *v.* (**-oes, -oed, -o•ing**) **a.** to repeat or imitate. **b.** to produce an echo.

e•col•o•gy /ĭ kŏl′ ə jē/ *n.* (**ec•o•log•i•cal** *adj.*) the science of the relationships between organisms and their environments.

ec•o•nom•ic /ĕk′ ə nŏm′ ĭk, ē′ kə-/ *adj.*
(**ec•o•nom•i•cal•ly** *adv.*) not wasteful or extravagant; prudent and thrifty in management; financially rewarding.

e•con•o•my /ĭ kŏn′ ə mē/ *n.* (**-mies** *pl.*) the careful or thrifty use or management of resources, such as income, materials, or labor.

e•di•tion /ĭ dĭsh′ ən/ *n.* **a.1.** the entire number of copies of a publication printed from a single typesetting or other form of reproduction. **a.2.** a single copy from this group. **b.** one closely similar to an original; version: *The boy was a smaller edition of his father.* **c.** all the copies of a single press run of a newspaper: *the morning edition.*

ed•i•to•ri•al /ĕd′ ĭ tôr′ ē əl, -tōr′-/ *n.*
a. an article in a publication expressing the opinion of its editors or publishers. **b.** a commentary on radio or television expressing the opinion of the station or network.

ed•u•cate /ĕj′ ə kāt′/ *v.* (**-cates, -cat•ed, -cat•ing**) **a.** to provide with knowledge or training, especially through formal schooling; teach. **b.** to provide with information; inform.
c. to teach or instruct a person or group.

ed•u•ca•tion /ĕj′ ə kā′ shən/ *n.* **a.** the knowledge or skill obtained or developed by a learning process. **b.** the field of study that is concerned with teaching and learning.

ef•fect /ĭ fĕkt′/ *n.* **a.** something brought about by a cause or agent; result. **b.** the way in which something acts upon or influences an object.
c. something that produces a specific impression or supports a general design or intention: *sound effects.* **—idioms. in effect. a.** in fact; actually.
b. in operation.

ef•fect /ĭ fĕkt′/ *v.* to cause or produce.

ef•fec•tive /ĭ fĕk′ tĭv/ *adj.* **a.** having an intended or expected effect. **b.** producing or designed to produce the desired impression or response:
an effective speech. **c.** operative; in effect: *The law is effective immediately.* [ME < OFr. < Lat. *effectus,* p.part. of e*fficere,* to effect: *ex-,* out + *facere,* to make.]

ef•fi•cient /ĭ fĭsh′ ənt/ *adj.* (**ef•fi•cient•ly** *adv.*)
a. acting directly to produce an effect: *an efficient cause.* **b.** acting or producing effectively with a minimum of waste, expense, or unnecessary effort. [ME < OFr. < Lat. *efficiens,* pr.part. of *efficere,* to effect.]

el•e•gance /ĕl′ ĭ gəns/ *n.* **a.** refinement and grace in movement, appearance, or manners.
b. rich in form, decoration, or presentation.

el•e•gant /ĕl′ ĭ gənt/ *adj.* **a.** characterized by or exhibiting elegance. **b.** excellent. [OFr.
< Lat. *elegans.*]

el•i•gi•ble /ĕl′ ĭ jə bəl/ *adj.* **a.** qualified, as for an office or position. **b.** desirable and worthy of choice, especially for marriage.

e•lim•i•nate /ĭ lĭm′ ə nāt′/ *v.* (**-nates, -nat•ed, -nat•ing**) (**e•lim•i•na•tion** *n.*)
a. to get rid of; remove. **b.1.** to leave out or omit from consideration; reject. **b.2.** to remove from consideration by defeating, as in a contest.

el•lipse /ĭ lĭps′/ *n.* a closed plane curve, composed of all the points that have the sum of their distances from two fixed points equal to a constant.

e•man•ci•pate /ĭ măn′ sə pāt′/ v. (-pates, -pat•ed, -pat•ing) to free from oppression, bondage, or restraint; liberate. [Lat. *emancipare*, *emancipat-: ex-*, out of, + *mancipium*, ownership < *manceps*, purchaser.]

em•bar•rass /ĕm băr′ əs/ v. (-rass•es, -rassed, -rass•ing) **a.** to cause to feel self-conscious or ill at ease; disconcert. **b.1.** to beset with difficulties. **b.2.** to hinder; impede. **c.** to complicate. [Fr. *embarrasser*, to impede < Sp. *embarazar* < Ital. *imbarazzare*, of Lat. orig.]

em•broi•der•y /ĕm broi′ də rē/ n. (-ies *pl.*) **a.** ornamentation of fabric with needlework. **b.** embellishment with fanciful details.

embroidery

em•er•ald /ĕm′ ər əld, ĕm′ rəld/ n. **a.** a brilliant, transparent green beryl used as a gemstone. **b.** a strong yellowish green.

e•mo•tion /ĭ mō′ shən/ n. a complex and usually strong feeling, as love and fear. [Fr. *emotion* < OFr. *esmovoir*, to excite < VLat. *exmovere* < Lat. *emovere*, to move out: *ex-*, out + *movēre*, to move.]

e•mo•tion•al /ĭ mō′ shə nəl/ *adj.* **a.** readily affected with or stirred by emotion. **b.** marked by or exhibiting emotion.

em•per•or /ĕm′ pər ər/ n. the male ruler of an empire.

en- a prefix that forms verbs: *endanger.* When en- is followed by **b, m,** or **p,** it becomes **em-.**

-en¹ a suffix that forms verbs from adjectives: *cheapen.*

-en² a suffix that forms adjectives from nouns: *wooden.*

-ence a suffix that forms nouns from verbs: *reference.*

en•close /ĕn klōz′/ v. (-clos•es, -closed, -clos•ing) **a.** to surround on all sides; close in. **b.1.** to place within a container. **b.2.** to insert in the same envelope or package. **c.** to fence in or place an enclosure around so as to prevent common use. [ME *enclosen* < OFr. *enclos.* p.part. of *enclore* < Lat. *includere*, to include: *in-*, in + *claudere*, to close.]

Pronunciation Key

ă	pat	ŏ	pot	th	**thin**
ā	pay	ō	toe	*th*	**this**
âr	care	ô	paw, for	hw	**which**
ä	father	oi	noise	zh	vision
ĕ	pet	ou	out	ə	about,
ē	be	ŏŏ	took		item,
ĭ	pit	ōō	boot		pencil,
ī	pie	ŭ	cut		gallop,
îr	pier	ûr	urge		circus

en•core /ŏn′ kôr′, -kōr′/ n. an additional performance in response to the demand of an audience. [Fr. again, still, yet.]

en•cour•age /ĕn kûr′ ĭj, -kŭr′-/ v. (-ag•es, -aged, -ag•ing) **a.** to inspire with hope, courage, or confidence; hearten. **b.** to give support to; foster. **c.** to stimulate. [ME *encouragen* < OFr. *encoragier: en-* (causative) < Lat. *in-*, in + *corage*, courage < Lat. *cor*, heart.]

en•cour•age•ment /ĕn kûr′ ĭj mənt, -kŭr′-/ n. the act of encouraging.

en•dan•gered /ĕn dān′ jərd/ *adj.* faced with the danger of extinction: *an endangered species.*

en•dorse /ĕn dôrs′/ v. (-dors•es, -dorsed, -dors•ing) **a.** to write one's signature on the back of (a check, for example) as evidence of the legal transfer of its ownership, especially in return for the cash or credit indicated on its face. **b.** to give approval of or support to; sanction.

en•dorse•ment /ĕn dôrs′ mənt/ n. **a.** an act of endorsing. **b.** something that endorses or validates, as a signature or voucher. **c.** support.

en•dur•ance /ĕn dŏŏr′ əns, -dyŏŏr′-/ n. the act, quality, or power of withstanding hardship or stress.

en•dure /ĕn dŏŏr′, -dyŏŏr′-/ v. (-dures, -dured, -dur•ing) **a.** to carry on through, despite hardships; undergo. **b.** to suffer patiently without yielding.

Eng•lish¹ /ĭng′ glĭsh/ *adj.* of, pertaining to, derived from, or characteristic of England, its people, or its culture.

Eng•lish² /ĭng′ glĭsh/ n. the people of England.

en•roll /ĕn rōl′/ v. **a.** to enter the name of in a register, record, or roll. **b.** to roll or wrap in. [ME *enrollen* < OFr. *enroller: en-*, in (< Lat. *in-*) + *rolle*, roll < Lat. *rotulus*, dim. of *rota*, wheel.]

-ent a suffix that forms adjectives and nouns: *effervescent; resident.*

en•ter•tain /ĕn′ tər tān′/ v. to hold the attention of; amuse.

entertain

en•thu•si•asm /ĕn thoo′ zē ăz′ əm/ n. **a.** great or intense feeling for a subject or cause. **b.** ardent eagerness; zeal.

en•vi•ron•ment /ĕn vī′ rən mənt/ n. (**en•vi•ron•men•tal** *adj.*) **a.** the circumstances or conditions that surround one; surroundings. **b.** an artistic or theatrical work that surrounds or involves the audience.

e•qua•tor /ĭ kwā′ tər/ n. the great circle circumscribing the earth's surface. It divides the earth into the Northern Hemisphere and the Southern Hemisphere.

e•qui•dis•tant /ē′ kwĭ dĭs′ tənt, ĕk′ wē-/ *adj.* equally distant.

e•qui•lat•er•al[1] /ē′ kwə lăt′ ər əl, ĕk′ wə-/ *adj.* having all sides or faces equal.

e•qui•lat•er•al[2] /ē′ kwə lăt′ ər əl, ĕk′ wə-/ n. **a.** a side exactly equal to others. **b.** a geometric figure having equal sides.

e•quip /ĭ kwĭp′/ v. (**e•quips, e•quipped, e•quip•ping**) **a.** to supply with necessities such as tools or provisions. **b.** to furnish with the qualities necessary for performance.

eth•nic /ĕth′ nĭk/ *adj.* of or pertaining to a religious, racial, national, or cultural group.

e•volve /ĭ vŏlv′/ v. (**-volves, -volved, -volv•ing**) **a.1.** to develop or achieve gradually. **a.2.** to work out; devise. **b.** *Biol.* to develop by evolutionary processes from a primitive to a more highly organized form. **c.** to experience evolutionary change. **d.** to undergo change or development. [Lat. *evolvere*, to unroll: *ex-* + *volvere*, to roll.]

ex- a prefix meaning: **a.** out; out of. **b.** former.

ex•ag•ger•ate /ĭg zăj′ ə rāt′/ v. (**-ates, -at•ed, -at•ing**) **a.** to enlarge or increase to an abnormal degree. **b.** to make greater than is actually the case; overstate: *exaggerated his own importance.* [Lat. *exaggerare: ex-* (intensive) + *aggerare*, to pile up < *agger*, pile.]

ex•am•ine /ĭg zăm′ ĭn/ v. (**-ines, -ined, -in•ing**) **a.** to inspect in detail. **b.** to observe or analyze carefully.

ex•am•i•na•tion /ĭg zăm′ ə nā′ shən/ n. **a.** the act of examining or the state of being examined. **b.** an exercise testing knowledge or skill.

ex•ca•vate /ĕk′ skə vāt′/ v. (**-vates, -vat•ed, -vat•ing**) **a.** to make a cavity or hole in; hollow out. **b.** to remove by digging or scooping out.

ex•cerpt /ĕk′ sûrpt′/ n. a passage or scene, as from a speech or book.

ex•clu•sive /ĭk skloo′ sĭv/ *adj.* not divided or shared with others.

ex•cuse[1] /ĭk skyooz′/ v. (**-cus•es, -cused, -cus•ing**) (**ex•cus•a•ble** *adj.*) **a.1.** to apologize for. **a.2.** to seek to remove the blame from. **b.1.** to grant pardon to; forgive: *excuse him for his clumsiness.* **b.2.** to make allowance for; overlook.

ex•cuse[2] /ĭk skyoos′/ n. **a.** an explanation offered to elicit forgiveness. **b.** a note explaining an absence.

ex•e•cute /ĕk′ sĭ kyoot′/ v. (**-cutes, -cut•ed, -cut•ing**) **a.** to carry out; put into effect. **b.** to perform.

ex•hi•bi•tion /ĕk′ sə bĭsh′ ən/ n. a display for the public, as of art objects, industrial achievements, or agricultural products.

ex•pand /ĭk spănd′/ v. to increase the size, volume, quantity, or scope of.

ex•pan•sion /ĭk spăn′ shən/ n. **a.** the act or process of expanding. **b.** an expanded part.

ex•pec•ta•tion /ĕk′ spĕk tā′ shən/ n. **a.** the act or state of expecting. **b.** eager anticipation. [Lat. *expectare*, to expect: *ex-*, out + *spectare*, to look at, freq. of *specere*, to see.]

ex•pe•di•ent /ĭk spē′ dē ənt/ *adj.* based on or marked by a concern for policy rather than principle.

ex•pe•di•tion /ĕk´ spĭ dĭsh´ ən/ *n.* **a.** a journey undertaken by an organized group of people with a definite objective. **b.** the group undertaking such a journey.

ex•pen•sive /ĭk spĕn´ sĭv/ *adj.* involving a large expenditure; costly.

ex•per•i•ment¹ /ĭk spĕr´ ə mənt/ *n.* something done to demonstrate a known fact, check the correctness of a theory, or see how well a new thing works; a test.

ex•per•i•ment² /ĭk spĕr´ ə mənt/ *v.* to conduct an experiment or experiments.

ex•per•i•men•tal /ĭk spĕr´ ə mĕn´ təl/ *adj.* **a.1.** based upon experiment. **a.2.** given to experimenting. **b.** of the nature of an experiment.

ex•per•tise /ĕk´ spûr tēz´/ *n.* **a.** expert advice or opinion. **b.** specialized knowledge or skill. [Fr. < OFr. < *expert,* experienced. < Lat. *expertus,* p.part. of *experiri,* to try.]

ex•plic•it /ĭk splĭs´ ĭt/ *adj.* **a.** expressed with clarity and precision. **b.** forthright and unreserved in expression.

ex•plore /ĭk splôr´, -splōr´/ *v.* (**-plores, -plored, -plor•ing**) **a.** to examine. **b.** to search into or range over for the purpose of discovery.

ex•plor•er /ĭk splôr´ ər, -splōr´-/ *n.* one who explores, especially one who explores a geographic area.

explorer

ex•tem•po•ra•ne•ous /ĭk stĕm´ pə rā´ nē əs/ *adj.* done with little or no preparation or practice; impromptu.

ex•treme /ĭk strēm´/ *adj.* (**ex•treme•ly** *adv.*) **a.** being in or attaining the greatest or highest degree; very intense. **b.** of the greatest severity; drastic. [ME < OFr. < Lat. *extremus.*]

ex•tro•vert also **ex•tra•vert** /ĕk´ strə vûrt´/ *n.* an individual interested in others or in the environment as opposed to or to the exclusion of self. [Lat. *extra,* outside < *exterus,* outward + Lat. *vertere,* to turn.]

fab•ric /făb´ rĭk/ *n.* **a.** a cloth produced especially by knitting, weaving, or felting fibers. **b.** the texture or quality of such cloth.

fa•cial¹ /fā´ shəl/ *adj.* of or concerning the face.

fa•cial² /fā´ shəl/ *n.* a treatment for the face, usually consisting of a massage and the application of cosmetic creams.

fac•sim•i•le /făk sĭm´ ə lē/ *n.* an exact copy or reproduction, as of a document. [Lat. *facsimile,* make (it) similar.]

fac•tion /făk´ shən/ *n.* a group of persons forming a united, usually troublesome minority within a larger group. [OFr. < Lat. *factio* < *factus,* p.part of *facere,* to do.]

fac•tu•al /făk´ chōō əl/ *adj.* of or containing facts.

fac•ul•ty /făk´ əl tē/ *n.* (**-ties** *pl.*) **a.** a special ability or skill. **b.** a body of teachers as distinguished from their students.

far-fetched /fär´ fĕcht´/ *adj.* strained or improbable.

fa•ther-in-law /fā´ thər-ĭn-lô´/ *n.* (**fa•thers-in-law** *pl.*) **a.** the father of one's husband or wife. **b.** *Archaic.* a stepfather.

fa•tigue /fə tēg´/ *n.* **a.** physical or mental weariness resulting from exertion. **b.** tiring effort or activity; labor. [Fr. < OFr. < *fatiguer,* to fatigue < Lat. *fatigare.*]

fear•less /fîr´ lĭs/ *adj.* (**fear•less•ly** *adv.*) (**fear•less•ness** *n.*) having no fear; brave.

fed•er•al /fĕd′ ər əl, fĕd′ rəl/ *adj.* of, pertaining to, or designating a form of government in which a union of states recognizes the sovereignty of a central authority while retaining certain powers of government.

fe•ro•cious /fə rō′ shəs/ *adj.* **a.** extremely savage; fierce. **b.** marked by unrelenting intensity; extreme: *a ferocious blizzard.*

feud /fyo͞od/ *n.* a bitter, prolonged quarrel, as between two families, individuals, or clans.

fi•an•cé /fē′ än sā′, fē än′ sā′/ *n.* a man engaged to be married. [Fr., p.part. of *fiancer,* to betroth < OFr. *fiancier* < *fiance,* trust < *fier* to trust < Lat. *fidere.*]

fi•an•cée /fē′ än sā′, fē än′ sā′/ *n.* a woman engaged to be married. [Fr., fem. of *fiancé,* fiancé.]

fierce /fîrs/ *adj.* (**fierc•er, fierc•est**) (**fierce•ly** *adv.*) (**fierce•ness** *n.*) **a.** having a savage and violent nature; ferocious. **b.** extremely severe or violent; terrible.

fi•es•ta /fē ĕs′ tə/ *n.* **a.** a festival or religious holiday, especially a saint's day celebrated in Spanish-speaking countries. **b.** any celebration or festive occasion. [Sp. < Lat. *festa,* neuter pl. of *festus,* joyous.]

fiesta

fi•nance /fə năns′, fī-, fī′ năns′/ *n.* the management of money, banking, investments, and credit.

fi•nan•cial /fə năn′ shəl, fī-/ *adj.* (**fi•nan•cial•ly** *adv.*) of, pertaining to, or involving finance, finances, or financiers.

first-per•son /fûrst′ pûr′ sən/ *adj.* **a.** describing a category of grammatical forms, such as verbs or pronouns, designating the speaker or writer of the sentence in which they appear. **b.** describing a literary style in which forms in the first person are used: *first-person narrative.*

fluc•tu•ate /flŭk′ cho͞o āt′/ *v.* (**-ates, -at•ed, -at•ing**) to vary irregularly: *prices fluctuating dramatically.* [Lat. *fluctuare, fluctuat-* < *fluctus,* a flowing < p.part. of *fluere,* to flow.]

flu•ent /flo͞o′ ənt/ *adj.* (**flu•en•cy** *n.*) (**flu•ent•ly** *adv.*) **a.** having facility in the use of language: *fluent in three languages.* **b.1.** flowing effortlessly; polished. **b.2.** flowing smoothly; graceful: *fluent curves.* [Lat. *fluens, fluent-,* pr.part. of *fluere,* to flow.]

flu•o•res•cence /flo͞o′ ə rĕs′ əns, flo͞o rĕs′-/ *n.* the emission of electromagnetic radiation, especially of visible light, resulting from the absorption of incident radiation and persisting only as long as the stimulating radiation is continued.

flu•o•res•cent /flo͞o′ ə rĕs′ ənt, flo͞o rĕs′-/ *adj.* exhibiting or capable of exhibiting fluorescence.

foot•age /fo͞ot′ ĭj/ *n.* a portion of motion-picture film, especially an amount of film depicting a specified event or kind of action: *news footage.*

for•give /fər gĭv′, fôr-/ *v.* (**-gives, -gave, -giv•en, -giv•ing**) to excuse for a fault or offense; pardon. [ME *forgiven* < OE *forgifan.*]

for•give•ness /fər gĭv′ nĭs, fôr-/ *n.* the act of forgiving; pardon.

for•mal¹ /fôr′ məl/ *adj.* (**for•mal•ly** *adv.*) **a.** following or adhering to accepted forms, conventions, or regulations: *a formal requirement.* **b.** done in proper or regular form. **c.** stiff or cold; ceremonious: *a formal manner.*

for•mal² /fôr′ məl/ *n.* **a.** an occasion or ceremony requiring formal attire. **b.** formal attire.

for•mat¹ /fôr′ măt′/ *n.* a plan for the organization and arrangment of a specified production.

for•mat² /fôr′ măt′/ *v.* (**-mats, -mat•ted, -mat•ting**) to produce (computer data, for example) in a specified form.

for•mer•ly /fôr′ mər lē/ *adv.* at a former time; once.

for•mu•la /fôr′ myə lə/ *n.* (**-las** or **-lae** /-lē′/ *pl.*) **a.** an established form of words or symbols for use in a ceremony or procedure. **b.** a mathematical statement, especially an equation, of a rule, principle, answer, or other logical relation.

for•tu•nate /fôr′ chən ĭt/ *adj.* (**for•tu•nate•ly** *adv.*) **a.** bringing something good and unforeseen. **b.** having unexpected good fortune; lucky.

four-fifths /fôr fifths/ *n. pl.* four parts of something that has been divided into five equal parts. *Marcie ate nearly four-fifths of the pie.*

frank•furt•er /frăngk′ fər tər/ *n.* a smoked sausage of beef or beef and pork made in long, reddish links. [after *Frankfurt am Main,* West Germany.]

fre•quen•cy /frē′ kwən sē/ *n.* (**-cies** *pl.*) **a.** the property or condition of occuring frequently. **b.** *Statistics.* **1.** the number of measurements in an interval of a frequency distribution. **b.2.** the ratio of the number of times an event occurs in a series of trials of a chance experiment to the number of trials of the experiment performed.

friend•ship /frĕnd′ shĭp′/ *n.* **a.** the condition of being friends. **b.** a feeling of warmth toward another; friendliness.

-ful a suffix meaning: **a.** full of: *eventful.* **b.** characterized by: *boastful.* **c.** having a specified tendency or capability: *mournful.* **d.** an amount or quantity that will fill: *cupful.*

fun•gus /fŭng′ gəs/ *n.* (**fun•gi** /fŭn′ jī′/ or **fun•gus•es** *pl.*) any of a group of plants, such as a mushroom, mold, yeast, or mildew, that have no green coloring and that obtain their nourishment from living or dead plant or animal substances.

fur•ther•more /fûr′ thər môr′, -mōr′/ *adv.* moreover; in addition.

-fy a suffix that forms verbs: *simplify.*

gar•de•nia /gär dēn′ yə/ *n.* a shrub having glossy evergreen leaves and large, fragrant, usually white flowers. [NLat., genus name, after Alexander *Garden* (1731–1790).]

gauge¹ /gāj/ *n.* **a.1.** a standard or scale of measurement. **a.2.** a standard dimension, quantity, or capacity. **b.** an instrument for measuring or testing. **c.** a means of estimating or evaluating; test: *a gauge of character.*

gauge

gauge² /gāj/ *v.* (**gaug•es, gauged, gaug•ing**) **a.** to measure precisely. **b.** to determine the capacity, volume, or contents of. **c.** to evaluate or judge: *gauge a person's ability.*

Pronunciation Key

ă	pat	ŏ	pot	th	**th**in
ā	pay	ō	toe	*th*	**th**is
âr	care	ô	paw, for	hw	**wh**ich
ä	father	oi	n**oi**se	zh	vi**s**ion
ĕ	pet	ou	**ou**t	ə	**a**bout,
ē	be	ŏŏ	t**oo**k		it**e**m,
ĭ	pit	ōō	b**oo**t		penc**i**l,
ī	pie	ŭ	cut		gall**o**p,
îr	pier	ûr	**ur**ge		circ**u**s

gem•stone /jĕm′ stōn′/ *n.* a precious or semi-precious stone that may be used as a jewel when cut and polished.

ge•ne•al•o•gy /jē nē ŏl′ ə jē, -ăl′ ə jē, jĕn′ ē-/ *n.* (**-gies** *pl.*) a record or table of the descent of a family, group, or person from an ancestor or ancestors.

gen•er•ate /jĕn′ ə rāt′/ *v.* (**-ates, -at•ed, -at•ing**) **a.** to bring into existence; produce. **b.** *Compuer Sci.* to produce a program by instructing a computer to follow given parameters with a skeleton program.

ge•net•ics /jə nĕt′ ĭks/ *n.* the biology of heredity.

ge•ol•o•gy /jē ŏl′ ə jē/ *n.* (**-gies** *pl.*) (**ge•o•log•i•cal** *adj.*) **a.** the scientific study of the origin, history, and structure of the earth. **b.** the structure of a specific region of the earth's surface.

gla•cial /glā′ shəl/ *adj.* **a.** of, pertaining to, or derived from a glacier. **b.** extremely cold; icy: *glacial waters.* **c.** having the appearance of ice. **d.** lacking warmth and friendliness: *a glacial stare.*

gnarled /närld/ *adj.* **a.** having gnarls; knotty or misshapen: *gnarled branches.* **b.** rugged and roughened, as from old age or work: *the gnarled hands of a carpenter.*

gour•met /gŏŏr mā′, gŏŏr′ mā′/ *n.* a connoisseur of fine food and drink. [Fr. < OFr., wine merchant's servant.]

gra•cious /grā′ shəs/ *adj.* **a.** characterized by kindness and warm courtesy. **b.** characterized by charm and beauty; graceful. **c.** characterized by elegance and good taste: *a gracious dinner.*

grad•u•ate[1] /grăj′ o͞o āt′/ *v.* (-ates, -ated, -at•ing) **a.** to be granted an academic degree or diploma. **b.** to grant an academic degree or diploma to.

grad•u•ate[2] /grăj′ o͞o ĭt/ *n.* one who has received an academic degree or diploma.

grad•u•ate[3] /grăj′ o͞o ĭt/ *adj.* of, for, or relating to studies beyond a bachelor's degree: *graduate courses.*

grad•u•a•tion /grăj′ o͞o ā′ shən/ *n.* **a.** the conferring or receipt of an academic degree or diploma marking completion of studies. **b.** a ceremony at which degrees or diplomas are conferred; commencement.

gram•mat•i•cal /grə măt′ ĭ kəl/ *adj.* **a.** of or relating to grammar. **b.** conforming to the rules of grammar. [LLat. *grammaticalis* < Lat. *grammaticus* < Gk. *grammatikos,* of letters < *gramma,* letter.]

grand•daugh•ter /grăn′ dô′ tər/ *n.* the daughter of one's son or daughter.

grid /grĭd/ *n.* **a.** a framework of parallel or crisscrossed bars; gridiron. **b.** a pattern of horizontal and vertical lines forming squares of uniform size on a map, chart, aerial photograph, or optical device, used as a reference for locating points.

guar•an•tee[1] /găr′ ən tē′/ *n.* **a.** something that ensures a particular outcome or condition. **b.** a promise or assurance, especially as to the quality or durability of a product or service. **c.** something given or held as security; pledge.

guar•an•tee[2] /găr′ ən tē′/ *v.* **a.** to assume responsibility for the debt, default, or miscarriage of. **b.** to assume responsibility for the quality or execution of. **c.** to give a guarantee for.

half-life /hăf′ līf, häf′-/ *n. Physics.* the time required for half the nuclei in a sample of a specific isotopic species to undergo radioactive decay.

ham•burg•er /hăm′ bûr′ gər/ *n.* **a.1.** ground meat, usually beef. **a.2.** a patty of such meat. **b.** a sandwich made with a hamburger patty, usually in a roll or bun. [short for *Hamburger steak,* after *Hamburg,* Germany.]

head•line /hĕd′ līn′/ *n.* **a.** the title or caption of a newspaper article, usually set in large type. **b.** a line at the head of a page or passage giving information such as the title, author, and page number.

head•phone /hĕd′ fōn′/ *n.* a receiver, as for a radio, held to the ear by a headband.

headphone

hem•i•sphere /hĕm′ ĭ sfîr′/ *n.* **a.** a half of a sphere bounded by a great circle. **b.** either the northern or southern half of the earth as divided by the equator or the eastern or western half as divided by a meridian.

herb /ûrb, hûrb/ *n.* any of various often aromatic plants used especially in medicine or as seasoning.

he•red•i•tar•y /hə rĕd′ ĭ tĕr′ ē/ *adj.* descending from an ancestor to a legal heir; passing down by inheritance.

he•ro•ic /hĭ rō′ ĭk/ *adj.* (**he•ro•i•cal•ly** *adv.*) **a.** having, displaying, or marked by the qualities appropriate to a hero; courageous: *heroic deeds.* **b.** impressive in size or scope; grand.

hes•i•tate /hĕz′ ĭ tāt′/ *v.* (-tates, -tated, -tat•ing) **a.1.** to be slow to act, speak, or decide. **a.2.** to pause in uncertainty; waver. **b.** to be reluctant: *He hesitated to ask for help.*

hes•i•ta•tion /hĕz′ ĭ tā′ shən/ *n.* the act or an instance of hesitating.

hin•der /hĭn′ dər/ *v.* **a.** to get in the way of; hamper. **b.** to obstruct or delay the process of.

hin•drance /hĭn′ drəns/ *n.* **a.** the act or condition of being hindered. **b.** one that hinders; impediment.

his•tor•i•cal /hĭ stôr′ ĭ kəl, -stŏr′-/ *adj.* (**his•tor•i•cal•ly** *adv.*) **a.** of, relating to, or of the character of history. **b.** based on or concerned with events in history. **c.** having considerable importance or influence in history; historic.

ho•mo•ge•ne•ous /hō′ mə jē′ nē əs, -jēn′ yəs/ *adj.* uniform in structure or composition throughout.

hon•es•ty /ŏn′ ĭ stē/ *n.* (-ties *pl.*) **a.** the quality or condition of being honest; integrity. **b.** truthfulness; sincerity.

hus•tle /hŭs′ əl/ *v.* (**-tles, -tled, -tling**) **a.** to jostle or shove roughly. **b.** *Informal.* to move hurriedly or urgently. **c.** *Informal.* to urge forward; hurry along.

hy•a•cinth /hī′ ə sĭnth/ *n.* **a.** a plant, perhaps a lily, gladiolus, or iris, that, according to Greek mythology, sprang from the blood of the slain Hyacinthus. **b.** a deep purplish blue to vivid violet. [Lat. *hyacinthus* < Gk. *huakinthos,* wild hyacinth.]

hy•phen /hī′ fən/ *n.* a punctuation mark (-) used to connect the parts of a compound word or between syllables of a word, especially of a word divided at the end of a line.

hy•pot•e•nuse /hī pŏt′ n o͞os′, -yo͞os′/ *n.* the side of a right triangle opposite the right angle.

hy•poth•e•sis /hī pŏth′ ĭ sĭs/ *n.* (**-ses** /-sēz′/ *pl.*) **a.** an explanation that accounts for a set of facts and that can be tested by further investigation; theory. **b.** something that is taken to be true for the purpose of argument or investigation; assumption.

-ible a form of the suffix **-able**.

-ic a suffix that forms adjectives meaning of or characteristic of: *allergic.*

i•de•al•ist /ī dē′ ə lĭst/ *n.* one whose conduct is influenced by ideals, especially when they conflict with practical considerations.

i•den•ti•fy /ī dĕn′ tə fī/ *v.* (**-fies, -fied, -fy•ing**) **a.1.** to establish the identity of. **a.2.** to ascertain the origin, nature, or definitive characteristics of. **b.** to associate or affiliate (oneself) closely with a person or group.

i•den•ti•ty /ī dĕn′ tĭ tē/ *n.* (**-ties** *pl.*) **a.** the distinct personality of an individual; individuality. **b.** *Math.* **1.** an equality satisfied by all values of the variables for which the expressions involved in the equality are defined. **b.2.** a unity.

i•dle¹ /īd′ l/ *adj.* (**i•dler, i•dlest**) (**i•dle•ness** *n.*) **a.1.** not in use. **a.2.** without a job; unemployed. **b.** lazy; shiftless. **c.** lacking foundation in fact.

i•dle² /īd′ l/ *v.* (**-dles, -dled, -dling**) **a.** to pass time without working or in avoiding work. **b.** to run at a slow speed or out of gear.

i•dol /īd′ l/ *n.* **a.** an image used as an object of worship. **b.** a person or thing that is blindly or excessively adored.

ig•ne•ous /ĭg′ nē əs/ *adj.* **a.** *Geol.* formed by solidification from a molten or partially molten state; used of rocks. **b.** of or pertaining to rock so formed.

ig•no•rance /ĭg′ nər əns/ *n.* the condition of being ignorant.

ig•no•rant /ĭg′ nər ənt/ *adj.* **a.** without education or knowledge. **b.** unaware or uninformed.

i•gua•na /ĭ gwä′ nə/ *n.* any of various large tropical American lizards of the family Iguanidae, often having spiny projections along the back. [Sp. < Arawak *iwana*.]

il•lus•trate /ĭl′ ə strāt′, ĭ lŭs′ trāt′/ *v.* (**-trates, -trat•ed, -trat•ing**) **a.1.** to clarify as by use of examples or comparisons. **a.2.** to clarify by serving as an example or comparison. **b.** to provide (a publication) with explanatory or decorative features.

iguana

i•mag•i•na•tive /ĭ măj′ ə nə tĭv, -nā′ tĭv/ *adj.* **a.** having a lively imagination, especially a creative imagination. **b.** created by, indicative of, or characterized by imagination or creativity.

im•me•di•ate•ly /ĭ mē′ dē ĭt lē/ *adv.* without delay.

im•mense /ĭ mĕns′/ *adj.* **a.** extremely large; huge. **b.** immeasurably vast; boundless.

im•par•tial /ĭm pär′ shəl/ *adj.* not partial or biased; unprejudiced.

im•passe /ĭm′ păs′/ *n.* **a.** a road or passage having no exit; cul-de-sac. **b.** a difficult situation offering no workable escape. [Fr.: *in-*, not (< Lat. *in-*) + *passer*, to pass < OFr.]

impasse

im•plic•it /ĭm plĭs′ ĭt/ *adj.* implied or understood, although not directly expressed.

im•pres•sion /ĭm prĕsh′ ən/ *n.* **a.** the effect, mark, or imprint made on a surface by pressure. **b.** an effect, feeling, or image retained as a consequence of experience. **c.** a vague notion, remembrance, or belief.

im•prove /ĭm prōōv′/ *v.* (**-proves, -proved, -prov•ing**) to advance to a better state or quality; make better. [ME *improven*, to enclose land for cultivation < AN *emprouwer*: OFr. *en-* (causative) + *prou*, profit < LLat. *prode*, advantageous.]

im•prove•ment /ĭm prōōv′ mənt/ *n.* **a.** the act or procedure of improving. **b.** a change or addition that improves.

in-¹ a prefix meaning without or not: *inaccurate*. When **in-** is followed by **l** or **r**, it becomes **il-** or **ir-** respectively. Before **b, m,** or **p,** it becomes **im-.**

in-² a prefix meaning in, within, or into: *inbound*. When **in-** is followed by **l** or **r**, it becomes **il-** or **ir-** respectively. Before **b, m,** or **p,** it becomes **im-.**

in•a•bil•i•ty /ĭn′ ə bĭl′ ĭ tē/ *n.* lack of ability or means.

in•an•i•mate /ĭn ăn′ ə mĭt/ *adj.* (**in•an•i•mate•ly** *adv.*) **a.** not having the qualities associated with active, living organisms; not animate. [Lat. *animare, animat-*, < *anima*, soul.]

in•ci•den•tal•ly /ĭn′ sĭ dĕn′ tl ē/ *adv.* **a.** by chance, casually. **b.** apart from the main subject; parenthetically.

in•cred•i•ble /ĭn krĕd′ ə bəl/ *adj.* too implausible to be believed; unbelievable.

in•di•cate /ĭn′ dĭ kāt′/ *v.* (**-cates, -cat•ed, -cat•ing**) **a.** to demonstrate or point out: *indicate a route*. **b.** to state or express briefly. [Lat. *indicare, indicat-*, to show: *in-*, in + *dicare*, to proclaim.]

in•el•i•gi•ble /ĭn ĕl′ ĭ jə bəl/ *adj.* not qualified for an election to an office or position.

in•ex•pen•sive /ĭn′ ĭk spĕn′ sĭv/ *adj.* not high in price; cheap.

in•fec•tion /ĭn fĕk′ shən/ *n.* invasion by microorganisms of a bodily part in which conditions are favorable for growth, production of toxins, and subsequent injury to tissue. [ME *infecten* < Latin *infectus*, p.part. of *inficere*, to stain: *in-*, in + *facere*, to do.]

in•fer /ĭn fûr′/ *v.* (**-fers, -ferred, -fer•ring**) to conclude from evidence or premises. [OFr. *infer* < Lat. *inferre*, to bring in, deduce: *in-*, in + *ferre*, to bear.]

in•fer•ence /ĭn′ fər əns/ *n.* **a.** the act or process of inferring or deriving a conclusion from facts or premises. **b.** something inferred, especially a conclusion derived by inference.

in•fla•tion /ĭn flā′ shən/ *n.* **a.** the act of inflating or the state of being inflated. **b.** *Econ.* an abnormal increase in available currency and credit beyond the proportion of available goods, resulting in a sharp and continuing rise in price levels.

in•flu•ence¹ /ĭn′ flōō əns/ *n.* a power indirectly or intangibly affecting a person or a course of events. [ME < OFr. < Med. Lat. *influentia* < Lat. *influens*, pr.part. of *influere*, to flow in: *in-*, in + *fluere*, to flow.]

in•flu•ence² /ĭn′ flōō əns/ *v.* (**-enc•es, -enced, -enc•ing**) to have power over; affect.

in•flu•en•tial /ĭn′ flōō ĕn′ shəl/ *adj.* having or exercising influence.

in•form•a•tive /ĭn fôr′ mə tĭv/ *adj.* providing or disclosing information; instructive.

in•i•tial¹ /ĭ nĭsh′ əl/ *adj.* occurring at the very beginning; first.

in•i•tial² /ĭ nĭsh′ əl/ *n.* (often **initials.**) the first letter or letters of a person's name or names, used as a shortened signature or for identification.

in•i•tial³ /ĭ nĭsh′ əl/ *v.* (**-tials, -tialed, -tialled, -tial•ing, -tial•ling**) to mark or sign with initials.

in•sist /ĭn sĭst′/ *v.* (**in•sis•tence** *n.*) to be firm in a demand or course; refuse to yield. [Lat. *insistere*, to persist: *in-*, on + *sistere*, to stand.]

in•spect /ĭn spĕkt'/ *v.* to examine carefully and critically, especially for flaws. [Lat. *inspectare*, freq. of *inspicere*, to look into: *in-*, in + *specere*, to look.]

in•stant•ly /ĭn' stənt lē/ *adv.* at once; immediately.

in•struc•tive /ĭn strŭk' tĭv/ *adj.* conveying knowledge or information; enlightening.

in•stru•men•tal /ĭn' strə mĕn' tl/ *adj.* **a.** serving as a means or agency; implemental. **b.** performed on or written for a musical instrument.

in•te•ger /ĭn' tĭ jər/ *n.* a member of the set of positive whole numbers (1, 2, 3, . . .), negative whole numbers (-1, -2, -3, . . .), and zero (0).

in•tense /ĭn tĕns'/ *adj.* extreme in degree, strength, or size.

in•ter•act /ĭn' tər ăkt'/ *v.* (**in•ter•ac•tive** *adj.*) to act on each other.

in•ter•mis•sion /ĭn' tər mĭsh' ən/ *n.* **a.** a respite or recess. **b.** the period between the acts of a theatrical performance. [Lat. *intermissio* < *intermissus*, p.part. of *intermittere*, to intermit: *inter-*, at intervals + *mittere*, to let go.]

in•ter•pret /ĭn tûr' prĭt/ *v.* **a.** to explain to oneself the meaning of. **b.** to offer an explanation. **c.** to serve as an interpreter for speakers of different languages.

in•ter•rupt /ĭn' tə rŭpt'/ *v.* **a.** to break the continuity or uniformity of. **b.** to hinder or stop by breaking in upon. [ME *interrupten* < OFr. *interrupte*, interrupted < Lat. *interruptus*, p.part. of *interrumpere*, to break off: *inter-* between + *rumpere*, to break.]

in•trigue¹ /ĭn' trēg', ĭn trēg'/ *n.* a secret or underhanded scheme; plot. [Fr. < Ital. *intrigo* < *intrigare*, to perplex < Lat. *intricare*: *in-*, in + *tricae*, perplexities.]

in•trigue² /ĭn trēg'/ *v.* (**-trigues, -trigued, -trigu•ing**) **a.** to engage in intrigue; plot. **b.** to arouse the interest or curiosity of.

in•tro•vert¹ /ĭn' trə vûrt', ĭn' trə vûrt'/ *v.* to turn or direct inward. [Lat. *intro*, to the inside + Lat. *vertere*, to turn.]

in•tro•vert² /ĭn' trə vûrt'/ *n.* a person whose thoughts and interests are directed inward.

Pronunciation Key

ă	pat	ŏ	pot	th	thin
ā	pay	ō	toe	*th*	this
âr	care	ô	paw, for	hw	which
ä	father	oi	noise	zh	vision
ĕ	pet	ou	out	ə	about,
ē	be	ŏŏ	took		item,
ĭ	pit	ōō	boot		pencil,
ī	pie	ŭ	cut		gallop,
îr	pier	ûr	urge		circus

in•ven•tive /ĭn vĕn' tĭv/ *adj.* (**in•ven•tive•ness** *n.*) adept or skillful at inventing; creative.

inventive

in•volve /ĭn vŏlv'/ *v.* (**-volves, -volved, -volv•ing**) **a.** to contain or include as a part. **b.** to have as a necessary feature or consequence; entail. **c.** to occupy or engross; absorb. [ME *involven* < OFr. *involver* < Lat. *involvere*, to enwrap: *in-*, in + *volvere*, to roll, turn.]

i•sos•ce•les /ī sŏs' ə lēz'/ *adj.* having two equal sides: *an isosceles triangle.*

i•so•tope /ī' sə tōp/ *n.* one of two or more atoms whose nuclei have the same number of protons but different numbers of neutrons.

is•sue¹ /ĭsh' ōō/ *n.* something produced, published, or offered.

is•sue² /ĭsh' ōō/ *v.* (**-sues, -sued, -su•ing**) **a.** to go or come out. **b.** to circulate or distribute in an official capacity: *issue uniforms to the players.* **c.** to publish.

-ity a suffix that forms nouns meaning a quality or condition: *authenticity.*

-ive¹ a suffix that forms adjectives meaning tending toward, performing, or accomplishing something: *disruptive.*

-ive² a suffix that forms nouns meaning something that performs or accomplishes something: *sedative.*

jos•tle /jŏs′ əl/ *v.* (**-tles, -tled, -tling**) **a.** to come in contact or collide. **b.** to make one's way by pushing or elbowing. **c.** to vie for an advantage or position.

jus•ti•fy /jŭs′ tə fī/ *v.* (**-fies, -fied, -fy•ing**) to demonstrate or prove to be just, right, or valid.

key•board[1] /kē′ bôrd′, -bōrd′/ *n.* a set of keys, as on a piano, an organ, or a typewriter.

key•board[2] /kē′ bôrd′, -bōrd′/ *v.* to set (copy) by means of a keyed typesetting machine.

knife /nīf/ *n.* (**knives** /nīvz′ *pl.*) a cutting instrument consisting of a sharp blade with a handle.

knoll /nōl / *n.* a small rounded hill or mound; hillock.

lab•o•ra•to•ry /lăb′ rə tôr′ ē, -tōr′ ē, lə bŏr′ ə trē, -tə rē/ *n.* (**-ries** *pl.*) a room or building equipped for scientific experimentation or research.

la•bor un•ion /lā′ bər yōōn′ yən/ *n.* an organization of wage earners formed for the purpose of serving the members' interests with respect to wages and working conditions.

lar•i•at /lăr′ ē ət/ *n.* a long rope with a running noose for catching livestock; lasso. [Sp. *la reata: la,* the + *reatar,* to tie again. *(re-,* again + *atar,* to tie).]

lariat

lar•ynx /lâr′ ĭngks/ *n.* (**la•ryn•ges** /lə′ rĭn′ jēz/ or **lar•ynx•es** *pl.*) the upper part of the respiratory tract between the pharynx and the trachea, having walls of cartilage and containing the vocal cords.

lat•i•tude /lăt′ ĭ tōōd′, -tyōōd′/ *n.* **a.** extent; breadth. **b.1.** the angular distance north or south of the equator, measured in degrees along a meridian, as on a map or globe. **b.2.** a region of the earth considered in relation to its distance from the equator.

laun•dry /lôn′ drē, län′-/ *n.* (**-dries** *pl.*) **a.** soiled or laundered clothes and linens; wash. **b.** a place where laundering is done.

league /lēg/ *n.* **a.** an association of states, organizations, or individuals for common action; alliance. **b.** an association of sports teams or clubs that compete chiefly among themselves. **c.** a class of competition: *out of his league.*

leg•is•la•tion /lĕj′ ĭ slā′ shən/ *n.* a proposed or enacted law or group of laws.

le•o•tard /lē′ ə tärd′/ *n.* (often **leotards.**) **a.** a snugly fitting, elastic one-piece garment that covers the torso, worn especially by dancers or acrobats. **b. leotards.** tights [after Jules *Léotard* (1830–1870).]

-less a suffix that forms adjectives meaning without or free of: *nameless.*

lik•a•ble /lī′ kə bəl/ *adj.* pleasing; attractive.

liq•ue•fy /lĭk′ wə fī/ *v.* (**-fies, -fied, -fy•ing**) to cause to become liquid, especially: **a.1.** to melt (a solid) by heating. **a.2.** to condense (a gas) by cooling. **b.** to become liquid. [OFr. *liquefacere: liquere,* to be liquid + *facere,* to make.]

lob•by[1] /lŏb′ ē/ *n.* (**-bies** *pl.*) (**lob•by•ist** *n.*) **a.** a hall, foyer, or waiting room at or near the entrance to a building such as a hotel or theater. **b.** a public room next to the assembly chamber of a legislative body.

lob•by[2] /lŏb′ ē/ *v.* (**-bies, -bied, -by•ing**) to try to influence legislators, expecially in favor of a special interest.

lon•gi•tude /lŏn′ jĭ tōōd′, -tyōōd′/ *n.* the angular distance on the earth or on a globe or map, east or west of the prime meridian at Greenwich, England, to the point on the earth's surface for which the longitude is being ascertained, expressed either in degrees or in hours, minutes, and seconds.

-ly[1] a suffix that forms adjectives and means: **a.** characteristic of: *sisterly.* **b.** appearing or occurring at specified intervals: *weekly.*

-ly² a suffix that forms adverbs and means:
a. in a specified manner: *gradually.* **b.** at a
specified interval: *hourly.*

lyr•i•cal /lĭr′ ĭ kəl/ *adj.* expressing feeling or
emotion, especially deep personal emotion, in a
direct and affecting manner.

ă	pat	ŏ	pot	th	**th**in
ā	pay	ō	toe	*th*	**th**is
âr	care	ô	paw, for	hw	**wh**ich
ä	father	oi	noise	zh	vision
ĕ	pet	ou	**ou**t	ə	**a**bout,
ē	be	ŏŏ	took		item,
ĭ	pit	ōō	boot		penc**i**l,
ī	pie	ŭ	cut		gall**o**p,
îr	pier	ûr	**ur**ge		circ**u**s

mag•nan•i•mous /măg năn′ ə məs/ *adj.*
noble of mind and heart, especially generous in
forgiving. [Lat. *magnanimus: magnus,* great +
animus, soul.]

mag•nif•i•cent /măg nĭf′ i sənt/ *adj.* (**mag•
nif•i•cent•ly** *adv.*) **a.** splendid in appearance;
grand: *a magnificent palace.* **b.** outstanding of
its kind; superlative. [Lat. *magnificens, magnifi-
cent-,* var. of *magnificus-: magnus,* great +
facere, to make.]

mag•ni•fy /măg′ nə fī′/ *v.* (**-fies, -fied, -fy•ing**)
a. to make greater in size; to enlarge. **b.** to cause
to appear greater or seem more important; exaggerate. **c.** to increase the apparent size of, especially by means of a lens. [ME *magnifien* < OFr.
magnifier < Lat. *magnificare* < *magnificus,* magnificent: *magnus,* great + *facere,* to make.]

mag•no•lia /măg nōl′ yə/ *n.*
a. tree or shrub with large,
showy, usually white or pink
flowers. **b.** the flower of the
magnolia. [NLat. *Magnolia,*
genus name, after Pierre
Magnol (1638–1715).]

magnolia

main•tain /mān tān′/ *v.* **a.** to
continue; carry on. **b.** to preserve or keep in a
given existing condition, as of efficiency or repair:
maintain two cars.

main•te•nance /mān′ tə nəns/ *n.* **a.1.** the
action of maintaining. **a.2.** the state of being
maintained. **b.** the work of keeping something
in proper condition.

man•age /măn′ ĭj/ *v.* (**-ag•es, -aged, -ag•ing**)
a. to direct or administer (a business, for example). **b.** to contrive or arrange. [Ital. *maneggiare*
< VLat. **manidiare* < Lat. *manus,* hand.]

man•age•ment /măn′ ĭj mənt/ *n.* **a.** the act,
manner, or practice of managing, supervising, or
controlling. **b.** the person or persons who manage a business establishment, organization,
or institution.

ma•neu•ver¹ /mə nōō′ vər, -nyōō′/ *n.* a physical movement or way of doing something requiring skill and dexterity. [Fr. *manoeuvre* < OFr.
maneuvre, manual work < Med. Lat. *manuopera*
< Lat. *manu operari,* to work by hand.]

ma•neu•ver² /mə nōō′ vər, -nyōō′/ *v.* to
manipulate into a desired position or course.

man•i•cure¹ /măn′ ĭ kyōōr/ *n.* treatment of the
hands and fingernails, including shaping, cleaning, and polishing of the nails. [Fr.: Lat. *manus,*
hand + Lat. *cura,* care.]

man•i•cure² /măn′ ĭ kyōōr/ *v.* (**-cures, -cured,
-cur•ing**) **a.** to care for (the fingernails) by shaping, cleaning, and polishing. **b.** to clip or trim
evenly or closely.

ma•nip•u•late /mə nĭp′ yə lāt′/ *v.* (**-lates,
-lat•ed, -lat•ing**) **a.** to operate or control by
skilled use of the hands; handle. **b.** to influence
or manage shrewdly or deviously. [< Fr. *manip-
ule,* handful < Lat. *manipulus* < *manus* hand.]

man•ner•ism /măn′ ə rĭz′ əm/ *n.* **a.** a distinctive behavioral trait; idiosyncrasy. **b.** exaggerated or affected style or habit, as in dress,
speech, or art. [ME < OFr. *maniere* < VLat.
*manuaria < Lat. *manuarius,* of the hand
< Lat. *manus,* hand.]

man•u•al¹ /măn′ yōō əl/ *adj.* **a.** of, pertaining to,
or done by the hands. **b.** employing human rather
than mechanical energy: *manual labor.* [ME <
OFr. *manuel* < Lat. *manualis* < *manus,* hand.]

man•u•al² /măn′ yоо̄ əl/ *n.* **a.** a small reference book, especially one giving instructions. **b.** a keyboard of an organ played with the hands.

man•u•fac•ture /măn′ yə **făk′** chər/ *v.* (**-tures, -tured, -tur•ing**) **a.** to make or process (a raw material) into a finished product, especially by means of a large-scale industrial operation. **b.** to concoct or invent; fabricate: *manufacture an excuse.* [< OFr., a making by hand < LLat. *manufactus:* Lat. *manus,* hand + Lat. *facere,* to make.]

man•u•script /măn′ yə skrĭpt′/ *n.* **a.** a typewritten or handwritten version of a book, article, document, or other work, especially the author's own copy, prepared and submitted for publication in print.

mas•quer•adeˡ /măs′ kə **rād′**/ *n.* **a.** a costume party at which masks are worn; masked ball. **b.** a disguise or false outward show; pretense: *a masquerade of humility.* [OFr. *mascarade* < OSp. *mascarada,* poss. < Ar. *maskharah,* buffoon.]

mas•quer•ade² /măs′ kə **rād′**/ *v.* (**-ades, -ad•ed, -ad•ing**) **a.** to wear a mask or disguise, as at a masquerade. **b.** to go about as if in disguise; have or put on a deceptive appearance.

mast•head /măst′ hĕd′/ *n.* the listing in a newspaper, magazine, or other publication of information about its staff and operation.

ma•te•ri•alˡ /mə **tîr′** ē əl/ *n.* **a.** the substance or substances out of which a thing is or can be constructed. **b. Materials.** tools or apparatus for the performance of a given task: *writing materials.* **c.** yard goods or cloth.

ma•te•ri•al² /mə **tîr′** ē əl/ *adj.* **a.** composed of or pertaining to physical substances; relating to matter. **b.** of or concerned with the physical as distinct from the intellectual or spiritual.

math•e•mat•ics /măth′ ə **măt′** ĭks/ *n.* (*used with a sing. verb.*) the study of numbers, forms, arrangements, and sets, and of their relationships and properties.

mat•i•nee /măt′ n **ā′**/ *n.* a dramatic or musical performance given in the daytime, usually in the afternoon. [Fr. *matinée* < *matin,* morning.]

me•chan•i•cal /mĭ **kăn′** ĭ kəl/ *adj.* (**me•chan•i•cal•ly** *adv.*) **a.** of or pertaining to machines or tools. **b.** acting or performing like a machine; automatic. *The speaker's delivery was mechanical.*

me•chan•ics /mĭ **kăn′** ĭks/ *n.* (*used with a sing. or pl. verb.*) the functional and technical aspect of an activity. *The mechanics of football are learned with practice.*

me•di•a /mē′ dē ə/ *n. pl.* See **medium**.

me•di•anˡ /mē′ dē ən/ *adj. Statistics.* relating to or constituting the middle value in a distribution.

me•di•an² /mē′ dē ən/ *n. Statistics.* the middle value in a distribution, above and below which lie an equal number of values.

med•i•cal /mĕd′ ĭ kəl/ *adj.* of or pertaining to the study or practice of medicine.

me•di•um /mē′ dē əm/ *n.* (**-dia** *pl.*) **a.** an intervening substance through which something is transmitted or carried on. **b.** an agency by which something is accomplished, conveyed, or transferred. **c.** a means of mass communication, as newspapers, magazines, or television.

mega- a prefix meaning: **a.** large: *megadose.* **b.** one million: *megahertz.*

meg•a•phone /mĕg′ ə fōn′/ *n.* a funnel-shaped device used to direct and amplify the voice.

megaphone

me•nag•er•ie /mə **năj′** ə rē, mə **năzh′**-/ *n.* **a.** a collection of live wild animals on exhibition. **b.** the enclosure in which wild animals are kept. [Fr. *ménagerie* < *ménage,* ménage.]

-ment a suffix that forms nouns and means: **a.** an action or process: *government.* **b.** a condition: *amazement.* **c.** the product, means, or result of an action: *entanglement.*

me•sa /mā′ sə/ *n.* a flat-topped elevation with one or more clifflike sides, common in the southwestern United States. [Sp. < OSp. < Lat. *mensa,* table.]

met•a•mor•phic /mĕt′ ə **môr′** fĭk/ *adj.* characteristic of, pertaining to, or changed by metamorphism.

met•a•mor•phism /mĕt′ ə **môr′** fĭz′ əm/ *n.* an alteration in composition, texture, or structure of rock masses caused by great heat or pressure.

met•ri•cal /mĕt′ rĭ kəl/ *adj.* (**met•ri•cal•ly** *adv.*) of, pertaining to, or composed in rhythmic meter.

micro- a prefix meaning: **a.** small or smaller: *microcosm.* **b.** an instrument or technique for working with small things: *microscope.*

mi•cro•or•gan•ism /mī′ krō ôr′ gə nǐz′ əm/ *n.* an animal or plant of microscopic size, especially a bacterium or a protozoan.

mi•cro•phone /mī′ krə fōn′/ *n.* an instrument that converts acoustical waves into an electric current, usually fed into an amplifier, recorder, or broadcast transmitter.

mi•cro•scope /mī′ krə skōp′/ *n.* an optical instrument that uses a combination of lenses to produce magnified images of small objects, especially of objects too small to be seen by the unaided eye. [NLat. *microscopium:* MICRO- + *scopium,* scope.]

microscope

mid•point /mǐd′ point′/ *n.* **a.** the point of a line segment or curvilinear arc that divides it into two parts of the same length. **b.** a position midway between two extremes.

mim•ic[1] /mǐm′ ǐk/ *v.* (**-ics, -icked, -ick•ing**) to copy or imitate closely, especially in speech, expression, and gesture; ape.

mim•ic[2] /mǐm′ ǐk/ *n.* **a.** one who imitates, especially **a.1.** a mime. **a.2.** a person who copies or mimics others, as for amusement. **b.** a copy or imitation.

min•i•a•ture[1] /mǐn′ ē ə choŏr′, mǐn′ ə chər/ *n.* **a.** a copy or a model that represents something in a greatly reduced size. **b.** something small of its class.

min•i•a•ture[2] /mǐn′ ē ə choŏr′, mǐn′ ə chər/ *adj.* on a small or greatly reduced scale: *miniature furniture.*

mi•rage /mǐ räzh′/ *n.* **a.** an optical phenomenon that creates the illusion of water, often with upside-down reflections of distant objects. It is caused by distortions that occur as light passes between alternate layers of hot and cool air. **b.** something that is illusory or insubstantial. [Fr. < *mirer,* to look at < Lat. *mirari,* to wonder at.]

mis•chie•vous /mǐs′ chə vəs/ *adj.* **a.** playful; teasing. **b.** causing harm, injury, or damage: *mischievous falsehoods.*

mis•sive /mǐs′ ǐv/ *n.* a letter or message. [< ME (*letter*) *missive,* sent (by superior authority) < Med. Lat. (*littere*) *missive* < neuter of *missivus,* sent < Lat. *mittere,* to send.]

mis•take[1] /mǐ stāk′/ *n.* **a.** an error or fault. **b.** a misconception or misunderstanding.

mis•take[2] /mǐ stāk′/ *v.* (**-takes, -took, -tak•en, -tak•ing**) to make a mistake; err.

mix-up /mǐks′ ŭp′/ *n.* a state of confusion; muddle.

mode /mōd/ *n. Statistics.* the value or item occurring most frequently in a series of observations or statistical data.

mono- or **mon-** a prefix meaning one, single, or alone: *monocle.*

mon•o•cle /mŏn′ ə kəl/ *n.* an eyeglass for one eye. [Fr. < LLat. *monoculus,* having one eye: Gk. *monos,* one + Lat. *oculus,* eye.]

mon•o•gram[1] /mŏn′ ə grăm′/ *n.* a design composed of one or more letters, usually the initials of a name. [LLat. *monogramma* < Gk. *monogrammon: monos,* single + *gramma,* letter < *graphein,* to write.]

mon•o•gram[2] /mŏn′ ə grăm′/ *v.* (**-grams, -grammed, -gram•ming**) to mark with a monogram.

mo•nop•o•ly /mə nŏp′ ə lē/ *n.* (**-lies** *pl.*) exclusive control by one group of the means of producing or selling a commodity or service. [Lat. *monopolium* < Gk. *monopōlion: monos,* one + *pōlein,* to sell.]

mon•o•rail /mŏn′ ə rāl′/ *n.* **a.** a single rail on which a vehicle or train of cars travels. **b.** a railway system using a monorail.

mon•o•tone[1] /mŏn′ ə tōn′/ *n.* **a.** a succession of sounds or words uttered in a single tone of voice. **b.** sameness or dull repetition in sound, style, manner, or color.

mon•o•tone[2] /mŏn′ ə tōn′/ *adj.* **a.** of, pertaining to, or characteristic of sounds emitted at a single pitch. **b.** of or having a single color. [< Gk. *monotonos,* monotonous: *monos,* one + *tonos,* tone.]

mo•not•o•nous /mə nŏt′ n əs/ *adj.* **a.** sounded or spoken in an unvarying tone. **b.** repetitiously dull or lacking in variety. [Gk. *monotonos: monos,* one + *tonos,* tone.]

mo•not•o•ny /mə nŏt′ n ē/ *n.* **a.** uniformity or lack of variation in pitch, intonation, or inflection. **b.** wearisome sameness. [Gk. *monotonia < monotonos,* monotonous: *monos,* one + *tonos,* tone.]

mos•qui•to /mə skē′ tō/ *n.* (**-toes** *pl.*) any of various winged insects of which the females bite and suck blood from animals and human beings. Some kinds transmit diseases such as malaria and yellow fever. [Sp. < dim. of *mosca,* fly < Lat. *musca.*]

moth•er-in-law /mŭ*th*′ ər ĭn lô/ *n.* (**moth•ers-in-law** *pl.*) the mother of one's wife or husband.

mo•ti•vate /mō′ tə vāt′/ *v.* (**-vates, -vat•ed, -vat•ing**) to provide with an incentive or motive; impel. [ME *motive,* motive < OFr. *motif < motive,* causing motion < LLat. *motivus* < Lat. *movēre,* to move.]

mus•tang /mŭs′ tăng′/ *n.* a wild horse of the North American plains, descended from Spanish horses. [Sp. *mesteño,* stray animal < OSp. *mesta,* association of cattle owners < Lat. *miscere,* to mix.]

mu•tu•al /myōō′ chōō əl/ *adj.* **a.** having the same relationship to the other: *mutual friends.* **b.** directed and received in equal amount: *mutual respect.* **c.** possessed in common: *mutual interests.*

nar•rate /năr′ āt′, nă rāt′/ *v.* (**-rates, -rat•ed, -rat•ing**) (**nar•ra•tor** *n.*) **a.** to give an account or description. **b.** to supply a running commentary for a motion picture or other performance.

nar•ra•tive[1] /năr′ ə tĭv/ *n.* **a.** a narrated account; story. **b.** the act, technique, or process of narrating.

nar•ra•tive[2] /năr′ ə tĭv/ *adj.* **a.** consisting of or characterized by the telling of a story: *narrative poetry.* **b.** of or pertaining to narration: *narrative skill.*

nav•i•ga•tion /năv′ ĭ gā′ shən/ *n.* the theory and practice of navigating, especially the charting of a course for a ship or aircraft.

nec•es•sar•i•ly /nĕs′ ĭ sâr′ ə lē/ *adv.* of necessity; inevitably.

-ness a suffix that forms nouns and means a state, condition, or quality: *rudeness.*

net•work /nĕt′ wûrk′/ *n.* a group or system of electric components and connecting circuitry designed to function in a specific manner.

nev•er•the•less /nĕv′ ər *th*ə lĕs′/ *adv.* none the less; however.

news•cast /nōōz′ kăst:, nyōōz′-/ *n.* a radio or television broadcast of events in the news.

news•print /nōōz′ prĭnt′, nyōōz′-/ *n.* inexpensive paper made from wood pulp, used chiefly for printing newspapers.

news•reel /nōōz′ rēl′, nyōōz′-/ *n.* a short motion picture dealing with recent news events.

news•room /nōōz′ rōōm′, -rŏŏm′, nyōōz′-/ *n.* a room, as in a newspaper office or a radio or television station, in which news is prepared for release.

news•stand /nōōz′ stănd′, nyōōz′-/ *n.* a shop or open booth at which newspapers and periodicals are sold.

newsstand

no•ble[1] /nō′ bəl/ *adj.* (**-bler, -blest**) (**no•bly** *adv.*)
a. superior in nature or character; exalted: *a noble ideal.* **b.** grand and stately in appearance; majestic: *noble mountain peaks.*

no•ble[2] /nō′ bəl/ *n.* a member of the nobility.

nos•tal•gi•a /nŏ stăl′ jə, nə-/ *n.* a bittersweet longing for things, persons, or situations of the past.

no•tice•a•ble /nō′ tĭ sə bəl/ *adj.* (**no•tice•a•bly** *adv.*) readily observed; evident.

no•ti•fy /nō′ tə fī/ *v.* (**-fies, -fied, -fy•ing**) to give notice to; inform: *notified his client.* [ME *notifien* < OFr. *notifier* < Lat. *notificare,* to make known: *notus,* known (p.part. of *noscere,* to come to know) + *facere,* to make.]

no•tion /nō′ shən/ *n.* **a.** a belief; opinion. **b.** a fanciful impulse; whim. [Lat. *notio* < *noscere,* to come to know.]

nu•mer•a•tion /nōō′ mə rā′ shən, nyōō-/ *n.* the act or process of counting or numbering; enumeration.

nu•mer•i•cal /nōō mĕr′ ĭ kəl, nyōō-/ *adj.* **a.** of or pertaining to a number or series of numbers: *numerical order.* **b.** expressed in or counted by numbers: *numerical strength.*

nu•tri•ent[1] /nōō′ trē ənt, nyōō′-/ *n.* something that nourishes, especially a nourishing ingredient in a food.

nu•tri•ent[2] /nōō′ trē ənt, nyōō′-/ *adj.* providing nourishment.

ob- a prefix meaning toward, in front of, or against. When **ob-** is followed by **c, f,** or **p,** it becomes **oc-, of-,** or **op-** respectively. When it is followed by **m,** it is reduced to **o-.** [NLat. < Lat., toward, against < *ob,* toward.]

oc•cur /ə kûr′/ *v.* (**-curs, -curred, -cur•ring**) **a.** to take place; come about. **b.** to come to mind. [Lat. < *occurrere: ob,* toward + *currere,* to run.]

oc•cur•rence /ə kûr′ əns/ *n.* **a.** an act or instance of occurring. **b.** something that takes place; incident.

o•mit /ō mĭt′/ *v.* (**-mits, -mit•ted, -mit•ting**) to fail to include; leave out. [ME *omitten* < Lat. *omittere: ob,* away + *mittere,* to send.]

op•por•tu•ni•ty /ŏp′ ər tōō′ nĭ tē, -tyōō′-/ *n.* (**-ties** *pl.*) a favorable or advantageous combination of circumstances; suitable occasion or time.

or•a•tor /ôr′ ə tər, ŏr′-/ *n.* a person skilled in the art of public speaking.

or•ches•tra /ôr′ kĭ strə/ *n.* (**or•ches•tral** *adj.*) **a.** a large group of musicians who play together on various musical instruments, usually including strings, woodwinds, brass instruments, and percussion instruments. **b.** the instruments played by such a group of musicians.

orchestra

or•di•nal[1] /ôr′ dn əl/ *adj.* being of a specified position in a numbered series: *an ordinal rank of seventh.*

or•di•nal[2] /ôr′ dn əl/ *n.* an ordinal number.

or•gan•i•za•tion /ôr′ gə nĭ zā′ shən/ *n.* **a.** the state or manner of being organized. **b.** a number of persons or groups having specific responsibilities and united for a particular purpose.

or•gan•ize /ôr′ gə nīz′/ *v.* (**-iz•es, -ized, -iz•ing**) to put together into an orderly, functional, structured whole.

or•i•gin /ôr′ ə jĭn/ *n.* **a.** a point of origination; source. **b.** *Math.* the point of intersection of coordinate axes, as in the Cartesian coordinate system.

-ous a suffix that forms adjectives and means full of or having: *joyous.*

out•ra•geous /out rā′ jəs/ *adj.* **a.** being an outrage; grossly offensive. **b.** extravagant; immoderate; extreme.

o•val[1] /ō′ vəl/ *adj.* resembling an egg in shape. **b.** resembling an ellipse in shape.

o•val[2] /ō′ vəl/ *n.* an oval form or figure.

o•va•tion /ō vā′ shən/ *n.* **a.** enthusiastic and prolonged applause. **b.** a show of public homage or welcome.

pa•go•da /pə gō′ də/ *n.* **a.** a religious building of the Far East, especially a many-storied Buddhist tower, erected as a memorial or shrine. **b.** a structure, such as a garden pavilion, built in imitation of a pagoda.

pains•tak•ing /pānz′ tā′ kĭng/ *adj.* taking great pains; careful.

par•a•chute[1] /păr′ ə shōōt′/ *n.* a foldable umbrella-shaped device used to slow the fall of persons or objects from great heights.

parachute

par•a•chute[2] /păr′ ə shōōt′/ *v.* (**-chutes, -chut•ed, -chut•ing**) to descend by means of a parachute.

par•a•phrase[1] /păr′ ə frāz′/ *n.* a restatement of a text or passage in another form or other words, often to clarify meaning.

par•a•phrase[2] /păr′ ə frāz′/ *v.* (**-phras•es, -phrased, -phras•ing**) to express in a paraphrase.

pa•ren•the•sis /pə rĕn′ thə sĭs/ *n.* (**-ses** *pl.*) either or both of the upright curved lines, ( ), used to mark off explanatory or qualifying remarks in writing or printing.

par•tial•ly /pär′ shə lē/ *adv.* to a degree; not totally.

par•tic•u•lar[1] /pər tĭk′ yə lər/ *adj.* **a.** separate and distinct from others; specific. **b.** worthy of note; exceptional. [ME < *particuler* < OFr. < LLat. *particularis* < Lat. *particula,* dim. of *pars,* part.]

par•tic•u•lar[2] /pər tĭk′ yə lər/ *n.* an individual item, fact, or detail.

par•tic•u•lar•ly /pər tĭk′ yə lər lē/ *adv.* **a.** to a great degree; especially. **b.** with particular reference or emphasis; specifically.

pas•ser•by /păs′ ər bī′/ *n.* (**pas•sers•by** *pl.*) a person who passes by, often by chance.

pass•word /păs′ wûrd′/ *n.* a secret word or phrase which indicates that the speaker is to be admitted.

pat•i•o /păt′ ē ō, pä′ tē ō′/ *n.* (**-os** *pl.*) **a.** an inner, roofless courtyard. **b.** a space for dining or recreation, usually paved, that adjoins a residence. [Sp. < OSp. < Lat. *patēre,* to be open.]

pe•cu•liar /pĭ kyōōl′ yər/ *adj.* (**pe•cu•liar•ly** *adv.*) **a.** unusual or eccentric; odd: *peculiar behavior.* **b.1.** exclusive; unique. **b.2.** belonging distinctively or primarily to one person, group, or kind.

pen•cil sharp•en•er /pĕn′ səl shär′ pə nər/ *n.* a small mechanical device that shaves the end of a pencil into a point for writing: *I need to use the pencil sharpener to sharpen my new pencils.*

per•cep•tion /pər sĕp′ shən/ *n.* insight, intuition, or knowledge gained by perceiving.

per•fec•tion /pər fĕk′ shən/ *n.* the state, quality, or condition of being perfect.

peri- a prefix meaning around, about, or enclosing: *periscope.*

per•i•scope /pĕr′ ĭ skōp′/ *n.* any of several instruments in which mirrors or prisms allow observation of objects that are not in a direct line of sight.

per•mis•si•ble /pər mĭs′ ə bəl/ *adj.* that can be permitted; allowable.

per•sist /pər sĭst′, -zĭst′/ *v.* **a.** to hold firmly and steadfastly to a purpose, state, or undertaking despite obstacles, warnings, or setbacks. **b.** to continue in existence; last. [Lat. *persistere: per-* (intensive) + *sistere,* to stand.]

per•son•al /pûr′ sə nəl/ *adj.* **a.1.** done, made, or performed in person: *a personal appearance.* **a.2.** done to or for or directed toward a particular person: *a personal favor.* **b.** concerning a particular individual and his intimate affairs, interests, or activities; intimate: *I have something personal to tell you.* **c.** of or pertaining to the body or physical being: *personal cleanliness.*

per•son•nel /pûr′ sən ĕl′/ *n.* **a.** the body of persons employed by or active in an organization, business, or service. **b.** an administrative division of an organization concerned with the body of persons employed by or active in it.

per•spec•tive /pər spĕk′ tĭv/ *n.* an idea of the relative importance of something; point of view.

phon•ics /fŏn′ ĭks/ *n.* (*used with a sing. verb*) **a.** the study or science of sound; acoustics. **b.** the use of phonetics in the teaching of reading.

phos•phate /fŏs′ fāt′/ *n. Chem.* a salt or ester of phosphoric acid.

phys•i•cal /fĭz′ ĭ kəl/ *adj.* of or pertaining to the body, as distinguished from the mind or spirit; bodily.

phys•i•ol•o•gy /fĭz ē ŏl′ ə jē/ *n.* the biological science of essential and characteristic life processes, activities, and functions.

pic•nic[1] /pĭk′ nĭk/ *n.* (**pic•nick•er** *n.*) a meal eaten outdoors on an excursion.

pic•nic[2] /pĭk′ nĭk/ *v.* (**-nics, -nicked, -nick•ing**) to go on or participate in a picnic.

pic•tur•esque /pĭk′ chə rĕsk′/ *adj.* **a.** of or suggesting a picture: *picturesque rocky shores.* **b.** strikingly expressive or vivid: *picturesque language.* [Fr. *pittoresque* < Ital. *pittoresco* < *pittore*, painter < Lat. *pictor* < *pingere*, to paint.]

pis•ton /pĭs′ tən/ *n.* a solid cylinder or disk that fits snugly into a larger cylinder and moves back and forth under fluid pressure.

play•wright /plā′ rīt′/ *n.* one who writes plays; dramatist.

poll[1] /pōl/ *n.* a survey of the public or of a sample of the public to acquire information or record opinion.

poll[2] /pōl/ *v.* **a.** to receive or record the votes of: *poll a jury.* **b.** to queston in a survey; canvass.

pol•lut•ant /pə lōōt′ nt/ *n.* a waste material that contaminates air, soil, or water.

pol•y•he•dron /pŏl ē hē′ drən/ *n.* a solid bounded by polygons.

Pronunciation Key

ă	pat	ŏ	pot	th	**th**in
ā	pay	ō	toe	*th*	**th**is
âr	care	ô	paw, for	hw	**wh**ich
ä	father	oi	noise	zh	vision
ĕ	pet	ou	out	ə	about,
ē	be	ŏŏ	took		item,
ĭ	pit	ōō	boot		pencil,
ī	pie	ŭ	cut		gallop,
îr	pier	ûr	urge		circus

pos•i•tive /pŏz′ ĭ tĭv/ *adj.* (**pos•i•tive•ly** *adv.*) **a.** characterized by or displaying certainty. **b.** admitting of no doubt. **c.** determined or settled in opinion or assertion; confident: *a positive manner.*

pos•si•bil•i•ty /pŏs′ ə bĭl′ ĭ tē/ *n.* (**-ties** *pl.*) the fact or state of being possible. [ME < OFr. < Lat. *possibilis* < *posse,* to be able.]

pos•si•ble /pŏs′ ə bəl/ *adj.* capable of happening, existing, or being true.

po•ta•to /pə tā′ tō/ *n.* (**-toes** *pl.*) a plant native to South America and widely cultivated for its starchy, edible tubers.

potato

po•ten•tial[1] /pə tĕn′ shəl/ *adj.* capable of being but not yet in existence.

po•ten•tial[2] /pə tĕn′ shəl/ *n.* **a.** the inherent ability or capacity for growth, development, or coming into being. **b.** something possessing the capacity for growth or development.

prag•ma•tism /prăg′ mə tĭz′ əm/ *n.* a practical way of solving problems.

pre- a prefix meaning before: *precaution.* When **pre-** is followed by a vowel, it may appear with a hyphen: **pre-empt, pre•empt.**

pred•a•tor /prĕd′ ə tər, -tôr′/ *n.* an animal that lives by preying upon others.

pre•dict /prĭ dĭkt′/ *v.* (**pre•dict•a•bil•i•ty** *n.*) (**pre•dict•a•ble** *adj.*) (**pre•dict•a•bly** *adv.*) **a.** to tell about or make known in advance: *predict the weather.* **b.** to foretell what will happen; prophesy.

pre•fer /prĭ fûr/ v. (-fers, -ferred, -fer•ring) to choose as more desirable; like better. [ME *pre-ferren* < OFr. *preferer* < Lat. *praeferre: prae,* before + *ferre,* to bear.]

pref•er•ence /prĕf′ ər əns, prĕf′ rəns/ n. **a.** the exercise of choice. **b.** the state of being preferred.

pre•miere /prĭ mîr′, myâr′/ n. the first public performance, as of a movie or play. [Fr. < fem. of *premier,* first.]

pre•mi•um /prē′ mē əm/ n. **a.** an unusual or high value: *put a premium on honesty and hard work.* **b.** the amount paid or payable, often in installments, for an insurance policy.

pres•ent•ly /prĕz′ ənt lē/ adv. in a short time; soon.

prim•i•tive /prĭm′ ĭ tĭv/ adj. (prim•i•tive•ly adv.) **a.** pertaining to an earliest or original stage or state. **b.** of or pertaining to early stages in the evolution of human culture: *primitive societies.*

prin•ci•pal¹ /prĭn′ sə pəl/ adj. (prin•ci•pal•ly adv.) first, highest, or foremost in importance, rank, worth, or degree.

prin•ci•pal² /prĭn′ sə pəl/ n. **a.** one who holds a position of presiding rank, especially the head of a school. **b.** a main participant in a given situation.

pri•or /prī′ ər/ adj. preceding in time or order: *a prior commitment.* **—idiom. prior to.** before.

priv•i•lege /prĭv′ ə lĭj/ n. a special advantage, immunity, permission, right, or benefit granted to or enjoyed by an individual, class, or caste. [ME < OFr. < Lat. *privilegium,* a law affecting one person: *privus,* single + *lex,* law.]

pro-¹ a prefix meaning: **a.** favor or support. **b.** acting as; substituting for: *pronoun.* When **pro-** is followed by a capital letter, it appears with a hyphen: *pro-American.* [ME < Lat. *pro,* for.]

pro-² a prefix meaning before or in front of: *prologue.* [< Gk. *pro,* before, in front of.]

pro•ces•sion /prə sĕsh′ ən/ n. a group of persons, vehicles, or objects moving along in an orderly and formal manner, usually in a long line. [ME < OFr. < Lat. *processio,* advance < *pro-cedere,* to advance: *pro-,* forward + *cedere,* to go.]

pro•duc•er /prə dōō′ sər, -dyōō′-, prō-/ n. one who finances and supervises the production of a play or other public entertainment.

pro•fes•sion•al¹ /prə fĕsh′ ə nəl/ adj. engaged in a specific activity as a source of livelihood.

pro•fes•sion•al² /prə fĕsh′ ə nəl/ n. **a.** one who has an assured competence in a particular field or occupation. **b.** one who earns his or her livelihood as an athlete. [ME *profession,* vow made on entering a religious order < OFr. < Lat. *professio,* declaration < *profiteri,* to declare.]

pron•to /prŏn′ tō/ adv. Informal. without delay; quickly. [Sp. < Lat. *promptus.*]

prop•a•gan•da /prŏp′ ə găn′ də/ n. material distributed for the purpose of winning people over to a given doctrine, often without regard to truth or fairness.

prop•er•ty /prŏp′ ər tē/ n. (-ties pl.) **a.1.** a possession. **a.2.** possessions collectively. **b.** something to which its owner has legal title. **c.1.** a characteristic trait or peculiarity. **c.2.** a quality serving to define or describe an object or substance. **c.3.** a characteristic attribute possessed by all members of a class.

pro•por•tion•al /prə pôr′ shə nəl, -pōr′-/ adj. **a.** properly related in size or other measurable characteristics. **b.** *Math.* having a constant ratio.

pro•pose /prə pōz′/ v. (-pos•es, -posed, -pos•ing) **a.** to put forward for consideration, discussion, or adoption; suggest: *propose new methods.* **b.** to form or make a proposal, especially of marriage.

pros•pect¹ /prŏs′ pĕkt/ n. **a.** something expected; possibility. **b.** the location or probable location of a mineral deposit. [ME *prospecte* < Lat. *prospectus,* distant view < p.part. of *prospicere,* to look out: *pro-,* forward + *specere,* to look.]

pros•pect² /prŏs′ pĕkt/ v. to search for or explore (a region) for gold or other mineral deposits.

pro•trac•tor /prō trăk′ tər, prə-/ n. a semicircular instrument for measuring and constructing angles.

protractor

pseu•do•nym /sōōd′ n ĭm′/ n. a fictitious name assumed by an author; pen name.

Spelling Dictionary

pub•lic•i•ty /pŭ blĭs′ ĭ tē/ *n.* information that concerns a person, group, event, or product and that is given out through various communications media to attract public notice.

pur•sue /pər sōō′/ *v.* (**-sues, -sued, -su•ing**)
a. to follow in an effort to overtake or capture; chase. **b.** to strive to gain or accomplish. **c.** to proceed along the course of; follow.

pur•suit /pər sōōt′/ *n.* **a.** the act or an instance of chasing or pursuing. **b.** the act of striving. **c.** a vocation, hobby, or other activity regularly engaged in.

pyr•a•mid /pĭr′ ə mĭd/ *n.* **a.** a polyhedron with a polygonal base and triangular faces meeting in a common vertex. **b.** a massive monument found especially in Egypt, having a rectangular base and four triangular faces culminating in a single apex, and serving as a tomb or temple.

pyramid

quad•rant /kwŏd′ rənt/ *n.* any of the four areas into which a plane is divided by the reference axes in a Cartesian coordinate system, designated first, second, third, and fourth, counting clockwise from the area in which both coordinates are positive.

qual•i•ty /kwŏl′ ĭ tē/ *n.* (**-ties** *pl.*) **a.** the essential character of something; nature. **b.1.** an inherent or distinguishing characteristic; property. **b.2.** a personal trait, especially a character trait. **c.1.** superiority of kin: *an intellect of unquestioned quality.* **c.2.** degree or grade of excellence: *yard goods of low quality.*

ques•tion•a•ble /kwĕs′ chə nə bəl/ *adj.*
a. open to doubt or challenge; problematic. **b.** not yet determined or specified; uncertain.

quick•wit•ted /kwĭk′ wĭt′ ĭd/ *adj.* mentally alert and sharp; keen.

Pronunciation Key

ă	pat	ŏ	pot	th	**thin**
ā	pay	ō	toe	*th*	**this**
âr	care	ô	paw, for	hw	**which**
ä	father	oi	noise	zh	vision
ĕ	pet	ou	**out**	ə	about,
ē	be	ŏŏ	took		item,
ĭ	pit	ōō	boot		pencil,
ī	pie	ŭ	cut		gallop,
îr	pier	ûr	**ur**ge		circus

ra•di•o•ac•tive /rā′ dē ō ăk′ tĭv/ *adj.* of or exhibiting radioactivity.

ra•di•o•ac•tiv•i•ty /rā′ dē ō ăk tĭv′ ĭ tē/ *n.* the process or property by which atomic nuclei emit radiation.

ra•ven[1] /rā′ vən/ *n.* a large bird, *Corvus corax,* having black plumage and a croaking cry. [ME < OE *hraefn.*]

ra•ven[2] /rā′ vən/ *adj.* black and shiny.

re- a prefix meaning: **a.** again; anew: *reassemble.* **b.** back; backward: *recall.* When **re-** is followed by **e,** it may appear with a hyphen: *re-elect.*

read•i•ly /rĕd′ ə lē/ *adv.* **a.** promptly. **b.** willingly. **c.** easily.

re•al•is•tic /rē′ ə lĭs′ tĭc/ *adj.* **a.** tending to or expressing an awareness of things as they really are. **b.** accurately representing what is depicted or described.

re•al•i•ty /rē ăl′ ĭ tē/ *n.* (**-ties** *pl.*) **a.** the quality or state of being actual or true. **b.** the totality of all things possessing actuality, existence, or essence.

re•ap•pear /rē ə pîr′/ *v.* (**re•ap•pear•ance** *n.*) to come into view again.

rea•son•a•ble /rē′ zə nə bəl/ *adj.* (**rea•son•a•bly** *adv.*) **a.** capable of reasoning; rational. **b.** not excessive or extreme; fair: *reasonable prices.*

re•ceive /rĭ sēv'/ *v.* (-ceives, -ceived, -ceiv•ing)
a. to acquire or get something; be a recipient.
b. *Electronics.* to convert incoming electromagnetic waves into visible or audible signals.

rec•og•ni•tion /rĕk'əg nĭsh'ən/ *n.* **a.** the act of recognizing or condition of being recognized.
b. attention or favorable notice: *recognition for their many achievements.*

rec•og•nize /rĕk'əg nīz'/ *v.* (-niz•es, -nized, -niz•ing) (**rec•og•niz•a•ble** *adj.*) **a.** to know to be something that has been perceived before.
b. to know or identify from past experience or knowledge. **c.** to perceive or acknowledge the validity or reality of.

rec•on•cile /rĕk'ən sīl'/ *v.* (-ciles, -ciled, -cil•ing) **a.** to reestablish friendship between.
b. to settle or resolve. **c.** to make compatible or consistent.

re•con•sid•er /rē'kən sĭd'ər/ *v.* to consider again, especially with intent to alter or modify a previous decision.

re•fer /rĭ fûr'/ *v.* (-fers, -ferred, -fer•ring) (**re•fer•ral** *n.*) **a.** to direct to a source for help or information. **b.** to pertain; concern: *questions referring to yesterday's lecture.* **c.** to turn to, as for information or authority. [ME *referen* < OFr. *referer* < Lat. *referre: re-*, back + *ferre*, to carry.]

ref•e•ree¹ /rĕf'ə rē'/ *n.* **a.** one to whom something is referred, especially for settlement or decision.
b. *Sports.* an official supervising the play; umpire.

referee

ref•e•ree² /rĕf'ə rē'/ *v.* (-rees, -reed, -ree•ing) to act as referee.

ref•er•ence /rĕf'ər əns, rĕf'rəns/ *n.* **a.** an act of referring. **b.** an allusion to an occurrence or situation. **c.1.** a note in a publication referring the reader to another passage or source. **c.2.** the passage or source so referred to. **d.1.** a person who is in a position to recommend another or to vouch for his or her fitness, as for a job. **d.2.** a written statement about a person's qualifications, character, and dependability.

re•frain /rĭ frān'/ *n.* a phrase or verse repeated at intervals throughout a song or poem, especially at the end of each stanza.

re•gard•less¹ /rĭ gärd'lĭs/ *adj.* heedless; unmindful. [ME *regarden*, to regard < OFr. *regarder: re-*, back + *guarder*, to guard, of Germanic origin.]

re•gard•less² /rĭ gärd'lĭs/ *adv.* in spite of everything; anyway.

re•hears•al /rĭ hûr'səl/ *n.* **a.** the act or process of practicing in preparation for a performance, especially for a public performance. **b.** a verbal repetition or recital.

re•mark•a•ble /rĭ mär'kə bəl/ *adj.* (**re•mark•a•bly** *adv.*) **a.** worthy of notice.
b. extraordinary; uncommon.

re•mem•brance /rĭ mĕm'brəns/ *n.* **a.** the act of remembering. **b.** something remembered; reminiscence. **c.** a memento; souvenir.

re•miss /rĭ mĭs'/ *adj.* **a.** lax in attending to duty; negligent. **b.** exhibiting carelessness or slackness.

rep•e•ti•tious /rĕp'ĭ tĭsh'əs/ *adj.* characterized by or filled with repetition, especially needless or tedious repetition.

rep•li•ca /rĕp'lĭ kə/ *n.* **a.** a copy or reproduction of a work of art, especially one made by the original artist. **b.** a copy or reproduction. [Ital. < *replicare*, to repeat < Lat. to fold back: *re-*, back + *plicare*, to fold.]

rep•re•sen•ta•tive /rĕp'rĭ zĕn'tə tĭv/ *n.*
a. one that serves as a delegate or agent for another. **b.1.** a member of a governmental body, usually legislative, chosen by popular vote. **b.2.** in the United States, a member of the House of Representatives or of a state legislature.

re•quire•ment /rĭ kwīr'mənt/ *n.* **a.** something that is required; necessity. **b.** something obligatory; prerequisite. [ME *requiren*, to require < OFr. *requere* < VLat. *requaerere* < Lat. *requirere: re-*, again + *quaerere*, to seek.]

res•i•den•tial /rĕz'ĭ dĕn'shəl/ *adj.* **a.** of, relating to, or having residence. **b.** of, suitable for, or limited to residences.

re•sign /rĭ zīn'/ *v.* **a.** to submit (oneself) passively; accept as inevitable. **b.** to give up (a position), especially by formal notification; quit.

re•sist /rǐ zǐst′/ *v.* **a.** to strive or work against; oppose actively. **b.** to remain firm against the action or effect of; withstand. **c.** to keep from giving in to or enjoying. [ME *resisten* < Lat. *resistere: re-,* against + *sistere,* to place.]

re•sis•tance /rǐ zǐs′ təns/ *n.* **a.1.** the act of resisting. **a.2.** the capacity to resist. **b.** a force that tends to oppose or retard motion.

res•o•lu•tion /rĕz′ ə lōō′ shən/ *n.* **a.** the state or quality of being resolute; firm determination. **b.** the act of resolving to do something. **c.** a course of action determined or decided upon. [Lat. *resolutus,* p.part. of *resolvere,* to untie: *re-,* back + *solvere,* to untie.]

re•solve¹ /rǐ zŏlv′/ *v.* (**-solves, -solved, -solv•ing**) **a.** to make a firm decision about. **b.** to find a solution to. **c.** to bring to a usually successful conclusion. [ME *resolven,* to dissolve < Lat. *resolvere,* to untie: *re-,* back + *solvere,* to untie.]

re•solve² /rǐ zŏlv′/ *n.* **a.** firmness of purpose; resolution. **b.** a fixed purpose.

res•o•nate /rĕz′ ə nāt′/ *v.* (**-nates, -nat•ed, -nat•ing**) **a.** to exhibit or produce resonance or resonant effects. **b.** to resound.

re•spect¹ /rǐ spĕkt′/ *v.* **a.** to feel or show deferential regard for; esteem. **b.** to relate or refer to; concern. [Lat. *respicere, respect-: re-,* back + *specere,* to look.]

re•spect² /rǐ spĕkt′/ *n.* **a.** a feeling of deferential regard; esteem. **b.** a particular aspect, feature, or detail.

re•strict /rǐ strǐkt′/ *v.* to keep within limits; confine. [Lat. *restringere, restrict-,* to restrain: *re-,* back + *stringere,* to bind.]

résumé /rĕz′ ŏŏ mā′/ *n.* a summary, especially a brief record of one's personal history and experience submitted with a job application. [Fr. < p.part. of *résumer,* to summarize < OFr. *résumer,* to resume.]

re•tract /rǐ trăkt′/ *v.* **a.** to take back; disavow. **b.** to draw back or in. [ME *retracten* < OFr. *retracter* < Lat. *retractare,* to handle again, freq. of *retrahere,* to draw back: *re-,* back + *trahere,* to draw.]

Pronunciation Key

ă	pat	ŏ	pot	th	**th**in
ā	pay	ō	toe	*th*	**th**is
âr	care	ô	paw, for	hw	**wh**ich
ä	father	oi	noise	zh	vi**s**ion
ĕ	pet	ou	**ou**t	ə	**a**bout,
ē	be	ŏŏ	took		it**e**m,
ĭ	pit	ōō	boot		penc**i**l,
ī	pie	ŭ	cut		gall**o**p,
îr	pier	ûr	**ur**ge		circ**u**s

rev•o•lu•tion /rĕv′ ə lōō′ shən/ *n.* **a.1.** orbital motion about a point, especially as distinguished from axial rotation: *the planetary revolution about the sun.* **a.2.** a single complete cycle of such orbital or axial motion. **b.** a sudden or momentous change in any situation. [ME *revolucioun* < OFr. *revolution* < LLat. *revolutio* < Lat. *revolvere,* to turn over: *re-,* back + *volvere,* to roll.]

re•volve /rǐ vŏlv′/ *v.* (**-volves, -volved, -volv•ing**) **a.** to orbit a central point. **b.** to turn on an axis; rotate. [ME *revolven* < Lat. *revolvere,* to turn over, to roll back: *re-,* back + *volvere,* to roll.]

rhet•o•ric /rĕt′ ər ĭk/ *n.* **a.** the study of the elements, as structure or style, used in writing and speaking. **b.** the art of effective expression and the persuasive use of language.

ri•dic•u•lous /rǐ dǐk′ yə ləs/ *adj.* deserving or inspiring ridicule; absurd or preposterous; laughable.

ri•val•ry /rī′ vəl rē/ *n.* (**-ries** *pl.*) **a.** the act of competing or emulating. **b.** the state or condition of being a rival.

ro•de•o /rō′ dē ō, rō dā′ ō/ *n.* (**-os** *pl.*) **a.** a cattle roundup. **b.** a competition in which cowboys display skills such as riding broncos or lassoing. [Sp. < *rodear,* to surround < Lat. *rotare,* to rotate < *rota,* wheel.]

rodeo

ro•tate /rō′ tāt/ *v.* (**-tates, -tat•ed, -tat•ing**) **a.** to turn or spin on an axis. **b.** to proceed in sequence; alternate. **c.** to plant or grow (crops) in a fixed order of succession.

rus•tic /rŭs′ tĭk/ *adj.* **a.** of, pertaining to, or typical of country life. **b.** simple and unsophisticated.

sal•a•ry /săl′ ə rē, săl′ rē/ *n.* (**-ries** *pl.*) a fixed compensation for services, paid to a person on a regular basis. [ME *salarie* < Lat. *salarium,* money given to Roman soldiers to buy salt < *sal,* salt.]

sam•ple /săm′ pəl/ *n.* a set of elements drawn from and analyzed to estimate the characteristics of a population.

sam•pling /săm′ plĭng/ *n. Statistics.* a sample.

sanc•tu•ar•y /săngk′ cho͞o ĕr′ē/ *n.* (**-ies** *pl.*) a reserved area in which animals are protected.

sap•phire /săf′ īr′/ *n.* **a.** any of several relatively pure forms of corundum, especially a blue form used as a gemstone. **b.** the blue color of a gem sapphire.

sar•casm /sär′ kăz′ əm/ *n.* **a.** a sharply mocking or ironic remark. **b.** the use of sarcasm.

sat•in /săt′ n/ *n.* a smooth fabric, as of silk or rayon, woven with a glossy face and a dull back. [prob. from *Zaitun,* after a city in China.]

sat•ire /săt′ īr′/ *n.* **a.** a literary work in which human vice or folly is attacked through irony, derision, or wit. **b.** the branch of literature comprising such works.

sax•o•phone /săk′ sə fōn′/ *n.* a wind instrument with a single-reed mouthpiece and a usually curved conical metal tube, available in a variety of sizes. [after Adolphe *Sax* (1814–1894), its inventor.]

sca•lene /skā′ lēn′, skā lēn′/ *adj.* having three unequal sides. Used of triangles.

scen•er•y /sē′ nə rē/ *n.* (**-ies** *pl.*) (**scen•ic** *adj.*) **a.** a landscape. **b.** the painted backdrops on a theatrical stage.

sched•ule¹ /skĕj′ o͞ol, -əl/ *n.* **a.** a printed or often written list of items in tabular form. **b.1.** a program of forthcoming events or appointments. **b.2.** a student's program of classes. **c.** a timetable of departures and arrivals.

sched•ule² /skĕj′ o͞ol, -əl/ *v.* (**-ules, -uled, -ul•ing**) **a.** to make up a schedule for. **b.** to plan or appoint for a certain time or date.

sci•en•tif•ic /sī′ ən tĭf′ ĭk/ *adj.* (**sci•en•tif•i•cal•ly** *adv.*) of, relating to, or employing the methodology of science.

score•board /skôr′ bôrd′, skōr′ bōrd′/ *n.* a large board for indicating the score of a game.

sea•far•ing¹ /sē′ fâr′ ĭng/ *n.* a sailor's calling.

sea•far•ing² /sē′ fâr′ ĭng/ *adj.* following a life at sea.

se•cu•ri•ty /sĭ kyo͝or′ ĭ tē/ *n.* (**-ties** *pl.*) **a.** freedom from risk or danger; safety. **b.** freedom from doubt, anxiety, or fear; confidence. **c.** something that gives or assures safety. **d.** something deposited or given as assurance of the fulfillment of an obligation; pledge.

sed•i•men•ta•ry /sĕd′ ə mĕn′ tə rē, -mĕn′ trē/ *adj. Geol.* of or pertaining to rocks formed from sediment or from transported fragments deposited in water.

seek /sēk/ *v.* (**seeks, sought** /sôt/, **seek•ing**) to try to locate or discover, search.

seis•mic /sīz′ mĭk/ *adj.* of, subject to, or caused by an earthquake or earth vibration.

seis•mo•graph /sīz′ mə grăf′/ *n.* an instrument for automatically detecting and recording the intensity, direction, and duration of a movement of the ground, especially of an earthquake.

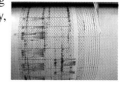

seismograph

self-em•ployed /sĕlf′ ĕm ploid′/ *adj.* working for oneself, rather than for an employer.

self-es•teem /sĕlf′ ĭ stēm′/ *n.* pride in oneself.

self-taught /sĕlf′ tôt′/ *adj.* having taught oneself without formal instruction or the help of others.

sen•si•tive /sĕn′ sĭ tĭv/ *adj.* **a.** responsive to external conditions or stimulation. **b.** susceptible to the attitudes, feelings, or circumstances of others. **c.** quick to take offense; touchy. **d.** easily irritated. **e.** registering very slight differences or changes of conditions.

sep•a•rate¹ /sĕp′ ə rāt′/ *v.* (**-rates, -rat•ed, -rat•ing**) (**sep•a•rate•ly** *adv.*) **a.1.** to set or keep apart. **a.2.** to space apart; scatter. **a.3.** to sort. **b.** to become divided into components or parts.

sep•a•rate² /sĕp′ ər ĭt, sĕp′ rĭt/ *adj.* **a.** set apart from others; detached. **b.** independent. **c.** not shared; individual.

se•quel /sē′ kwəl, -kwĕl′/ *n.* **a.** something that follows; continuation. **b.** a literary work complete in itself but continuing the narrative of an earlier work.

set•ting /sĕt′ ĭng/ *n.* **a.** the context and environment in which a situation is set. **b.** the time and place in which a literary or a dramatic work is set.

shelf /shĕlf/ *n.* (**shelves** *pl.*) a flat, usually rectangular structure of a rigid material, as wood, glass, or metal. It is usually fixed to a wall or other vertical surface and used to hold or store objects.

si•er•ra /sē ĕr′ ə/ *n.* **a.** a rugged range of mountains having an irregular or serrated profile. [Sp. < Lat. *serra,* saw.]

si•es•ta /sē ĕs′ tə/ *n.* a rest or nap, usually taken after the midday meal. [Sp. < Lat. *sexta (hora),* sixth (hour) < *sextus,* sixth.]

sig•ni•fy /sĭg′ nə fī′/ *v.* (**-fies, -fied, -fy•ing**) **a.** to serve as a sign of. **b.** to have meaning or importance.

sil•hou•ette¹ /sĭl′ oo ĕt′/ *n.* **a.** a drawing consisting of the outline of something, especially a human profile, filled in with a solid color. **b.** an outline of something that appears dark against a light background.

sil•hou•ette² /sĭl′ oo ĕt′/ *v.* (**-ettes, -et•ted, -et•ting**) to cause to be seen as a silhouette; outline. [Fr. < Etienne de *Silhouette* (1709–1767).]

si•mul•ta•ne•ous /sī′ məl tā′ nē əs, sĭm′ əl-/ *adj.* (**si•mul•ta•ne•ous•ly** *adv.*) happening, existing, or done at the same time.

sit•u•a•tion /sĭch′ oo ā′ shən/ *n.* **a.** the place in which something is situated; location. **b.** a combination of circumstances at a given moment; a state of affairs: *the international situation.* **c.** a position of employment; post.

skew /skyoo/ *adj. Math.* neither parallel nor intersecting. Used of straight lines in space.

so•ci•ol•o•gy /sō′ sē ŏl′ ə jē, -shē-/ *n.* the study of human social behavior, especially the study of the origins, organization, institutions, and development of human society.

-some a suffix that forms adjectives and means being or tending to be: *burdensome.*

son•net /sŏn′ ĭt/ *n.* a 14-line poetic form usually made up of an octave and a sestet embodying the statement and the resolution of a single theme.

sought /sôt/ *v.* past tense and past participle of **seek.**

sou•ve•nir /soo′ və nîr′, soo′ və nîr′/ *n.* something serving as a token of remembrance; memento. [Fr., memory < *souvenir,* to recall < Lat. *subvenire,* to come to mind: *sub-,* under + *venire,* to come.]

souvenir

spa•cious /spā′ shəs/ *adj.* **a.** providing or having much space or room; extensive. **b.** vast in range or scope: *a spacious view.*

spa•ghet•ti /spə gĕt′ ē/ *n.* a pasta made into long, solid strings and cooked by boiling.

spa•tial /spā′ shəl/ *adj.* of, pertaining to, involving, or having the nature of space.

spe•cies /spē′ shēz, -sēz/ *n.* (**spe•cies** *pl.*) **a.1.** a group of similar animals or plants that are regarded as of the same kind and that are able to breed with one another. **a.2.** an animal or plant belonging to such a group, identified by a scientific name consisting of two Latin terms. **b.** a kind, variety, or type.

spe•cif•ic /spĭ sĭf′ ĭk/ *adj.* (**spe•cif•i•cal•ly** *adv.*) **a.** explicitly set forth; definite. **b.** pertaining to, characterizing, or distinguishing a species. **c.** special, distinctive, or unique, as a quality or attribute. **d.** intended for, applying to, or acting upon a particular thing.

Spelling Dictionary

spec•ta•cle /spĕk′ tə kəl/ *n.* **a.** a public performance or display. **b.** an object of interest.
c.1. something seen or capable of being seen.
c.2. the sight of something. **d. spectacles.**
glasses. [ME < OFr. < Lat. *spectaculum* <
spectare, to watch, freq. of *specere,* to look at.]

spec•tac•u•lar /spĕk tăk′ yə lər/ *adj.* of the
nature of a spectacle; sensational. [Lat. *spectaculum,* spectacle < *spectare,* to watch, freq. of
specere, to look at.]

spec•ta•tor /spĕk′ tā′tər/ *n.* an observer of an
event. [Lat. *spectator* < *spectare,* to watch, freq.
of *specere,* to look at.]

sphere /sfîr/ *n.* **a.** *Math.*
a three-dimensional surface
all points of which are equi-
distant from a fixed point.
b. a spherical object or figure.
c. an area of power, control,
or influence; domain.

sphere

spoon•ful /spoon′ foŏl′/ *n.* (**-fuls** *pl.*) the amount
a spoon holds.

sports•cast /spôrts′ kăst′, spōrts′-/ *n.* (**sports•
cast•er** *n.*) a radio or television broadcast of a
sports event or of sports news.

square root /skwâr′ root′, -root′/ *n.* a divisor of
a quantity that when squared gives the quantity.

stage•hand /stāj′ hănd′/ *n.* a person who works
backstage in a theater.

stam•pede[1] /stăm pēd′/ *n.* **a.** a sudden headlong
rush of startled animals. **b.** a sudden headlong
rush of a crowd of people. [Sp. *estampida,*
uproar < *Prov.* < *estampier,* to stamp, of
Germanic orig.]

stam•pede[2] /stăm pēd′/ *v.* (**-pedes, -ped•ed,
-ped•ing**) **a.** to move in a headlong rush.
b. to act on impulse.

stan•za /stăn′ zə/ *n.* one of the divisions of a
poem, composed of two or more lines usually
characterized by a common pattern of meter,
rhyme, and number of lines.

sta•tion•ar•y /stā′ shə nĕr′ē/ *adj.* **a.1.** not
moving. **a.2.** not capable of being moved; fixed.
b. unchanging.

sta•tion•er•y /stā′ shə nĕr′ē/ *n.* **a.** writing
paper and envelopes. **b.** writing materials and
office supplies.

stat•is•ti•cian /stăt ĭ stĭsh′ ən/ *n.* **a.** a mathe-
matician specializing in statistics. **b.** a compiler
of statistical data.

sta•tis•tics /stə tĭs′ tĭks/ *n.* **a.** (*used with a sing.
verb*). the mathematics of the collection, organization, and interpretation of numerical data,
especially the analysis of population characteristics by inference from sampling. **b.** (*used with a
pl. verb*). a collection of numerical data.

ster•e•o•phon•ic /stĕr′ē ō fŏn′ ĭk, stîr′-/ *adj.*
of or used in a sound-reproduction system that
uses two or more separate channels to give a
more natural distribution of sound.

steth•o•scope /stĕth′ ə skōp′/ *n.* an instrument
used for listening to sounds produced within the
body. [Fr. *stéthoscope:* Gk. *stēthos,* chest + Fr.
-scope, -scope.]

straight•edge /strāt′ ĕj′/ *n.* a rigid flat rectangular bar, as of wood or metal, with a straight
edge for testing or drawing straight lines.

strict /strĭkt/ *adj.* **a.** precise; exact. **b.** complete;
absolute: *strict loyalty.* **c.** kept within narrow
and specific limits: *a strict application of a law.*
d. imposing an exacting discipline. [Lat. *strictus*
< p.part. of *stringere,* to bind tightly.]

struc•ture[1] /strŭk′ chər/ *n.* **a.** something made up
of a number of parts that are held or put together
in a particular way. **b.** the way in which parts are
arranged or put together to form a whole.

struc•ture[2] /strŭk′ chər/ *v.* (**-tures, -tured,
-tur•ing**) to give form or arrangement to.

stud•y hall /stŭd′ ē hôl′/ *n.* **a.** a schoolroom
reserved for study. **b.** a period set aside for
study.

sub•stan•tial /səb stăn′ shəl/ *adj.* **a.** of,
pertaining to, or having substance; material.
b. ample; sustaining. **c.** considerable in importance, value, degree, amount, or extent.

sub•ter•ra•ne•an /sŭb′ tə rā′ nē ən/ *adj.*
situated or operating beneath the earth's surface;
underground.

suc•ces•sive /sək sĕs′ ĭv/ *adj.* following in
uninterrupted order or sequence.

suede /swād/ *n.* leather with a soft napped surface. [Fr. *suède* < *Suède,* Sweden.]

suf•fi•cient /sə fĭsh′ ənt/ *adj.* as much as is needed; enough; adequate: *sufficient food for survival.*

suit•a•ble /soo′ tə bəl/ *adj.* (**suit•a•bil•i•ty** *n.*) (**suit•a•bly** *adv.*) appropriate to a given purpose or occasion.

su•per•fi•cial /soo′ pər fĭsh′ əl/ *adj.* **a.** of, affecting, or being on or near the surface. **b.** concerned with only what is apparent or obvious. **c.1.** apparent rather than actual or substantial. **c.2.** trivial; insignificant.

sup•port¹ /sə pôrt′, -pōrt′/ *v.* **a.** to bear the weight of, especially from below. **b.** to hold in position so as to keep from falling, sinking, or slipping. **c.** to provide for or maintain, by supplying with money or necessities. **d.** to aid the cause of by approving, favoring, or advocating.

sup•port² /sə pôrt′, -pōrt′/ *n.* **a.1.** the act of supporting. **a.2.** the state of being supported. **b.** one that supports. **c.** maintenance or subsistence.

sur- a prefix meaning: **a.** over; above; upon. **b.** addition.

sur•name¹ /sûr′ nām′/ *n.* a person's family name as distinguished from his or her given name.

sur•name² /sûr′ nām′/ *v.* (**-names, -named, -nam•ing**) to give a surname to.

sur•prise¹ /sər prīz′/ *v.* (**-pris•es, -prised, -pris•ing**) (**sur•pris•ing•ly** *adv.*) **a.** to encounter suddenly or unexpectedly; take or catch unaware. **b.** to cause to feel wonder, astonishment, or amazement.

sur•prise² /sər prīz′/ *n.* **a.** the condition of being surprised; astonishment. **b.** something that surprises, as an unexpected encounter, event, or gift. [ME *surprysen,* to overcome < OFr. *surprendre, surpris-: sur-,* over + *prendre,* to take < Lat. *praehendere,* to seize.]

sur•ren•der¹ /sə rĕn′ dər/ *v.* **a.** to relinquish possession or control of to another because of demand or compulsion. **b.** to give up in favor of another. **c.** to give up or abandon: *surrender all hope.* **d.** to give oneself up, as to an enemy.

sur•ren•der² /sə rĕn′ dər/ *n.* the act or an instance of surrendering. [ME *sorendren* < OFr. *surrender: sur-,* over + *rendre,* to deliver.]

sur•vey /sər vā′, sûr′ vā′/ *v.* (**sur•vey•or** *n.*) **a.** to inspect carefully; scrutinize. **b.** to determine the boundaries, the area, or the elevations of (land or structures on the earth's surface).

sus•pect¹ /sə spĕkt′/ *v.* **a.** to surmise to be true or probable; imagine. **b.** to have doubts about; distrust: *suspected his motives.*

sus•pect² /sŭs′ pĕkt′, sə spĕkt′/ *adj.* open to or viewed with suspicion. [Lat. *suspectare,* freq. of *suspicere,* to watch: *sub-,* from below + *specere,* to look at.]

sus•pi•cious /sə spĭsh′ əs/ *adj.* **a.** arousing or apt to arouse suspicion; questionable: *suspicious behavior.* **b.** tending to suspect; distrustful: *a suspicious nature.* **c.** expressing suspicion: *a suspicious look.*

sym•bol /sĭm′ bəl/ *n.* **a.** something that represents something else by association, resemblance, or convention, especially a material object used to represent something invisible. **b.** a printed or written sign used to represent an operation, element, quantity, quality, or relation, as in mathematics or music.

sym•me•try /sĭm′ ĭ trē/ *n.* (**-tries** *pl.*) **a.** correspondence of form and arrangement of parts on opposite sides of a boundary, such as a plane or line or around a point or axis. **b.** beauty as a result of balance or harmonious arrangement.

symmetry

sym•phon•ic /sĭm fŏn′ ĭk/ *adj.* pertaining to or having the character or form of a symphony.

sym•pho•ny /sĭm′ fə nē/ *n.* (**-nies** *pl.*) **a.** *Mus.* a usually long sonata for orchestra, consisting of four related movements. **b.** an instrumental overture or interlude, as in early opera. **c.** anything characterized by a harmonious combination of elements. [ME *symphonie,* harmony < OFr. < Lat. *symphonia* < Gk. *symphōnia* < *symphōnos,* harmonious: *syn-,* together + *phōnē,* sound.]

syn- or **sym-** a prefix meaning: **a.1.** together; with: *symphony.* **a.2.** united. **b.** same; similar.

syn•chro•nize /sĭng′ krə nīz′, sĭn′-/ *v.* (**-niz•es, -nized, -niz•ing**) to cause to operate with exact coincidence in time or rate. [Lat. *synchronos* < Gk. *synkhronos: syn-,* same + *khronos,* time.]

syn•thet•ic /sĭn thĕt′ ĭk/ *adj.* **a.** *Chem.* produced by synthesis, especially not of natural origin; manufactured. **b.** not genuine; artificial; devised.

tab•u•late /tăb′ yə lāt′/ *v.* (**-lates, -lat•ed, -lat•ing**) to arrange in tabular form; condense and list.

tan•ger•ine /tăn′ jə rēn′, tăn′ jə rēn′/ *n.* **a.** a widely cultivated citrus tree bearing edible fruit having an easily peeled deep-orange skin and sweet, juicy pulp. **b.** the fruit of the tangerine. **c.** a strong reddish orange to strong or vivid orange. [< Fr. *Tanger,* Tangier, Morocco.]

team•mate /tēm′ māt′/ *n.* a fellow member of a team.

tea•spoon•ful /tē′ spoon′ fool′/ *n.* (**-fuls** *pl.*) the amount a teaspoon will hold.

tech•nol•o•gy /tĕk nŏl′ ə jē/ *n.* (**-gies** *pl.*) **a.** the application of science, especially to industrial or commercial objectives. **b.** *Anthropol.* the body of knowledge available to a civilization that is of use in fashioning implements, practicing manual arts and skills, and extracting or collecting materials.

tele- a prefix that means distance: *telegraph.*

tel•e•gram /tĕl′ ə grăm′/ *n.* a communication transmitted by telegraph.

tel•e•phone[1] /tĕl′ ə fōn′/ *n.* an instrument that reproduces or receives sound, especially speech at a distance.

tel•e•phone[2] /tĕl′ ə fōn′/ *v.* (**-phones, -phoned, -phon•ing**) to communicate by telephone.

tel•e•scope[1] /tĕl′ ə skōp′/ *n.* **a.** an instrument for collecting and examining electromagnetic radiation. **b.** an arrangement of lenses or mirrors or both that gathers visible light, permitting direct observation or photographic recording of distant objects. **c.** any of various devices, such as a radio telescope, used to detect and observe distant objects by their emission, transmission, reflection, or other interaction with invisible radiation. [NLat. *telescopium* or Ital. *telescopio,* both < Gk. *teleskopos,* far seeing: *tele,* at a distance + *skopos,* watcher.]

telescope

tel•e•scope[2] /tĕl′ ə skōp′/ *v.* (**-scopes, -scoped, -scop•ing**) **a.** to cause to slide inward or outward in overlapping sections, as the cylindrical sections of a small hand telescope. **b.** to make shorter or more precise; condense.

tem•per•a•ment /tĕm′ prə mənt, tĕm′ pər ə-/ *n.* the manner of thinking, behaving, or reacting characteristic of a specific individual. [ME < Lat. *temperamentum* < *temperare,* to temper.]

tem•per•a•ture /tĕm′ pər ə choor′, tĕm′ prə-/ *n.* **a.** the degree of hotness or coldness of a body or environment. **b.** an abnormally high temperature caused by illness; fever. [Lat. *temperatura,* composition < *temperare,* to mix.]

ter•ri•to•ri•al /tĕr′ ĭ tôr′ ē əl/ *adj.* of or pertaining to a territory or to its powers of jurisdiction.

tes•ti•mo•ni•al /tĕs′ tə mō′ nē əl/ *n.* **a.** a formal or written statement testifying to a particular truth or fact. **b.** a written affirmation of another's character or worth. **c.** something given as a tribute for a person's service or achievement.

text•book /tĕkst′ book′/ *n.* a book used as a standard work for the formal study of a particular subject.

the•o•rem /thē′ ər əm, thîr′ əm/ *n.* *Math.* **a.** a proposition that is provable on the basis of explicit assumptions. **b.** a proven proposition.

the•o•ry /thē′ ə rē, thîr′ ē/ *n.* (**-ries** *pl.*)
a. systematically organized knowledge applica-
ble in a relatively wide variety of circumstances,
especially a system of assumptions, accepted
principles, and rules of procedure devised to
analyze, predict, or otherwise explain the nature
or behavior of a specified set of phenomena.
b. an assumption or guess based on limited
information or knowledge.

the•sis /thē′ sĭs/ *n.* (**-ses** /sēz/ *pl.*) a hypothetical
proposition, especially one put forth for the
sake of argument or one to be accepted
without proof.

thief /thēf/ *n.* (**thieves** /thēvz/ *pl.*) a person who
steals.

third-per•son /thûrd′ pûr′ sən/ *adj.* describing
a set of grammatical forms used in referring to a
person or thing other than the speaker or the one
spoken to.

thir•teen-year-olds /thûr tēn′ yîr ōlds/ *n. pl.*
a group of young adolescents who are thirteen
years old: *They invited the whole class of
thirteen-year-olds to their party.*

thor•ough /thûr′ ō/ *adj.* (**thor•ough•ly** *adv.*)
a. exhaustively complete. **b.** painstakingly accurate or careful. **c.** completely satisfactory in
all respects.

thought•ful /thôt′ fəl/ *adj.* (**thought•ful•ly** *adv.*)
(**thought•ful•ness** *n.*) **a.** occupied with thought;
contemplative. **b.** well thought-out; well considered. **c.** showing regard for others; considerate.

thought•less /thôt′ lĭs/ *adj.* (**thought•less•ly**
adv.) (**thought•less•ness** *n.*) **a.** careless; unthink-
ing. **b.** inconsiderate; inattentive.

three-fourths /thrē fôrths/ *n. pl.* three parts of
something that has been divided into four equal
parts: *Three quarters are three-fourths of a dollar.*

-tion a noun suffix that means action or process.

to•ma•to /tə mā′ tō, -mä′-/ *n.* (**-toes** *pl.*)
a. a plant native to South America, widely
cultivated for its edible, fleshy, usually red fruit.
b. the fruit of this plant.

to•pog•ra•phy /tə pŏg′ rə fē, tō-/ *n.* (**-phies**
pl.) detailed and precise description representing
the exact physical features of a place or region
on a map.

Pronunciation Key

ă	pat	ŏ	pot	th	**th**in
ā	pay	ō	toe	*th*	**th**is
âr	care	ô	paw, for	hw	**wh**ich
ä	father	oi	noise	zh	vi**s**ion
ĕ	pet	ou	out	ə	**a**bout,
ē	be	oͦo	took		item,
ĭ	pit	o͞o	boot		pencil,
ī	pie	ŭ	cut		gallop,
îr	pier	ûr	urge		circus

tor•na•do /tôr nā′ dō/ *n.*
(**-does** or **-dos** *pl.*)
a rotating column of air
usually accompanied
by a funnel-shaped
downward extension of
a cumulonimbus cloud
and having a vortex
several hundred yards
in diameter whirling
destructively at speeds

tornado

up to 300 miles per hour. [Alteration of Sp.
tronada, thunderstorm < *tronar,* to thunder
< Lat. *tonare.*]

tor•ti•lla /tôr tē′ yə/ *n.* a thin, round unleavened
bread, usually made from cornmeal and served
hot with various toppings of ground meat or
cheese. [Mex. Sp. < Sp., omelet < Sp. *torta,*
cake < LLat. *torta,* a kind of bread.]

tox•ic /tŏk′ sĭk/ *adj.* **a.** of or caused by a toxin or
poison. **b.** harmful, destructive, or deadly.

tra•di•tion /trə dĭsh′ ən/ *n.* **a.** the passing down
of elements of a culture from generation to generation, especially by oral communication.
b. a mode of thought or behavior followed by a
people continuously from generation to generation; custom or usage. **c.** a time-honored practice or a set of such practices.

trans•mis•sion /trăns mĭsh′ ən, trănz-/ *n.*
a.1. the act or process of transmitting. **a.2.** the
state of being transmitted. **b.** something transmitted, as a voice or message. **c.1.** an automo-
tive assembly of gears and associated parts by
which power is transmitted from the engine to a
driving axle. **c.2.** a system of gears. [Lat. *trans-
missio,* a sending across < *transmitter,* to transmit: *trans,* across + *mittere,* to send.]

Spelling Dictionary

trans•mit /trăns mĭt', trănz-/ *v.* (**-mits, -mit•ted, -mit•ting**) to send from one person, thing, or place to another; convey. [ME *transmitten* < Lat. *transmittere: trans,* across + *mittere,* to send.]

trem•or /trĕm' ər/ *n.* **a.** a quick shaking or vibrating movement. **b.** an involuntary trembling motion of the body. **c.** a nervous quiver; thrill. **d.** a tremulous sound; quaver.

trend /trĕnd/ *n.* **a.** a direction of movement. **b.** a general inclination or tendency; to have a general tendency; tend.

tri•al /trī' əl, trīl/ *n.* **a.** *Law.* the examination of evidence, charges, or claims made in a case in court. **b.** the act or process of testing, trying, or putting to the proof by actual or simulated use and experience. **c.** made, done, used, or performed during the course of a trial or trials.

tro•phy /trō' fē/ *n.* (**-phies** *pl.*) something received as a symbol of victory or achievement, often preserved as a memento.

trophy

tux•e•do /tŭk sē' dō/ *n.* (**-dos** or **-does** *pl.*) **a.** a man's usually dark jacket with satin or grosgrain lapels worn for formal or semi-formal occasions. **b.** a complete outfit including a tuxedo jacket, black trousers with a stripe down the side, and a black bow tie. [After *Tuxedo* Park, New York.]

twen•ti•eth /twĕn' tē ĭth/ *n.* **a.** the ordinal number that matches the number 20 in a series. **b.** one of 20 equal parts.

U

un-[1] a prefix meaning not or contrary to.

un-[2] a prefix meaning: **a.** reversal of action. **b.** release or removal from: *unburden.* **c.** intensified action: *unloose.*

un•ac•cept•a•ble /ŭn'ăk sĕp' tə bəl/ *adj.* not acceptable, especially not satisfactory or pleasing.

u•nan•i•mous /yōō năn' ə məs/ *adj.* **a.** sharing the same opinions or views; being in complete harmony or accord. **b.** based on or characterized by complete assent or agreement. [Lat. *unanimus: unus,* one + *animus,* mind.]

un•a•void•a•ble /ŭn' ə voi' də bəl/ *adj.* not able to be avoided; inevitable.

un•com•fort•a•ble /ŭn kŭm' fĕr tə bəl, -kŭmf' tə bel/ *adj.* **a.** experiencing discomfort; uneasy. **b.** causing discomfort.

under- a prefix meaning: **a.** location below or under: *underground.* **b.** inferiority in rank or importance: *undersecretary.* **c.** degree, rate, or quantity that is lower or less than normal: *underestimate.* **d.** secrecy or treachery: *underhand.*

un•der•es•ti•mate[1] /ŭn dər ĕs' tə māt'/ *v.* (**-mates, -mat•ed, -mat•ing**) to make too low an estimate of the quantity, degree, or worth of.

un•der•es•ti•mate[2] /ŭn dər ĕs' tə māt'/ *n.* an estimate that is or proves to be too low.

un•e•mo•tion•al /ŭn' ĭ mō' shə nəl/ *adj.* **a.** not easily stirred or moved. **b.** involving little or no emotion; rational.

un•ex•pect•ed /ŭn' ĭk spĕk' tĭd/ *adj.* coming without warning; unforeseen.

uni- a prefix meaning one or single: *unilateral.*

u•ni•fy /yōō' nə fī'/ *v.* (**-fies, -fied, -fy•ing**) to make into a unit; consolidate; to become unified. [OFr. *unifier* < LLat. *unificare:* Lat. *unus,* one + Lat. *facere,* to make.]

un•in•ter•est•ed /ŭn ĭn' trĭs tĭd, -ĭn' tə rĕs' tĭd/ *adj.* **a.** without an interest: *uninterested parties.* **b.** not paying attention.

u•nique /yōō nēk'/ *adj.* **a.** being the only one of its kind; sole. **b.** being without an equal. [Fr. < Lat. *unicus,* sole < *unus,* one.]

u•ni•son /yōō' nĭ sən', -zən/ *n.* an instance of agreement; concord. —*idiom.* **in unison.** in complete agreement; harmonizing exactly. [OFr. < Med. Lat. *unisonus,* in unison: Lat. *unus,* one + Lat. *sonus,* sound.]

u•nite /yōō nīt'/ *v.* (**-nites, -nit•ed, -nit•ing**) **a.** to bring together so as to form a whole. **b.** to combine (people) in interest, attitude, or action. [ME *uniten* < LLat. *unire* < Lat. *unus,* one.]

u•ni•verse /yōo′ nə vûrs′/ *n.* **a.** all existing things, including the earth, the heavens, the galaxies, and all therein, regarded as a whole. **b.** the sphere or realm in which something exists or takes place. [ME < OFr. *univers* < Lat. *universum,* neuter of *universus,* whole: *unus,* one + *versus,* p.part. of *vertere,* to turn.]

u•ni•ver•si•ty /yōo′ nə **vûr′** sĭ tē/ *n.* (**-ties** *pl.*) an institution for higher learning with teaching and research facilities comprising a graduate school and professional schools that award master's degrees and doctorates and an undergraduate division that awards bachelor's degrees. [ME *universite* < OFr. < Med. Lat. *universitas* < LLat., a society < Lat., the whole < *universus,* whole: *unus,* one + *versus,* p.part. of *vertere,* to turn.]

un•mis•tak•a•ble /ŭn′ mĭ **stā′** kə bəl/ *adj.* obvious; evident.

un•nec•es•sar•y /ŭn **nĕs′** ĭ sĕr′ē/ *adj.* not necessary; needless.

un•rea•son•a•ble /ŭn **rē′** zə nə bəl/ *adj.* **a.** not governed by reason. **b.** exceeding reasonable limits; immoderate.

up•date /ŭp dāt′/ *v.* (**-dates, -dat•ed, -dat•ing**) to bring up to date: *update a textbook.*

ur•gent /ûr′ jənt/ *adj.* (**ur•gent•ly** *adv.*) **a.** compelling immediate action; imperative: *a crisis of an urgent nature.* **b.** conveying a sense of pressing importance: *an urgent message.* [ME < OFr. < Lat. *urgens,* p.part. of *urgere,* to urge.]

u•su•al /yōo′ zhōo əl/ *adj.* (**u•su•al•ly** *adv.*) **a.** such as is commonly or frequently encountered, experienced, observed, or used. **b.** habitual or customary; particular.

vac•u•um¹ /văk′ yōom, -yəm, -yōo əm/ *n.* (**-u•ums** or **-u•a** *pl.*) **a.** the absence of matter. **b.** a state of emptiness; void. **c.** *pl.* **vacuums.** a vacuum cleaner.

vac•u•um² /văk′ yōom, -yəm, -yōo əm/ *v.* to clean with or use a vacuum cleaner.

vague /vāg/ *adj.* (**vague•ly** *adv.*) **a.** not clearly expressed or outlined: *vague instructions.* **b.** not thinking or expressing oneself clearly: *She was vague about her future plans.* [OFr. < Lat. *vagus.*]

va•ri•e•ty /və rī′ ĭ tē/ *n.* (**-ties** *pl.*) **a.** the condition or quality of being various or varied; diversity. **b.** a number or collection of varied things, especially of a particular group; assortment: *brought home a variety of snacks.*

veg•e•tar•i•an /vĕj ĭ **târ′** ē ən/ *n.* **a.** a person who practices or advocates vegetarianism. **b.** consisting primarily of vegetables and vegetable products; containing little or no animal food: *a vegetarian diet.*

ve•hi•cle /vē′ ĭ kəl/ *n.* **a.** a device, such as a car or sled, for carrying passengers, goods, or equipment; conveyance. **b.** a medium through which something is conveyed, transmitted, expressed, or achieved.

vehicle

ver•i•fy /vĕr′ ə fī′/ *v.* (**-fies, -fied, -fy•ing**) **a.** to prove the truth of by the presentation of evidence or testimony; substantiate. **b.** to determine or test the truth or accuracy of, as by comparison, investigation, or reference: *conduct experiments to verify a hypothesis.*

ver•sa•tile /vûr′ sə təl/ *adj.* **a.** capable of doing many things well. **b.** having varied uses or serving many functions. [Fr. < Lat. *versatilis* < *versare,* freq. of *vertere,* to turn.]

ver•sion /vûr′ zhən, -shən/ *n.* a description, narration, or account related from a specific point of view: *Her version of the accident differed from his.* [OFr. < Med. Lat. *versio,* act of turning < Lat. *vertere,* to turn.]

ver•tex /vûr′ tĕks/ *n.* (**-tex•es** or **-ti•ces** *pl.*) **a.** the highest point of something; apex. **b.** the point at which the sides of an angle intersect.

vet•er•i•nar•i•an /vĕt′ ər ə **năr′** ē ən, vĕt′ rə-/ *n.* a person trained and authorized to treat animals medically. [Lat. *veterinarius,* pertaining to beasts of burden, *veterinus* < *veterinae,* beasts of burden.]

vi•bra•tion /vī **brā′** shən/ *n.* a single complete vibrating motion; quiver.

vi•cious /**vĭsh′** əs/ *adj.* **a.** characterized by violence or ferocity: *a vicious storm.* **b.** savagely aggressive; dangerous: *a vicious shark.*

vi•su•al /**vĭzh′** oo əl/ *adj.* (**vi•su•al•ly** *adv.*) **a.** serving, resulting from, or pertaining to the sense of sight. **b.** capable of being seen by the eye; visible. **c.** optical.

vol•ca•no /vŏl **kā′** nō, vôl-/ *n.* (**-noes** or **-nos** *pl.*) **a.** a vent in the earth's crust through which molten lava and gases are ejected. **b.** a mountain formed by the materials ejected from a volcano.

volcano

war•rant /**wôr′** ənt, wŏr′-/ *n.* **a.** authorization or certification; sanction, as given by a superior. **b.** justification for an action; grounds. **c.** something that assures, attests to, or guarantees some event or result; proof.

weap•on /**wĕp′** ən/ *n.* an instrument used in offensive or defensive combat.

well-known /wĕl′ nōn′/ *adj.* widely known; familiar or famous.

wil•der•ness /**wĭl′** dər nĭs/ *n.* an unsettled, uncultivated region left in its natural condition, especially: **a.** a large wild tract of land covered with dense vegetation or forest. **b.** an extensive area, as a desert or ocean, that is barren or empty; waste.

wild•life /**wīld′** līf′/ *n.* wild animals and vegetation, especially animals living in a natural, undomesticated state.

wis•dom /**wĭs′** dəm/ *n.* **a.** understanding of what is true, right, or lasting. **b.** common sense; good judgment.

with•draw•al /wĭth **drô′** əl, wĭth-/ *n.* the act or process of withdrawing, as: **a.** a retreat or retirement. **b.** a detachment, as from emotional involvement. **c.** a removal from a place or position of something that has been deposited.

wit•ness¹ /**wĭt′** nĭs/ *n.* **a.** one who has seen or heard something. **b.** one who furnishes evidence.

wit•ness² /**wĭt′** nĭs/ *v.* **a.** to be present at or have personal knowledge of. **b.** to provide or serve as evidence of. **c.** to testify to; bear witness.

word pro•ces•sing /wûrd′ **prŏ′** sĕs′ ĭng/ *n.* a system of producing typewritten documents by use of automated typewriters and electronic text-editing equipment.

wres•tle /**rĕs′** əl/ *v.* (**-tles, -tled, -tling**) **a.** to contend by grappling and attempting to throw one's opponent, especially under certain contest rules. **b.1.** to contend; to struggle: *city planners wrestle with budget cuts.* **b.2.** to strive in an effort to master: *wrestle with one's conscience.*

USING THE Thesaurus

The **Writing Thesaurus** provides synonyms—words that mean the same or nearly the same—and antonyms—words that mean the opposite—for your spelling words. Use this sample to identify the various parts of each thesaurus entry.

- **Entry words** are listed in alphabetical order and are printed in boldface type.

- The abbreviation for the **part of speech** of each entry word follows the boldface entry word.

- The **definition** of the entry word matches the definition of the word in your **Spelling Dictionary**. A **sample sentence** shows the correct use of the word in context.

- Each **synonym** for the entry word is listed under the entry word. Again, a sample sentence shows the correct use of the synonym in context.

- Where appropriate, **antonyms** for the entry word are listed at the end of the entry.

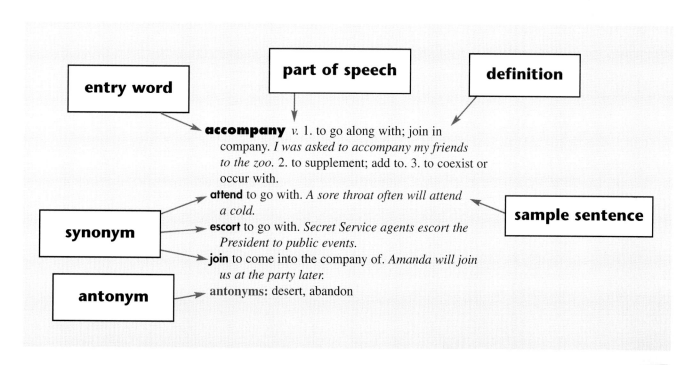

entry word

part of speech

definition

accompany *v.* 1. to go along with; join in company. *I was asked to accompany my friends to the zoo.* 2. to supplement; add to. 3. to coexist or occur with.

attend to go with. *A sore throat often will attend a cold.*

escort to go with. *Secret Service agents escort the President to public events.*

join to come into the company of. *Amanda will join us at the party later.*

antonyms: desert, abandon

synonym

antonym

sample sentence

accompany *v.* 1. to go along with; join in company. *I was asked to accompany my friends to the zoo.* 2. to supplement; add to. 3. to coexist or occur with.

attend to go with. *A sore throat often will attend a cold.*

escort to go with. *Secret Service agents escort the President to public events.*

join to come into the company of. *Amanda will join us at the party later.*

antonyms: desert, abandon

accomplish *v.* 1. to succeed in doing; bring to pass. 2. to reach the end of; complete. *I always accomplish what I set out to do.*

achieve to carry out; do. *You have to work hard to achieve your goals.*

complete to finish. *Please complete the test and hand in your papers.*

finish to complete. *Ted must finish washing the dishes before he begins his homework.*

fulfill to carry out; finish. *Terry will fulfill her part of the task before we finish ours.*

succeed to do well. *Will she succeed in running a mile in three minutes?*

antonyms: foil, thwart, frustrate

accustomed *adj.* 1. usual; characteristic; normal. *Alicia worked with her accustomed thoroughness.* 2. in the habit of. *Jack had become accustomed to sleeping late on weekend mornings.*

characteristic distinctive. *Bob has a characteristic laugh.*

common usual. *Political upheaval is common in that region.*

customary usual. *The Bensons sat at their customary table.*

familiar common. *The old town looked strangely familiar to him.*

habitual done by habit. *Dawn is a habitual nail biter.*

usual customary. *It is usual for the baby to take a nap at two o'clock.*

antonyms: unaccustomed, unusual, unfamiliar, uncommon

actual *adj.* 1. existing in fact or reality. 2. current. 3. based on fact. *The book was said to be an actual account of a spy's secret missions.*

certain sure. *I am certain that it will rain today; I read all the reports.*

definite sure. *She was quite definite about her decision to take the job.*

genuine real. *The expression of happiness on his face was genuine.*

real genuine. *He was astounded to discover that the rock contained real gold.*

tangible real; able to be touched. *Rumors and hearsay are not tangible evidence.*

true real. *Knowing when to keep a secret is a true test of friendship.*

antonyms: unreal, untrue, fake

adapt *v.* to adjust to a specified use or situation. *The cat was able to adapt quickly to its new surroundings.*

accommodate to make suitable to a particular situation. *She learned to accommodate herself to the variable weather.*

adjust to change to fit. *The seat belts adjust automatically to fit each passenger.*

fit to adjust. *Ask the tailor at the store to fit your suit before you take it home.*

modify to change somewhat. *George will modify the sailboat to make it lighter and faster.*

suit to make fit. *A judge will decide how to suit the punishment to the crime.*

admiration *n.* a feeling of pleasure, wonder, and approval. *He sat looking at the painting, lost in admiration.*

awe wonder and fear. *The view from the edge of the Grand Canyon filled them with awe.*

delight joy; pleasure. *His delight at seeing me made me feel good.*

esteem regard; good opinion. *He was held in high esteem by his colleagues.*

pleasure delight; joy. *The puppy made the children squeal with pleasure.*

regard esteem. *She was worried that the professor's low regard of her work would affect her class standing.*

wonder feeling of amazement. *She gazed in wonder at the lights of the city spread out below her.*

antonyms: disgust, hatred

admire *v.* 1. to regard with pleasure, wonder, and approval. 2. to have a high opinion of; esteem or respect. *I admire his ability to remain calm and competent in all situations.* See **respect**.

admission *n.* 1.a. the act of admitting or allowing to enter. 1.b. the state of being allowed to enter. 2. the right to enter; access. 3. the price required or paid for entering; entrance fee. 4. a voluntary acknowledgment that something is true. *His admission of the error helped to resolve the conflict.*

access right to enter or use. *Despite their protests, the reporters were denied immediate access to the scene of the crime.*

admittance right or permission to enter. *The pass allowed us admittance backstage after the show.*

entrance permission to enter. *Entrance is restricted to club members.*

antonyms: rejection, exclusion

advantageous *adj.* affording benefit or gain; useful. *Investing money in those stocks was an advantageous move.*

beneficial helpful; favorable. *Proper diet and exercise are beneficial to a person's health.*

profitable having real value. *Terry worked hard to make her pet-sitting service a profitable venture.*

rewarding satisfying. *Working as a volunteer at the hospital is a rewarding activity for Denise.*

worthwhile having merit or value. *Bob contributed to the wildlife group because it seemed like a worthwhile cause.*

antonyms: harmful, unfavorable, injurious, ruinous, destructive

advise *v.* 1. to offer advice to; counsel. 2. to recommend; suggest. 3. to inform; notify. *Howard always waits until the last minute to advise a person of a decision.* See **notify**.

admonish to advise; warn. *The flight attendant had to admonish the passenger to fasten his seat belt.*

consult to talk over. *Doris will consult with her doctor about possible treatments.*

counsel to give advice to. *Her job is to counsel students on career choices.*

inform to tell. *Janice must inform me that she is no longer a member of the committee.*

notify to let know. *The bank will notify me if my account is overdrawn.*

recommend to advise. *She would often recommend that we invest our money in stocks.*

suggest to propose. *I suggest that we buy a house now while interest rates are low.*

agreeable *adj.* 1. to one's liking; pleasing; pleasant. 2. ready to consent or submit. *If you want to go downtown, I'm agreeable.*

pleasant pleasing. *We had a pleasant day at the zoo.*

pleasing pleasant. *Tom has a very pleasing personality; he gets along with everyone.*

willing consenting. *Julio is always willing to play with the baby.*

antonyms: disagreeable, unpleasant, unwilling, reluctant

ambitious *adj.* 1. full of, characterized by, or motivated by ambition. *The ambitious man would stop at nothing to gain fortune and power.* 2. greatly desirous; eager. 3. showing or requiring much effort.

aspiring desiring strongly. *She is an aspiring actress.*

desirous desiring; eager. *He is desirous of making your acquaintance.*

eager desiring strongly. *Melinda was eager to learn to play the guitar.*

enterprising bold; daring to take risks. *Building a treehouse was an enterprising project for the two boys.*

antonyms: apathetic, humble, modest

apparent *adj.* 1. readily seen; open to view; visible. 2. readily understood or perceived; plain or obvious. 3. appearing as such but not necessarily so. *His ability to speak Spanish was an apparent advantage in getting the job.*

clear easily seen. *From the third floor there is a clear view of the lake.*

conspicuous easily seen. *The footprint by the back door was a conspicuous clue.*

evident clear; plain. *It was evident to all but Cindy that the party was over.*

obvious easily seen; clear. *I cannot believe that Tim could make such an obvious mistake.*

open exposed; not secret. *The argument had not yet turned into open warfare.*

plain easily perceived. *It was plain that there would be no picnic because of the rain.*

antonyms: concealed, obscure, mysterious

appetite *n.* 1. a desire for food or drink. 2. a physical desire. 3. a strong wish or urge. *All of his life, Thomas Jefferson displayed an appetite for learning.*

craving strong desire; longing. *Thanksgiving dinner satisfies my craving for turkey and cranberries for an entire year.*

desire strong wish; craving. *After seeing the toys in the window, the children were filled with desire.*

hunger desire for food; craving. *Hunger made him dream of steak and potatoes.*

longing desire. *Her longing to see the child overcame her fear of being seen.*

urge force or impulse. *Quentin resisted the urge to run away from the barking dog.*

appliance *n.* a device or instrument, especially one operated by electricity and designed for household use. *The refrigerator is a major household appliance.*

apparatus tool for a particular use. *He hung hammers, saws, and other carpentry apparatus on the walls of his garage.*

device something made for a particular use. *That round piece of flexible plastic is a clever device for opening jars.*

instrument mechanical device; tool. *A surgeon uses many special instruments to perform an operation.*

tool instrument used in doing work. *A wrench is a mechanic's tool, while a pen is a writer's tool.*

assemble *v.* 1. to bring or gather together into a group or whole. 2. to fit or join together the parts of. *It took me three hours to assemble the computer desk.*

build to put together; construct. *Ken and his friends are trying to build a treehouse.*

collect to gather together. *The children banded together to collect cans of food for the homeless.*

congregate to come together in a group. *The ducks tend to congregate under the willow by the pond.*

construct to put together; build. *My father and my brother construct houses for a living.*

convene to gather together. *The Fifth Cell Wall Congress was to convene in Edinburgh, Scotland, last August.*

gather to bring together. *I tried to gather all the library books into one pile.*

antonyms: disperse, disassemble

assess *v.* to evaluate; appraise. *He must assess the situation before he decides what to do.*

appraise to consider the value or importance of. *The judges will appraise each contestant's cooking skills.*

calculate to estimate. *Joy wanted to calculate how many days it would take her to finish the book.*

estimate to judge; form an opinion about. *The foreman estimated that he would need four workers to unload the truck in an hour.*

evaluate to find out the value or importance of. *The scientist planned to evaluate the impact of pollution on the marshlands.*

gauge to judge; estimate. *Sam could not gauge the distance between his house and mine without measuring.*

attain *v.* to gain, reach, or accomplish by mental or physical effort. *She worked hard to attain her goal of becoming a doctor.*

accomplish to carry out; finish. *Anna can accomplish the task with great ease.*

achieve to complete successfully. *Hard work will help you achieve your goals.*

acquire to get; obtain. *Marcia must acquire a new swimsuit while she is in Florida.*

obtain to gain or acquire. *How did Shirley obtain her new bicycle?*

reach to arrive at, get to. *I could not reach a decision based on the information.*

secure to obtain; get. *He tried to secure the position by meeting with the boss after working hours.*

antonyms: fail, lose

attempt *n.* 1. an effort or try. 2. an attack; assault. *He feared there would be an attempt on his life.*

effort good try. *She made an effort to finish the marathon.*

endeavor serious effort. *He approaches every endeavor with determination.*

enterprise bold project. *Designing and selling clothes is a risky enterprise.*

try test; attempt. *I promised my mother I would give cooking a try.*

attentive *adj.* 1. paying attention; observant. 2. mindful of the well-being of others; considerate. *Julio was very attentive to his great-aunt.*

alert watchful. *It is hard to stay alert when you are tired.*

considerate thoughtful of people. *Carrying Mrs. Johnson's bags was a considerate thing for Erin to do.*

mindful heedful; careful. *Be mindful of the traffic when you cross the street.*

observant watchful. *It is important for a police officer to be observant.*

thoughtful thinking of others; considerate. *Sending a sympathy card was a thoughtful gesture.*

watchful observant; careful. *The watchful dog kept guard in the backyard.*

basis *n.* 1. a supporting element; foundation. 2. the chief component of something. 3. the essential principle. *Trust is the basis of a good partnership or any relationship.*

foundation base. *They poured the concrete for the foundation of the new building yesterday.*

groundwork foundation. *The notes I took at the library provided the groundwork for my science report.*

boundaries *n.* something that indicates borders or limits. *The boundaries of the farm were marked by fieldstone walls.*

borders lines separating countries, states, or other areas. *We crossed the borders of ten different countries during our vacation trip in Europe.*

frontiers borders. *Sol likes to explore new frontiers.*

limits bounds. *The streets were narrow and crowded within the limits of the city.*

bravado *n.* a pretense of courage; false bravery. *The lizard's hissing and charging are really just a show of bravado.*

bluster loud talk with empty threats. *The man's bluster did not worry the police officer; she knew it did not mean anything.*

boasting overpraise of one's talents or possessions. *The two boys tried to outdo each other with their boasting of their strength and prowess.*

bombast grand, pompous language. *There were some good ideas hidden under the bombast in his speech.*

bragging boasting. *After much bragging about his town, the mayor went on to criticize the neighboring city.*

heroics melodramatic words or actions used only for effect. *Such heroics were out of place in a sensible debate.*

swaggering noisy boasting. *Susie thought that his swaggering was annoying.*

antonyms: modesty, humility

briefly *adv.* 1. in a short time. 2. to a short length or extent. *She spoke briefly before announcing the guest of honor.* See **presently**.

concisely in a few meaningful words. *They asked him to give his opinion of the situation as concisely as possible.*

shortly in a short time; in a few words. *He promised to speak with me shortly.*

succinctly concisely. *She is known for being able to state complex problems succinctly.*

antonyms: gradually, slowly, deliberately

canyon *n.* a narrow chasm with steep cliff walls, formed by running water; gorge. *The awestruck hikers looked cautiously into the mile-deep canyon.*

dell small valley with trees. *We enjoyed hiking in the dell.*

glen small, narrow valley. *In Scotland, a lake is a loch and a valley is a glen.*

gorge narrow valley between mountains. *After the rainstorm, the water rushed through the gorge.*

gully small ravine; deep ditch. *In the fall the gully was filled with leaves, branches, and other debris.*

ravine deep, narrow valley made by running water. *Do not walk in a ravine if it looks as if it might rain.*

vale valley. *In poems, a valley is often called a vale.*

valley low land between mountains. *The village was nestled in the valley between Casper Mountain and Black Mountain.*

caption *n.* a title, short explanation, or description accompanying an illustration or photograph. *The caption under the photograph identified the location as Paris, France.*

heading word or words at the beginning of a page, chapter, etc. *Read the headings to get an idea of what the chapter is about.*

title name of a picture, book, poem, etc. *The title of the book was* We Struck It Rich: The California Gold Rush of 1848.

chronic *adj.* 1. of long duration; continuing; constant. 2. prolonged; lingering, as certain diseases. 3. subject to a disease or habit for a long time. *Jay's grandmother has chronic arthritis.*

confirmed habitual. *Don had often declared that he was a confirmed cat hater.*

constant never stopping. *The constant noise kept me awake all night.*

continual without stopping. *The continual dripping of the faucet annoyed Eric.*

habitual done by habit. *Habitual shoppers should avoid the new mall.*

inveterate habitual. *Mrs. Perkins has a reputation as an inveterate busybody.*

perpetual never stopping. *The children were a perpetual source of joy to their grandparents.*

unending without end. *The stream of complaining customers seemed unending.*

antonyms: fleeting, temporary

chronicle *n.* a chronological record of historical events. *Much of our historical knowledge comes from chronicles that were kept by people of ancient times.*

account detailed statement. *The newspaper account of the fire included the names of the ten victims.*

annals history. *The association's annals are kept by the librarian.*

history account of events. *Can you tell us the history of this campaign?*

memoir record written from personal knowledge. *The teacher wrote a memoir of her days in a one-room schoolhouse.*

record written account. *Let the record show that the witness refuses to answer my questions.*

story account of an event or events. *The story of the shipwreck was the lead on the evening news.*

colleague *n.* a fellow member of a profession, staff, or academic faculty; associate. *He and a colleague at the university worked on the experiment together.*

accomplice person who helps another in a wrong act. *Terry's brother was her accomplice in the kitchen mess last night.*

ally helper; partner. *My sister has always been my ally.*

associate partner; companion. *Darryl and I were associates at the same law firm for three years.*

companion comrade; a person who shares in another's activities. *Cheryl and Alan are often dinner companions when he is in town.*

comrade partner; coworker. *He wanted to be with his comrades for the rally.*

confederate ally; partner. *The police knew that the thief had a confederate in the job.*

coworker person who works with another. *Her coworkers at the office gave her a surprise birthday party.*

partner person who invests with others in a company or business. *When Jane wanted to open a restaurant, she asked Henry to be her partner.*

combine *v.* 1. to bring into a state of unity. 2. to join (two or more substances) to make a single substance; mix. *If you combine blue paint with red paint, you will get purple paint.*

blend to mix. *Chris is careful to blend the milk and the eggs by adding the milk a little at a time.*

join to put together. *At camp we all were asked to join hands and sing songs around the fire.*

mix to put together as one. *The directions said to mix 1 cup of water, 1 cup of oil, and 1 teaspoon of ground mustard.*

unite to join together. *The thirteen colonies had to unite to fight the British.*

antonyms: divide, separate, split

comfort *v.* 1. to soothe in time of grief or fear; console. *The teacher tried to comfort the crying child.* 2. to ease physically; relieve.

console to ease; relieve. *It is hard to console someone who has lost a relative.*

relieve to reduce; ease. *A heating pad can relieve sore muscles.*

soothe to calm; quiet. *The singing and laughing helped soothe the campers' fears.*

antonyms: irritate, annoy, aggravate, embarrass, upset, burden, hamper

commence *v.* 1. to begin; start. *The debate will commence promptly at seven o'clock.* 2. to come into existence; have a beginning.

begin to start. *Open your test booklets and begin working on item one.*

inaugurate to begin officially or formally. *The completion of the transcontinental railroad served to inaugurate the era of the railroads in America.*

initiate to begin. *Carl was the one who tried to initiate reduced-price passes for senior citizens and students.*

originate to begin; come into being. *The idea for the play did originate in a writing class.*

start to begin. *Remember to always start with the first problem.*

antonyms: end, finish, terminate

commend *v.* 1. to represent as worthy, qualified, or desirable; recommend. 2. to express approval of; praise. *The coach always tries to commend the efforts of the entire team.*

applaud to praise; approve. *Jessie wanted to applaud her brother's decision to go to college.*

extol to praise. *He should extol the virtues of hard work.*

laud to praise. *The mayor was happy to laud the citizen's rescue of the drowning child.*

praise to express approval of. *My mother and father praise my desire to learn to paint.*

recommend to speak of favorably. *I recommend that you take the scenic route rather than the interstate highway.*

antonyms: blame, censure

commentary *n.* 1. a series of explanations or interpretations. 2. something that explains or illustrates. *The reporter delivered his commentary on the White House press conference.*

editorial newspaper or magazine article expressing the editor's or publisher's opinion on a topic. *The editorial in today's paper spoke out against corruption.*

essay written composition presenting the author's views. *The teacher asked us to write an essay on our role in the democratic process.*

review report offering a critical evaluation of a work. *In my book review, I discussed both the merits and flaws of the author's first-person narrative.*

companies *n.* 1. groups; gatherings. 2. business enterprises; firms. *Many companies have offices in several major cities.*

associations groups of people joined together. *Over the years Ava has belonged to many different associations.*

bands numbers of persons or animals joined together. *Long ago this region was home to many bands of outlaws.*

bodies groups of persons or things. *Congress is the largest of all our government bodies.*

businesses commercial enterprises. *Most of the businesses on Main Street have been there for thirty years.*

corporations groups of people with charters to operate businesses as separate legal entities. *Big corporations often have lobbyists who work for their interests in Washington, D.C.*

firms two or more people in business together. *Jeff has worked for three law firms since he finished law school.*

groups numbers of persons or things joined together. *Groups of children were working on different projects.*

parties groups of people joined together. *The restaurant is too small to seat parties of six or more people.*

partnerships two or more people who agree to contribute to and profit from a business. *He did not want to form any partnerships because he liked to work on his own.*

compel *v.* to force, drive, or constrain. *My parents try to compel me to explain my actions.*

coerce to force. *Ali tried to coerce the group into choosing him as the leader.*

commit to pledge. *Alicia and Joan always commit themselves to new programs of diet and exercise.*

constrain to force. *Dorothy had to constrain the dog from chasing the little rabbit.*

demand to request firmly. *I demand to see the manager of the store!*

drive to force. *The desire for success seemed to drive him to work harder than everyone else.*

force to make happen by force. *The company tried to force the man to resign his position.*

impel to force. *The approaching test date might impel Cathy to study harder.*

insist to stand firm on some issue. *The teacher often insists that the students work in groups.*

motivate to impel; move to act. *The teacher could motivate her students to read by scheduling additional reading periods.*

oblige to force. *The school will oblige its students to wear uniforms.*

antonym: coax

compete *v.* to strive or contend with another or others, as for profit or a prize; vie. *Twenty people signed up to compete in the relay race.*

contend to fight; vie. *The first five racers will contend in the first heat.*

contest to fight for; challenge. *The determined Central High team tried to contest the results of every single race today.*

dispute to fight; contest. *An underdog team from Monroe High seemed to dispute every heat.*

oppose to fight; struggle. *The coach from Jefferson will hotly oppose the decision to limit the number of entrants.*

rival to compete with. *The cheering squads must rival each other in screaming, shouting, and singing.*

vie to compete. *Earl Williamson and Guillermo Martinez will once again vie for first-place points in every race.*

antonym: support

complicate *v.* 1. to make or become complex, intricate, or perplexing. *David's arrival right after Hugh's seemed to complicate things even more.* 2. to twist or become twisted together.

confound to confuse; perplex. *Sylvia will confound you with her mastery of the game.*

confuse to mix up; bewilder. *The babble of different languages at the airport could confuse a tourist.*

perplex to puzzle; confuse. *The structure of a car's engine does perplex me.*

concentrate *v.* 1. to direct or draw toward a common center; focus. 2. to converge toward or meet in a common center. 3. to direct one's thoughts or attention. *I concentrate on going through all the problems on the test at least once.*

converge to come together to a central point. *On a warm summer day, a crowd might converge on the city park.*

focus to concentrate. *He must focus his attention on the speaker.*

antonyms: dissipate, disperse

confer *v.* 1. to bestow (an honor, for example). *The president will confer a medal on the hero.* 2. to hold a conference; consult together.

advise to counsel. *It is good to advise the rafters to wear their life jackets at all times.*

bestow to give. *The mayor will bestow the keys to the city on the visiting head of state.*

consult to talk over. *The patient decided to consult with his doctor about the available treatments for his condition.*

converse to talk. *Ed and Matt converse regularly about current events.*

deliberate to talk over. *The jury members could deliberate their verdict for more than a week.*

discuss to talk over. *The study group might discuss the topics they can investigate together as their semester project.*

donate to contribute. *Millions of people donate money to the Red Cross for the emergency relief fund.*

give to present. *The book promises to give the true story behind the political campaign last November.*

grant to give formally. *The Spanish king would grant large tracts of land to his nobles.*

talk to discuss. *Dan and Tom met to talk about where they would like to go on vacation.*

conscientious *adj.* thorough and painstaking; careful. *Rhonda is known at the office as a conscientious worker.* See **deliberate**.

careful thorough; exact. *She was careful to draw the pattern to the correct size.*

meticulous very careful about details. *Joanie keeps meticulous records of her weekly expenses.*

painstaking exacting. *It was painstaking work to glue the vase together.*

scrupulous very careful. *My father was scrupulous in his planning of the garden.*

thorough very careful. *He did a thorough job of assembling the model.*

antonyms: negligent, careless

considerable *adj.* 1. large in amount, extent, or degree. *It is of considerable importance that you listen to him.* 2. worthy of consideration; important; significant. See **substantial**.

consistent *adj.* in agreement; compatible. *His speech was consistent with his earlier remarks on pollution.*

compatible agreeing. *The two people seemed quite compatible.*

constant not changing. *His constant loyalty is one of his redeeming qualities.*

faithful accurate. *She wanted to produce a replica that was faithful to the original.*

harmonious agreeing. *We felt very comfortable among such harmonious people.*

suitable fitting; proper. *A dress would be suitable for the occasion.*

unwavering steady; constant. *Dogs are known for their unwavering devotion to their owners.*

antonym: inconsistent

copies *n.* 1. imitations or reproductions of something original; duplicates. 2. specimens or examples of printed text or pictures. *At least twenty copies of the lithograph were sold at the art gallery.*

carbons copies made with carbon paper. *The files were filled with carbons of letters the manager had sent to the salespeople.*

duplicates exact copies. *You should always keep duplicates of business letters.*

facsimiles exact copies. *The autographs of the presidents were very good facsimiles of the originals.*

imitations likenesses. *Even the art experts found it hard to tell the real paintings and the imitations apart.*

replicas copies. *Charlie likes to build replicas of old sailing vessels.*

reproductions copies. *The company makes reproductions of eighteenth-century American furniture.*

transcripts copies. *To apply for the job, I had to send transcripts of my high school and college records.*

antonym: originals

copy *v.* 1. to make a copy of. 2. to follow as a model or pattern; imitate. *It is wrong to copy from someone else's paper.*

duplicate to make a copy of. *Can you duplicate this material by tomorrow?*

reproduce to make a copy of. *This machine can reproduce a letter in two seconds.*

correction *n.* 1. the act or instance of correcting. *I had to make a correction in my paper.* 2. something offered or substituted for a mistake or fault.

alteration a change. *An author can make an alteration in the manuscript.*

amendment a change for improvement. *At his request, she made an amendment in the article.*

improvement a change for the better. *Everyone agreed that the new title was an improvement over the old one.*

revision a change; alteration. *Kay got annoyed when the publishers asked for dozens of revisions in the copy.*

courtesy *n.* 1. polite behavior; gracious manner or manners. *My mother always insisted that we treat others with courtesy.* 2. a polite gesture or remark.

civility polite behavior. *Civility is essential if you have a job in which you deal directly with customers.*

consideration thoughtfulness for others. *She showed consideration for her elderly neighbor by carrying his grocery bags up the stairs.*

manners polite ways of behaving. *Good manners require that you write a "Thank-you" note after you receive a gift.*

politeness good manners; polite behavior. *He is known for his charm and politeness.*

thoughtfulness consideration. *Kim's thoughtfulness made a difficult time a little easier for the children.*

antonyms: rudeness, incivility, thoughtlessness

defect *n.* 1. the lack of something necessary or desirable for completion or perfection; deficiency. 2. an imperfection; fault. *A defect in the wiring caused the fan to overheat and short out.*

blemish flaw. *The water spot was the only blemish on the table's polished surface.*

deficiency lack of something necessary or desirable. *Scurvy is caused by a deficiency of vitamin C in the diet.*

failing fault; weakness. *One of my failings is an inability to speak in public.*

fault flaw that spoils perfection. *A fault in the plaster caused the wall to collapse.*

imperfection fault. *The imperfection in the china cup was so tiny that it could not be seen without a magnifying glass.*

shortcoming fault; flaw. *Great-aunt Sarah is quick to point out one's shortcomings while ignoring one's virtues.*

deliberate *adj.* 1. done or said on purpose; intentional. 2. careful and thorough in deciding or determining. *He weighed all the factors before making a deliberate choice.* See **conscientious.**

careful done with thought and effort. *Arlene wants to do a careful job of restoring the water-damaged painting.*

cautious very careful. *She is cautious about the toys she gives to the baby.*

intentional done on purpose. *The insult was intentional; he knew what he was saying.*

methodical done according to a plan. *Dale approached each task in a methodical way.*

premeditated planned beforehand. *The attorney contended that the crime was premeditated.*

purposeful having an aim or intent. *She moved forward with a purposeful air.*

thorough very careful. *He was very thorough in cleaning up after the flood.*

antonyms: unintentional, haphazard, careless

deliver *v.* to take to the intended recipient. *Dan delivers groceries after school.* See **transmit.**

convey to take from one place to another. *Airplanes convey mail across the country.*

transfer to move from one place to another. *Trucks are generally used to transfer goods from one city to another.*

deluxe *adj.* particularly elegant and luxurious; sumptuous. *Ted chose the deluxe sedan over the standard one.*

comfortable giving comfort. *The down coat is soft, warm, and comfortable.*

luxurious very comfortable and beautiful. *The Waldorf-Astoria is a luxurious hotel.*

rich elegant; expensive. *Velvet and satin are rich materials.*

sumptuous magnificent; rich. *The cruise ship provides five sumptuous meals every day.*

antonyms: uncomfortable, poor

demonstration *n.* 1. the act of making evident or proving. 2. conclusive evidence; proof. 3. an illustration or explanation, as of a theory or product, by practical application. *Dave made extra money by giving demonstrations of vacuum cleaners.* 4. a public display of group opinion, as by a rally or march.

display showing; exhibit. *In the display, the jewelry was arranged by color.*

exhibition display; public show. *There are art exhibitions every summer weekend in the village square.*

presentation offering; exhibition. *One critic had seen at least fifteen different presentations of that play.*

descend *v.* 1. to move from a higher to a lower place. 2. to come down from a source; derive. *Paul is descended from an old New England family.*

drop to let fall; cause to fall. *I tried not to drop the glass pitcher on the kitchen floor.*

fall to drop down. *Every autumn the leaves fall from the trees.*

plunge to jump down. *The swimmer took a running start and plunged into the pool.*

sink to fall slowly. *The ship began to sink after it hit an iceberg.*

antonyms: ascend, rise, soar, climb

diagram *n.* 1. a plan, sketch, drawing, or outline designed to demonstrate or explain how something works or to clarify the relationship between the parts of a whole. *He drew a diagram of his idea for a new lamp on the back of a paper napkin.* 2. a chart or graph.

chart information in lists, pictures, tables, or diagrams. *The chart in the science book shows the life cycle of a wood tick.*

depiction drawing; painting; description. *His depiction of a Canada goose was very lifelike and natural.*

figure picture; drawing; illustration. *Figure A shows the parts of an internal combustion engine.*

graph diagram showing the relationship between two quantities. *You can draw a graph showing the increase in the company's profits over the last ten years.*

illustration picture, diagram, or map used to explain or decorate. *The illustration on page 42 shows one of Georgia O'Keeffe's flower paintings.*

representation likeness; picture. *Alicia was upset because she felt that the representation of her face was unflattering.*

disappointment *n.* the act, condition, or feeling of not satisfying a hope, desire, or expectation. *Andy felt a pang of disappointment when he realized that the bicycle he wanted to buy was gone.*

chagrin feeling of humiliation. *Much to her chagrin, Connie could not remember the words to the song.*

frustration feeling caused by being thwarted. *The baby howled in frustration when he could not reach the toy.*

antonyms: satisfaction, fulfillment

disastrous *adj.* causing widespread destruction and distress. *Hurricane Hugo's sweep across the mainland had disastrous results for thousands of people.*

calamitous causing misery. *The region had been hit by a series of calamitous fires.*

destructive causing ruin. *The recent earthquake in California was not as destructive as the one in 1906.*

dreadful terrible. *The state of the city after the typhoon was dreadful.*

ruinous bringing ruin. *The stock market crash was ruinous to his career.*

antonyms: beneficial, useful

dismiss *v.* 1. to discharge, as from employment. 2. to direct or allow to leave. *The general will dismiss the troops.* 3. to discontinue consideration of; drop.

discard to throw away. *Paul had to discard his old track shoes.*

discharge to let go. *The doctor said he would discharge the patient in two weeks.*

reject to throw out as useless. *You can't reject all the bananas because a few have brown spots.*

release to let go. *Dana will release the trout into the river.*

distract *v.* to cause to turn away from the original focus of attention or interest; divert. *The television can distract her from her studies.*

divert to turn aside. *The interruption will divert their attention from his red face.*

fluster to confuse. *Don't fluster Mrs. Conners by singing off-key.*

upset to disturb. *Please don't upset the children by mentioning the lost puppy.*

antonyms: concentrate, attend

drastic *adj.* 1. taking effect violently or rapidly. 2. quite severe or radical in nature; extreme. *The boss took drastic steps to curb excessive spending.*

extreme more than usual. *I thought the decision to ban all imports of fruit from that country was extreme.*

radical extreme. *Giving up his job as a stockbroker and going to work as a laborer represented a radical change for Bob.*

ruthless cruel. *The ruthless dictator imposed heavy taxes on the people.*

severe strict; harsh. *The company placed severe restrictions on access to the computer.*

stringent severe; strict. *Vanessa protested the more stringent curfew rules.*

antonyms: relaxed, indulgent, lenient

dynamic *adj.* characterized by vigor and energy; forceful. *Jackson has a dynamic personality.*

active energetic; busy. *Clara took an active role in establishing the social center.*

energetic active; vigorous. *She did the housework in her usual energetic fashion.*

forceful strong; vigorous. *His forceful manner can be overwhelming at times.*

intense vigorous; extreme. *December is a time of intense activity for merchants.*

vigorous active; forceful. *Even at ninety-one, George was the most vigorous dancer in the group.*

antonyms: languid, passive, sluggish

education *n.* 1. the knowledge or skill obtained or developed by a learning process. 2. the field of study that is concerned with teaching and learning. *Jesse plans to major in education in college and become a first-grade teacher.*

instruction lessons; teaching; education. *Ed had to have forty hours of classroom instruction and eighty hours of flight time before he could get his pilot's license.*

learning knowledge. *Thomas Jefferson was a man of wide and varied learning.*

schooling instruction; education. *Formal schooling may end when you leave school, but education is a lifelong process.*

training practical instruction. *Josie completed her nurse's training at a hospital in her hometown.*

tuition teaching; instruction. *The quality of the tuition at the state university is very high.*

antonyms: illiteracy, ignorance

effect *n.* 1. something brought about by a cause or agent; result. 2. the way in which something acts upon or influences an object. 3. something that produces a specific impression or supports a general design or intention. *The sound effects in the movie really made you think you were on a safari in Africa.*

consequence result; effect. *He did not want to face the consequences of his rudeness.*

force power to influence or control. *He delivered the opening address at the political convention with force and passion.*

intent meaning; significance. *She was puzzled by the intent of the question.*

meaning intent; significance. *I had to read the card three times before I finally grasped its meaning.*

outcome result; consequence. *The reporters waited outside the courtroom to hear the outcome of the trial.*

power influence; right. *The courts have the power to award custody of a child to either parent in a divorce case.*

result something that is caused. *The result of the fight was a bloody nose.*

antonym: cause

elegant *adj.* 1. characterized by or exhibiting either (a) refinement and grace in movement, appearance, or manners, or (b) tasteful richness in form, decoration, or presentation. *Ann gave an elegant dinner for the visiting politician and his entourage.* 2. excellent.

graceful pleasing in movement, form, or proportion. *Angela is a graceful ballet dancer.*

stylish fashionable. *Henry's new apartment was modern and very stylish.*

antonyms: crude, ugly, tasteless

eliminate *v.* 1. to get rid of; remove. 2.a. to leave out or omit from consideration; reject. 2.b. to remove from consideration by defeating, as in a contest. *His opponent tried to eliminate Tony in the first heat.*

exclude to leave out. *The tougher requirements will exclude any student who has not had a recent physical.*

expel to drive out. *Blowing air into the tube will expel the liquid trapped inside.*

omit to leave out. *The list of cast members did mistakenly omit Anna's name.*

reject to refuse; throw out. *Levon decided to reject the possibility that he might not be chosen for the school play.*

remove to get rid of. *A careful inspection will remove all suspicion from the employee.*

antonyms: include, accept

embarrass *v.* 1. to cause to feel self-conscious or ill at ease; disconcert. *She turned bright red at his question when he meant to embarrass her.* 2.a. to beset with difficulties. 2.b. to hinder; impede. 3. to complicate.

annoy to disturb; trouble. *Don't annoy your classmates, please.*

confuse to mix up; bewilder. *Driving on the left side of the road in England did confuse me.*

trouble to disturb. *Jim's reckless behavior does trouble his sister.*

vex to trouble; annoy. *Sean did not mean to vex the professor with his questions.*

antonyms: comfort, console

encourage *v.* 1. to inspire with hope, courage, or confidence; hearten. 2. to give support to; foster. 3. to stimulate. *My mother always encourages me to do the best I can in everything I try.*

promote to contribute to; further. *Proper food, adequate sleep, and moderate exercise will promote good health.*

support to favor; lend strength. *Alice supports Ben's decision to try out for the soccer team.*

urge to push forward. *Jamie urged me to run for class president.*

antonyms: discourage, daunt, depress, intimidate, dissuade, prevent, obstruct

endurance *n.* the act, quality, or power of withstanding hardship or stress. *Pioneers must have great endurance to begin new lives in forbidding places.*

perseverance determination to achieve a purpose. *Dana won a scholarship with hard work and perseverance.*

persistence refusal to give up. *Alex has the persistence of a bull terrier.*

stamina strength to endure. *Athletes need physical stamina to last through a game.*

tenacity stubbornness. *Owen finished the marathon on tenacity alone.*

antonyms: weakness, cowardice

examination *n.* the act of inspecting, observing, or analyzing, or the state of being inspected, observed, or analyzed. *After careful examination of the store, the police officer concluded that two people were involved in the robbery.*

inquiry search for information. *Shortly after beginning the inquiry, the police arrested two possible suspects in the Riverside district.*

inspection careful examination. *A close inspection revealed that the robbers had worn gloves.*

investigation detailed search or examination. *Several detectives were assigned to the robbery investigation.*

scrutiny close study or examination. *All store employees were kept under close scrutiny after a series of robberies.*

exclusive *adj.* not divided or shared with others. *The club was very exclusive; members had to be voted in by other members.*

single for only one. *That victory was the single most important event in her life so far.*

sole for only one person or group. *The grant gave him the sole right to mine the land for all ores.*

antonyms: general, common

excuse *v.* 1.a. to apologize for. 1.b. to seek to remove the blame from. 2.a. to grant pardon to; forgive. *The manager was able to excuse the worker's tardiness the first time.* 2.b. to make allowances for; overlook. See **forgive**.

exhibition *n.* a display for the public, as of art objects, industrial achievements, or agricultural products. *The exhibition at the museum featured paintings by Monet.* See **demonstration**.

expertise *n.* 1. expert advice or opinion. 2. specialized knowledge or skill. *We need his expertise in furniture restoration.*

knowledge familiarity with a subject. *Her knowledge of horticulture helped make her garden a showplace.*

skill expertness. *It takes skill to be able to paint a portrait.*

specialty special profession, trade, field, etc. *Dwayne's specialty is sixteenth-century English poetry.*

technique special method or system. *Jennie's technique for separating eggs is different from mine.*

facsimile *n.* an exact copy or reproduction, as of a document. *The letter was a good facsimile of the original.* See **copies**.

faculty *n.* 1. a special ability or skill. *Jimmy has an amazing faculty for remembering names and faces.* 2. a body of teachers as distinguished from their students.
  ability skill at doing something. *She has a remarkable ability to juggle five tasks at once.*
  aptitude talent; ability. *My mother thinks I have an aptitude for music because I can hum tunes after I hear them once.*
  capacity ability. *That teacher encourages her students' capacity for hard work.*
  competence ability. *I have always envied my brother's competence in math.*
  knack special skill. *Mia has a knack for making friends easily.*
  skill ability to do something. *It takes skill to wrap a present the way she does.*
  talent special ability. *Juan has a talent for training horses.*
  antonyms: inability, incapacity, ineptness, weakness, incompetence

far-fetched *adj.* strained or improbable. *The idea the stone could be turned into gold was a little far-fetched.*
  bizarre odd or fantastic. *Elly's costume was a bizarre combination of Little Red Riding Hood and a rock star.*
  curious odd or strange. *You can sometimes find very curious things at a garage sale.*
  strange odd or unusual. *Animals will often exhibit strange behavior before an earthquake occurs.*
  unusual rare. *It is unusual for Mr. Simon to be seen without a tie.*
  antonyms: typical, normal, everyday, ordinary, average, natural

fatigue *n.* 1. physical or mental weariness resulting from exertion. *Fatigue made it difficult for her to concentrate on the test.* 2. tiring effort or activity; labor.
  exhaustion extreme fatigue. *Many of the runners had to drop out of the marathon because of exhaustion.*
  lassitude weariness. *The disease is characterized by weight loss and lassitude.*
  tiredness weariness. *Monica's tiredness finally wore off after many relaxing days at the cottage.*
  weariness tiredness. *Weariness and hunger eventually drove the children into the house.*
  antonyms: energy, vigor, enthusiasm

ferocious *adj.* 1. extremely savage; fierce. 2. marked by unrelenting intensity; extreme. *On Friday the Northeast was crippled by a ferocious blizzard.*
  cruel causing pain. *It is cruel to laugh at someone in pain.*
  fierce savage; wild. *The fierce bear was protecting her cubs.*
  savage fierce; cruel. *A mistreated dog can become savage.*
  violent forceful; severe. *The battle was brief but violent.*
  wild savage. *It was rumored that a wild man lived in the mountain forest.*
  antonyms: tame, calm, mild

fluent *adj.* 1. having facility in the use of language. *Melanie is fluent in three languages.* 2.a. flowing effortlessly; polished. 2.b. flowing smoothly; graceful.
  flowing moving smoothly. *Her flowing poetry is much admired by the students in her classes.*
  glib speaking too smoothly. *Abby offered a glib reason for her tardiness.*
  polished smooth; refined. *After weeks of practice, his speaking style had become easier and more polished.*
  smooth even; polished. *The experienced politician made a smooth transition from the difficult issue to a safer one.*
  voluble talkative. *He is known as a voluble speaker who can easily talk for an hour.*
  antonyms: terse, silent, curt

forgive *v.* to excuse for a fault or offense; pardon. *I hope Cathy will forgive me for forgetting her birthday.*
  absolve to declare free from blame. *The council might absolve him of any connection with the embezzlement.*
  acquit to declare not guilty. *The jury can acquit the defendant.*
  excuse to pardon; forgive. *If you will excuse me, I have to leave to make a telephone call.*
  pardon to make allowance for. *Grandmother will certainly pardon your behavior if you apologize to her.*
  antonyms: blame, condemn, censure

gracious *adj.* 1. characterized by kindness and warm courtesy. *The gracious hostess made sure that her guests enjoyed the dinner.* 2. characterized by charm and beauty; graceful. 3. characterized by elegance and good taste. See **elegant**.

benevolent kind; charitable. *It was a benevolent gesture to give money to the children's home.*

benign kind; gracious. *Her benign face encouraged people to trust her.*

charming pleasing; attractive. *They thought the small boys were charming.*

courteous thoughtful; polite. *The courteous girl gave her seat on the bus to the blind man.*

graceful pleasing. *She rejected the invitation in a graceful manner.*

kind friendly; gentle. *He was kind to the new child in the class.*

antonyms: ungracious, unkind, discourteous, impolite, rude

guarantee *v.* 1. to assume responsibility for the debt, default, or miscarriage of. 2. to assume responsibility for the quality or execution of. 3. to give a guarantee for. *The moving company guaranteed that the furniture would be delivered Friday.*

ensure to make sure or certain. *Elena knew her grades and test scores would ensure her a place at the university.*

pledge to give one's word; promise. *Dan and Tom each pledge to give up smoking for a month.*

promise to give one's word; pledge. *His parents promise to take him to a baseball game for his birthday.*

secure to make sure or certain. *The team members did everything they could to secure a victory.*

warrant to promise. *The building contractor warrants that construction of all his buildings will last for fifty years.*

hesitate *v.* 1.a. to be slow to act, speak, or decide. 1.b. to pause in uncertainty; waiver. 2. to be reluctant. *He seemed to hesitate to ask for help.*

delay to postpone; stop for a while. *Snow will delay the flight to Chicago for five hours.*

falter to waver; hesitate. *Despite the long years of training, Carmen's resolution to become a doctor never faltered.*

fluctuate to vary; waver. *Prices on the stock market fluctuate with every little rumor.*

pause to stop for a while. *Debbie paused in her speech and looked straight at the audience for a moment.*

vacillate to move one way and then another. *During the campaign the politician seemed to vacillate on the major issues.*

waver to be uncertain or undecided. *Jane and I waver between voting "No" and voting "Yes" on the referendum.*

antonyms: resolve, determine, decide, continue

hindrance *n.* 1. the act or condition of being hampered or obstructed. 2. one that hinders; impediment. *Her younger sister was a hindrance to our secret meeting.*

hitch obstacle. *The dinner party proceeded without a hitch.*

impediment obstacle. *They refused to allow any impediment to block their marriage.*

obstacle something in the way. *She overcame every obstacle on her way to recovery from the operation.*

obstruction something in the way. *Receiving permission is not an obstruction to our plan to go fishing.*

antonyms: help, aid, support

honesty *n.* 1. the quality or condition of being honest; integrity. 2. truthfulness; sincerity. *Mr. Parker is known for his honesty in dealing with his customers.*

candor frankness in giving views or opinions. *Jason made his statement with more candor than his mother was comfortable with.*

frankness openness in giving thoughts. *Tanya said with great frankness that she did not like the new outfits.*

integrity honesty; sincerity; uprightness. *Integrity is an important quality in a politician or anyone else in public life.*

sincerity honesty; freedom from deceit. *Thank-you notes should be written with as much sincerity as possible.*

truthfulness honesty, sincerity. *The story of George Washington and the cherry tree tells about the value of truthfulness.*

antonyms: dishonesty, insincerity

hustle *v.* 1. to jostle or shove roughly. 2. informal. to move hurriedly or urgently. 3. informal. to urge forward; hurry along. *Streams of shoppers tried to hustle through the department store aisles.*

bustle to hurry busily. *People often bustle about in preparation for a party.*

hasten to speed; hurry. *The extra hours in the library certainly can hasten the completion of my report.*

hurry to move too quickly. *We must hurry or we will miss the bus!*

scramble to move hurriedly. *People had to scramble to get places in line.*

scurry to hurry. *The children had to scurry to put their toys away before dinner.*

scuttle to run; scurry. *We watched the crab scuttle across the sand and into the grass.*

idle *adj.* 1.a. not in use. 1.b. without a job; unemployed. 2. lazy; shiftless. *Susan likes to stay really busy; she is rarely idle.*

indolent not liking to work. *He led an indolent life, always expecting others to do the work.*

lazy not active. *Tom was too lazy to mow the lawn.*

sluggish moving slowly. *The river was sluggish on the warm summer day.*

antonyms: active, busy, energetic, industrious

immediately *adv.* without delay. *When the call came, she left immediately.*

directly at once. *Be sure to come home directly after the game.*

instantly at once. *He knew instantly that he had come to visit at a bad time.*

immense *adj.* 1. extremely large; huge. 2. immeasurably vast; boundless. *The universe is so immense that its size is impossible for us to comprehend.*

extensive large; far-reaching. *He was promised extensive powers in the new government in return for his contribution.*

great large; big. *A great mountain range stretched for many miles.*

huge large; very big. *The national debt is a huge amount of money.*

vast great; immense. *Millions of years ago, vast oceans covered much of what is now land.*

antonyms: small, tiny, minute

impartial *adj.* not partial or biased; unprejudiced. *My mother was impartial in dealing with my brother and me.*

fair just; honest. *Amy got more than her fair share of the apple.*

just right; fair. *Making us each pay half the cost was a just decision.*

unbiased fair; not prejudiced. *There is no such thing as an unbiased opinion.*

unprejudiced without prejudice; fair. *It is important for a judge to be unprejudiced.*

improve *v.* to advance to a better state or quality; make better. *Dan knows that he needs to improve his reading skills.*

progress to develop; move ahead. *A baby will progress from crawling to walking.*

reform to make better. *Dorothea Dix worked to reform the prison system in the nineteenth century.*

antonyms: ruin, deteriorate, decline, regress

incredible *adj.* too implausible to be believed; unbelievable. *The book told the incredible story of a man who survived for forty-five days in the desert.* See **remarkable**.

indicate *v.* 1. to demonstrate or point out. *He drew a line on the map to indicate a route.* 2. to state or express briefly.

demonstrate to show or prove. *Can you demonstrate the accuracy of your pitching?*

signify to mean or denote. *What does this dotted line on the map signify?*

insist *v.* to be firm in a demand or course; refuse to yield. *Cesar tried to insist that he was not the one who left the windows open.* See **compel**.

inspect *v.* to examine carefully and critically, especially for flaws. *I need to inspect the new car thoroughly.*

examine to look at carefully. *The collector needed to examine the stamp with a magnifying glass.*

investigate to examine; search. *The insurance company tried to investigate the cause of the fire.*

scrutinize to examine carefully. *It made me uncomfortable to have so many people scrutinize my work.*

instantly *adv.* at once; immediately. *Casey instantly realized that she had said the wrong thing.* See **immediately**.

interrupt *v.* 1. to break the continuity or uniformity of. 2. to hinder or stop by breaking in upon. *Please do not interrupt me when I am talking on the telephone.*

cease to stop. *The laughter will cease the minute the lights go out.*

discontinue to put a stop to; give up. *They found it necessary to discontinue that line of clothing.*

intrude to force in. *Why does Amy intrude on people's private conversations?*

suspend to stop for a while. *It was necessary for workers to suspend traffic on the bridge while they cleared the wreckage from the accident.*

antonym: continue

jostle *v.* 1. to come in contact or collide.
2. to make one's way by pushing or elbowing.
*We tried to jostle through the crowd in the
stadium.* 3. to vie for an advantage or position.
collide to crash together. *We saw the two cars
collide at the busy intersection.*
crowd to push; shove. *Excited fans will crowd
past the guards onto the field.*
elbow to move through by pushing. *The running
back elbowed his way through the defensive line
to make a touchdown.*
push to move forward forcefully. *He needed to
push his way to the front of the line.*
shove to push roughly. *The big boy might shove
the little children out of his way.*

knoll *n.* a small rounded hill or mound; hillock.
The house was built on the top of the knoll.
dune mound of sand. *The children chased each
other up and down the dune.*
hill raised portion of earth. *The old car had a hard
time making it up the hill.*
hillock little hill. *He was completely winded, even
though he had only climbed a hillock.*
mound small hill. *The pitcher returned to the
mound for the final inning.*

league *n.* 1. an association of states, organizations, or individuals for common action;
alliance. 2. an association of sports teams or
clubs that compete chiefly among themselves.
3. a class of competition. *Harry is a good
golfer, but he is not in the same league as
the professionals.*
alliance a joining together of people, groups, or
nations for some purpose. *In World War II the
United States was part of an alliance with western
European nations against Germany and Italy.*
association group of people joined together for
some purpose. *The bankers' association offers
scholarships for qualified students.*

coalition alliance for a special purpose. *The different political parties in the country formed a
coalition because no one party commanded a
majority of the votes.*
compact agreement. *The compact between the
two nations ended the twenty-year war.*
confederation a joining together in an alliance.
*The confederation of the colonies was necessary
to ensure their protection against larger nations.*
covenant agreement between people or groups.
*The temperance groups urged people to sign
covenants to stop drinking.*
organization group of people united for a purpose.
*Kathleen belongs to several social organizations
in her neighborhood.*
union group united for a special purpose. *The
environmental groups proposed a union to combine their forces.*

likable *adj.* pleasing; attractive. *She is one of the
most likable girls in school.*
agreeable pleasing. *His agreeable manners make
him a popular guest at parties.*
attractive inspiring liking; pleasing. *He made me
a very attractive job offer.*
congenial agreeable. *The visit was more congenial
than she thought it would be.*
pleasing pleasant. *Tad has a pleasing personality;
everyone likes him.*
popular liked by many people. *Angela was voted
the most popular girl in her class.*
antonyms: unpopular, disliked, disagreeable,
obnoxious

magnificent *adj.* 1. splendid in appearance;
grand. *The king lived in a magnificent palace.*
2. outstanding of its kind; superlative.
brilliant splendid. *He was dazzled by the brilliant
gleam of the jewels.*
excellent superior; better than others. *He was
awarded a grant for his excellent work
in biochemistry.*
exquisite lovely. *The flower arrangements on the
tables were exquisite.*
gorgeous splendid. *The shop was filled with
gorgeous dresses.*
grand beautiful in appearance; high in quality.
*Dora felt very shy when she saw the
grand surroundings.*
imposing impressive due to size or appearance.
*At six feet, six inches and 280 pounds, the
governor was an imposing figure.*

impressive able to have an effect on the mind and feelings. *The world-renowned doctor delivered an impressive speech.*

outstanding important; beyond others. *She was offered several scholarships because of her outstanding student academic record.*

splendid grand. *Cinderella was invited to a splendid ball at the palace.*

superb grand; first-rate. *The production of the play was really superb.*

superior excellent; better than others. *Eddie makes a superior apple pie.*

superlative above others; supreme. The Book of Kells *is a superlative example of illuminated manuscript.*

antonyms: poor, sordid, squalid, ugly, dull, plain, insignificant, common, inferior

magnify *v.* 1. to make greater in size; to enlarge. 2. to cause to appear greater or seem more important; exaggerate. 3. to increase the apparent size of, especially by means of a lens. *The scientist used the microscope to magnify the bacterium.*

amplify to enlarge; expand. *The city editor told the reporter to amplify the important points in his story on the mayoral campaign.*

augment to make larger in size or number. *She will augment her education classes by taking two for no credit.*

enlarge to make larger in size. *They tried to enlarge the photograph to make it easier to see the faces of the criminals.*

exaggerate to make something more than it is. *He did exaggerate when he said he traveled four thousand miles a week!*

glorify to make something more wonderful than it is. *Sheila tends to glorify all dogs.*

increase to make larger in number or power. *The profits may increase twofold in the next two years.*

overstate to exaggerate. *I think he overstated his ability to climb sheer rock walls.*

antonyms: diminish, decrease, shrink, downplay, understate

manage *v.* 1. to direct or administer (a business, for example). 2. to contrive or arrange. *He did manage to get an invitation to the exclusive party.*

administer to direct. *Both teachers were needed to administer the test this morning.*

arrange to plan. *How did you arrange to get two tickets on such short notice?*

conduct to direct. *They conduct all of their business by telephone.*

contrive to plot; scheme. *Elly contrived to get the seat next to the guest of honor.*

control to direct. *Shawn and Mike control the company's purchasing.*

devise to plot; scheme. *He must devise a way to make the fake jewels look like real ones.*

direct to guide; control. *The supervisor will direct the activities of the department.*

handle to direct. *Mr. Gomez will handle the introduction of a new computer system.*

plot to plan. *Chris had to plot how she would get into the hotel unseen.*

scheme to plot; plan. *They always scheme to get what they want without having to work for it.*

antonyms: mismanage, disarrange

menagerie *n.* 1. a collection of live wild animals on exhibition. 2. the enclosure in which wild animals are kept. *The roadside menagerie featured a coyote, a bear, a rattlesnake, and a prairie dog.*

circus traveling show of people and animals. *Al thought it would be exciting to be a clown in the circus.*

collection group of things belonging together. *The zoo has an outstanding collection of primates.*

zoo place where animals are kept. *In zoos today vanishing species of animals are preserved.*

miniature *adj.* on a small or greatly reduced scale. *My mother collects miniature furniture for her dollhouse.*

diminutive very small. *The gymnast was diminutive next to the football player.*

minute very small. *Microorganisms are so minute that they can be seen only through a microscope or other magnifier.*

small little; not big. *A toy poodle is a small dog.*

tiny very small. *A Yorkshire terrier is a tiny dog.*

wee very small. *My grandfather likes to tell stories of the days when he was a wee lad in Ireland.*

mistake *n.* 1. an error or fault. 2. a misconception or misunderstanding. *I made a wrong turn by mistake.*

blunder foolish mistake. *I made a second blunder when I mispronounced her last name.*

error incorrect action. *I did not have time to correct the error I made on my math test.*

miscalculation wrong estimate. *Because of my miscalculation, we missed the airplane.*

mix-up *n.* state of confusion; muddle. *Connie's inability to remember names and faces caused many mix-ups.*

chaos great disorder and confusion. *The early morning thunderstorm caused chaos on the expressways.*

mess difficulty. *He is known for his ability to clean up other people's messes.*

mistake misunderstanding; error. *I made a lot of mistakes in my speech because I was nervous.*

problem difficulty; things to be worked out. *Despite problems with the car, the weather, and the hotels, we enjoyed our trip to New York.*

monotonous *adj.* 1. sounded or spoken in an unvarying tone. 2. repetitiously dull or lacking in variety. *The landscape was a monotonous brown.*

dull tiresome; boring. *It was hard to stay awake through the dull movie.*

humdrum dull. *He thought he had a humdrum existence as a grocer.*

tedious long; tiring. *Packing and unpacking boxes is a tedious chore.*

tiresome tiring; boring. *Long car trips are often tiresome.*

uniform not varying. *All the clothes were a uniform color.*

unvaried all alike. *She longed to escape the round of unvaried tasks.*

antonyms: interesting, amusing, diverting

motivate *v.* to provide with an incentive or motive; impel. *His mother used a special treat to motivate Tim to finish his assignment.* See **compel**.

impel to cause to act. *The approaching deadline will impel her to work late.*

incite to urge on. *He was accused of trying to incite a riot at the rally.*

induce to lead on; persuade. *They used an ad to induce him to try a new kind of shampoo.*

influence to use power to urge on. *He tried to influence the judge's decision in the trial.*

spur to urge on. *Opposition only served to spur the movement to greater efforts.*

stimulate to spur on. *Preschools are designed to help stimulate a child's development.*

mutual *adj.* 1. having the same relationship to the other. 2. directed and received in equal amount. 3. possessed in common. *Our mutual interests include baseball and fishing.*

common joint; held by all alike. *It is a common belief that colds can be caused by cold weather.*

interchangeable able to be exchanged. *The drill I gave Dad for his birthday has interchangeable bits.*

reciprocal on both sides. *The two countries have had a reciprocal trade agreement since 1855.*

antonyms: single, singular

noble *adj.* 1. superior in nature or character; exalted. 2. grand and stately in appearance; majestic. *Many western travelers have been inspired by the noble mountain peaks of the Rockies.* See **elegant** and **magnificent**.

august majestic. *The judge seemed to her a wise and august personage.*

exalted raised high in power, honor, or rank. *The followers paid homage to their exalted leader.*

lofty grand. *He often expresses lofty sentiments in his poetry.*

majestic grand; stately. *She strolled into the room with a majestic air.*

stately dignified; grand. *England has many beautiful, stately mansions.*

sublime raised high in feeling, thought, or language. *Calvin was awestruck when he first saw the sublime coastal landscape.*

notify *v.* to give notice to; inform. *The lawyer had to notify his client that the trial was set to begin December 12.* See **advise**.

acquaint to let know. *She asked if someone could show her around and acquaint her with the building's layout.*

advise to inform. *Police officers are required to advise people of their rights.*

apprise to let know. *The tax accountant must apprise his clients of changes in the tax laws that would affect their returns.*

inform to tell. *I intended to inform the clerk that her rude behavior would be reported to the manager at once.*

notion *n.* 1. a belief; opinion. 2. a fanciful impulse; whim. *I got this notion that I would learn to play the harmonica.*

concept notion; idea. *The football coach discussed the concept of fair play.*

idea belief; opinion. *I had a great idea for a costume for the party.*

theory opinion; idea. *David has a theory about the best way to train a dog.*

thought what one thinks. *The essay is supposed to reflect your thoughts on the school elections.*

occurrence *n*. 1. an act or instance of occurring or happening. 2. something that takes place; incident. *The accident at that intersection was the fifth such occurrence this year.*

affair happening. *His graduation party was a wild affair.*

appearance a coming into sight. *The appearance of too many white blood cells in the blood sample alarmed the doctor.*

circumstance event; fact. *Getting the first place in line was a fortunate circumstance.*

event happening. *The opening of the Berlin Wall was a major historical event.*

incident event; happening. *She dismissed the fall as a minor incident.*

omit *v*. to fail to include; leave out. *The newspaper inadvertently omitted the telephone number in our classified ad.* See **eliminate**.

organization *n*. 1. the state or manner of being put together into an orderly, functional, structured whole. *She worked a long time on the organization of the office.* 2. a number of persons or groups having specific responsibilities and united for a particular purpose. See **league**.

arrangement ordered parts. *The arrangement of the furniture was intended to make the room wheelchair-accessible.*

design arrangement of color and details. *The design on the tablecloth was burgundy and blue paisley.*

pattern arrangement; design. *The child used a pencil to connect the pattern of dots.*

plan design; scheme. *We made a plan for the vegetable garden.*

scheme coordinated things or parts. *I wanted the color scheme for the bedroom to be blue and white.*

structure arrangement of parts. *The plot provides the structure of the story.*

system parts forming a whole. *The lightning knocked out our telephone system.*

outrageous *adj*. 1. being an outrage; grossly offensive. 2. extravagant; immoderate; extreme. *Steven's behavior at the party was outrageous.*

disgraceful bringing shame. *The child's conduct at the day camp was simply disgraceful, according to the counselor.*

excessive too much. *The management took steps to curb the excessive amount of talking in the theater.*

extravagant going beyond reasonable limits. *The actress is given to making extravagant gestures and movements.*

shameful bringing disgrace. *Aunt Hetty thought it was shameful that Uncle Dick was seen playing billiards in town.*

shocking very offensive. *The official showed a shocking lack of concern for the victims of the fire.*

antonyms: modest, sober, sedate, moderate, reasonable

particular *adj*. 1. separate and distinct from others; specific. 2. worthy of note; exceptional. *That discovery was of particular importance because it advanced cancer research.*

distinct definite. *Candace got the distinct impression that Larry was avoiding her.*

extraordinary unusual. *The* Voyager *missions provided extraordinary pictures of Jupiter and Saturn.*

individual separate; particular. *Each artist expresses an individual vision in his or her work.*

noteworthy remarkable. *Abby's dedication to her job is noteworthy.*

special singular; exceptional. *Jack's special hen laid golden eggs.*

specific particular; definite. *I had no specific reason for wanting to go there.*

unusual uncommon; rare. *It is unusual to see a canary this far north.*

antonyms: general, common, ordinary

peculiar *adj*. 1. unusual or eccentric; odd. *The man muttered to himself and exhibited other peculiar behavior.* 2.a. exclusive; unique. 2.b. belonging distinctively or primarily to one person, group, or kind. See **particular** and **exclusive**.

bizarre odd. *Are you going to work in that bizarre outfit?*

eccentric odd. *Great-aunt Agatha liked to be thought of as eccentric; she said it meant she was interesting.*

odd strange. *What seems odd to one person may seem perfectly normal to another person.*

strange odd. *It seems strange to me that Allison left without saying good-bye.*

uncommon unusual. *A comet streaking through the sky is an uncommon sight.*

antonyms: usual, common, ordinary

picturesque *adj.* 1. of or suggesting a picture. 2. strikingly expressive or vivid. *Charles Dickens is noted for the picturesque language he used to describe Victorian London.*

colorful exciting; interesting. *Years at sea had made him a colorful character.*

graphic picture-like; vivid. *His graphic description made the picture really come alive for me.*

interesting attention-holding. *The baby found the mobile very interesting.*

scenic having beautiful scenery. *Vermont is crisscrossed by scenic highways.*

striking attention-getting. *The scenery along Highway 1 is particularly striking.*

vivid lively; interesting. *The vivid tale enthralled the children.*

antonyms: uninteresting, dull

prefer *v.* to choose as more desirable; like better. *Barbara Ann likes baths; I prefer showers.*

choose to take one thing over another. *Which candidate did the voters choose?*

elect to choose; select. *I elected to wait until tomorrow to do the laundry.*

favor to approve; prefer. *Clay seemed to favor the Cortland apples over the Red Delicious apples.*

pick to choose; select. *Why did you pick that particular puppy?*

select to choose. *After trying on ten sweaters, Joe selected the navy blue one.*

antonyms: exclude, dislike

premium *n.* an unusual or high value. *My parents always put a premium on honesty.*

bonus something given in addition to what is expected. *The workers were given a bonus of $100.*

prize a reward won in competition. *Helen won first prize in the spelling bee.*

reward something given for special behavior or service. *Lee offered a $10 reward for information on the missing cat.*

presently *adv.* in a short time; soon. *Presently Dwayne will leave for school.* See **briefly**.

shortly in a short time. *Mr. Anderson will see you shortly.*

soon in a short time. *My father said that dinner would be ready soon.*

antonym: later

prior *adj.* preceding in time or order. *She turned down my invitation, saying she had a prior commitment.*

earlier before this time. *My earlier proposal was rejected.*

first coming before all others. *Anita took her first trip to Spain last summer.*

preceding coming before. *The preceding television program was sponsored by a national foundation.*

previous coming before. *He had seen that man on a previous occasion.*

privilege *n.* a special advantage, immunity, permission, right, or benefit granted to or enjoyed by an individual, class, or caste. *Mark always considered it a privilege to work for the senator.*

advantage something favorable or beneficial. *His height was an advantage in playing basketball.*

benefit advantage. *One of the benefits of this job is the opportunity to travel.*

franchise privilege or right granted to a particular person or company. *He was given the franchise to sell plastic doilies in the Midwest.*

immunity exemption from something. *The witness was offered immunity from prosecution if she would testify.*

permission consent to do something. *I had to have my parents' permission to go on the field trip.*

prerogative special right or privilege. *It is a person's prerogative to make up his or her own mind.*

right something that is due to a person. *A democracy guarantees certain rights to all its citizens.*

pursue *v.* 1. to follow in an effort to overtake or capture; chase. *The police had to pursue the car thief to the state line.* 2. to strive to gain or accomplish. 3. to proceed along the course of; follow.

chase to go after; to catch. *Every morning the cat would chase the squirrel around the backyard.*

follow to pursue. *The bears follow the fish up the river and catch them near the dam.*

hunt to look for. *Cheryl likes to hunt through every store in town for the perfect gift for her mother.*

search to look for. *I will search the whole house until I find my black glove.*

seek to look for. *Let's play a game; you hide and I will seek you.*

stalk to pursue carefully. *We watched the fox quietly and patiently stalk the field mouse.*

trace to follow; trail. *Computer records can be used to trace missing people.*

track to follow; trail. *Lee was able to track Henry to the record store at the mall.*

antonyms: avoid, desert, escape, retreat

questionable *adj.* 1. open to doubt or challenge; problematic. *Joey's choice of outfit was questionable at best.* 2. not yet determined or specified; uncertain.

debatable not decided. *Whether we will go on vacation this year is debatable.*

doubtful open to question; uncertain. *I was doubtful about Serena's ability to sing at such a large gathering.*

dubious uncertain. *Charlie has a dubious future as an artist.*

uncertain doubtful. *She was uncertain about whether they had met before.*

antonyms: certain, sure, positive

quick-witted *adj.* mentally alert and sharp; keen. *Sally is quick-witted in a crisis; she always knows what to do.*

bright quick-witted; clever. *Joe had the bright idea of gluing the lamp back together again.*

clever smart; intelligent. *The clever baby can put the puzzle pieces together.*

intelligent quick to learn and understand. *Apes are intelligent animals.*

antonyms: stupid, dumb, slow, dim-witted

reasonable *adj.* 1. capable of reasoning; rational. 2. not excessive or extreme; fair. *That particular store has very reasonable prices.*

logical able to reason. *Abby always plans her projects in a logical, step-by-step fashion.*

moderate not extreme. *David has a moderate lifestyle and lives well within his means.*

rational able to reason; sensible. *Was it the act of a rational human being to eat four pepperoni pizzas?*

sane normal; rational. *Off the football field, he behaves like a sane person.*

sensible having good sense. *The only sensible course was to apologize and leave as quickly as possible.*

antonyms: unreasonable, illogical, irrational, intolerable, unsound

remarkable *adj.* 1. worthy of notice. 2. extraordinary; uncommon. *Mary has a remarkable facility for learning foreign languages.*

extraordinary very unusual. *Donald's grandmother lived to the extraordinary age of 106.*

incredible unbelievable. *It seems incredible to me that she could do such a thing.*

notable important. *The annual charity ball is a notable event of the season.*

rare unusual. *An eclipse of the moon is a rare occurrence.*

uncommon unusual. *Chester is an uncommon cat; he can open and close doors.*

unusual not usual. *It is unusual for Annie to stay at work past five o'clock.*

antonyms: common, usual, ordinary

replica *n.* 1. a copy or reproduction of a work of art, especially one made by the original artist. 2. a copy or reproduction. *He was noted for his replicas of well-known sculptures.* See **copies**.

requirement *n.* 1. something that is required; necessity. 2. something obligatory; prerequisite. *A requirement of the course is a paper on an aspect of American foreign policy.*

claim something demanded. *After the accident several people filed claims with the insurance company.*

demand something claimed. *Tony's schedule of sports and activities puts many demands on his time and energy.*

need something wanted. *The company had a need for qualified accountants.*

requisite something needed. *Love and attention are requisites for babies.*

resign *v.* 1. to submit (oneself) passively; accept as inevitable. 2. to give up (a position), especially by formal notification; quit. *Mr. Mores decided to resign from his job as a salesman to go back to school.*

abandon to give up completely. *Sheila had to abandon the attempt to haul the box upstairs by herself.*

abdicate to give up; resign. *A king may abdicate his throne.*

cede to give up. *The farmer had to cede his land to the state for a highway.*

forego to give up; do without. *I must forego butter and sour cream on my baked potato.*

quit to give up. *Jay quit his after-school job to join the chess club.*

relinquish to give up; let go. *I reluctantly relinquished my request for the last piece of pie.*

renounce to give up; do without. *Cynthia had to renounce her claim on the grand prize.*

submit to yield. *The king occasionally submitted to the wishes of his wife.*

surrender to give up; yield. *The knight was able to force his opponent to surrender.*

yield to give up. *We yield the right-of-way at this intersection.*

resist *v.* 1. to strive or work against; oppose actively. 2. to remain firm against the action or effect of; withstand. 3. to keep from giving in to or enjoying. *I had to resist the temptation to yell back at the rude cabdriver.*

assail to attack. *She tried to assail the speaker's claim that no one wanted the pollution laws enforced to their full extent.*

attack to begin fighting. *The politician began to attack her opponent's position on income tax increases.*

oppose to fight against. *The student council will oppose the plan to limit access to the gym after school hours.*

rebuff to reject. *He tried to rebuff the notion that he had done anything improper.*

refrain to hold back. *Sue decided to refrain from telling George that he was right.*

withstand to hold out against. *We feared the house might not withstand the fierce wind.*

respect *v.* 1. to feel or show deferential regard for; esteem. *My family has always respected my need for privacy.* 2. to relate or refer to; concern.

admire to think highly of. *Cecil admired her ability to remember the minute details of every contract.*

esteem to think highly of. *I esteem her opinion; she is often right.*

honor to think highly of; respect. *The professor's students honored her in a special farewell dinner.*

revere to honor; respect. *Native American cultures revere the land and its resources.*

venerate to revere; respect. *They venerated their ancestors and their homeland.*

antonyms: dislike, hate, loathe, abhor, detest

revolve *v.* 1. to orbit a central point. *Earth revolves around the sun.* 2. to turn on an axis; rotate.

circle to move in a ring. *The dog spied the cat and began to circle the tree.*

orbit to move in a path around a heavenly body. *There are dozens of satellites that orbit Earth.*

roll to turn over and over. *The dog rolled the ball back to the child.*

rotate to move in a circle. *When you turn the handle, the wheels rotate.*

spin to turn around. *If you twist it just right, the top will spin for five minutes.*

turn to rotate. *Every time the mobile turned, the baby smiled and giggled.*

rustic *adj.* 1. of, pertaining to, or typical of country life. *Built to look like a rustic barn, the house would have fit in better in the country.* 2. simple and unsophisticated.

country of the country. *Their country ways included being friendly to strangers and helpful to everyone.*

plain simple; uncomplicated. *The plain clapboard house could be clearly seen from miles away.*

rural in the country. *Many people prefer the quieter rural life.*

simple plain; natural. *They enjoyed the simple pleasures of farm life.*

unsophisticated simple; natural. *Some city people regard country life as unsophisticated.*

antonyms: urban, city, sophisticated

salary *n.* a fixed compensation for services, paid to a person on a regular basis. *Dave receives a 5 percent increase in salary every year.*

earnings money earned. *The government requires that you report your earnings.*

income money from work, investments, etc. *They could live very well on their combined incomes.*

pay money for work. *When she left the company to start her own, she had to take a cut in pay.*

wages money for work. *Angie receives the wages from her part-time job every Friday afternoon.*

souvenir *n.* something serving as a token of remembrance; memento. *Tess bought a picture made of seashells as a souvenir of her Florida trip.*

keepsake something kept in memory of the giver. *The gold flower charm was a keepsake from her friend Stacy.*

memento reminder; remembrance. *The shelves in Dana's room are filled with mementos of her travels.*

remembrance souvenir; keepsake. *The portrait in the hall was a remembrance from her grandmother's house.*

reminder something to help one remember. *He kept the smooth stone as a reminder of the river trip.*

spacious *adj.* 1. providing or having much space or room; extensive. 2. vast in range or scope. *The huge windows offer a spacious view of the surrounding mountains.*

ample roomy; large. *The day-care center is ample enough for one hundred children.*

capacious roomy; large. *Troy needs a capacious storage place for his collection of model trains.*

extensive large. *He planned an extensive addition to the house.*

huge very big. *The living room in the new house is huge.*

vast immense. *The city covers a vast amount of land.*

antonyms: crowded, cramped, small

spectacular *adj.* of the nature of a spectacle; sensational. *The view from the top of the tower is spectacular.* See **magnificent**.

stampede *v.* 1. to move in a headlong rush. 2. to act on impulse. *The storm caused the cattle to stampede to the river.*

flee to run away. *Amy wanted to flee, but her feet felt too heavy to move.*

frighten to drive away by scaring. *The big dog will frighten the cats away.*

panic to lose control through fear. *I always panic when I am in a small space.*

scare to frighten away. *The forest fire began to scare away the campers.*

stationary *adj.* 1.a. not moving. 1.b. not capable of being moved; fixed. *A building is a stationary object.* 2. unchanging.

inactive not active. *The broken leg kept him inactive all summer.*

motionless not moving. *The cat sat motionless, watching the birds on the patio.*

antonyms: active, energetic

strict *adj.* 1. precise; exact. 2. complete; absolute. 3. kept within narrow and specific limits. *Judge Dawson is known for his strict application of the law.* 4. imposing an exacting discipline.

accurate correct; exact. *The clock kept very accurate time.*

exact correct; accurate. *She was careful to take the exact amount of medicine.*

inflexible rigid; unyielding. *She tends to be inflexible on matters of money.*

precise correct; accurate. *The floor plan was drawn using precise measurements.*

rigid not changing. *Mr. Porteous is very rigid in his views on punctuality.*

severe stern; harsh. *We have had five severe winters in a row.*

stern firm; hard. *His stern face indicated that we were in terrible trouble.*

stiff not easily bent. *The man felt stiff and uncomfortable around children.*

unyielding not giving way. *Doris has an unyielding desire to become a dancer.*

antonyms: inexact, inaccurate, imprecise, flexible, yielding, compliant

substantial *adj.* 1. of, pertaining to, or having substance; material. 2. ample; sustaining. 3. considerable in importance, value, degree, amount, or extent. *He owes the IRS a substantial sum of money.*

actual existing; real. *As it turned out, the actual event was not as frightening as she had feared it would be.*

ample more than enough. *We have ample time to plan our next tour.*

considerable much; important. *I put a considerable amount of time and effort into my paper on children's literature.*

firm solid; hard. *Jeff stood firm against the pushing of the excited crowd.*

important having significance or value. *Getting a driver's license is an important event in a teenager's life.*

material physical. *The material world mattered to her more than the spiritual.*

real existing; actual. *The real reason they left is that they did not want to see him.*

significant important. *The visit was significant because it was the first time he had met his in-laws.*

sizable large. *Grandfather placed a sizable portion of turkey on my plate.*

solid firm; hard. *After the earthquake, the citizens could no longer depend on having solid ground under their feet.*

stable firm; steady. *Even with the extra weight on it, the platform remained stable.*

antonyms: insubstantial, immaterial, trivial, minor, insignificant, unstable, unsound, unimportant

Writing Thesaurus

sufficient *adj.* as much as is needed; enough; adequate. *The castaways had sufficient food to survive for several weeks on the island.*

adequate as much as is needed. *He was provided with adequate food and hotel accommodations.*

ample as much as is needed. *Five dollars is ample money for lunch.*

enough as much as is needed or wanted. *Does she have enough money with her to pay for the theater tickets?*

satisfactory adequate; good enough. *We agreed upon a satisfactory amount for a weekly allowance.*

antonyms: insufficient, inadequate

support *v.* 1. to bear the weight of, especially from below. 2. to hold in position so as to keep from falling, sinking, or slipping. *Denise struggled to support the ladder that Harold was climbing on.*

bear to hold up. *The roof could not bear the weight of that many men.*

sustain to hold up. *The bridge's towers help to sustain the weight of many vehicles.*

antonyms: drop, demolish, crush

surrender *v.* 1. to relinquish possession or control of to another because of demand or compulsion. 2. to give up in favor of another. 3. to give up or abandon. *After the opposing team got a fourth touchdown in the first quarter, we surrendered all hope of victory.* 4. to give oneself up, as to an enemy. See **resign**.

capitulate to surrender. *I will capitulate now only if you promise me a rematch next week.*

relinquish to give up. *Prince John was made to relinquish his claim to the crown.*

yield to give up. *He was forced to yield to the stronger wrestler.*

antonyms: win, defeat, conquer, vanquish, triumph, succeed

thieves *n.* people who steal. *The thieves left dozens of fingerprints in the house.*

bandits robbers or thieves, usually a group. *According to legend, Robin Hood and his men were bandits who lived in Sherwood Forest.*

burglars people who enter buildings to steal. *Dead bolts and alarm systems can help deter burglars.*

muggers people who attack and rob people. *Muggers will hesitate to attack several people traveling together.*

pickpockets people who steal from people's pockets. *In* Oliver Twist, *Fagin was the leader of a gang of pickpockets.*

robbers people who take things by force. *The police caught the robbers when they tried to sell the stolen merchandise.*

thoroughly *adv.* 1. exhaustively, completely. 2. painstakingly, accurately. 3. satisfactorily, completely. *After reading every book she could find on koalas, Sue was thoroughly familiar with the animal.*

carefully in an exacting way. *Zia dug around the roots of the plant carefully before transplanting it.*

completely entirely. *Jack was completely exhausted after working sixteen hours at his computer.*

entirely completely. *Whether we go on or turn back is entirely up to you.*

totally wholly; entirely. *The village was totally destroyed by the volcanic eruption.*

thoughtfulness *n.* regard for others; consideration. *She showed her thoughtfulness by sending cards to her friends on all kinds of occasions.* See **courtesy**.

tornado *n.* a rotating column of air usually accompanied by a funnel-shaped downward extension of a cumulonimbus cloud and having a vortex several hundred yards in diameter whirling destructively at speeds up to 300 miles per hour. *The tornado that hit our town last spring uprooted trees and overturned mobile homes.*

cyclone tornado. *In* The Wizard of Oz, *a cyclone picked up Dorothy's house and carried it to Oz.*

twister informal name for a tornado. *Ellen lives in a part of the country where twisters are very common.*

waterspout tornado occurring over a body of water. *The people on the boat stared in amazement at the huge waterspout twirling on the horizon.*

whirlwind windstorm in which the air whirls around violently. *The whirlwind picked up all the leaves and debris and pulled them up into the air.*

transmit *v.* to send from one person, thing, or place to another; convey. *It is easy to transmit a cold from one person to another.*

carry to take from one place to another. *She will carry the baby to the car.*

convey to carry from one place to another. *Trucks convey goods across the country.*

dispatch to send off for a reason. *The colonel will dispatch a messenger to carry important information to headquarters.*

forward to send on. *The post office will forward her letters to her new address.*

send to cause to go from one place to another. *If you misbehave once more, the principal may send you home.*

transfer to move from one place to another. *My mother got transferred every two years when I was growing up.*

transport to carry from one place to another. *Buses were used to transport the children to the summer camp.*

underestimate *v.* to make too low an estimate of the quantity, degree, or worth of. *Tom and Joe always underestimate the amount of time they need to spend studying for the math tests.*

belittle to make seem less. *I belittle my writing because it does not seem good enough to take seriously.*

depreciate to devalue; lessen. *An appliance begins to depreciate as soon as it leaves the store.*

underrate to put too low a value on. *I think the coaches underrate Ed's pitching ability.*

undervalue to put too low a value on. *People tend to undervalue the importance of fiber in their diet.*

unexpected *adj.* coming without warning; unforeseen. *The invitation to the grand ball was unexpected.*

abrupt sudden. *The conversation came to an abrupt halt when Joey mentioned that he had his pet snake with him.*

sudden happening without warning. *Anna was hit by a sudden gust of wind.*

surprising causing astonishment. *Why do you find it so surprising that I can play the piano without being able to read music?*

unanticipated not thought of beforehand. *Sharon is experiencing some unanticipated side effects from the chemotherapy.*

unforeseen not known beforehand. *The tremendous demand for tickets was unforeseen by the new theater owners.*

antonyms: expected, foreseen, anticipated, gradual

uninterested *adj.* 1. without an interest. *They were uninterested parties in the lawsuit.* 2. not paying attention.

inattentive paying no attention. *I must apologize for being inattentive during the council meeting.*

indifferent having no interest. *Jason loved the movie, but Jane was indifferent.*

unconcerned not interested. *He seemed unconcerned about his own safety.*

antonym: interested

unique *adj.* 1. being the only one of its kind; sole. 2. being without an equal or equivalent. *The study tour was a unique opportunity to see Russia.*

alone with nothing more. *Money alone cannot guarantee happiness.*

only sole. *Andy is an only child.*

peerless unequaled. *Dave's peerless performance on the court brought the spectators to their feet.*

singular only one. *The signing of the treaty was a singular event in the course of Western European history.*

sole one and only. *She was the sole support of her mother and her brothers.*

unequaled no equal. *The Great Barrier Reef is a place of unequaled beauty.*

antonyms: common, usual

unite *v.* 1. to bring together so as to form a whole. 2. to combine (people) in interest, attitude, or action. *The neighbors needed to unite to fight street crime.*

associate to connect. *I associate red hearts with Valentine's Day.*

blend to mix together completely. *Have you ever tried to blend oil and water?*

combine to join things together. *The teacher combines kindness with firmness in handling her class of preschoolers.*

compound to mix; combine. *The scientist tried to compound several elements in her most recent experiment.*

connect to join; link. *The diagram showed Part A connected to Part G.*

couple to join together. *Dad will couple the car and the trailer.*

fuse to blend. *The fire can fuse the coins into a single mass.*

incorporate to add or blend. *Remember to incorporate the new information in your weekly report.*

join to combine. *We should join forces with our neighbors to fight the zoning changes.*

link to join; connect. *He did not want his name linked with the plan.*

antonyms: separate, sever

urgent *adj.* 1. compelling immediate action; imperative. 2. conveying a sense of pressing importance. *The caller left an urgent message.*

immediate without delay. *The Red Cross can bring immediate aid to the victims of natural disasters.*

imperative necessary; urgent. *It is imperative that we find the missing key.*

insistent demanding attention. *The dog's insistent barking warned the family of uninvited guests.*

pressing needing immediate attention. *After the storm, our most pressing need was fresh batteries.*

antonyms: unimportant, insignificant, trivial

usually *adv.* 1. commonly or frequently encountered, experienced, observed, or used. 2. habitually or customarily; particularly. *The baby usually takes a nap every day at about two o'clock.*

commonly generally. *Children commonly start school at the age of five.*

frequently often. *I frequently use my lunch hour to run errands.*

generally most of the time. *Claudia is generally able to handle any kind of domestic problem.*

ordinarily generally. *Juan ordinarily attends computer classes on Saturday.*

regularly in a fixed manner; habitually. *Exercising regularly is an important part of a healthy lifestyle.*

antonyms: rarely, infrequently, seldom

vague *adj.* 1. not clearly expressed or outlined. *The vague instructions made it hard to know how to put the kit together.* 2. not thinking or expressing oneself clearly. *She was vague about her future plans.*

dim not distinct. *The lighting in the room was too dim for me to see her face clearly.*

indefinite not clear. *The precise date of the exam is indefinite.*

obscure not clear. *Tina found the meaning of the poem obscure.*

uncertain indefinite. *He sounded uncertain when Jan asked him what his plans for the summer were.*

unsure uncertain. *Leon is unsure of his future with the company.*

antonyms: clear, definite, specific

verify *v.* 1. to prove the truth of by the presentation of evidence or testimony; substantiate. 2. to determine or test the truth or accuracy of, as by comparison, investigation, or reference. *A good scientist will conduct numerous experiments to verify a hypothesis before publishing a new theory.*

prove to show to be right and true. *You will have to prove your theory.*

substantiate to establish by evidence. *The insurance agent had to see the damage to substantiate our claim.*

antonyms: disprove, refute, invalidate

versatile *adj.* 1. capable of doing many things competently. 2. having varied uses or serving many functions. *That versatile tool can be used as a hammer, a screwdriver, or a wrench.*

adroit having skill with the body or the mind. *No matter what the question, she was adroit in providing answers.*

all-around able to do many things. *Jean is a good all-around student; she handles all her subjects equally well.*

competent able. *She is a competent driver.*

dexterous having skill with the hands or the mind. *Maria is dexterous from years of playing the piano.*

diverse varied; different. *The people at the convention were a diverse group.*

diversified varied. *His diversified interests meant that he did not spend much time on any one activity.*

multifarious many, varied. *For multifarious reasons, she had to drop out of the play.*

skillful having skill. *He is a skillful electrician.*

sundry several; varied. *He finally finished the report after sundry excuses.*

well-known *adj.* widely known; familiar or famous. *J.P. Thatcher is well-known in literary circles.*

celebrated much talked about. *Joe was eager to get the autograph of the celebrated actress.*

famous noted; acclaimed. *Janice is famous for her apple pies.*

renowned famous. *The renowned pianist is playing a concert on Saturday night.*

antonyms: unknown, obscure, modest

witness *v.* 1. to be present at or have personal knowledge of. 2. to provide or serve as evidence of. 3. to testify to; bear witness. *Mrs. Garson witnessed the robbery that took place on First Street last Tuesday.*

notice to see or detect. *Kate noticed that the fish seemed to prefer the dried flakes.*

observe to see. *Matt could observe that the birds preferred the cracked corn.*